THE REFORMATION
IN GERMANY

Volume One

LORTZ, Joseph. The Reformation in Germany, tr. by R. Walls.
   Herder and Herder, 1968. 2v tab bibl 67-29675. 22.50 set
This two-volume history takes its place among the other standard
works on the subject. Father Lortz is the most respected German
Catholic historian of the Reformation. The volumes were first published in Germany in 1939–40; however, this translation is based upon
the 1949 edition. Adequate index; excellent bibliography including
German titles. The book is noteworthy for its objective and sympathetic view of the Reformation from the pen of a Roman Catholic
priest. The translation makes available in easy reach the work of an
important Reformation historian and will be extremely valuable to any
serious student. A reader who desires a thorough, accurate, and
scholarly account of the Reformation in Germany could find no better
place to begin than with Lortz.

CHOICE   NOV. '69

History, Geography &
Travel

Europe

JOSEPH LORTZ

The Reformation in Germany

VOLUME ONE

Translated by Ronald Walls

LONDON

DARTON, LONGMAN & TODD

NEW YORK

HERDER AND HERDER

DARTON, LONGMAN & TODD LTD
64 Chiswick High Road, London W4

HERDER AND HERDER, NEW YORK
232 Madison Avenue, New York 10016

Vol 1 of *Die Reformation in Deutschland*
was first published in 1939; Vol 2 in 1940.
This is a translation of the revised edition published
in 1949. The Author's Foreword, the Postscript and
Bibliography are new.

This Translation
© 1968 Darton, Longman & Todd Ltd
First published 1968

Library of Congress Catalog Card Number: 67–29675

Printed in Great Britain by Richard Clay
(The Chaucer Press) Ltd, Bungay, Suffolk

CONTENTS

AUTHOR'S FOREWORD

The publisher of the English version of my book *Reformation in Germany* has asked me for a foreword for my English readers. I welcome this opportunity. There are three things I want to say.

To begin with: I am very glad that after some delay and several complications this translation has finally been published. I had no opportunity to check the English text and I fully realise the difficulty of the translator's work. I hope that it will prove to be faultless. I want to thank him as well as the publishers who have taken so much trouble to ensure a successful start for my book.

Furthermore I want to state that this book does not give a complete history of the Reformation as such. It deals, as the title says, with the events in Germany, the country of the origin of the Reformation and with its centre, the personality of Martin Luther, the genius who initiated what later became an all-European tragedy. The presentation ends more or less with the year 1555, the date of the Treaty of Augsburg, which finally settled that there would be in future separate Christian denominations instead of One Church. Consequently the great historical facts of the expansion of the Reformation throughout Europe are hardly mentioned. Calvin and Zwingli had little influence on German development, although their importance for England and France was very considerable. It would have been an interesting task to give an outline of those spiritual and political forces which created the Reformation in England and became eminent factors in the building up of the United States of America,[1] and also to examine the different roots of the separation from Rome in England and in Scotland, etc.

Finally I must draw the attention of the reader to the fact that this book was written nearly thirty years ago (1938–39). Since that time the situation of Christianity has changed greatly. Unforeseen

[1] I have tried to do this in a small volume *Die kleine Reformationsgeschichte* which will shortly be published by Herder, Freiburg i. Br.

developments have taken place in the relationships between individual Christians. Above all, the World Council of Churches and the Second Vatican Council have created an atmosphere of understanding which was not then anticipated. I have tried to sketch this new situation in a few specially written new paragraphs added to the last chapter of Volume II.

BOOK ONE

Presupposition:
On the Eve of A New Epoch

The New Religious Pattern

ONE

The Causes of the Reformation

I

Christianity divided is a self-contradiction. This, however, has been the state of Christianity since the Reformation. Quite apart from the eastern schism, for the past four hundred years a fundamental split has persisted in a Christianity that formerly was one. During this space of time a far greater number of Christians – a far greater number of non-Catholic Christians indeed – have lived than during the whole of the first fifteen Christian centuries.

From this fact emerges the real question which a Christian must put to the Reformation historian: What was the meaning and the historical purpose of the Reformation?

To answer this question we require knowledge not only of the course but also of the foundation of the Reformation. Without this knowledge the course itself remains incomprehensible. Enquiry into *the causes of the Reformation* is thus essential to a study of the history of the Reformation.

What we have in mind is not primarily the answering of questions about how particular developments led up to the Reformation, but rather the answer to the preliminary question as to how any Church revolution such as was accomplished in the sixteenth century could have been possible at all, and how it was, in a deeper sense, necessary. That the Reformation should have occurred is by no means self-evident. On the contrary: to arrive at a deeper understanding of what it was, we must first become quite clear as to how it was possible for it to happen; we must try to relive the strange, the colossal, trial of strength which called in question the absolutely fixed norm of Christian faith and government that directed with divine authority the entire life of individuals and communities.

The study of history is rewarding only in so far as underlying reasons are grasped. The events of history must be raised above the level of more or less arbitrary emergence from the stream of time and of episodic appearance and disappearance. It must become characterised by a certain inner necessity – not an absolute necessity, but one that leads us to expect the appearance of the historical fact to arise with inner logicality out of previous events, thus, in turn, making possible its further advance.

Such demonstration explains the genesis of an historical event: it does not justify its substance. Only a naïve, materialist and fatalist interpretation of history simplifies the problem so as to suggest that great events in the history of the human race always bear within themselves their absolute metaphysical justification. Only an attitude weakened by relativism, and unsure of its own strength, imagines that due honour can be done to the great ones of history only by unreserved, if temporally restricted, assent. In contrast to such an attitude the Christian judgment – which is also profoundly human – allows plenty of room in the historical fact for man's subjective merit or subjective guilt, and consequently makes it possible for us to judge a past epoch and yet maintain perfect reverence for it and a real sense of involvement in it. *Demonstration of a deep historical logic does not decide concerning truth or error, merit or guilt.* The contrary opinion is part of the stock in trade of undogmatic, and hence eternally vacillating, liberalism. Because, indeed, error plays its vast and positive role in history, because the *felix culpa* is even part of the underlying powers of history, we must affirm that there can be a fulness of meaning in the historical sense that yet does not manifest truth. Cause and guilt are, after all, not the same thing. Guilt always embraces cause: cause may include guilt, but need not.

Upon this basis alone can we proceed to an *essential* critique of world-shattering victorious movements. One of these is the Reformation. Conversely: to claim that the fact of the Reformation provides its ultimate justification is to hand Christianity over to the eternal flux of historical process, and so to deny the absoluteness of Christianity.

The age of the Reformation was marked by a complexity and diversity of life hitherto unknown. In a measure likewise unknown until then, personalities of second and third stature appeared on the stage of history and drew the masses into the course of events. The great precondition of all modern history: numbers, numbers of individuals, that is, caught up in the historical process, and in turn reacting upon it in some way or other, and upon each other in a variety of ways, is indeed a characteristic of Reformation history. The history of the preaching friars, of theology, of the mercenaries, of the peasants' wars, provides an indication of this factor. An even better indication lies in the fact that this period was the first to be decisively touched by that power which first made possible any sort of real public opinion, any spiritual mass-movement – the art of printing.

The full significance of this appears when we recognise that the Reformation period was heir to the close of the fifteenth century – a period of countless interwoven antitheses. These antitheses for their part were the result of centuries-old dissolutions and rebuildings, and as such not only characterise or even dominate the image of life at that time but also make this whole life an antithesis from its very foundations upwards.

We have already hinted that comprehending the causes that we wish to trace is no narrow schoolroom exercise. It must be set in a much more imposing framework. The fulness of meaning we mentioned signifies that an historical phenomenon follows a recognisably planned development, and, to that extent, explains itself. On the other hand, comprehension of the historical cause reaches out far beyond the actual and immediate causation. It includes comprehension of foundation, precondition and preparation.

In terms of this broad significance, comprehension reaches out even further, beyond the limits of strict proof and, even more, beyond all awareness of the connection between cause and effect. That is to say: there can be an historical cause that is quite basic and comprehensive, and yet the subject of one of its dependent historical processes need not be in a position to discover the direct connection between cause and effect, to uncover the channels along which the effect runs. Thus, in his own development and in the construction and expansion of his Church, Luther made use of a host of earlier events and precursors without himself and his age being aware of their connection with them.

Much deeper than consciously perceived stimuli is the far less precisely controllable primeval reaction-chain that reaches down into the heritage that is in man's blood, and to his spiritual milieu. Such invisible stimuli, however, do not rule out scientific examination. The ultimate reason for this is that history is an objective manifestation of the inner consequence of once-uttered ideas and of definite facts, and also an objective manifestation of the will of God. History, viewed as a whole, is, despite the decisive influence of genius, something far out of the reach of the will and the desires of men.

Consequently it is scientifically justifiable to include in the series of causes of a later phenomenon, great facts that have characterised whole centuries, even if no precisely documented connection is directly or mediately demonstrable, presupposing, that is, that a strong interior relationship of the two-sided spiritual-intellectual structure exists, and that the development in question runs its course within the same milieu.

To speak in concrete terms: if the attitude of complete adherence to the Roman Church, characteristic of the twelfth and thirteenth centuries, is succeeded in the sixteenth century by an attitude that is largely independent, even hostile, this change compels us to look for an explanation in causes that include events in all phases, which have loosened this adherence and encouraged this freedom.

The concept of cause must be sharply distinguished from the notion that the effect, or principal effect, of an idea must always be measured against the image which the creators of that idea possess of it in their minds. With respect to content, reforming zeal within the Church, expressed, for example, in the 'devotio moderna' (cf. p. 151), is the exact antithesis to the heretical Reformation; but because that reforming zeal set itself vigorously and successfully against prevailing formalism ('Judaism', as Erasmus and Luther were to call it), and stressed and strengthened the importance of the individual conscience, it became, quite against its will, an important cause of the Reformation. It propagated an intellectual attitude bearing a formal resemblance to that of Luther, and which was therefore capable of being filled with the substance of Luther's attitude – a thing which would have been impossible within Church circles apart from the influence of Luther.

Our problem is not simply to explain how Luther's personal development was possible but to show how this man was able to claim the allegiance of a huge section of the population of Europe, to show how the Reformation was possible as a world-historical phenomenon, capable of setting its imprint upon the whole range of life, religious and secular, in its own age and in the centuries which followed.

No century is merely a termination or a transition. The concrete variety of life in every era contradicts such a conception; the late Middle Ages were more than just autumn or just early spring. They had an intrinsic meaning of their own. Whoever wishes to give a complete description of any period must above all comprehend it as it is at its centre, without antecedent consideration of its precedents and its consequences.

But every period is also a transition to another; and many parts of history are so strongly marked by this character that we may describe them as typical periods of transition. One of such periods is the later and concluding Middle Ages, that is, the period from about 1300 until the end of the fifteenth century. All serious quarrel over this conception disappears if one considers the late Middle Ages in their relation to the period of the Reformation and to the Reformation itself. For the late Middle Ages are, in general, the cause of the Reformation, and it is evident that an extraordinary number of powerful forces at work in that period can be easily classed together under that designation.

The mighty change which the Reformation effected in the total life of Europe – ecclesiastical, religious, scientific, political and economic – was one half the result of a change and disintegration which set in around 1300. The other half was Luther.

II

If we define 'causes' as 'presuppositions', there is indeed a summary, but penetrating and most illuminating formula which answers our question. The Reformation was caused by the disintegration of the basic principles and basic forms upon which the Middle Ages were built.

The principal question is that of the disruption of the unity of the Middle Ages; for the Reformation was without doubt essentially the break-up of this unity, or, better, the revolutionary consummation of this break-up.

The shortest formula for the empirical situation in so far as it appears as a preparation for the Reformation goes something like this: the unity of western Christianity had gone; the *una civitas christiana* had already vanished. This meant that the unity of dogma and of Church life – still manifestly present – had surrendered in essence the substratum which supported their existence. The separation of the individual components of Europe and of the Roman Catholic Church (the rise of nations, in fact) had advanced so far that the lever could be applied with good prospect of achieving disruption. This state of affairs was brought to light by Luther, and he, indeed, was the first to allow it to lead right into schism.

Evidence for the pre-Reformation break-up of Christian unity or for the threat of its imminent disappearance is not difficult to produce.

(*a*) Avignon (the pope, formerly truly a universal figure, now very nearly became a French court bishop); the schism of the west (split of the entire western Church into two camps mutually excommunicating each other); the nationally conceived reform councils based upon a radically separatist idea of a council (see p. 25f.); the Renaissance popes as Italian princes. In contrast to the cohesion of medieval universalism these phenomena present a series of logically increasing expressions of religious nationalism.

(*b*) The national-political division of Europe, the rise of great national monarchies in the west, the emergence therein of national Churches, and, in Germany, the gradual tendency towards the erection of territorial Churches.

(c) The refusal of the west to respond to the papal call to war against the enemy of Christendom; the inevitable hardening of this refusal on account of the political relations of both popes with the Turks (Innocent VIII as paid gaoler of the captive brother of the Turkish sultan, and Alexander VI). The fall of Constantinople in 1453 was the expression of a Europe become disunited: it no longer mobilised its united strength towards a common end.

(d) The expulsion of heretical Bohemia from the common Christian heritage.

The beginnings of a new sense of unity which European humanism brought were powerless against the disappearance of western, Christian unity; they hastened it, in fact, for on the whole humanism moved towards secularisation, that is, the dissolution of the more spiritual Middle Ages (cf. pp. 12 and 61 f.).

This break-up of European unity in the pre-Reformation period must not be linked or confused either with Janssen's one-sided over-evaluation, or with Denifle's one-sided under-evaluation of the late Middle Ages. It is obvious, rather, that this disruptive process was making room for a reconstruction, for the evolution of something that was both new and of value. This development was deliberately fostered by the Church itself in the great work of educating the nations of Europe, the result of which was bound to be the maturity of these nations, and their accepting adult responsibility. The achieving of this aim necessarily brought about an alteration in the relationship of attachment to the Church that had grown up in the early Middle Ages. The decisive question was: Would the transition result in people, hitherto accustomed only to being led, entering into a relationship of free co-operation; or would the changed conditions result in animosity and schism?

We know the answer. But why was the result animosity and schism?

The growth of the European nations was burdened, among other things, by a dangerous unevenness. The foundation was the linking together of religion and political-social life to become a single whole. With the co-operation and leadership of the Church in the course of many centuries secular society fought doggedly and consistently towards ever greater independence. This was in accordance with natural necessity and, as we have said, with the purpose of all true education. But the Church, although she had established and fostered this independence, was not entirely happy about it. By the Church we mean the socially and economically privileged priestly estate, the bishops, the church courts, the great religious orders, living and exercising their care of souls in the cities, and the Roman curia. Two classes within the same vital social organism grew at quite a different tempo and, to some extent, in different directions: a spiritual breach was easy, if not inevitable. On the other hand, the Church tolerated a carelessness in the expression of religious opinions, which gave too much latitude to freedom, and became a dangerous temptation. We must take account of certain dominant humanist views which were at work in this process.

The line of development is evident: the Reformation is an expression of Europe's attainment of intellectual and religious independence. It is the revolutionary declaration of the coming of age of the Christian people of Europe. As early as 1300 polemical writings on Church politics were full of the revolt of the laity in every form, and so basic that they simply could not be overlooked.

Not only did the basic mental and religious attitudes which characterised the Middle Ages change but so did the forms of expression they had known in the Church and the world. Medieval institutions were passing away. Concerning the Church, we think of everything that comes under the heading of the disintegration of its concept as an apostolic, religious entity, and under the heading of ecclesiastical abuses in the widest sense of the word. Concerning the world, we think of the colossal reorganisation in the social, cultural and political spheres. (Political: the impotence of the empire and the emperor, its diminution as a result of the loss of large frontier areas; the separation and enmity between countless emergent territories and regions.)

In the battle against this disorder and reorganisation in world and Church there arose those power currents which governed

German history in the period of confessional division. But these did not arise merely from this battle. They arose essentially from their own roots. It was this latter fact alone which made the Reformation no mere episode, but an epoch in German history. The violence of its convulsion in the religious sphere even made it an epoch in world history.

In fact at the beginning of the sixteenth century this disintegration of medieval principles in every area of national-political, ecclesiastical, religious and scientific life had gone so far, reaching the Church and striking against her, that in broad outline the framework of the Reformation seemed to have been prepared. Seen as a religious and ecclesiastical event the Reformation is the denial of the visible Church, rooted and grounded in the objective teaching authority and in the sacramental priesthood; and it is the acceptance of a religion of conscience erected upon the judgment of the individual with regard to the biblical word. That is to say: along these two lines of its development, the Reformation replaced the basic medieval attitudes of objectivism, traditionalism and clericalism by those of subjectivism, spiritualism and laicism. This was a development, therefore, which took up, united, and carried on with surprising intensity tendencies of the late medieval interplay of forces. The Reformation was a revolutionary revolt against the papal Church by a theological lay movement. Everything which prepared the enmity of the laity against papacy and Church belongs to the causes of the Reformation.

In the intellectual sphere the most far-reaching effect was produced by that slowly emerging force which we like to call the subjectivist tendency, although it was still centuries removed from modern subjectivism. This development had begun in the moment when the western mind began to adopt its own independent attitude towards the Christian message, to pose bold questions and to give answers unheard of before. This happened at first within, but soon outside, the Church. The two epoch-making figures, both belonging to the high Middle Ages, are Bernard of Clairvaux and Peter Waldo.

An historical analysis of the intellectual, ecclesiastical, political and social situation at the turn of the sixteenth century yields, further, the precise reflection of this disintegration: a very strong, widespread and dangerous dissatisfaction with prevailing conditions and, moreover, strong agitation (see p. 113 f.) and a corresponding demand for reform that had already become violent. In reality the Lutheran Reformation, which grew into a denunciation of the former way of life, became an outlet for all this. But at the decisive point, namely, opposition to the Church as the supporting power of the Middle Ages, the demand for reform was expressed with extraordinary sharpness, and here it developed an unusually explosive power, which in its turn reverberated to unusual lengths.

The tension expressed vis-à-vis the Church possessed such great explosive power because a thorough reform had been due for three hundred years; indeed, Innocent III had made reform the theme of the fourth Lateran council. Furthermore, in spite of the manifestly great achievements and persons (in the papacy, episcopacy, clergy, monasticism, civil life, in piety, theology and art) a consistent decadence had set in within this development and, in spite of all the excellence, it could not be concealed or smoothed over. No matter how one may extol the value of fourteenth-century mysticism; no matter how we now concede many Christian features to the Renaissance, the sequence Avignon–schism–Renaissance is, seen as a whole, a development of religious debilitation, a dangerous disintegration of Christian and priestly life, a perilous eclipse of the Catholic idea. Indeed, when the Church was in danger of its life, in the two-, and then three-headed papacy, had not the self-seeking of the highest senate of the Church and of some of the popes prevented the initiation of the long-overdue reform? Certainly one can concede to Möhler that 'by rebuilding upon the existent foundations (of the Church), according to the laws of continuity, a new and better time' could have been ushered in; but, in virtue of the inner consistency of the concrete situation at the beginning of the sixteenth-century, there was not much prospect of this possibility becoming a reality. Conversely, the many, vain, centuries-old attempts at reform and the countless, frequently successful revolts against the Church's authority made things ripe for a radical break-through. People had had more than enough. They wanted to make an end of it. A radical revolution was bound to find many enthusiastic adherents.

The distribution of forces is seen even more in the fact that the absolute necessity of reform was a profound conviction in all trends and circles within the Church, all of whom were possessed by an intense longing for some sort of renewal.

The call for a reformation in head and members was, to be sure, vastly different from a merely polemical antipapal or anti-Church movement. It was first of all the positive expression of the conviction which penetrated to the very roots of western consciousness that the profoundest order of the Church had become distorted, and which imperiously demanded a transformation; there was also the conviction that this transformation would come through a tremendous revolution – an apocalyptic chastisement willed by God. This expectation was characterised by both longing and fear. From the most diverse quarters, in all spheres of life, this revolutionary mood had grown as a wish, a fear, a plan, as a prophecy, as an already living movement. Conditions were intolerable; a fundamental change had to come. The tyranny had to be broken. In a time of famine, with great frankness in his cathedral pulpit Geiler von Kayserberg (d. 1510) incited the people of Strasburg to take grain from the rich by force. It was this same, truly Catholic and deeply devout Geiler who knew that 'Christianity was distorted from top to bottom, from the pope to the sacristan, from the emperor to the shepherd'.

No revolution could be too radical to prevent many from finding at once, in this longing and fear, a proof of its justification. Luther, at first intensely earnest, then bold and obstinate, then reckless, in attack, found here an unusually well-prepared soil.

III

And yet, despite all we have said, the onset of the Reformation had not become self-evident. Its appearance and the world-historical shattering of Christianity which it precipitated, remain primarily a mystery. But we make a mystery no more accessible to understanding by hushing up whatever constitutes its incomprehensibility. It is better to emphasise the enigma which it conceals. By going beyond the quite inadequate forms of explanation hitherto provided, and realistically investigating the origin of the Reformation we are now, it is true, progressively illuminating its tragic genesis; but at the same time too much stress has been laid on one

angle. It is time now to do justice to irrational factors. The complex of causes of the Reformation had so throughly come to a head
that the breaking of a storm became almost an absolute necessity.
But in spite of this, much of the undiluted essence of the Church,
much of the heroic spirit of Christianity remained. It is false to
describe the process as though the disintegration took place without any opposition, and even falser to trace back such a dissolution
simply to an act of malice. The Reformation was a battle for the
authentic form of Christianity; its emergence was not a self-evident fact; less still was it self-evident that the struggle was to be
resolved by the greater part of western Christendom turning
against the Church.

One of the indispensable preconditions of reaching an understanding of the development of the Reformation, and of assessing
its value, is that we clarify the magnitude of the cleavage represented by the Reformation, in terms of these two problems. Only
then will sufficient light be cast on Luther's responsibility for the
Reformation schism.

There were two fundamental preconditions for the possibility
of the Reformation: first, that the question be asked, whether the
existent and ruling papal Church, believed to be of divine right,
were in fact the true representation of Christianity.

We can sense at once the colossal development which was necessary before there could be any question of the Reformation. That
is to say, doubt had to be raised not simply over this or that aspect
of the ecclesiastical system: the whole presentation of the faith had
to be rejected, and a fresh total conception of Christianity produced, capable of capturing the mind – almost overnight – of the
majority of the members of the Church. For things to have reached
such a state it was necessary that there should have been a prior,
interior decadence in the religious and ecclesiastical heritage of the
nations of Europe. Even the compelling power of Luther's oratory
could not have found such an echo, had the beginnings of his views
not somehow been familiar for a long time to the European mind.

It was, therefore, in the nature of things that this radical questioning should grow but slowly. Above all, before it had clearly
emerged into consciousness, before it had been formulated, or
grasped in its full import, it lay for long inarticulate within the
secret, inner trend of the thoughts and deeds which determined

the movement of history. From the awakening of the strongly
personal piety within the Church in the twelfth-century the way
led through the destructive struggle of the Church with the 'enlightened' Frederick II to the antipapal disintegration of the late
Middle Ages. Ever more consciously, the contrast became expressed between the Roman Church and Christendom, between curia
and papacy, between papal church and early Christian Church.
To this one can add the name of Philip IV of France, the poverty
controversy, nominalism Occam, *Defensor Pacis*, conciliar ideas, the
Waldensians, the Cathars, Wycliffe, Huss, Hussites. What a vast,
many-sided movement away from the Church then becomes visible.

And this movement of defection can be traced back to roots
lying much further in the past.

Thus, for example, the whole tragic interconnection of justification, duty and fate in the course of the history of the world and
of the Church had already become manifest in that great movement which the Church had been conducting – since the time of
Gregory VII – for the liberation of its religious and spiritual principle from secular control. For this mighty process developed, at
the same time, into a clericalisation of the Church, that is, to an
exclusion of the laity from active participation in the government
of the Church (strained relations with the ruling priestly caste
arose and then changed to enmity), and to a de-sacralisation of the
secular–political sphere. This process of secularisation contained
also a bitter and self-perpetuating opposition between the Germanic and the papal, ultimately between Rome and Germany.
From then on the interests even of the German Church were very
often no longer those of the papacy. Pure faith, in terms of which
it was possible to make a sharp division between papal politics and
the papal, Catholic religion, provided a means of softening that
opposition; but in real life this faith was not strong enough to keep
friction permanently away from vital interests. Even at that time
the great flight of churchmen and their concept of the Church
into a 'purely ecclesiastical' sphere (beyond real life in the actual
political realm) was not particularly good for the Church.

The investiture controversy, in its broadest sense, inaugurated
the rise of the medieval Church. Without it the great achievements
of the Church in the high Middle Ages could scarcely have been
realised. But, by the law of original sin, even the constructive

elements in history are doomed to contain within themselves the seeds of their own corruption, which leads to new burdens, new trials and to new decisions. And so here too the investiture controversy became the cause of the decline of the Church, in the sense of a severe and lasting weakening of things papal and ecclesiastical.

This happened in a roundabout way through the concept of power which Gregory VII had introduced into the papal programme, but which so many of his successors had not succeeded in keeping on the high plane of heroic, religious devotion. Out of human weakness and egotism, by means of politics, law and greed they brought about that secularisation that led even further away from true Christianity, and which we know as the exaggerated curialism of the late Middle Ages, with its completely exaggerated views of direct papal jurisdiction over the temporal goods and laws of the Church and world.

In the meantime, the behaviour of the higher clergy had led the political rulers to turn a dangerous opinion into an axiom: the Church, that is its papal and episcopal incumbents, were to be fought like any other political, judicial and financial power. The battle against the pope, so often reckless in tone and in practical dealings (the pope figuring as 'Antichrist', 'son of wickedness', 'blood sucker', 'oppressor'), prepared the ground. As soon as this battle became allied with dogmatically false propositions people could easily, or at least more easily, find justification for false dogma in the long-familiar legitimacy of the battle. One cannot see, for example, how in 1412 in Prague the papal bulls could have been consigned to the flames if people had not long been accustomed to that grim battle. The inner distortion (or emptiness) of the meaning of ecclesiastical institutions made independence from them easy, in spite of the fact that dogma was considered just as binding as ever. However, that this one-sided bond could never have developed and sustained sufficient strength to save the essential supreme authority of the Church, is taught by daily experience and proved extensively by history. This acceptance of dogma, and loyalty to the externals of the Church tend to be the last things to go, but once they do begin to go, their decline is very rapid. Suddenly they seem to lose their meaning. One day staunch Catholicism is there and is being emphatically lauded; the next day it is gone.

And hence it came about, that that fundamental doubt (cf. p. 14) which had grown so slowly, spread out still more slowly into the masses. But in reality, as already indicated, in every sphere of life the ties with the Church became slacker and less absolute. That is to say, the impossibility of seriously calling the Church in question progressively dissolved, and the possibility of a radical transformation became more evident.

At the beginning of modern times the dissolution or obscuring of the Catholic idea assumed dangerous proportions, threatening life in two ways: it appeared first of all in the aggressive, heretical form of Hussitism and in the various, heretical (or quasi heretical) forms of apocalypsism, spiritualism and communistic socialism; and it also appeared under the guise of a scarcely perceptible, inner decomposition – in the indifferentism and immorality of Renaissance culture, in the secularisation of curialism, in the dangerous, intra-theological disintegration of what was Catholic in Occamism, and, most decisively, in the a-dogmatic and anti-dogmatic relativism of humanist, enlightened education and theology.

And yet it is precisely here that the mysterious element in the subsequent Reformation schism becomes evident. The Church was still the dominant power of the time, the acknowledged guardian and leader, the moulder, so men thought, of both public and private life. Proof of this can be adduced from many sides. The Christian faith was still the central point of all life, and it was taught and dispensed by the priests of the Roman pope; in science, theology, philosophy, law, as in social life, including the administration of justice, and charitable activity, the leadership of the clergy was not seriously called in question. Even the life of the state seemed conceivable only on a foundation of Church order.

And it is not as if this dominance was purely exterior. Precisely in this does the incomparably provocative and alluring paradox of the period fully disclose itself. We can sense this if we contrast the deep, truly evangelical, Church piety, the religious Church art of the years from 1500 to 1520, with the almost instantaneous defection of such wide circles to Luther.

At the same time we must interpret that proposition about the still unbroken dominance of the Roman Church over life in a very restricted sense, if we wish to avoid reaching an enormously false conclusion. In fact, fundamentally, the papal church was no longer the ruler and guide. Hussitism had torn away an entire country, Bohemia, from the western Church community and from the empire. But the decisive factor was that the visible and invisible foundations of life, out of which this dominance of the Church had first grown, had altered most radically. A breaking away from the Church on a gigantic scale, in part visible, in greater part invisible, had taken place; the power of the tradition of the Church as a demand for, and affirmation of, unquestioning obedience to the Church, had been essentially weakened.

Great revolutions are possible only where serious vacuums have formed within a dominant way of life. The vacuums suck alien, hostile forces in from outside, and these rush with elemental power into that which has become empty. The façade still stands, asserting its rights; but because it is itself in the wrong, and has become too superficial, the alien forces advance of themselves. Then there arises that apparently inexplicable, and yet basically natural process of the victory of new ideas over ancient, established power.

We will come to know the details of this process of undermining. Amongst the general causes we list, as always, the destruction of one's own substance by oneself, through the consumption of capital, instead of increasing one's substance and living upon the interest from capital. For example, spiritual capital was used up through the exaggerated use of spiritual weapons. This was one of the furthest-reaching causes, and one which had been longest at work in preparation. Here one must take account of the total process, extending over centuries, of the struggle between papacy and empire, with its excommunications, its antipopes and its large-scale invective. At the beginning of the preparation for the coming religious–ecclesiastical revolution stands the damage to the irreplaceable, religious, mystical aura which surrounded the pope as a completely other-wordly power. With every step into the sphere of politics, especially with every victorious step, the pope more and more became one ruler amongst many others. The twelfth and thirteenth centuries, too, contributed to this development, even although the life of faith was still advancing, and the purely spiritual substance of the hierarchy was still strong – as a result, maybe, of the mighty warnings uttered by St Bernard and St Francis. But then came Boniface VIII, Philip the Fair and the shattering incident of Anagni, after which, to all outward appearance, there remained in the most power-conscious of all popes, no trace of any likeness to God. Europe was left only with the profound experience that papal power, even in spiritual things, had very narrow limits. Then came the undignified haggling between Philip the Fair and Clement V – pope turned French court bishop and finally, Avignon, the emperor Louis the Bavarian and then the schism.

And we must not forget that not only the wholesale application of the highest spiritual punishments automatically diminished their effectiveness but that in the midst of a ceaselessly growing, extraordinarily rich self-awareness on the part of national states, provinces, and of the middle-class laity, Rome always linked very real political and economic demands with spiritual punishments. If the papacy, by an interdict on entire countries, could simply write them off (Bezold), then, whether this was formally justified or not, the situation had become quite impossible, so that the deepest, invisible foundation of faith, which presented Church and papacy as divine things, was severely threatened and dangerously weakened. Contemporaries knew well that in reality the papacy was identified with these things. The man, harshly affected by some punishment, distinguished between a secular and a dogmatic position, and yet did not distinguish. The wrath of the stricken was directed against individual popes, but very easily against the papacy as well.

In accordance with the universal character of the Church these developments applied almost equally to all of Europe. The Reformation, however, arose in Germany. Why?

The problem is very complicated and must, therefore, be approached from different angles. A provisional answer, leaving many elements (chiefly Luther) out of account, would run something like this: in Germany in the Catholic period there was never sufficient national fulfilment within the Church. What we mean is this: in Spain, France and England a present, although dangerous (cf. England) remedy against the common threat of an explosion in Church stability and European unity had been provided in time by the formation, with papal approval and within the unity of the Church, of national Churches, allowing considerable satisfaction of national interests within the Church. In these countries the explosive force was paralysed by this satisfaction, but the Germans were not satisfied and so the tendency towards rebellion in all the movements we have mentioned became, for the most part, concentrated in Germany. Because in Germany national interests had not been sufficiently satisfied by Rome there resulted a twofold intensification of the danger, making it easier for the breach to take place there than elsewhere. On the other hand, the political development in the kingdoms to the west made possible the political form of the Church just mentioned.

Certainly, in accordance with the basic law of all development, including the preliminary stages of all revolutions, the far-reaching disintegration mentioned above was in many ways still latent. Many of the faithful were close to the point where any further step was bound to lead them away from the foundation of the Church, to separate them from it in fact, but they had no idea that this was so. The period was uniformly Catholic, and yet that unity was threatened at its foundations. It was precisely this interior, unconscious disintegration that characterised the situation; and it was precisely this circumstance which made the attack, when launched with such force by Luther, such a destructive blow.

A bitter proof of the correctness of this thesis is to be found in the incomprehensibly rapid change in attitude to the Church, the clergy, the mass and ceremonies, amongst large groups in all classes of society. The special value formerly – in spite of every protest – conceded everywhere as a matter of course to the sacral priesthood with all its radiance, collapsed, in many places overnight. One day the great patrician families of Nuremberg were calmly donating new, wonderful, costly altars and numerous splendid statues in honour of the saints; next day they were dragging out of the cloister the child whom they had dedicated to the life of perfection as a nun under the seal of the threefold vows of the Church – rescuing her from the net of godless human ordinances, from the sacrilege of papistical idolatry. This is a saddening, insoluble riddle. But here too we come to know what a spiritual façade without adequate substance, and what the sudden process of spiritual crystallisation or spiritual collapse mean. The attitude of respect collapsed all the sooner on account of its having been retained in spite of all, simply from habit, without reflection or deeper motivation, and not really possessed. Spiritual possession presupposes increase. In the widest circles of the faithful who were absolutely loyal to the Church, this increase was out of the question. The spiritual riches of the gospel and the liturgy were unknown to many loyal members of the Church. And, as will be seen, this was true not least of the uneducated masses who enjoyed insufficient religious care. For the moment the intensive illumination of the breaches by embittered criticism together with a radically simplified new presentation must suffice to explain the subjectively inadequate assurance of the old inheritance.

Widespread ignorance of the extent of Luther's dogmatic opposition to the Church as well as the concealment from the people of the apostasy taking place suggest, and Catholic life, heroically maintained and then blossoming anew, proves, that the processes indicated had not been entirely victorious; but this is no denial of the fact that in countless places the process, as we have described it, had run its course.

One has only to consider side by side, the indicated 'necessity' of the Reformation and the mystery of its advent, in order to raise the question: Why had this condition of coexistence and confrontation not already been resolved at the end of the fifteenth century by the outbreak of a reformation?

This question seeks to uncover the positive strength of the Reformation. And that was Luther. In spite of the absolute rule of the Church over life, in spite of flourishing, pure, Christian piety, the Reformation was prepared for within the Church by the latent inner disintegration we have mentioned. But it only became possible through the Reformer himself.

For a correct understanding of the foregoing account and of that which will follow, it is necessary to bear in mind that every total presentation of such comprehensive events must be stylised. The reader must therefore remember that the concrete circumstances of pre-Reformation times were an extraordinarily colourful assortment, far beyond anything we can describe here. They frequently vary, not only from region to region but also from place to place within these regions.

TWO

Prologue in Church History
(1300–1450)

The schism in the Christian Church, which we call the Reformation, could not have happened if the state and Church of the west had still possessed the strength of medieval, universal unity. In particular, since the foundation of the schism was pre-eminently an event in Church history, it could not have happened had the medieval papacy still exercised its universal authority over the people. It is necessary, therefore, to clarify the break-up and inner weakening of this specifically medieval, political, universal papacy.

The origin of the Middle Ages and the configuration of their basic characteristics resulted in the fact that the Middle Ages, in the classic sense of the period of full bloom of the Church, were only possible through the co-operation of the two mutually dependent supreme authorities: that is the co-operation of the universal, specifically medieval empire and the specifically medieval universal papacy.

The break-up of this organic co-operation, maintained in spite of all sorts of tensions, even hostile tensions, meant also the collapse of the specifically medieval absolute authority of the papacy; this collapse inaugurated the late Middle Ages or, what amounts to the same thing, the emergence of modern times. But the collapse had already begun in the period when the universal partner of the papacy, the medieval empire, disappeared with the ruin of the Hohenstauffen – partly through their own fault as well as through the machinations of the papacy. But the destruction of the Hohenstauffen enemy was, in the last analysis, no victory for the papacy. In the first place this destroyed the active balance necessary to the European medieval world, as its structure then was; that is to say, it in fact weakened the power of the Church. Secondly, the ruin of the Hohenstauffen was accomplished (as the completion of a very long development which had already begun with the Church reform party concerned with the pseudo-Isidorean forgeries of the ninth century, and with the Cluniac reformers) by the obvious reliance of the papacy on France, and therefore on a non-universal, modern, national, political and particularist power, which forthwith strove, as a natural consequence, to control the Church.

This development was decisively encouraged by Philip IV of France – who must be repeatedly mentioned – and his struggle against the inopportune and grandiosely exaggerated claims of Boniface VIII. The climax of this process was Avignon. The battle of Philip IV against Boniface VIII was not an episode but a watershed in world history. Thereafter the specifically medieval papacy no longer existed.

What has this to do with the German Reformation? It is a decisive factor, if we define 'cause' in that more penetrating sense in which it was defined in the first chapter. Obviously it is not true that the outcome of this struggle made a revolutionary Church reform necessary, but probably without it and its consequences the Reformation would not have been possible. For the process included a mighty weakening of the papacy and the Church, resulting in fresh weaknesses constantly emerging in the realm of Church politics and in political and religious life. Every great weakening of this century must be taken into account, if we wish to understand the condition of the Church which Luther was one day to attack. For every weakening produces a diminution of substance, provokes criticism and, in addition, multiplies the prospects of successful attack. All this is truer than ever when the attacks are of the cataclysmic type we have mentioned.

Decisive also for the victory of the Reformation was the concept of the modern, autonomous state, not subject to the Church. A start was made in Sicily by Frederick II; then the beginnings of the creation of the concept and its corresponding realisation are to be found in Philip IV, more precisely, in the work of his lay jurists and in his own political scheme. From the point of view of Church politics, Avignon became the test-case. And through a logical inversion as through a logical sequence there developed out of the German struggle against Avignon the further formation of the concept of the autonomous state in a directly antipapal sense. This took place within the circle of the Franciscan Spirituals, who remained united to the last against the Avignon papacy, and through the epoch-making work of the Parisian professors Marsiglio of Padua – who had fled to Louis the Bavarian – and John of Jandun, authors of *Defensor Pacis*, and through the work of the English Franciscan, William of Occam, who also had fled to Bavaria. The ideas of the *Defensor Pacis* including the conciliar view which it shared with Occam, and the independent and liberal attitude towards clerical claims, formed part of the decisive foundations of the pre-Reformation dissolution in Europe and in the Church. For this reason these ideas became part of the essential armoury of the Reformers, and with them they disclosed, for the first time, their full explosive force.

The political, national dissolution we have mentioned now ran its course everywhere in such a way that it became mingled with an anti-Church criticism, bearing the clearly recognisable tendency, already mentioned, to move away from the ecclesiastical–political and the moral spheres to the sphere of dogma – the tendency, that is, to become a fundamental criticism of the dogmatic primacy. Luther's system, in turn, was to place the full-stop at the end of this development.

This transition in the form of criticism is not without its inner logic. The linking in a personal union of the specifically medieval, time-conditioned papacy, of the political, papal plenitude of power (*potestas directa in temporalia*) with the absolute primacy of the teaching authority, not conditioned by time, is the beginning of this process, the elaboration of curialism the commentary upon it.

In the most diverse ways the popes placed their spiritual power at the service of their temporary political aims. This was understandable and often necessary. But it was just as often effective in obliterating the boundaries between the conditional, temporal power of the pope and his absolute power, especially when, at the end of the Middle Ages, excessive exploitation of the spiritual penalties of excommunication and interdict was indulged for the sake of purely secular interests. This confusion of interests injected a reverse tendency into the reaction of the protagonists: criticism of the temporally conditioned papacy became a criticism of the dogmatic primacy.

As early as the fourteenth century this criticism had assumed the acute form already mentioned. The central motif of antipapal attack, the conciliar idea, had emerged. This was the theory that not the pope but the general council was leader and representative of the Church; and the council was superior to the pope and directed him. It was an idea which moved out of the realm of theory to capture with great power the most varied spheres of life. If there ever was a centrifugal, decentralising force of this kind in the Church before Luther's time it was this. Having been formulated in the *Defensor Pacis* it was brought to life by an inner necessity in the schism; it was encouraged not only from without, by the enemies of the papacy, but from within by the papacy itself, which for years had seemed to contradict itself through schism, so that the life of the Church – its unity – seemed no longer capable of being saved by any other means.

The experience of European schism left an indelible mark upon the consciousness of the western Church. The experience, that is to say, of a papacy divided in two for forty years; two papacies mutually excommunicating each other and the world, tearing Christendom apart, down to individual states, dioceses, cloisters and families, and finally laying a double financial burden upon Christendom, and almost sucking it dry. Such an experience could never be completely erased from western consciousness; its consequences certainly could never disappear. Severe theoretical and practical damage had been done to the dogmatic concept. All too often people have allowed the unexpected external rise of the Renaissance papacy to blind them to the disintegrating and profound effects of the conciliar idea and its continuance.

In order to end the apparently irresolvable conflict between Eugene IV (1431–47) and the Council of Basel, the empire decided that a new, and irreproachably general, council should assemble in a German city. Eugene IV naturally rejected this idea, but the

B

empire countered by summoning a German national council, at which the conciliar rights laid down at Constance were accepted, and a pragmatic sanction obtained. In 1482 Margrare Albert Alcibiades declared that if the worst came to the worst he would appeal to a general council. In fact in Germany there were never so many appeals made to a council as in the years immediately following the promulgation of the bull *Execrablis*, in which the conciliar idea was condemned in 1460 by Pius II, formerly its zealous champion. Before the diet at Worms in 1495 the Saxon nobleman Hans von Hermannsgrün proposed to the emperor that the pope be refused obedience and a German patriarchate erected, if, for example, Alexander VI should transfer the imperial crown to the French; for a general council would be the appropriate court for calling the pope to account.

Conversely, the paralysing fear of the Renaissance popes of a general council, as well as the continuance of the conciliar idea in contemporary French Gallicanism and in Anglicanism, and finally, the effectiveness of the idea when Luther took it up, prove the same thing. It even became possible for cardinals of the Church to threaten schism in the midst of the Reformation storm, under Adrian VI and Clement VII. There was the appeal to a general council against Clement VII by the rebellious Cardinal Pompeo Colonna, his plan eventually to take the tiara by force, and the fear of Clement VII that this Colonna could bring him before a council or have himself elected as antipope. Charles V threatened Clement VII with a council. Charles' counsellor, Gattinara, planned to make himself pope through a council after the deposition of Clement VII. The council to which the antipapal state document of Charles V against Clement VII appealed, was, to be sure, to be summoned by the pope, but the antithesis between pope and council was abundantly clear. Had not Charles V written to the cardinals, 'If His Holiness does not want to summon a council, should not the cardinals convoke it according to legal right?' And again, the English chancellor, Cardinal Wolsey, conceived the plan that for the time when Clement VII was a prisoner in Rome, all the free cardinals should assemble in Avignon and take over the government of the Church in place of the pope. It was also taken for granted that if at the death of Clement VII the imperial cardinals should elect a pope, France and England would set up an antipope. Cardinal Salviati, who issued the summons to Avignon, feared a schism. The deliberations of the royal council of Castile were dominated by the conciliar idea. Vital tradition followed the same line in the university of Paris, a centre still exerting an important influence upon ecclesiastical views at the beginning of the sixteenth century. There they had not forgotten Gerson.

In his memorandum of 1520 John Faber, O.P., demanded, in the interest of the pope himself, that he should not take a 'single step which, in the tacit judgment of honest men, might appear unworthy of him. Since now the struggle against Luther appears to be laden with all manner of dubious, personal motives, it is obviously most expedient to leave the settlement of the entire affair to men who are above all suspicion. Admittedly decision in matters of faith is the special prerogative of the pope, and no one should take this right from him. Yet, from love of the common good, he will leave this matter to others, to men of distinguished learning, who are quite above any suspicion that they might, from fear or hope, flatter the pope to the damage of evangelical truth, or that they might, from temporal interest, incline to the side of the opposition party. . . . They should read through Luther's writings with care, listen to the man himself, and their judgment, whatever it is, should be accepted. Taught by these men, Luther will sincerely admit his error and republish his works, corrected by himself, so that the great value of his seeds of evangelical truth be not destroyed on account of a few trifling instances. . . . If some are not pleased by these proposals, then it is probably best to leave the decision to the next general council.' In 1520 Cochlaeus, who had just become an avowed Catholic in Rome, in his answer to *Martin Luther's Vicious Appeal from the Pope to a Future Council*, deduced the absolute power of the pope purely from Scripture, with such a lack of restraint, as though there had never been a victorious conciliar idea. But in 1523 he became convinced in Rome (Adrian VI had just died and Cochlaeus could now see how directly the curia strove against reform) that only a council would be of any use since the pope would never succeed in carrying through a reform alone. But this position is none other than that which since the eighth decade of the fourteenth century had brought victory to the moderate conciliar idea of loyal churchmen, and which had finally ended with the summoning of the Council of Pisa (1409) by the cardinals who were doubtful of the goodwill and power of the popes.

Do we fully realise how deeply the unity of the Church had been attacked and how weak it remained? No matter how much the idea of a council and conciliar theory here and there were made to serve crass self-interest, they were the expression of the now universal awareness of the untenability of the Church's condition. This awareness had not, in fact, disappeared after the cessation of the schism, but had become stronger and more general. The feeling that the heart of the evil was located in the curia and that therefore the curia or its head, the individual pope, could not bring about thorough changes, had encouraged the ripening of the conciliar idea; and now, at the beginning of the Reformation, this feeling was again as full of life as ever.

We cannot discount as one of the causes of the German Reformation the notion of the papacy as an Italian and foreign power. It will be seen that the growth of German national consciousness in the stormy years of the Reformation was linked with this feeling. The strengthening of this impression in Germany, however, is in turn linked with the hundred years' dependence of the papacy on France, and with the resultant and long-term financial exploitation of the German Church by Avignon and France, in favour of the papal curia, whether through the management of benefices, or through extraordinary taxation. Through Innocent IV, who excommunicated the Hohenstauffen Frederick II on French soil at Lyons, through the many French cardinals and the series of French popes at the end of the thirteenth century, through the overthrow of Boniface VIII, the road had led to the enslavement of Avignon and the continuance of this enslavement by a majority of French cardinals, and finally to the schism of the west.

It is obvious how much the break-up of the specifically, medieval, universal position of the papacy within power-politics laid the foundation in many ways of a profound, inner weakening of the papacy and consequently of the Church. However, every inner weakening of the Church, which, like this one, may be declared to be of importance, prepares the ground for the emergence of radical criticism and its success.

From the high Middle Ages on, this weakening of the papacy

was paralleled by a second weakening which represents, even more directly, a religious and ecclesiastical loss.

Through a legitimate, a necessary, development the pope had become first a landowner, then a political prince and then a prince of the world. Again through a legitimate development, there grew up at the papal court, in connection with the increase of papal authority a mighty, juridical, political, administrative apparatus, which soon fulfilled a fiscal function as well. That is to say, through justifiable developments, control of law, politics and finance were drawn into church administration. Again the foundation was provided by the utterly religious programme of Gregory VII, which had developed out of monastic reform. Even at the height of the Middle Ages under Innocent III, for the pope personally, power, law, politics and wealth were united in a great sense of responsibility before God, which increased all the more as the pope's fulness of power and consciousness of power appeared to raise him ever closer to God.

At the same time, law, politics, taxes and administrative apparatus, in the service of selfish men, became a dead weight and developed a logic of their own. The inner dialectic of things made itself felt to the detriment of the Church; on a vast scale there resulted a politicising, a tendency to legalism and worldliness in ecclesiastical administration, and hence to a thoroughgoing secularisation of the private and public life of the Church.

Out of harmless, justifiable and necessary taxes there developed in the papal curia, at first gradually and then in a flood, the buying and selling of spiritual offices, corruption and simony, the whole fiscally managed system of benefices with its attendant expectancies, pluralities, nepotism, luxury and immorality.

Each of these three series of developments in turn contains a whole series of foci of infection; not until just before the Reformation do they reveal their whole poisonous strength. Once again they diminish the irreplaceable, religious feeling of veneration of the papacy and of the popes, as something incomparable, something elevated above this world, and therefore unimpeachable. And so, people fought and criticised this ruler amongst rulers as they did any other, using the same weapons of furtive and lying diplomacy, calumny, forged documents and false prophecies. The ever-growing pressure of papal taxes, used to pay foreigners and maintain splendid courts, aroused the anger of the taxpayers and the desire and effort to escape from this pressure.

Immediately before the Reformation, under the Renaissance popes, in direct antithesis to the increasingly violent demand for reform by all groups in society and in the Church, from the most varied reasons, these abuses multiplied until a point of disintegration was reached, which threatened the very life of the Church. They were intensified and supported by a far-reaching break-up of the concept of spiritual life through moral and religious abuses in the higher and lower clergy, in the monasteries and in the people; through an intellectual revolution in the Renaissance and humanism; through the danger of schism in the form of national Churches; through the enormous weakening of things ecclesiastical and Catholic. We shall return later to the content and effect of this process; but let us note at once that it is easy but pointless to doubt the correctness of this account by pointing to the fact that the people in the fourteenth and fifteenth centuries were obviously still perfectly happy under Rome, and that – as admitted above – in spite of the enormous shocks of two or three centuries the Church at the beginning of the sixteenth was still the dominant power of the time. For here, ultimately, we face the problem of every serious analysis of life – its complexity. It is not solved by describing the condition reached, in such a way that, according to inclination, one aspect is suppressed through stronger emphasis upon the other. It is much more a question of exposing the evolutionary trend, the *direction towards*, what is new, that which is in process of becoming. That alone is a more or less satisfactory account of the complexity of life.

Now, the new factor, that which was logically on the increase in these decades, was not a strengthening of the religious idea of the papacy, of the Church, of the priestly life or of Catholicism as unchangeable, firmly established truth; it was not contentment with and adherence to the Church; but the diminution of these ideas and an enormous increase of criticism.

THREE

Political Powers and Social Stratification in Germany before the Reformation

I

The peculiarity of the medieval state, and hence the possibilities of its history, were bound up in great measure with the vague delimitation of spheres of influence within the complex hierarchy of powers upon which it rested. The heart of the intra-political process consisted in the competitive struggle of these various powers for predominance or at least survival.

In fifteenth-century Europe this struggle entered a decisive stage, at that time reaching its virtual conclusion in many states. Ranke rightly characterised this interplay of political forces by saying that the nations had achieved a consciousness of their individuality, of themselves. In England, France, Spain and Poland, to some extent in Hungary, this consciousness was strong enough to exhibit its unity in a central government which forced the particular powers into dependence upon it.

Germany faced the same problem. But there it was not solved. The concept of the empire, whose meaning and destiny was to be at one and the same time universal and national, was too vague and therefore too weak. On the other hand, the princely and non-princely territories and local powers of diverse forms had grown mightily. The reform struggle of the opposition parties in 1461, 1484, 1495 ff., is most important as an expression of the need to gather together the imperial powers in a greater unity than before, and as a proof of the beginnings of a national sense of unity – important, therefore, for the solution of one of the great themes of Reformation history. For the most part, however, this consciousness unfortunately developed along with the simultaneous rejection of the political assertion that the reforms be conceived as affecting the estates of the realm. It is understandable that this roundabout way led neither to a clarification of the concept of the empire, which had gradually become so inorganic, nor to its unification. What did happen was that, as a result of territorial egoism and imminent confessional schism, achievement lagged hopelessly behind rational objectives. After more than fifty years of strife, Charles V, when he abdicated, was to face essentially the same situation in this respect, as did his grandfather at the epoch-making diet of Worms in 1495.

On the other hand, the course of German history in the era of confessional division was closely bound up with the fact that the wearer of the imperial crown was the representative of a family dynasty which dominated the other German princes. The individual, who as Charles V was overlord of the German territorial princes and of the free cities, in the exercise of his imperial office was ultimately dependent on Habsburg, Burgundian and Spanish power. This power brought him assistance, money and soldiers, but aroused the envy, fear and opposition of his colleagues, the German territorial princes.

This unusual Habsburg complex of powers not only manifested itself as a secure possession but also, in the political sphere, frequently in the form of unrealised claims. The foundation of this power had been laid by the feeble Frederick III in his treaty (1463) with King Corvinus of Hungary, and with Burgundy. For, in spite of all reverses and accidents, both countries were finally won, and both acquired a universal historical significance. In connection with the war to liberate Europe from the Turks (and also with the rise of the Habsburg Empire, no longer truly universal but only national after the time of Ferdinand I), this alliance with Hungary became the germ of the modern Austro-

Hungarian dual monarchy. Finally the marriage of the eighteen-year-old, completely impecunious Archduke Maximilian with Mary of Burgundy became nothing less than the source from which the world empire of Charles V arose: the son of Mary of Burgundy and Maximilian, Philip the Handsome, married the heiress of Aragon and Castile, Juana, daughter of Ferdinand the Catholic. This marriage produced the future emperor Charles and his brother Ferdinand. The union of Habsburg, Burgundy and Spain produced that empire upon which, after the acquisition of over-seas possessions, the sun never set; it included the Habsburg family lands in Austria, possessions in southern Germany, Burgundy with the most important and richest provinces in the Netherlands, southern Italy and Spain.

It was this very predominance of family power that aroused and increased the opposition of the electors and the princes. They did not want to allow the Habsburgs to rise to such power that they might turn them into vassals of the empire, of the emperor indeed, through privileges granted to the French (later to the Spanish). Until the world-historical revolution before the Schmalkald War, the main centre of purely political opposition was that provided by the antagonism between the two neighbours, Wittelsbach and Habsburg.

In the Habsburg state system and hence in the history of central Europe in the time of Maximilian and Charles V, Burgundy formed the pivot. It was only this large-scale structure stretching from the North Sea to the Alps, economically and culturally most highly developed in the Flanders provinces, that made the Habsburgs a European power, and Charles V a world power. But without the pivot the structure remained a disconnected framework, easily weakened.

The possibilities of conflict to which this state system was exposed, are easily recognisable. They were rooted in the natural antagonism between Habsburg and France in their struggle for Burgundy and Italy. Under Maximilian, however, they were activated chiefly by his exaggerated personal plans with regard to France, plans that were carried out with insufficient stability.

Under Charles V, when Spain and southern Italy completed the encirclement of France, conflict on a large scale for the first time became unavoidable. The same fate of encirclement threatened the states of the Church, that is the papacy which in a sense had become a dynasty. The old, anti-imperial inclination of the popes towards France received a fresh and natural stimulus.

The expansionist tendencies of France worked in the opposite direction. They flared up in Burgundy also, a duchy indubitably containing former French fiefs, and then in Naples (the kings of France being the successors to the extinct line of Anjou).

To recapture the crown of Naples was the aim of the fantastic 1494 campaign of Charles VIII against Naples, when he was announced as God's scourge by Savonarola. Once again France won Naples in 1506. To be sure this was in the end a mere episode. From the turn of the century it is Spain which finally appears as the decisive power in southern Italy. The French advances during the third decade of the century did not alter this fact. But forced surrender was by no means the same thing as a French renunciation of her southern Italian claims, and consequently contributed nothing to slackening the tensions between France and Habsburg-Spain.

With the campaign of Charles VIII to southern Italy, Italy became the subject of major European politics, and in a significant degree the scene of the quarrel. Italy was torn apart by internal quarrels and visited by many wars in the interests of foreign nations, at a time when, like no other country in the world, it was producing a wealth of intellect and artistic genius. With this there began the perplexing and often senseless, rapid change of ownership of important parts of Italy, chiefly of Milan, which in 1494 was French, in 1495 was won back, became French again in 1499, only to be lost again, and then was won by Francis I after the defeat of the Swiss at Marignano; thereafter it remained a bone of contention between Francis I and Charles V until 1544 (peace of Crépy).

It was in Italy too in the fifteenth century, that there had arisen out of this battle of all against all, the edifices of five great states. Through its growing power on the mainland Venice had become an important factor in the battle for upper Italy; through her maritime power, Venice had at times been nothing less than the deciding factor in the war against the Turks. Milan's importance lay in its key position as a connecting link with Rome; Naples' value lay partly in its being a bridgehead connecting Spain with the Habsburg lands, via north Italy, and partly – along with Milan – in its being a corner-post in the encirclement of the Church state.

This Church state was politically the most significant element in the peninsula, partly in a secular political sense on account of the national, Italian, dynastic character which it had acquired under the Renaissance popes, and on account of the expansion which the powerful and belligerent Julius II had bestowed on it; partly, however, on account of its connection with the papacy and its far-reaching non-political and political and, not least, financial, world power. Its importance became specially obvious as a decisive factor in the struggle between the Habsburgs and France. In its abandonment of the empire and its turning to aid the French it was to fulfil in tragic fashion its political role of world-historical dimensions.

A similar role, but on a much smaller scale, was played by England, in the history of the German Reformation. England dominated the sea routes around France, and was in a position to complete the encirclement of that country, at all events, to tie up considerable French forces, or else release them against the emperor.

And finally there was the great foreign political factor in the history of Christian Europe – the Turks. The foundation of national consolidation in Spain was in reality completed in 1492 by the conquest of Granada, the last Moorish possession in the peninsula. But this repulsion of Islam in the south-west was balanced by its strengthening in the Mediterranean and its menacing advance from the east after the fall of Constantinople in 1453.

Islam, 'the infidel', was officially *the* enemy of Christian Europe. In reality nothing more mercilessly revealed how far the political and religious unity of Europe had declined and how great the crass political egotism of the individual European states had become, than the handling of the Turkish menace by the German princes (with the exception of those directly threatened), by Pope Alexander VI, from time to time even by Clement VII, by Venice, by Zapolya in Hungary (and his Bavarian allies) and by the French. The picture is one of treaty-breaking and utter faithlessness which makes a mockery of the idea of a unified and Christian Europe, as well as of the Christian conviction of individual leaders.

II

The political potentialities of an historical situation wait for some leader who will turn them into realities. It has already been indicated that an important role in the activation of the above developments fell to Maximilian. In fact, the whole political struggle for power which affected the history of the Reformation in Germany was, in a decisive measure, an inheritance from this emperor. His unique, by no means straightforward personality was added as an equally important, sometimes more important, factor, to the general political circumstances. He released formative historical forces of great magnitude, which would not have been released without him.

It says something for the strength of this personality that the electoral princes did what for centuries nothing less than the power of the reigning emperor or the privileges which he granted could have elicited from them: they elected the son of a completely powerless, fugitive emperor (Frederick III) as king of the Romans. He alone, the youthful consort of the heiress of Burgundy, who had first to fight for the inheritance of his wife, seemed able to vanquish Corvinus, the Hungarian robber of Habsburg lands, then residing in Vienna (peace of Pressburg, 1491).

The nickname, 'the last of the knights', which stuck to him, well expresses the essentials of Maximilian's character and deeds. It expresses the charm of his warlike, personal courage and the attraction of his appearance as he fought in the first line of battle, calling the soldiers, whom he knew how to unite, his 'sons'; it also suggests the romantic element in his sense of history. It fits just as well the unexpected and adventurous-theatrical quality of his political plans. Maximilian was full of sudden movements, in setting things up, in allowing them to fall, in forgetting objectives of great importance. For example, in a most unimperial manner he was quick to declare to the estates in Freiburg in 1498 and in Augsburg in 1500 that he would rather throw the crown at his feet than wait for others to do so. He moved at an unevenly quick tempo, a spiritual brother of those humanists of his time, whom he valued so highly, who so often wrote 'in haste', upon their letters; he belonged to that 'hasty epoch', as Luther called it. He had great but also inconsistent and inconstant versatility. When this was expressed in his private life in his curious, many-sided interests and manual skills (painting, hunting, fishing and even cooking), it was more interesting than great, at all events it was harmless. It moved him to study the art of artillery, and to recount, in history and historical novels, the fame of his family and of himself; but the same propensity entered the sphere of state policy and exercised a far-reaching effect upon his own time and that which followed, both theoretically and in military practice. Through the national-humanistic history and novel writing which he demanded and encouraged, and which recorded his own deeds in the great story of Germany's past, he significantly encouraged the national consciousness for which he provided a living, attractive centre, in his own person.

If, however, it is the same forces which shape policy both at home and abroad, then it is here alone that they are tested; and we can hardly say they would have passed the test.

It is beyond dispute that Maximilian, through augmenting the power of the Habsburg family (Tyrol, lower Austria, alliance with Hungary), through the Burgundian marriage and his battle for the Burgundian inheritance, created the possibility of the fairy-tale rise of Habsburg power under Charles V, and also set up an important bastion around Germany, which was only surrendered to the French by the treachery of the rebellious German princes in 1552. Nevertheless, the fact remains that his large-scale policy succeeded in providing a settlement neither in Italian nor in French affairs.

If Maximilian could still claim considerable success or, put otherwise, if he was able to avoid falling into even worse chaos, he often had astonishing luck to thank for this, a luck which will be met again in similar and yet very different form as companion of his grandson, Charles V.

The height of fantasy was reached in his plan to make himself pope, and so at last achieve genuine unity for the Christian west.

More realistic and all the more ominous were his fantastic plans for France: his plan to marry the heiress of Brittany and thereby tear this province away from France; the obstinacy with which, all his life, he clung to the idea of winning back the duchy of Burgundy which lay outside the empire. The abandonment of these plans must have shown that, in Maximilian, the holder of the imperial power took precedence over the particular dynastic designs of the heir of Charles the Bold. It is true that his dynastic policy was never separated from the concept of the empire, but as a whole his policy followed the line of the rapidly rising territorial powers. In this respect he was the most significant phenomenon of this kind before Brandenburg-Prussia.

Again, the peculiarity of Maximilian's personality made it impossible for him either to avoid or to do without this overloading. Reasonable restraint with respect to Burgundy appeared to him as an abandonment of his knightly honour and reputation. He lost Switzerland and surrendered Prussia in order to win Brittany; he married his daughter in Spain (1495–97), and laid the foundation for the alliance of his grandson with Hungary and Bohemia (1515); his plans were grandiose, but boundless and inorganic, and hence overburdened and threatened on all sides. This is true also of his evaluation and handling of the German territorial princes. He did not recognise the limits of his power, and failed to form an adequate estimate of the power of his enemies; he made no attempt to gain a clear conception of what was necessary for the substance and continuation and, even more, for the urgent, inner constitutional renewal of the empire (in fact, he saw no necessity for this), and of what further territorial claims were a luxury.

He remained – as someone has said – the knight of the small battles, whom fate had set in the midst of great combinations, which he then began to settle with splendid self-confidence and knightly verve, but, all too often, piecemeal, without a sufficiently constructive plan.

It is only this manner of approaching major politics as a knightly adventurer which can explain how Maximilian bit into Flanders and, in spite of the calls for help from his threatened and then pursued father, permitted the Austrian family power to break up completely, without fulfilling his duty as the elected king of the Romans (from 1486 on). This also explains why he brought to an end the reconquest of the Habsburg lands with that indecisive peace of Pressburg on account of the fantastic, problematic and internationally poisonous plan for acquiring Brittany.

In these things Maximilian was the opposite of his statesmanlike, incomparably more important, and consistently dogged grandson, Charles. Not only did Charles take over from Maximilian this fateful, inorganic inheritance with its insufficiently consolidated inner structure and its multifarious external burdens but, as a result of significant increase in the power of the Spanish inheritance, he saw dangerous opposition growing against his world-empire, and his power being decisively pushed out of Germany, although at the same time that power was on the increase. And so, for Charles, the demand for the whole of Burgundy meant much more than an extension of the dynastic power; it was to serve the construction of a universal imperial power.

That inconsistent policy governed by Maximilian's personality stood in contrast to the systematic programme of the king with respect to the needs and rights of the empire in Italy and with respect to the inner necessity of resisting the hereditary French enemy. But this programme would have been a contradiction of what has just been described, only if Maximilian himself had remained true to these things. However, he himself entered into an alliance in his quickly fluctuating manner with the French, whom he had so forcibly represented as the hereditary enemy. Not without justice, the estates of the empire saw in this a dangerous lack of orientation.

In spite of this, the adversaries in the empire, the territorial powers, had the least right to criticise the emperor. Despite his wavering, which clearly arose from the needs of his dynastic policy (in Flanders), the emperor still recognised the fateful importance of the French danger; and he recognised it because he understood its connection with the political role of the contemporary papacy. He saw the danger of a French emperor whose inevitable counterpart would have been a French pope. Without doubt France did present this danger; and it was presented by the papacy as well, for the power of the papal, Italian principality would not have sufficed, even under Julius II, to withstand the pressure of a French emperor who encircled the states of the Church. All this was true quite apart from the fact that the traditional, immanent

French powers had by no means disappeared from the fabric of the curia.

If this danger had become a reality, it would have meant nothing less than the dissolution of the empire. But even this danger of a French emperor was not perceived by the greater number of the German territorial princes. The subsequent, dishonourable incidents of bribery in the struggle of Francis I for the imperial crown provide just as much proof of this as do the later, complicated negotiations of the German princes with the emperor's French enemy, up to the betrayal of the league of princes in 1552.

III

The centrifugal development of Germany in contrast to the unified development of the great monarchies in the west is an expression of the triumphant egotism of the separate estates in Germany and, conversely, an expression of the lack of an absolute power. The predominance of this egotism with respect both to the empire and to the emperor was the most important factor in the political development of Germany in the whole Reformation period; indeed, apart from Luther, it was the most important factor in the development of Church politics. This intrigue was, none the less, elevated to a higher level in that a kind of consciousness of the unity of the nation emerged and elicited attempts to turn this unity into a practical, political power.

The most significant beginnings of this, however, were to be found in the concept of the emperor. In spite of all the dynastic egotism of Maximilian and later of Charles V, it would be unjust to overlook the extent to which the idea and interests of the empire governed their plans and negotiations. And we can never lose sight of the fact that a radical victory of the centrifugal territorial powers would have been equivalent to the collapse of the empire. The distressing thing was that the emperor was not the empire, and that the empire remained the intermediary between monarchy and confederation, in which the estates were not subservient but participating members in the government in contrast to the national monarchies. Moreover, here the social strata are to be understood as estates, only in a limited sense. When, after 1388, the cities fell out of national politics, and much later, the knights and peasants too, the empire became a union of princes. Until the period of humanism and the Reformation, what was or was not the unity of the empire rested upon the greater or lesser consent of the princes, a consent that was easily influenced by petty egotism.

To this must be added the dualism between empire and emperor, which had been increasing since the fifteenth century. Gradually the personal power of the emperor departed from the empire. By the end of the fifteenth century even the Habsburg family possessions did not completely and always belong to the empire. Under Charles V this process became quite obvious in the efforts to release the Netherlands from their obligations towards the empire while leaving their rights unimpaired. It is self-evident that in terms of sentiment as of practical politics this dissolution was encouraged by the mighty power of Charles in Spain, and then by his enmity towards the German Reformation.

Behind this particularistic egotism of the princes towards one another, which condemned the empire to impotence, there were attempts at reform, that is, attempts to mobilise the forces of the empire.

Above all there was the reform work carried out after 1486 by the elector of Mainz, Count Berthold von Henneberg. To condemn him, along with the majority of princes about that time, of gross class egotism, is to be most unjust, for he saw the empire as unequivocally based upon the estates. His reforms were always aimed at exalting the empire. For him the fundamental thing was the desire and the ability soberly to weigh up the political possibilities. Henneberg is the antithesis to Maximilian's arbitrary volatility. Henneberg wanted to protect the empire against this very arbitrariness, and also against the instability of territorial particularism. If he could succeed in ensuring that imperial projects had to be laid before the imperial estates as a whole, that is that the emperor did not have to play one estate off against another, then this also would promote the unity of the empire.

The work of reform of Berthold of Mainz is tied up with the existence and the power of the electoral council. With its help were carried out those discussions, the most famous episode in which was the diet of Worms (1495). Contrary to the foreign policy of Maximilian who wanted support against Charles VIII (the latter's campaign against Naples destroyed Maximilian's Italian plans), the reform party proceeded with the very necessary, domestic political arrangements in such a manner that they would have been of epoch-making importance for the realisation of imperial unity, had they been lasting.

The following things were resolved: (a) there should be a universal, and, for the first time, a lasting territorial peace; (b) there should be an imperial supreme court, distinct from the royal supreme court, with the right of proclaiming the ban of the empire, with a permanent meeting-place (no longer travelling about with the royal court), and a fixed salary for its members; (c) there should be a 'common penny', i.e. a common tax. The German diet of the estates would form the executive.

Clearly such a compromise was so disadvantageous to the emperor that he was obliged to try to make the decreed arrangement ineffective. In reality his power still proved to be the stronger because the estates did not have the desire to adapt themselves to a common goal and to make sacrifices for it.

By 1498, contrary to the settlement of 1495, Maximilian had set up his own privy council in opposition to the imperial supreme court. But in 1500 the diet at Augsburg accomplished the real inauguration of a permanent imperial executive of twenty members from the estates, the 'regents of the empire', meeting in Nuremberg and having competence over the matters hitherto reserved to the diet. The distribution of votes (two royal, six electoral, two princely, two municipal, two for the counts and prelates, six for the knights and doctors) put the king in a hopeless minority. On the other hand, the interests of the estates represented by the other members were vitiated by such contradictions, that fruitful operation was unthinkable. However one may evaluate Maximilian's aims, a king with overwhelming family power still remained, as in the coming century, the only force capable, in some degree, of effectively representing the unity of the empire, and of curbing the 'hordes of German princes'. Once again the imperial régime disintegrated of its own accord. With the rising antipathy of the electors and princes against the king, both the domestic and foreign political power of the empire waned. Then the defeat of the Palatinate in the struggle for the Landshut possessions (Maximilian as arbitrator between Wittelsbach and the Palatinate), the election of a near relative of the king to be the elector of Trier, and, in 1504, the death of Berthold von Henneberg, brought about the collapse of opposition from the electoral princes.

Now it was Maximilian who led the reform of the empire. The organisation of the imperial supreme court was finally realised.

How feeble was the foundation that had been created, how vague in inner organisation, the epoch-making diets of the Reformation period were to show by the multifarious, confused antagonisms between the estates. The unwieldiness of the state machinery and the lack of unity in the administration were unimaginable. There was an enormous distance between an imperial decree and its execution, and endless opportunities of leaving things undisturbed or of direct sabotage (Eder). Even Charles V promised an imperial government at the electoral capitulation (an innovation at that time). The realisation of this was discussed at Worms in 1521, where the estates referred back to the draft of 1500, Charles at the same time ensuring that great respect be shown for the emperor's power. Although more parts of a unified administration for the empire were added, the empire remained without a precise constitution during the Reformation, its most difficult crisis. With its hazy delimitation of political powers inherited from the period of the truly medieval, feudal state, it was to pass through the decisive struggle of its history, in the full tide of revolution from the Middle Ages to modern times.

The struggle was embodied in the diets. They had become the great power factors from which we can read the history of the public reform movement. They now became genuine diets of the empire, which became visible in them. Thereby, however, they became such focal points and exchange centres of German life, that they are to be reckoned the most important power centres for the emerging German consciousness of community. Just as the Frankfurt book fair provides a highly important intellectual exchange, so the diets provided a constantly recurring gathering point for political, ecclesiastical, economic, national and dynastic discussions, led by the few representatives who held power, or by their counsellors educated in Roman law.

As the course of events showed, the formation of a genuine German consciousness of community became a really shamefully difficult affair. A real national consciousness in Germany was effected neither during the Reformation nor during the Counter-Reformation. At the beginning of the Reformation period we see a highly significant wave of unifying sentiments flaring up; but, in spite of positive elements, we must conclude that it followed a too negative direction. Furthermore, the common national consciousness which was stirred up significantly at that time came to nothing after the failure of the Peasants' War in 1525, as a result of the calculating power of the princes, and the restriction of their interest to their own territories. In this social group, however, no positive community could arise without pressure from a central, royal or imperial power upon the territories, or without a sacrifice from their side. The first failed; the second was lacking in a degree possible at that time in Germany alone. In its place, throughout the whole epoch, there flourished a non-national egotism, which regarded the lowest form of bribery as perfectly honourable.

The Germany which in 1517 heard Luther's theses on indulgences is thus politically very difficult to define. If one may link up the fulness of that which was still in process of becoming, still seething in confusion, to a centre of power that in some measure represented this Germany, that centre was the Germany of Maximilian.

This means that, in spite of all the uneven, sometimes contradictory lines of development, a great part of Germany had been stirred in a fruitful way by a strong personality. In Maximilian the unifying force of a powerful personality also made itself felt even where it possessed neither specially distinguished ideas nor a consistent programme. We see the Maximilian, who was so closely united to his common soldiers, the man who, by his romantic attraction, touched what was most important in the people – their heart and imagination, the imagination of those who took part in his campaigns and shared in his plans, the imagination of the leaders in the various social orders, which he aroused by disclosing the historical origins of his race, going back into the grey dawn of antiquity.

In the many-sided, so often confused, search for cohesion in the nation, humanism, too, was of some importance, humanism with its ideas of world citizenship, its friendships that cut across social divisions, and its prolific letter-writing. The great, truly universal force which encouraged this tendency was the art of printing. For us today it is difficult to imagine the isolation of men (and the attendant freedom of ideas) before the appearance of printing, an isolation that was matched, indeed, by an essential stereotyped similarity and absence of agitation; but just as difficult to conceive is the quite enormous significance of the multiplication of intellectual contacts, immeasurably increased by printing. The printed word rarely achieves the stirring power of the personality expressing itself in speech and gesture. And yet, when Luther preached he spoke at most to hundreds. But within a few days 4,000 copies of his *To the Christian Nobility* were sold. They were reprinted quickly and often. How many people heard Luther's voice? In this way, too, the impulse towards unification was increased. The unifying effect of Luther's 'standard speech' in his Bible could never have resulted from the distribution of manuscripts. Book-printing made it possible for the first time, for all of Germany to fall under the influence of a single man – Luther in the first years of his public life.

On the other hand, there were consolidating rather than centrifugal forces at work. Whereas the definite formation of imperial unity, possessing its necessary executive (through the creation of an imperial finance machinery, an imperial army and a civil service) did not succeed, more local needs demanded the establishment of systems which created their own executives. Immediately these became a threat to the unity of the empire. After the formation of the Hanseatic League of earlier times (a severe threat to the empire), there appears in our period (apart from the estates with their private associations outside the diets) the Swabian League, representative of the territorial peace and of the empire, and the emperor's strongest support.

Alongside the dynastic elements in the empire (amongst which we include the Church lands in their variously graded independence and freedom) stand the democratic elements: the world of the burgesses and the peasants in distinction to that of the princes and noblemen.

Economically, the cities were by far the most powerful part of the empire. They could have substantially increased the domestic and foreign political power of the empire if, as in Italy, they had been administered politically instead of preponderantly economically. But they had remained far from world politics ever since their confederations were suppressed in 1388 in the struggle with the knights and the confederation of princes, until they sought inclusion in the reform of the empire in 1487, an attempt which was an important expression of growing national consciousness.

Meantime, however, the struggle of the territorial lords to extend their rule throughout the whole breadth of their territories had long since grown into a struggle to incorporate the cities with their flourishing monetary systems. Out of this grew the stubborn opposition of the princely estates to granting the cities representation in the diets; but at the same time the greater involvement of the cities in the financial burden of imperial enterprises grew also. But precisely in this was the non-political and predominantly economic attitude of the cities, and their jealous watch over their special interests, a permanent obstacle to unity. Their political importance was the automatic result of their frequent divisions amongst themselves. Only the later confessional principle partly overcame this division; often this was achieved in an exemplary way, as in the Strasburg of Jacob Sturm, although even in the Schmalkald League the states were still more a burden and impediment than a centre of power. Only Magdeburg, as a result of a concentration of special conditions, rose to historical importance.

Nevertheless, the German cities were nothing less than the determining factor in the development of the collective life of Germany in this period. They created the models, the roots and the stimuli for that which later became the function of the modern state in war, finance, civil service and the planned concern of governments for the rights of the community and the individual.

In particular, the needs and stimuli of the rich middle class produced, in schools and universities, the intellectual and cultural forces which became fateful for the problems of the declining fifteenth century, and of the sixteenth century. Capitalism, humanism and the art of the German Renaissance, the explosive power of late medieval piety, the ferment set off by printing, the rise of an increasingly powerful public opinion – all of these things would have been impossible outside the cities, upon the culture of which the Italians, Aeneas Sylvius Piccolomini (mid-fifteenth century) and Machiavelli (beginning of the sixteenth), passed astonishingly favourable judgment.

The middle class of the German cities around 1500–20 was no longer a vague, fluctuating entity. It had long since become a ruling, self-assured and self-contained power, conscious of its own worth in trade, commerce, art and ecclesiastical policy. A genuine shift of social power on a grand scale had taken place, turning the merchants and artists into the leading class of society. One need only name the great leaders of the economy, the Fuggers, and the Welsers, or the pioneers in German printing and the book trade. Until 1520 this middle class was still endowing countless ecclesiastical benefices, building some of the best buildings in the history of art (the Fugger Chapel in Augsburg introduced Renaissance architecture into Germany), tirelessly and lavishly enriching the stock of church treasures, and also decorating the façades and interiors of their houses with great works of art. And even if we must still admit the characteristic difference between German woodcuts and Italian steel engravings, it is undeniable that the German middle class adorned itself not only with luxury but also with good taste. This is proved by the statuette of a young woman in fashionable clothes and with slightly affected posture by a Regensberg master around 1510–20 (now in the German museum in Berlin). And then there is the impressive gallery of heads of prominent citizens and their wives, of burgomasters, guild members and humanists. We need go no further than to the portraits of one artist – Dürer. The types of citizen seem to be inexhaustible, as is shown by the work of Riemenschneider. What strength without coarseness! What a wealth of form! What self-assurance! What genius with severity is to be seen in the head of Jacob Fugger, what daring in the portrait of an unknown person – possibly the tailor Hans Dürer!

I am writing these pages in Münster in Westphalia. If I want to gain a lively impression of what the pre-Reformation middle class was, of the strength, the verve, the polish it once called its own, I have only to look at the magnificent collection of bourgeois façades which stand in the chief market-place, witnesses of the fourteenth, fifteenth and sixteenth centuries, amongst them, perhaps the most beautiful of its kind in Germany (Wackernagel), the spendid town hall, the façade of which, with its cross-gable from the fourteenth century, is an unusual, bold and unsurpassably fine creation. With what symbolic emphasis this token of bourgeois self-assurance stands facing its counterpart, the cathedral close of the higher clergy.

There is another detail which may not be overlooked, a detail which influenced the coming intellectual, economic and religious battles: the different strata in the population were no longer clearly distinguished and articulated. Their characteristics had largely become blurred, and they found themselves in a process of mixing together. The peasant was becoming a city-dweller, artisans, citizens, nobles, were all changing places. The outward sign of this was the slightness in the difference in dress between the different classes.

The cities fulfilled a special role in the fateful antithesis between the new monetary economy and the old natural economy, in which not only the peasants but also the knights and the imperial knightly class had their place. In economic life, too, the most important sign was the intermingling of old traditions and newly emerging factors. Amongst the peasants and the middle class and most of the knights and aristocracy, the agrarian and guild systems were dominant. With the change over to a monetary economy this pattern of life was disrupted by a specifically modern, capitalist, commercial enterprise – great merchants, great banks and monopoly. Sharp contrasts had already developed. These became all the sharper as, in a short time, the new forms experienced a turbulent forward surge, exhibiting all the dark side of a too rapid development, with which only a few could keep step: great wealth piled up in a few hands, a broad class of prosperous city merchants, and along with this the creation of a city proletariat, filled with envy and jealousy against the rich merchants.

The change of the Germans after the thirteenth century, from being a peasant people with an agrarian economy to becoming a nation with a monetary economy and cities, etc., was infinitely more than a change in their material economy and the exterior forms of commerce. It was nothing less than a mighty revolution in the foundations of life, in the sense that the complete transformation of material existence moulds the impulses, the content and, above all, the formal attitudes of intellectual life. This was not accomplished immediately but was all the more impressive for its being a transformation from the foundations upwards.

It was in the cities, too, that, for the first time, it was thought necessary to suppress feuds – that barbaric evil which so astonishingly and tenaciously survived, a blatant contradiction, within an advanced civilisation. This tenacious reaction is explicable only as the frantic effort of one estate, the knights who had fallen into the background, to stay alive by whatever means. The prohibitions of 1466, 1467 and 1472 were of no use; those of 1495, 1500 and 1505–7 were unsatisfactory. The situation precipitated a last trial of strength. Sickingen led it in 1523 and was put down.

The knights like the peasants (together with the city proletariat) were the really discontented classes in the empire in this period. Without doubt both found themselves slipping from a high standard of living to a lower one. For this very reason (although obviously in different ways) they are the social detonators of the period.

In both cases it was principally the south and the west that were affected. In the north and north-east the social structure was less disrupted, simply because the property was less divided, the density of population thinner, and there were fewer imperial cities. In the much more thickly settled central and southern Frankish regions, where the land had been more intensively exploited for a much longer time, and divided up into a far greater number of separate properties, the knights possessed less and required more; for they were enraged by the standard of living in the neighbouring wealthy cities, a thing which could not happen to the same extent in the north. The knight no longer fulfilled any function in harmony with his real nature. The mercenaries and artillery had taken over his warlike activities, and performed them far better. On the other hand, his own castle was no longer able to withstand artillery.

The knights became debtors to the city-dwellers. This was the very thing which nourished the pride of position of the bearer of an ancient name, and fanned his envy of the emerging wealthy bourgeoisie. What was worse, not only did the wealth of many knights decrease, but wretched poverty invaded their castles.

Only very few of these knights (unusually well endowed with children) were successful in counteracting this decline by taking service with princes or cities, by doing the work of clerks (if they were educated, and then in unequal competition with lawyers), or of cavalrymen, or by raising and commanding a troop.

From the standpoint of the empire's unity the knights constituted an irremovable threat of disorder of various sorts. Unity could
be achieved only against them, not with them. All reforms designed by a central authority to create a permanent system of taxation, commerce and domestic order in general, ran counter to the
interests of the knights. They had long since surrendered their universal purpose and become almost completely high-handed and
selfish. Indeed, they lived from the very fact that no great,
superior executive was there to oppose them, that the conflict of
interests, was decided in petty territorial quarrels. It was here alone
that they could show their strength. To the extent that these
knights still formed an imperial knighthood, they suffered from
the malady which crippled Germany's power – division. The few
attempts to give the knighthood some semblance of unity (Hans
von Schwarzenberg, Sickingen) remained episodic. Just as in
Germany the political structure in general, through the multiple
autonomy of those in power, moved away – to its own injury –
from the centralised view of political power held in Spain, France
and England, so too the knighthood there was not united, as in
these other countries, by common, overriding national aims.
Turned in upon themselves they succumbed to petty jealousies
and the competition for power. Since they no longer supported or
represented the empire, their sole interest was themselves and their
class. They refused to shoulder any financial burden (rejection of
the 'common penny', 1495) and to give up their right to carry
the sword as they pleased (rejection of the territorial peace).
They played their part, rather, in a particularly active way, in
the general selfish and – from the point of view of the empire –
centrifugal, development of the estates.

This is true of Sickingen, too, who worked his way up under
Maximilian. He far surpassed the others. He knew how to lead
an army, and he made use of modern weapons. At the imperial
election and on the arrival of Charles in Germany he entered into
major politics. His feud with Trier was the signal for a general
uprising of the knights. But in the last analysis he was no more
than a knightly speculator. He served now France, now the emperor, he ridiculed the ban of the empire when it was raised
against himself, but helped to execute it against Ulrich of Würt-

temberg (1519); and the plan, which he hatched with Hutten, to seize the property of the Church 'in order to provide an opening for the gospel', was palpable robbery. His declaration of war on Trier alters nothing in the slightest. And from the religious angle, too, it is scarcely possible to explain away his hybrid character. Sickingen's catastrophe is of historic significance: his downfall affected the whole knighthood, and rightly so.

Quite clearly, public insecurity encouraged agitation. Agitation, arising from various causes, has been described as one of the chief marks of the period (p. 113 f.). This is true of all classes in society: the educated (experiencing a new intellectual ferment), the devout and also the peasants.

Like the knights, the peasants faced an epoch-making revolution, which seemed to be fomented from many sides: by the galling widespread derision of peasant stupidity, by the praise accorded to his cunning, and also to his poverty, willed by God ('the peasant is the closest to our Lord God'), and his labour as the foundation and crowning glory of all mankind and, indeed, of the empire. Besides this it was fomented by the stream of religious agitation in socialistic, spritualistic and apocalyptic ideas which took deep root amongst the peasants, and the literary presentation of which, directly or indirectly, espoused the cause of the common man. Above all, the revolution was caused by economic oppression and the restrictions imposed on personal freedom. In addition, the prescriptions of Roman law, which gave more weight to authentic documents than to concrete tradition, and which appeared to the peasant as something arbitrarily new, and therefore perfidious, helped on the revolution (Eder). In order to evaluate fully the significance of the agitation this generated, we must note that in 1500 the peasantry constituted at least three-quarters of the population of the empire, and were, after all, numerically the leading class. The remarkable migration into the cities did not at that time oppress the countryside, but did increase the city proletariat, and hence augmented the disruptive forces.

In this account we do not wish to overlook those elements of discontent which arose from forced taxes bound up with ecclesiastical usage. More will be said about them later. This applies both to city and countryside. Demands of the clergy, arising, for example, from ostentatious rivalry (e.g. in the display of candles in the office of the dead), led here and there to economic overburdening, the abolition of which by the Reformation was gladly anticipated.

The most important mark of the endlessly divided disposition of power in the empire was lack of balance. At every point that unanimity was lacking which could have directed the full potential of domestic and foreign policy along one straight line. And so development displayed chaotic variety and changeability. The political muddle at home, this condition of weakness, this unsteady fluctuation of policy, of necessity strengthened in many the feeling of dissatisfaction, even of insecurity, and produced the conviction that the usual remedies were no longer of any avail.

If we set these forces in the context of the manifold social, intellectual, ecclesiastical and religious unrest of the time, we perceive the double connection which domestic political disintegration (the failure of imperial reform) had with the processes of reform in the Church. In the first place the grouping of forces which would take up the battle for or against the old and the new faith was already fixed; that is to say, fundamentally and ultimately the emperor was on one side, the territorial princes on the other. Secondly, disillusionment allowed radical ideas to germinate, or, if already grown, to gain in strength.

We must, therefore, vigorously reject the notion that imperial reform was a question of narrowly delimited individual questions isolated from life as a whole. Basically it was a question which deeply affected everybody and everything: Would the empire survive the revolt of the princes? The survival of the empire, however, was very much bound up with the security and saving of all Europeans, who still had a lively consciousness of the empire in many respects, although this consciousness had been clouded for 200 years. In other words, the battle for the reform of the empire displayed the serious crisis in late medieval Germany; this was counterbalanced by a second – the threatening reform of the Church. The desire for a reform of the empire was deeply rooted in the whole thought and feeling of the period. It was passionately formulated and, as was self-evident to the rulers of the Middle Ages, in the particular, intellectual, moral and economic situation of the fifteenth century, could not be separated from religion.

It was demanded in the name of divine compassion (as in the *Reformatio Sigismundi* written at the time of the council of Basel and frequently printed at the end of the century). As in the religious sphere, failure to initiate reform in the political and state sphere aggravated the clamant discontent. 'The explosive power of Luther's movement would be incomprehensible apart from the years-old conviction of the need for reform in the empire' (Eder).

There is one element in the sequence of events that was of particularly far-reaching significance. All of these deficiencies built up into a chaos of constantly changing possibilities of solving the political problem, until the political scene fluctuated in a manner that often appeared absurd, but which was in truth quite unscrupulous. This element was the theoretical and practical Machiavellianism of the time, that is, its unscrupulous, selfish way of thinking and acting. At the beginning of the sixteenth century no class in society was free from this fault. Only a very few individuals rose above this to display greater purity of character. Sense of obligation was lacking everywhere, disloyalty was rampant.

Now we find ourselves asking the question: Will the coming Reformation regulate and control this chaos, or will it strengthen the authority of the individual?

FOUR

Intellectual Life in Germany before the Reformation

Our aim cannot be to describe the whole of the intellectual life of this period, even in outline; but we must describe the intellectual atmosphere of the time, stressing particularly those areas which were operative as causes in constructing the Reformation world.

I

Seen positively, the chief intellectual content of the period may be given the collective title, 'humanism'. The penetration into Germany of the Italian Renaissance movement, which had grown up in the south, presents us with a host of unsolved questions on points of detail. But the sheer possibility of this penetration and its transformation into a genuine German product are relatively easy to explain; for Renaissance and humanism are not closed systems but merely definitions of content. They are, above all, a way of being and of thinking, expressing itself as a movement, a setting of aims, a new point of departure. In the south the cry 'Back to the sources!', meant a return to Rome, but wherever it resounded this cry obviously led, in general, to a reflection on the origins of one's own values. With Germans in German surroundings, in an age which was searching for a sense of its individuality, interest centred around German sources, and all the more, because one of the great Roman authorities, Tacitus, in his *Germania* had praised the Germans so highly, and presented them to the Romans as an example.

We have already said that the most general mark of this period was the acute exaggeration of its transitional character, and the attendant multiplicity of contradictions. This is true, and not just of a limited area. One has only to think of the philosopher, reformer, cardinal and man of prayer, Nicholas of Cusa on the Moselle, and at the same time of arid scholasticism, on the one hand, and the traffic in indulgences of 1517, on the other, to become aware of quite unusual tensions in the spiritual, religious and ecclesiastical spheres.

Unfortunately, however, the earnestness and depth of Nicholas of Cusa was not characteristic of the period. Viewed as a whole, the development tended towards externalism and superficiality, in spite of the powerful release of new life. Even humanism, which resisted the multiplication of concepts, forms and theses, which proliferated in the sphere of the Church and of scholastic philosophy, was itself, unfortunately, to a great extent the heir of this excessively formal intellectual attitude, by reason of its often empty exuberance and stereotyped ideals of form, its turning away from grand objectivity to petty subjectivity.

In spite of this, at first the Italian fifteenth century produced the very proper effect of a mighty, high-spirited intoxication, a boundless sense of vitality with wide horizons, which thrilled the world anew, a new urge to accomplish the greatest tasks, fully confident of possessing the necessary strength, a high ideal of knowledge and feeling; it was a colossal, intoxicated and intoxicating outburst. To be sure, it was essentially dependent upon human power, upon human power alone; and hence it was not only human, but humanist.

As is well known, this applied to ecclesiastical circles as well, especially in the curia, where the sensual and naturalistic pushed its way so victoriously into the foreground, that the cross and the Crucified had of necessity to retreat, because it would have been blasphemous to place them alongside the portrayals of naked, pagan beauty.

This wave, with its pagan and classical content, never fully penetrated Germany. But the new surge and the revolution did, in the form of new attitudes and new styles. The victorious sensation of a timely, new beginning, brought with it a growing independence of the traditional, and created an inclination towards the new, indeed, towards the radically new. This very inclination is one of the most decisive elements in the conditions necessary for any revolutionary movement. To this extent here was one of the chief causes of the Reformation, in fact, in a certain sense it was the *conditio sine qua non* of the Reformation revolution.

The Renaissance and humanism entered the acute stage of their development in Germany around 1450. From then on Germany, too, shared in an emphatic way in the basic apocalyptic experience, which from the beginning had characterised the Renaissance in Italy. The idea of world decline and world renewal, so decisively expressed by the Calabrian Abbot Joachim of Flora (d. 1204), and fostered by the personality and preaching of Saint Francis, had caught the imagination of many classes in society, as a result of the overthrow of the Hohenstauffen and the medieval papacy, and the withdrawal of the papacy to Avignon, and the dispute of the Franciscan-Joachimite Zelanti. This excitement was very much alive in the second half of the fifteenth century, both in the expectation of an apocalyptic chastisement as well as in the enthusiastic salutation of this wonderful century in which it was a joy to be alive. Just as Italy had experienced the warning-sign of a Savonarola and later of a Michelangelo (not without an echo north of the Alps), so Germany heard the impressive admonitions of Cardinal Nicholas of Cusa (d. 1464) and the mighty preaching of penance and renewal by the Franciscan John Capestrano (d. 1456). The apocalyptic ideas in the preaching of the piper Hans Böhm of Niklashausen, in the so-called *Reformatio Sigismundi*, in the various agitated works of Dürer; the influential ideas of Geissler, the idea of the 'Angel Pope' (a representative of whom appeared in 1446 at the Council of Basel 'to root out the wicked and bind Satan', and who was burned), the increasing prophecies of doom, the 'Revolutionary from the upper Rhine', pilgrimage-fever and the search for miracles, inflammatory plays like the new *Nollart* of 1488, in which a trial of the estates was held, and in which the pope was threatened with the destruction of Rome as God's punishment upon the depraved clergy; all of these things, about which we will have to speak repeatedly, reveal the rank growth of apocalyptic excitement which penetrated all levels of society. The revolutionary effusions of that violent anti-clerical Hans Böhm who, directed by the Mother of God, demanded the slaying of parsons, made a powerful impression. They were carried throughout all the states by inflammatory songs. Like an epidemic the number grew, of those who were smitten and made a pilgrimage to him at Niklashausen (1476).

On the other hand, humanism created a much more joyful mood. Cusa himself, a man of versatile nature, with an optimism curiously derived from the Middle Ages, was a source for this current. A powerful desire for a humanity reshaped within a re-fashioned era dominated the thought of the German arch-human-ist Conrad Celtis (d. 1508). People felt themselves moved by the great irreducible and indescribable primary value of 'the new'. The sun of classical beauty had risen again; men tasted the sweet poison of form and of unrestrained enjoyment, which Celtis, speaking for many, called 'virtue'. With strange blindness, people felt themselves far superior to the scholastic surroundings of an age just past; Erasmus scoffed at the antiquated Gothic and called its exponents Goths; Henry Bebel described traditional methods as barbarism.

People largely subscribed to the Socratic error that knowledge is virtue, and hence that the educated are better people than the rest of mankind. The overestimation of learning or simply of re-finement as an almost all-powerful factor in the transformation of the world reached astonishing heights; and this idea persisted far into the Reformation. It was highly significant that Luther, in 1521 at Worms at the hearing before the elector of Trier, said: 'I am only one of the least; twenty others more *learned* could speak for me.'

Just as Pico della Mirandola (of the Platonic Academy in Florence) enthusiastically spoke about the manifold life with which the heavenly Father had endowed man, so that he might mould himself on a grand scale (God said to Adam: 'I have made you neither mortal nor immortal so that you might be your own sculptor and tutor, fashioning yourself according to the image and nature of your choice'), so the century was greeted jubilantly in Germany by von Hutten, by Capito, by Eck and Erasmus. Bebel,

c

later an adherent of Luther, saw a new German era emerging: now all at once, through God's mercy, men everywhere were returning to a better life, to the classical study of languages; and now, for sure, ancient Christian virtue, the primitive purity of the Christian faith, was being regained. At the same time hymns in praise of Erasmus were being composed, and these were more exuberant in Germany than anywhere else in the world. This indicates something else of vast importance. A man was required – a leader. People awaited him.

No matter how German humanism subscribed to the fundamental viewpoints (for example, to Stoic–Neo-Platonic popular philosophy, moralism, reduction to essences, the more or less universally accepted norms of style, the common veneration for Erasmus and his achievement, and consequently to that which made humanism a European affair, familiar, indeed, even to the Turkish Sultan Mohammed II), in Germany humanism possessed genuine power of producing new forms. This is shown not least by the fact that it became a German, national movement. That, by so doing, it lost Italian power and smoothness of form and took on instead a German solidity and firmness of line, does not indicate a lower value, but only a characteristic difference in style. That its greatest achievement in Erasmus was cosmopolitan, and that the value of Hutten's call to battle was seriously suspect from the national point of view, clearly demonstrate the limits of it capabilities. It is also strange, and in a way suspicious, that many national humanists combined enthusiasm for their national, German individuality with an outspoken expression of homelessness ('where you die is immaterial; everywhere the same road leads from the earth to Jupiter's hall' – Celtis).

On the other hand, the humanist ideal of community education cut across existing social divisions in some degree. It became a force that created community. People gained a sense of an 'intellectual total Germany', a feeling which was fostered by the organisation of humanist circles, such as Celtis founded as he moved here and there on his typical wanderings.

And then, the consciousness of having saved the Church at Constance was still alive amongst the Germans. The enormous weight of the religious and intellectual figure of Nicholas of Cusa, the 'apostle of the new era', was still a living force. The personality and activity of the emperor Maximilian, the mercantile, and hence the cultural, superiority of the Germans, the intellectual world-power of Erasmus of Rotterdam, were present realities. The Brethren of the Common Life (especially the school of John Cele, d. 1417 in Zwolle), who encouraged humanism, were also admirers of the German past. We find a great deal of work being done on Germanic history, based upon Tacitus' presentation of it in the *Germania*, and through collections of sources and writings from the German past (compiled systematically, for example, by Celtis). There was resistance to French encroachment upon German border territories (Wimpfeling and Brant). Wimpfeling in particular worked hard to produce a national consciousness. Bebel collected German proverbs and planned a great, German, complete edition. Maximilian offered rewards for old documents. Important chronicles were discovered. Cochlaeus – like Eck primarily a humanist – in his *Theodoric*, quite overcomes his aversion to the heretical Arian, and is full of joyful enthusiasm for the old Germanic hero.

Perhaps the clearest revelation of the weakness of the great Erasmus is his essential dissociation from native land and from nationality. Here, too, he was the theoretician, the a-political man, who fell prey to the beautiful Socratic error. Indeed, even his longing for peace, and his criticism of the princes of his era, who had not made peace between Church and state, arose more out of his reading of the classics than from the political experience of his time (Huizinga).

Erasmus never had a permanent dwelling-place; he would not have endured such a tie: 'I want to be a citizen of the world, common to all, or . . . rather, a stranger to all.' Hence, besides strengthening German self-consciousness, he became also a serious impediment to German humanism as a national force. It is true that he made statements which were a concession to national feeling – he wanted to see the Bible translated into the common tongues which he despised – but such isolated statements tell us nothing about his real attitude. Erasmus remained a-national. Admittedly, if one wishes, conversely, to describe him as a representative of medieval universalism, one must sharply emphasise the extent to which, in him, revelationary, Christian universalism had become secularised cosmopolitanism.

German national consciousness, as it appears in humanism and as it understood itself, is above all an awareness of the marked difference, the contradiction, between the German and the Roman. This fact gradually comes to light in all the humanists – Sebastian Brant, Cochlaeus, Hutten and Erasmus.

Here is one of the points at which German humanism became a most important detonator in the medieval, ecclesiastical system. This is true in two ways, for here national anti-Roman feeling joined forces with that religious and ecclesiastical hatred of Rome, which was to constitute a good half of the life force of the Reformation.

Since Petrarch's time, Italian humanism had grown accustomed to opposing scholasticism, to indulging in derisive criticism of the religious life and of the most important curial claims – at least these things formed the starting-point of humanist discussion. After Lorenzo Valla, criticism changed to fundamental challenge. In Germany this was specially fostered by the awareness that a great theological wave had been happy to make use of the German language, with powerful effect (Ekkehard, Tauler and Seuse). This happened in spite of the essentially positive relationships of German mysticism to scholasticism – a relationship which did not exist in Italy. In a characteristic way it was an expression of the strength of pressing national needs within the narrower sphere of the Church. This movement itself, in its more restricted presentation by the great friars and the mysticism of the fifteenth century, appears strongly associated with specifically German impulses. We shall see in Luther what a profound effect this consciousness could have.

Scholasticism had become the official protectress of the Church's point of view. Although many Christian humanists did not surrender one iota of the Christian faith, the tension between humanism and scholasticism remained. The danger that this would lead to a contradiction of fundamental Catholic teaching was often very close. All too often the highly developed scholastic forms of thought had become equated with the content of the Church's teaching. Logically, the new humanist manner of thinking developed a hostility towards the content of scholasticism also; that is, towards the theology of the Church, and then, as a result, to the Church itself. In Italy, as we recalled, the radical awakening of classicism had turned many humanists into pagans. Wimpfeling rightly protested against this abuse, which rested on a false conclusion; but this conclusion was part of the line of development, as the German arch-humanist was soon to show. Celtis completely freed himself from all the obligations which hitherto had been considered essential. However much the universal Agricola (Rudolf Huesmann from Groningen) surpassed Celtis in nobility, intelligence and character, sounder as were the many humanist educators who co-operated with the nationally minded Wimpfeling and his friend Ulrich Zasius, and insignificant as was the general penetration of the Italian restoration of paganism into German humanism, in the end, besides Erasmus, it was those humanists of the Erfurt circle, who enthusiastically imitated Celtis' lack of restraint, who wove a visible, tangible and permanent pattern into the fabric of the time. With his abandoned freedom Celtis more than the others revealed a latent aim of humanism – to break loose from the Church. This did not mean simply a hostile separation from the Church but a tendency towards lay independence.

Humanist criticism contained frightful exaggerations and false conclusions; but at the same time it rightly castigated much that was unhealthy in the life of the Church. Undeniably, however, for most people the heart of a matter becomes identified with its outer shell, the thing itself with its abuses. That is to say, impetuous revolt of the new against a Church in many ways corrupt, an anticurial attitude, antagonism to scholasticism, hatred of monastic life, a rationalistic this-worldliness, seemed to many to be the logical and welcome conclusion. And so, humanism became one of the great and most effective causes of the Reformation. Jacob Sturm of Strasburg admitted having become estranged from the Church by the sharp criticism of Geiler, Wimpfeling and Brant. Were those critics who remained loyal to the Church, was the Christian conscience, to remain silent in face of corruption within the sanctuary; or should people expect this corruption merely to express itself with a little more caution and reserve? That would be to reject the true thesis because of a false conclusion, and to want to harness according to the book the true strength and genuine anger of an agitated world.

I have no intention of denying the religious, Christian and

ecclesiastical potential of the Renaissance and of humanism. The close connection of the Renaissance with the Middle Ages, its slow emergence from them, its share in the Erasmian reform (Erasmus, Fisher of Rochester, Thomas More), in Luther's pre-heretical education, and in the counter-Reformation, cannot be overlooked. Nor by any means do we intend to accept all the radical words of the humanists as ready cash. Many intended their assertions to be taken quite loosely. With these excited propagandists one must clearly distinguish between their intellectual life and their own awareness of it, which they expressed so noisily in their words. In spite of its evolution, their substance was still deeply rooted in their inheritance, in medieval thought. It was failure to make this distinction that led to the one-sidedness of the imitators of Jacob Burckhardt.

As is well known, it was not as if humanism stopped short at the mendicant orders, which it loved to insult. It is true that Erasmus felt he could commend the humanist Dominican, John Faber of Augsburg, only by sharply distinguishing him from the rest of his order. But it was precisely the reviled Dominicans (after the Reuchlin affair, the Tetzel business and Luther's attacks on Prierias and Hoogstraeten, commonly represented as stupid and hypocritical or even as 'fat, dirty swine') who had maintained a healthy Thomistic open-mindedness, which did not see humanism as hostile but as a fulfilment. We will become still better acquainted with the fruitfulness of this union of old and new in the Carthusians of Cologne. At the beginning of the Reformation, at the university of Rostock there were humanist Dominicans who felt no temptation to apostasy. Their prior, a professor in the university and a man of far-reaching influence, was none other than the distinguished Cornelius de Sneckis.

Italy, Spain and Germany supply proof of the ambiguity of humanism, and of its capacity to enter into the most varied associations. In Germany the older humanism, for example, exhibited (in harmony with the coexistence of scholasticism and humanism in the schools and in some universities) a prevalent tendency to join forces with the *via antiqua* of the realists. In later years, before the Reformation powerfully forced interests to follow a new direction, Eck provides important proof of this. Eck, the realist, was in raptures over the princes of humanism. As late as 1518 he could still write: 'Almost all learned men, apart from a few monks and theologians, are Erasmians.'

None the less, the question was posed repeatedly: Where is the decisive factor? Where is the secret, deepest tendency of the new and where is it leading? Was rediscovered classicism essentially pagan, or was it 'Christian', as Aristotle seemed to be for scholasticism, and Cicero and his circle for early humanism? Was the Christian humanist movement, viewed as a whole, a sanctification of the world, or a secularisation of the holy? Was humanism a lay movement or not, was it an expression of the advance of people now mature but dissatisfied? Was it a coming of age? Was the character of the new that it integrated itself into the tradition of the Church – as all intellectual life in the west had hitherto done – or was it that it now set itself up as an independent power in opposition to the as yet unchallenged absolute ruler? The question is not: How many genuine humanists remained Christian? but rather: What was bound to result from the fundamental attitude of humanism if taken to its logical conclusion, if allowed to turn its innovation into an absolute value?

Humanism was the advancement and affirmation of a free humanity. It offered a solution of the basic problem of the time – the problem of Christian freedom, of the coming of age of the Christian man. This came about, however, not predominantly in a manner consonant with revelation but much more in a more or less worldly, naturalistic, anthropocentric form.

A contradiction of this thesis is provided least of all by the ecclesiastical, curial humanists in Germany. Few of them, indeed, were theologically and religiously genuinely Catholic. Many of them were like Erasmus, wanting peace, fearing tumult and desiring a papacy that distributed benefices in the interest of the marvellously flourishing new learning – and in their own interest. At all events, their number diminished rapidly as a result of the Reformation movement. In 1520 when Cochlaeus praised the world-wide dignity of the Apostolic See from earliest times, according to Adelmann, a canon of Augsburg, he aroused 'the suspicion of all learned and honest Germans'. By this time things had gone so far, that in many places anyone who defended the curia was presumed to have dishonourable motives.

It is part of the function of history to open our eyes to the variety of answers which men have given to the same few primary questions of life. The study of history looks impartially at a diversity of values. This is its constant strength, and its danger. Both of these aspects were displayed when the study of history (or what goes by that name) appeared for the first time in Europe. We already know one of the forces which was released: the discovery of national origins and hence of national character, and, as a result, a mighty increase in national energy. The danger was expressed by strong, often radical, spiritual independence of the representatives of the immediate past, who were, indeed, at the same time the representatives of still dominant, settled institutions. This abruptness and radicalism resulted in a largely unjustified and damaging breach. But the element decisive for the continuance of the course of events was the sense of freedom. The Renaissance and humanism became the first classical period of criticism in Europe. Corresponding to the comprehensive character of the Renaissance and humanism, this sense of freedom was expressed in all spheres of life. And everywhere, reserved criticism was supplemented by radical attack. Epoch-making examples are the disputing of the donation of Constantine and hence of one of the chief foundations of the power of the specifically medieval papacy; the collection of the deviations of the Greek text of the Bible from the official Latin text; and – even more directly impressive – the unprecedented, liberal views of Machiavelli in *The Prince*.

This sense of freedom, like the whole culture of the Renaissance, became the possession of only a small section of society. But this section indirectly gained widespread influence over the masses. This happened principally through political and moral life – as well as through canon law – which became a copy and model of that freedom from obligation which was apparent to all. Besides this, the advocates of this freedom from obligation did not speak a secret language. Whether they wrote in Latin, Italian or German, they created a type of literature which was much more accessible than the scholasticism of the Church; and through this they created a freer atmosphere, that was congenial to themselves.

To be sure all this did not yet directly damage the established institutions – the Church and the old faith. But it showed again and again in what dangerous measure the shell of life no longer validly represented its core, and indicated how far inner disintegration, or at least the process of loosening up, had already advanced. Many in this era, without realising it, had come to the point where any further advance would necessarily result in their abandoning the Church.

These things apply above all to Germany. There humanism was more democratic than in Italy. It operated incomparably more strongly through the schools, and therefore upon the people. There, too, the revolutionary power of humanist criticism was greater than in Italy, in spite of the fact that it appeared in a tamer form. Moreover, at that time the ponderous, conscientious Germans did not possess the positivistic agility to enable them to find a way of living with an existent contradiction. Italian Christian humanists succeeded in combining a bitter hatred of the clergy with a basic reverence for, or at least a 'correct' toleration of, the priesthood. The Germans were not nearly so good at this. This in part explains why the initially more radical and cynical opposition to the Church in Italy still allowed a fundamental loyalty to the Church to persist, and why this did not happen in the course of the German Reformation. Rather, in Germany the intellectual attitude created by humanist criticism provided powerful possibilities or carrying out a revolutionary thrust. From the outset, Luther's chances had been mightily increased by humanism. We will be able to evaluate this judgment only after we become acquainted with early German humanism in Erfurt, and its revolutionary intervention in the disputes of Church history.

Viewed in general, as time went by German humanism became more radical. None the less, we distort our understanding of its multiple character, of its danger to the Church, and of its embodiment of the future, if we divide it up chronologically. The moral and religious freedom of Celtis was never essentially exceeded in later German humanism. On the other hand, later German humanism also contained basic energies which made common cause with the aims of the older humanism that was loyal to the Church. The national, pedagogical, ecclesiastical style is all too often ascribed only to the older generation and thus reduced to a mere episode. People overlook the fact, however, that this type of humanism continued to live at the heart of the tragedy of the fight for

Church unity, and became a most significant starting-point for reform within the Church.

For the rest, it will not be surprising if we find it very difficult to define German humanism exactly with respect to its various aims. Not for nothing was it the essential part of a typical period of transition. Reformation history will repeatedly show us how little contemporaries were aware of the ultimate aims of the forces at work under their very eyes. We learn the same thing from German humanism. The pure scholars stood worlds apart from the humanist men of action. The theologically educated schoolman, Cochlaeus, had learned, in the Nuremberg circle of Pirkheimer, to sympathise with everything that was inspired by ancient Rome, and that wanted to have little to do with the Church. His national sentiment has been acknowledged as one of his conspicuous traits; and his later magnanimous fight for the old Church is regarded just as much as a fight for the Fatherland, threatened by the Reformation. In Bologna this man was for a long time the neighbour and close acquaintance of Ulrich von Hutten. And yet how deeply hidden from him were those initially secret, and then openly avowed, aims of national rebirth, as Hutten dreamed of them, and the means by which Hutten worked for them. If we search in his works to discover what the world and values of learning are, what humanism is, we learn that the first and last precondition of humanism is peace, tranquillity, regulated interior activity. Cochlaeus knew only the humanism of Erasmus. He knew nothing at all of Hutten's variety.

A striking contrast to the anti-Roman feeling of humanism and to its national impulses was presented by the prescription of Roman law in Germany. This was carried out between the mid-fifteenth and the mid-sixteenth century, in the period, that is, when hatred of Rome was undeniably at its height. And only here, in Germany, where the flame of anti-Roman feeling burned brightest, was Roman law taken over. Not everything Roman was taken over, not everything German set aside, but this foreign law as a whole triumphed. Lay courts, which formerly pronounced judgment according to the native traditions, disappeared, to be replaced by courts of learned jurists who proclaimed a uniform law – 'imperial' law.

This contrast is not so surprising, but is rather a mark of the time. In this single problem there comes to light that inner split which, in spite of everything, seriously burdened non-Italian, and particularly non-Latin, humanism. As on all other points the strength of German humanism, more precisely, of German, humanist, legal learning would have had to prove itself by overthrowing the Roman in favour of the German – a thing which Ulrich Zasius set about doing in an exemplary way, but which remained uncompleted thereafter.

The prescription of Roman law had long been prepared, for, in externals, the old imperial law of the Hohenstauffen was regarded as Roman. As soon as paid officials (found incipiently in the princely chanceries and in the German courts at the turn of the sixteenth century) began to acquire learning (one of the basic facts of the time, particularly with reference to the spread of the Reformation) the victory of Roman law was assured; for it was theoretically presented and presentable, and therefore learnable, in an incomparably clearer way than was the native law. Because of the fearful disunity in German law, all centralisation of legal terminology and practice was thrown back upon the one unified and thoroughly organised Roman law. German particularism proved itself the enemy of German law as soon as even the most elementary standardisation of the legal system was attempted, as, for example, in the imperial supreme court from 1495 onwards. The necessity of somehow arranging for appeals, resulted in the territorial courts and then in all the lower courts turning to the same Roman law.

So that we do not falsify the picture we must add that in the sixteenth century there were Germans who refused to attend an Italian university, and resisted Roman law. It is of some importance for the questions dealt with in this book, that Cochlaeus was one of these.

II

It is already evident from what has been said, that it is false to see humanism and later scholasticism merely as antitheses. It is hardly correct simply to place the edifying piety of late scholasticism and the personal, emotion-charged piety of humanism in two separate compartments. The return to the subject was common to both. Unfortunately, as yet we have no clear and comprehensive answer to the question as to how far the interior intensification of the vast body of edifying literature (which we have yet to meet) was or was not dependent on the emergence of the humanist feeling for life. On the other hand, it is unthinkable that any such dependence could have been complete. The piety of the fifteenth-century prayers for confession and for the dying are completely medieval and not humanist. There are still other points of relationship: the frivolous criticism of humanism, so often denoting a frivolous life, led many into scepticism. The same end was reached, but along a different road by the nominalism of Occam, with its separation of believing and knowing, a position directly represented by Pomponazzi in the Italian Renaissance. Through this separation he had introduced an almost systematic doubt (at least for many of his pupils) into the area of theological knowledge. Here was much more than independent reflection on revelation. This independence, although it was not intended to be so, became directly inclined towards the possibility of *thinking otherwise*.

That which in Occam, despite his unworthy sophistries (about which more below), had been the work of a great intellect, in his disciples lost its inner connection with its foundation, through a submission to orthodoxy (as with Biel), or else, amongst his incompetent pupils and anonymous masters, lost all serious meaning. Then arose that enormous concern with peripheral things, that pompous free-wheeling, that too subtle distinguishing and senseless multiplication of allegedly deep arguments, the exponents of which, amidst the verbiage of endless disputations, took themselves and their new-found would-be profundity too seriously, stubbornly pursuing their favourite adversaries on account of the merest trivialities. Eck thoroughly castigated the spiritlessness of this most recent theology, this 'preserve of monks', which was ridiculed everywhere. But if we read the theses which even a man like Eck extracted from the doctrine of angels and of the Trinity, and presented in disputations in Bologna and Vienna (1515 and 1516) we are as painfully disturbed by the absence of those great, truly rewarding problems which alone are important for religion, as we are amazed at the accumulation of logic-chopping, quoted from obscure sources, concerning the angels and the *relationes* in the

Trinity. And yet these are serious questions compared with those which Erasmus derisively castigated, or which Juan Luis Vives (d. 1540) pilloried with such vigorous scorn as heaps of nonsense over which endless time was lost in arid study. From Vives we learn how justified was the colossal ridicule of the *Epistolae vivorum obscurorum* and of Erasmus of much in this fossilised scholastic activity, and the degree in which the scholastics themselves provoked this mockery that was so harmful to the Church. It was a tale of wasted opportunities. The establishment fared as always: life marched on and the system stayed behind. The result was – as always – that the surging revolution enthusiastically affirmed the new, if only by rejecting the old and, above all, by being alive itself; and that the new was affirmed even where it was indubitably weaker and thinner in substance than the old.

We have already become too accustomed to these statements. Because they are too often made without proper differentiation, the danger arises of underestimating their fateful effect upon the approaching schism in the Church. This would be wrong. In 1520 the humanist Dominican, John Faber, took the matter more seriously: 'The world is tired of the sophistical logic-chopping of theology; it yearns after the springs of evangelical truth. If the way is not opened up, it will break through with violence.'

Moreover, nonsensical formulae and fruitless controversy did not appear only with the petty heirs to Occam's dialectic. For Occam himself, this philosophical theology had often radically lost its meaning. Certain theses in his *Centilogium* prove this: 'The head of Christ is the foot of Christ'; 'The eye of Christ is his hand'; 'At any given moment in time, God is not that God he was when there was no time'; 'The divine persons are not eternal'; 'The Father who has never died, could die.'

In these matters, the relation to Italy is similar to that which we discovered with regard to the classicising and paganising of life. Theological disintegration was much more acute in Italy than in Germany. But in Italy in spite of the disintegration there was also a solider Thomistic tradition in lay and ecclesiastical circles, from Savonarola to Cajetan. Germany lacked great truly fruitful representatives of this *via antiqua*.

It is not enough, when considering Germany, to follow the model of the Italian situation and, as is commonly done, to speak only of declining scholasticism and of humanism. Between them and above them stands the most powerful intellectual genius of the German fifteenth century – Nicholas of Cusa, with whom Janssen clear-sightedly began the history of the German people from the end of the Middle Ages. Unfortunately we cannot say that his deep perceptions were fruitful even in small measure. He had no worthy heirs. He was, perhaps, the only fully Catholic expression of the liberty of the Christian man, of the autonomy of the human spirit within, and in allegiance to, the Church, avoiding equally the superficiality of Erasmus and the one-sided depth of Luther. The immediate fruits of his efforts were confined to the sphere of attempts at religious and ecclesiastical reform. These attempts were of necessity unsatisfactory because, while the cardinal possessed great gifts of preaching and of pious exposition, these gifts did not amount to genius; and, moreover, his efforts were only partially directed towards these aims.

In spite of this, Nicholas of Cusa must be numbered as one of the great forces in the national and intellectual awakening of the Germans. After the defeat of the revolutionary conciliar idea of Basel he became the great German Catholic, living by his consciousness of homeland and nation, in mighty independence of and superiority to vulgar, ecclesiastical notions in philosophy and theology, seeking the new synthesis for which the time was ripe. By far the most powerful single intellectual force urging the Germans along the road towards awareness of their own character in the fifteenth century, he was at the same time loyal to the Church in the fullest sense of the word.

To be sure, we must not forget that the strict philosophy of late scholasticism and of Nicholas of Cusa remained confined to the specialists. Because of its technical language it did not affect the life of the fifteenth century nearly as much as did the creeds of the humanists. This fact is specially important for the very problems considered in this book; for the coming Reformation was to be very largely a popular movement.

III

In Germany the full inheritance of Celtis was handed on to the Erfurt circle gathered round Mutian, the sceptical canon of Gotha.

This circle included Helius Eobanus Hessus, the cynical composer of 'Christian' love letters in the style of Ovid, Crotus Rubeanus and, from time to time, Hutten. Early German humanism in its first generation on the Rhine (with the scholastic, humanist, national and pedagogical figures of Agricola, Langen and Zasius) and in its second generation on the Danube was radically outdone by these contemporaries of the Lutheran Reformation. The spirit of the classical age had moved in and destroyed Christianity. There was now complete estrangement from the Church, with ridicule and biting hatred not only of the countless abuses in the Church but of the Church itself. The all-important distinction between the ecclesiastical office and the person holding it was forgotten. The spirit by which this circle lived – judging by its leader, Mutianus Rufus – can be succinctly described as libertine rationalism. This rationalist element consisted in the rejection of religious faith in revelation, which was replaced by a personally determined and subjective insight into the secular cosmos. The value of the creative individual became grossly exaggerated. The libertine element was expressed, in word and action, in loose views concerning moral duties, turning that morality, which was the humanist substitute for religion, almost into its opposite. The source was Stoic, popular philosophy and it penetrated these new, humanist Christians scarcely less deeply than it had their pagan predecessors. Imitating so many of their predecessors, this circle again presented a basically false interpretation of Christianity: because Christianity is monotheism, all monotheism is Christianity. People forgot that Christianity is essentially redemption through Christ, and hence also the worship of Christ. The consequence was a relativist softening with a fatefully wide influence. The most diverse religions converge along the common line of the one permanent never-changing religion (Mutian) – the basis of which was obviously extremely narrow. To want to leave the uneducated with the external supports of the mediatory Church, but, with shortsighted arrogance, to consider oneself a gnostic humanist, was but an intrinsically false extension of this relativist softening.

For Germany, the invasion of what one can only call religious liberalism was at hand in this a-dogmatic and anti-dogmatic humanism. It was explicitly present in the renunciation of the dogmas of revelation. Therefore it can never be permanently opposed without a return to the fundamental dogmatic position from the denial of which it emerged. One is surprised at the amount of self-deception that was and is possible on this issue.

In the Reuchlin affair this humanist circle won considerable publicity. A noble man and a good cause were compromised by the dazzling wit of the Erfurt radicals.

In Reuchlin, the foremost German Grecist and Hebraist of his time, the uncle and educator of Melanchthon, we see, as in other humanists, the close relationships between German and Italian humanism. He considered as normative his connection with the cabbalistic theology of Pico della Mirandola from the school of the Platonic Academy in Florence – the true wellspring of the Christian Renaissance, of the *regeneratio christianismi*, of the 'philosophy of Christ'. But the controversy in which, as Hebraist and cabbalist, he engaged with the convert Jew, Pfefferkorn (a man consumed by a renegade's hatred of his former co-believers), is of interest more as a revelation of the alignments which were forming: the traditional Church on the one hand, a new age, a new feeling for life, on the other.

At this point both new and old disclose to us for the first time a rather unhappy mark of the times – a lack of good manners. Corresponding to the coarseness and brutality of the masses, an uncultivated tone pervaded the disputes and anathematisings which formed a large part of the total picture both in late scholasticism (between different schools and orders) and in humanism (between individuals). Not only were controversy and disputation in the blood of the representatives of both intellectual currents; all too frequently this degenerated into reviling and insults. It is astonishing how deeply this coarseness, corresponding, indeed, to the incomparably unrefined eating, drinking and other habits, even of the aristocracy in public, characterises the age. We find obscenity even in strict men like Geiler von Kayserberg and Wimpfeling, to say nothing of the repulsive and confused mixture of the sacred and the indecent in Eobanus Hessus, or of the risky style of Erasmus. Celtis could dedicate his frivolous *Amores* to the emperor Maximilian, and celebrate him as the 'despiser of the stinking cowls'. In analysing Luther's strength, as well as his religious limitations, we will have to deal seriously with the problem of this coarseness. How deeply it permeated the whole age is perhaps even better illustrated by the fact that even the outwardly very correct Erasmus occasionally succumbed to it, as when he pilloried the youthful Lee of England in the dispute about the New Testament, calling him a 'British viper, Satan, Englishman with a tail', whereby the real point at issue became completely obscured by reciprocal bitterness.

It is quite difficult to see beyond this invective to the very important role played by this acrimonious controversy itself in the development of the period, and in aggravating the state of conflict. Special importance attaches to the *disputations* that were common to humanism and late scholasticism. The interesting and loud echo sounded by the polemics of well-known figures within the contemporary learned world is the first sign of anything resembling powerful public opinion, the thing without which the coming controversies of the Reformation would have been unthinkable. Erasmus believed that 'his dispute with Faber had held the whole world in suspense', that no one sat down to table without deciding for or against the protagonists'. The whole of Germany, according to Erasmus, was literally in a rage against Lee. Likewise Luther considered these humanist discussions, that were so well known to the public, of such importance, that he feared a long silence between him and Erasmus might be misinterpreted. And so, without doubt, they had to keep in touch with one another.

The genuine disputations of the schools (for the reintroduction of which Luther strove energetically at a later date) have yet another special significance for our theme. When these developed into great public oratorical tournaments between masters they were accorded the status of a judgment upon truth, so that whoever or whatever had been defeated was regarded as no longer worthy of discussion. Obviously this was self-deception. But this conviction was to make itself felt at the early, ethical disputations of Luther, and again most decisively at the Leipzig disputation of 1519, and not least at Worms in 1521. Luther's demand to be refuted out of Scripture presupposed such a disputation. On the one hand, Aleander reports how the adherents of the Reformer justified their hero by arguing that he had not been permitted to dispute; on the other hand, he maintained that Luther had been refuted on more than six points in private argument with the official from Trier.

Another and deeper insight provided by Reuchlin's circle is the proof of the practical antithesis between the humanists of Erfurt, who gained such powerful support, and ecclesiastical circles.

Reuchlin had published the letters of all the celebrated men who sympathised with him in his bid to preserve valuable Jewish literature, and in his fight against the theologians of the university of Cologne who, it was alleged, accused him of heresy. Representative of these theologians were the grand inquisitor, Jacob van Hoogstraeten (d. 1527) in Cologne, and the master of the sacred palace in Rome, Sylvester Prierias (d. 1523), both of the order of preachers. The same end, to destroy decadent scholasticism and its monkish exponents, was sought by the fictitious letters of the unknown and obscure men (*Epistolae Obscurorum Virorum*, Part I, 1515). In barbaric Latin, addressed to the Cologne master of theology, Ortwin Gratius (secular priest), these allegedly scholastic writers discuss their private affairs and those concerning theology, the universities and the religious orders, in a manner and language which illustrates in the grossest, and yet most comical, way, the stupidity, the wantonness, the hypocrisy and deadly vanity within universities, cloisters and curia, within the whole scholastic-monastic world. With quite unrestrained exaggeration and utter falsehood, the Cologne masters, even the blameless Arnold von Tongern, were exposed. (In a letter that is not entirely above suspicion, in 1511 Reuchlin himself had written to Arnold praising his co-religious, Köllin, for his learning and sanctity, and also affirming his own loyalty to scholasticism and to the pope. Indeed, in 1512 he had addressed the men of Cologne with the familiar pronoun.) The second part of the *Letters of Obscure Men* (1517) gave vent to Hutten's revolutionary hatred of Rome. Bitter contempt was hurled at the pope, holy things were joined with obscenities; the Holy Coat at Trier was nothing but a lousy old doublet, and all other relics and indulgences were exposed to utter ridicule. The intrigues of the orders surrounding the curia were castigated. Scorn and the bitterest and most implacable criticism of the powers of the old Church characterised the whole affair. This second part of the letters clearly reveals the atmosphere of hatred into which, in the very same year, the voice of Luther resounded against Roman indulgences. Luther himself for the most part did not relish this style of battle. If he had experienced it later at the height of his hatred of Rome, he might well have greeted it with enthusiasm. But at this time he called the author a buffoon.

The *Letters of Obscure Men* were only the first in a long series of anti-Church pamphlets emanating from humanist circles. These pamphlets began to come thick and fast, creating a widespread anticlerical, antischolastic, anti-Roman, anti-ecclesiastical atmosphere, and fully preparing men's minds for a revolutionary break. In 1518 there followed the *Letters about our Professors at Louvain*, then Hutten's pamphlets, and the effusions of Willibald Pirkheimer against Eck.

In the Reuchlin controversy the new humanist circles stepped into the public eye for the first time with ranks closed. And immediately it became clear, with a compulsion possessed only by the self-evident, which were the outmoded and which the progressive, that is the victorious, forces. In Reuchlin the new learning was called in question; its propositions had been attacked; and humanism stood up for itself.

For the impetus of this battle unfortunately it mattered not at all whether the public image of scholasticism and monasticism was accurate, or whether the strength of monasticism was later to show itself greater than was here affirmed. The decisive thing was that the image presented and the judgment passed upon it was immediately victorious, and at a time, moreover, that was absolutely crucial for the solution of the question whether this development would run for, or against, the Church. After an inconclusive inquisition against Reuchlin in Mainz in 1513 under Jacob van Hoogstraeten, and Reuchlin's acquittal by the bishop's court at Speyer after he had already been condemned by no fewer than four of the old theological faculties (Paris, Louvain, Mainz, Erfurt), Reuchlin appealed to the pope. The ultimate official judgment of the curia was not pronounced until 1520, under the shadow of the Lutheran controversy. Like so much else at the time, this issue was affected by that fatal lack of Catholic clarity which has still to be discussed. Reuchlin was not officially condemned but he was silenced and ordered to pay the legal costs, about the calculation of which Joseph Schlecht gives us an illuminating account.

Undoubtedly the most energetic figure, who towers above the humanist circles that had produced a self-portrait in the *Letters of Obscure Men*, was that of Ulrich von Hutten. Scion of a Frankish, knightly family, this young man had been educated in a monastery against his will, had broken out of it, and committed his life to the formation of a radically free personality, to free 'learning' and to a free Fatherland. Not until 1520 when he joined in Luther's attack on the pope was he to begin to play his great role in world and Church history. Besides contributing his German polemical satire (the *Vadiscus*, 1520, an unrestrained lampoon upon curial immorality, simony and the exploitation of Germany), he joined Sickingen in holding the arms of free knights ready to 'make a way for the gospel'. As yet, however, he was still the wild, ebullient, humanist critic who, on the one hand it is true, in 1517 had published Valla's treatise on the spuriousness of the donation of Constantine, but who, on the other hand, in his satirical dialogues had vigorously helped to create that atmosphere of violent scorn, so deadly to all things loyal to the pope, and which so surely prevented Eck, Cochlaeus and Emser from effectively gaining the ear of the people at that time. For Hutten approached the people, directly, certainly those who could read. But German inflammatory writings were also read aloud (in the same way as, for example, letters intercepted from the enemy were read to the mercenaries in camp); offensive woodcuts were understood by everybody; aphorisms and metaphors were passed on by word of mouth.

It is hard to understand Hutten completely. He defies all systematisation; and it is for this reason that he presents such a wide open front to the attack of his critics. In his life, as in his literary work, there is so much that is inadequate, equivocal, inconsistent, morally inferior and deceitful, that it is possible to dismiss him utterly. And yet, he was a tremendous, living force which, in spite of all his patent deficiencies, lost nothing of its reality. Indeed, he is an extraordinary epitome of the seething confusion of the transition period from the end of the fifteenth century up to the third decade of the sixteenth century.

Hutten became of inestimable value for the victory of the Reformation. It is true that he did not succeed in turning his crusading idea into a bloody war 'against superstition, by the troopers and knights and all who value freedom and are bent on demanding freedom from Rome'. For Luther's cause to survive, however, it was essential that it become a focus for general discontent. If Luther was to conquer he had to win over public opinion. Hutten, the eloquent knight, the humanist, the German, the hater of Rome, contributed enormously to this end. In addition, since 1520 he had been infusing public opinion with a powerful spirit of aggression that was to prove of immense importance in further development. He seconded the motion of Luther who was at that time declaring: 'Emperor and princes must take arms against the Roman Antichrist and the Roman Sodom: we must wash our hands in their blood.'

This is by no means to say that Hutten felt the spiritual compulsion of Luther's religious aspirations. Hutten's religious requirements were small. He was unfamiliar with the details of Luther's ideas. Moreover, as his criticism of ecclesiastical abuses stopped short at the point where the interest of his fellow nobles was at stake (the nobility's monopoly of benefices), so he did not draw the conclusions of his pro-Lutheran, unrestrained writings to the emperor and to Aleander, but once more sought an alliance with the emperor. After the edict of Worms, however, he again abandoned this alliance.

The *Letters of Obscure Men* were a real and highly significant support to Luther in the coming strife. According to them, however, another man was the saviour – Erasmus of Rotterdam, prince of the learned world. They extolled him and his theology as the only means of salvation for the ills of the Church. In fact this was the hope of Erasmus and of many others.

In Erasmus there appeared the fulfilment of the theological, moral and religious beginnings of Christianity as re-formed according to the suggestions of Petrarch, and upon the foundation supplied by Marsiglio Ficino, following the synoptic gospels and St Paul, interpreted in a Neo-Platonic sense, and with the help of the moralism of late Stoic popular philosophy. However, this fulfilment did not lead to the rebirth of Christianity; rather, it threatened its very life, as we shall see presently.

FIVE

Religious Life before
the Reformation

I

The great national apostasy of the Church in Bohemia, which shook Europe to its foundations in the terrible Hussite wars, should not be overestimated in its subsequent effect upon the European sense of unity. There is a temptation to do this at least from the post-Reformation standpoint. The period itself saw Hussitism as splintering, not as schism. The return of important sections of the Hussite movement to the Church provides visible justification of this interpretation.

None the less it remained a powerful fact of experience for Europe that a nation of the Church had been able effectively to withstand both the empire and the crusading armies. The experience went deep, because in Prague Huss had so vigorously attacked the corruption of the indigenous clergy, and, by so doing, gained widespread approval.

In this region religious demands had been made and taught, which at first had been rejected as heretical in Germany and in the rest of Europe, but which were bound to have a disintegrating effect upon the Church, simply by reason of their triumphant presence in the European mind. This immediately became clear when, later, similar ideas were put forward from another source –

from Luther. Hussitism desired the rule of divine law over all of reality; its teaching grew out of the scriptural principle; the whole design was coloured and enhanced by the Czech national, and Bohemian social, individuality of a people who had been nationally, religiously and socially, aroused; all had been fructified in the blood of Huss, who died so courageously; and the legend emerged out of the radical will of 'God's warriors' to conquer and destroy the 'Godless', in a 'holy war'. In substance Hussitism almost completely anticipated the theological ideas of Luther. When he was making his way out of the Church, Luther did not know the writings of Huss. Huss, therefore, had no part in Luther's revolution; but no further proof is required to show how the way for Luther's victory had been prepared by Huss, because of the close relationship of their ideas. When Luther appeared, his advocacy of the scriptural principle, of the chalice for the laity, of clerical marriage, of a national colouring for the liturgy, was favourably received in many places. (Many at Worms inclined to the view that in Constance the safe conduct given to Huss had been violated.) Likewise the radical enthusiasm and quietist mysticism of the Taborites and the Moravian brethren were important, anticipatory and preparatory parallels to the later Protestant fanatics and Anabaptists.

These are not merely notional connections. The Hussites had had to be opposed throughout much of southern Germany and even in Prussia. The popular manifestos of the Taborites spread far and wide. They were in complete agreement with the ill-will to be found everywhere against the 'lords', i.e. the parsons, against whom the great manifesto of 1431 (addressed to the whole of Christendom) hurled a mountain of complaints, social and dogmatic.

It is obvious that a purely theological evaluation does not exhaust the historic impetus of these heretical movements. Even when considered from the viewpoint of Church history it would not be enough to see them simply as apostasy, or as God's rod of correction, and a monitory reproach upon a Church in drastic need of reform. They also expressed noteworthy Christian and religious impulses. It is precisely the Catholic, as representative of the all-embracing notion of providence, of the notion of the *logos spermaticos*, and of the *felix culpa*, who must guard against being satisfied with the dogmatic label, 'heresy' (utterly necessary as this may be), and against regarding heresy, *a priori*, as simply inferior in every respect. Within many heretically inclined, or at least religiously disruptive, movements, there are also many valuable expressions of religious revival. Individual Waldensian–Hussite wandering monks, who undoubtedly presented a protest against certain of the hierarchy, made just as strong an appeal as did the often brutally destructive and religiously fanatical Hussitism of the Taborites. Likewise we must estimate the sufferings of many condemned heretics as more than a religious–psychological factor. Even if the masses, who lived from sheer habit, and, without compassion, enjoyed the spectacle of an execution, were not deeply impressed by these things, and although every death did not possess the symbolic power of that of Huss, none the less Tertullian's axiom about the germinating power of Christian blood applied to those martyred in the cause of heretical Christianity. We cannot close our eyes to facts.

In discussing the social conditions in Germany before the Reformation it has already been shown that the weakening of the link with Rome, and the erosion of religious and ecclesiastical power in the late Middle Ages, were also represented, in an important way, by a multitude of social and religious movements. The converging of social discontent in city and country and amongst the lower nobility, with this rising, but to some extent, excited, piety, must be specially underlined. For it was precisely this religious attitude, with its major and minor element of absoluteness, with its interior fervour, and strict demands, that enabled the social tensions to develop into something really revolutionary and recklessly fanatical, and to produce a really explosive effect, in the deepest sense. The excitement we have mentioned was powerfully present, most of all in the impetuously advancing new movements – as we shall prove later.

What followed was the elaboration and organisation of existent explosive forces. Acute phenomena of disintegration appeared in the Church in the form of sectarian and heretical institutions. They paved the way both for the gravity of the Reformation and for its revolutionary protest, not least, for that pattern which was to characterise Reformation enthusiasm. In this we are concerned not with closely integrated and nameable associations but with intellectual currents and moods which appeared in the same fashion in several places, especially in south and south-west Germany, and along the Rhine. The common expression of the discontent behind all of these movements was the demand which, in varying degrees of clarity, they all made of the Church. Get back, they demanded, to a more authentic Christianity, through the restoration of apostolic simplicity. In this formula, which had been brandished in the face of the Church as early as the twelfth century, and in a quite extended measure in the thirteenth century, all the demands of the Reformation seem to resound in anticipation. It is a summary of all the causes that urged on the Reformation.

Here simplicity meant pruning the rank growth of theology and canon law, and also cutting away much of the power and fiscalism in the political life of the curia. The dissatisfaction was on the one hand religious and ecclesiastical, on the other, political and social. And it was this very combination of desires which provided that breadth of foundation which was the really dangerous thing about it.

Taking first place amongst the sources of this religious energy as of religious discontent was the simple word of God in the Bible, now being printed and read more and more in its whole context. The Bible extols poverty. In sharp contrast to this stood the Church, patron of culture, and possessing very great wealth. This wealth attached to a hierarchy that was almost totally out of touch with the lower clergy. In addition, the Church headed a society wherein it legitimated a class distinction that ran to outrageous inequality of privilege, utterly obliterating the reality of Christian brotherhood. This very absence of equality of rights gave birth to the notion of a natural condition of universal equality, and to the demand for Christian socialism. This sentiment reached out far beyond the purely economic sphere. It was expressed in frequent praise of the 'poor peasant' (cf. above, p. 51). It received encouragement from a religious angle through contempt of the science of the guilds, with which certain mystical circles contrasted the innate wisdom of the poor in spirit, which 'speaks of Your wonderful grace more eloquently than any wizard'.

From Joachim of Floris onwards, companion to the whole development, and, as always, expression of dissatisfaction with the present order, we find *apocalypsism*. Here, too, the Bible was the source – the Gospels, St Paul, the Apocalypse of St John, Daniel. With his preaching of the tripartite division of the span of history, Abbot Joachim had profoundly called in question the order of the present second epoch in world history. This order was described as merely temporary and therefore open to criticism. To await the ending of this epoch with its priestly Church became the legitimate attitude of those who placed their hope in the coming Spirit of perfection. 'Whatever Christ had experienced in his passion, death and resurrection, is enacted also in his body, the Church. In the second epoch the Church is afflicted and dies out.' Later on the idea of Antichrist and his precursors became central in apocalyptic imagery. Old prophecies were revived and rumoured far and wide amongst the people; new prophecies were invented. Wycliffe and Huss channelled the idea of Antichrist into theology as a mighty anti-ecclesiastical stream; and the idea was kept alive in the mind of the masses through many forms of popular literature, plays and pictorial art. There arose that atmosphere of eschatological expectancy, that is so pregnant of radical revolutionary developments.

Even incipient Reformation *spiritualism*, more precisely, Luther's spiritual view of the Church, had been largely prefigured. Joachim of Floris (or the pseudo-Joachimite writings) deserves to be first mentioned in this context also. It is the coming Church of the Spirit alone that is truly the Church. When, in succeeding centuries, the signs of decay in the visible Church became all too evident, flight from reality into the ideal of an invisible, holy Church very readily appeared as a way of salvation. Straightway Huss, with his inheritance from Wycliffe, became the normative voice, although we must never overlook the power of popular preaching as an additional factor. Wycliffe had declared the papacy to be superfluous, for Christ is the sole head of the Church. As a consequence of this view, a host of important institutions, of essential elements of faith, indeed, must go from the visible Church. The Bible becomes the one source of faith; the Catholic view of the sacraments, including the special priesthood and transsubstantiation, must be denied. The same thing happens to monasticism, to confession and to indulgences. It is true that Huss kept the Catholic notion of sacraments, but he adopted Wycliffe's spiritual view of the Church.

It is in Wycliffe especially, or in his remote influence upon the Bohemians, and through their mediation, that we are best able to examine the enormous weakening in the idea of the inviolability of the papacy: the actual, mainly victorious, attack had proved the possibility of a violation of the essential idea, and had introduced this process, consciously and unconsciously, into European thought, especially in the eastern part of the empire.

It is common to all of these views that they reject the absolute necessity of the constitution and visibility of the Church. We face not only the colossal efforts of late medieval piety to achieve a healthy interior life, but also one-sided spiritualising tendencies.

II

And now we are approaching the heart of our subject. The answers to the following questions were to be decisive for the fortunes of the Church in the coming storm. What was the extent of the religious strength or guilt with which she entered the struggle? To what extent did her weaknesses provoke the revolution and then hamper the battle against innovation? What kind of powers were they which enabled her to survive and ultimately to rebuild?

(At this point we are able to give only a partial answer to these questions. We shall give an exhaustive treatment of the theme, with respect to the problem of the religious strength of the old Church, only when, against the catastrophe now in full swing, we are able to catch glimpses of the beginnings of a new Catholicism. Cf. Book Two, Part Three.)

The mighty antipapal movement of the late Middle Ages, which originated in the concept of the autonomous state, and found representation in the conciliar idea and in the corresponding national and democratically convened reforming councils of Constance and Basel, had come to nothing. This was by no means a sheer victory for the Church. A salutary thorn had been removed from the Church's side, a thorn which might have led to timely reform within the Church. As things now stood, no satisfaction of justified demands for reform had been achieved; the papacy experienced not a religious but a political and ecclesiastical, revival; the total condition of the Church on the eve of the Reformation was still permeated by abuses. The Church had sold out to the world.

To understand the causes of this condition we must go back to Pope Gregory VII. The evil state of the Church before the Reformation is closely connected to his policy. To the extent, that is, that his policy ultimately overreached its desired goal and achieved the opposite of what this saintly pope of the eleventh century wished, and to begin with completely achieved. Let us explain. The normative centre of Gregory's policy was the notion of papal power. In itself, however, the notion of power is by no means so direct an expression of Christianity as is the idea of love, of service, even when – as with Gregory VII – it is designed merely to ensure the liberty of the Church. In the course of time its dead weight makes itself felt all the more as it becomes allied to the self-seeking that is never at rest in man. Similarly, human egoism was at work in the clericalisation of the Church, a process for which Gregory prepared the way in all good faith, but which had the fatal result of turning the laity more and more into objects managed by the clergy. As we have remarked already, this led to that secularisation of the Church along the road of law, politics and fiscalism, which we recognise in Avignon and the schism of the west.

A summary of these few indications leads us to a formula, rough and ready in form, no doubt, but pointing only to the possibility of coming revolution. It is a formula that had been repeated in one form or another by all the critics and reformers since the deeply Christian Franciscan Observantine member of the curia, Alvaro Pelayo (d. 1350, an exemplary bishop). It runs like this: the clergy have become the exploiters of the Church.

And so the time was ripe for some sort of violent reaction by the people thus separated from their pastors. The detailed features of this reaction depended upon the disposition of strength, weaknesses and requirements in the various departments of the Church. This must now be described.

III

The papacy, encountered by Luther and the Reformation, and in terms of which, for the most part, they themselves evolved, was the Renaissance papacy. It was and wished to be the leader of culture. Plainly in the forefront of its consciousness stood the *potestas*, the papal power, with respect chiefly to temporal things (the *temporalia*), that is jurisdiction, the system of benefices and politics. The outlook and activity of this curia was deeply impressed by a dangerous and exaggerated curialism. Having accepted political nepotism, since Callistus III, and most decidedly since Sixtus IV, the popes were representatives of their own families to a remarkable degree. The papacy had become a succession of dynastic familes, the patrimony of Peter an Italian princedom. In large measure its income had been diverted from universal ecclesiastical uses, and applied to the family, that is to the favourites of the wearer of the tiara. Along with the fiscalism in Church administration, founded at Avignon, elaborated during the schism, and applied during the Renaissance, there had swept into the curia a broad stream of simony and – allied to Renaissance culture – luxury, bringing much worldliness and immorality in its train. Frequently this fiscalism became a worship of mammon, and immorality in the narrowest and most serious sense did not stop short of the tiara itself.

Naturally, the language of the curia was still full of the now sacrosanct pious phrases, interwoven with unctuous superlatives and richly endorsed with scriptural citations; but the spirit which dictated these documents was far removed from the spiritual conception of the mystical body of Christ, even although around the year 1500 Alexander VI is said to have encouraged people to visit Rome by announcing 'the highest graces of a plenary indulgence'. This may indeed have been a symptom of decline. In curial practice the concept of the Church had become legalised, externalised, secularised. The Renaissance curia for the most part represented acute secularisation, which primitive and early Christianity would certainly have declared to be anti-Christian.

Legalism in the chair of Peter was not in itself the worst evil. The worst evil was despotism, which dominated the curia, spreading all the time, and often becoming quite unscrupulous. This led to a multiplication of favours (and often to simultaneous neglect of others – political jobbery) that made a mockery of holy things, and to the above-mentioned exploitation of spiritual penalties by the frequent use of interdict, even for purposes that stood in no relation to the power of the bann – i.e. exclusion from the life-giving body of the Church. In addition there arose considerable corrosion of the regular laws and authority so that dangerous confusion was bound to follow, and many evils could no longer be put right because the evil itself had become sanctioned in canon law through some privilege or other. Once again the price was being paid for the fact that Rome was so much a city of law and not a city of theology, that the popes were jurists and curial officials, not theologians. Dante had already complained of this, and a century and a half earlier Gerhoh of Reichensberg (twelfth century) had pointed threateningly to the blurring of the distinction between Church and curia, because people no longer spoke of the Roman Church, but of the Roman curia. Since that time this mentality had hardened and become even more blatant.

Avignon's craze for excommunication (Sanuto reckoned that in 1307 about half of Christendom lay under the bann) was followed by the mutual complete excommunication of the two sets of popes and their supporters in the schism. By now, that problem had been resolved; but the tendency, lightly to prolong the bann, had even increased. The excommunication of a prince to the fourth generation and the interdicting of his country on account of an economic dispute, the refusal of Christian burial to some poor soul because of his failure to pay some small debt, were by no means odd exceptions. In the fifteenth century when pacts were made between princes or cities the bann of excommunication was treated just like any other grievance, like some action which the contracting parties agreed to ignore and against which they pledged themselves to make common cause. Individuals acquiesced in or flouted the bann according to whether or not they were sufficiently powerful successfully to resist the effects of excommunication. Excommunication fell into exactly the same category as the bann of the empire. At Worms in 1521, with perfect justification, Aleander uttered the warning that it was an illusion to imagine that the Germans were now impressed by such a device. The bann of excommunication no longer aroused fear, only derision.

The buying and selling of spiritual offices within the curia (occasionally traffic in forged bulls), the sale even of the expectation of benefices, are an indication of the normal attitude to this financial system. (For example, Julius II promised a bishopric to Paris de Grassis, his master of ceremonies – a gratuity in reward for his most successful preparations for the opening ceremony of the Lateran Council.) From this situation inevitably arose the *cumulus*, i.e. the multiplication of several benefices in the possession of one person. In the case of specially favoured cardinals like the young Medici, later Leo X, these might be many and vast. The inner logic of this abuse led further, until this trade in simony was not content to stop at the plurality of such spiritual offices, each one of which was attached to pastoral obligations. The consequence was a colossal neglect of residential obligation and hence of pastoral care. In the literature of the period we are constantly meeting the cleric who, through his good connections, was able to procure a diocese or at least some kind of benefice without being there to administer it. In Germany the percentage of resident pastors was fearfully small – as little as seven per cent. Despite the huge supply of available clergy, compliant about the absence of pastoral care was possible and justified. It is this fact above all, i.e. the utter dissipation of pastoral resources that had run riot for a century, which must be kept in mind if we would form a true assessment of the Christian capital amongst those who were faithful to the Church at the start of the Reformation. Of necessity it had been greatly diminished, in many places, all but destroyed.

It is true that the practice of *cumulus* was canonically forbidden; but men were ingenious. In Roman a series of juridicial subterfuges – or subterfuges dressed up as juridical stipulations – were constructed, designed to justify and permit what was forbidden (prebend, incorporation, administration). Bearing this behaviour in mind, the words of 2 P. 2 : 3 come as quite a shock : 'And in their greed they will exploit you with false words.' Luther made full use of this in his address to the Christian nobility.

The popes heard purely economic disputes in their courts, and set up directly economic authorities within Christian countries (tariffs, for example). Maximilian said that the pope drew 'a hundred times' as much revenue from the empire as did the emperor. Charles V simply said: 'much more than the emperor'. The papal income from the curia was reckoned at some 220,000 guilders. Dispensations, privileges, indults and benefices reserved to the pope, accounted for about half of these. What Christendom felt most directly were the Church taxes, regular and extraordinary; and it was these which constantly aroused the strongest resentment everywhere.

Most oppressive of all were the annates. These were specific dues to the curia on the conferring of spiritual benefices, and they might run to half a year's income. In large dioceses these taxes represented a serious financial burden. If, as the result of translation or death, a vacancy occurred several times within a short space of time, this could mean a financial ruin for a diocese. As a result of the vacancies of 1482, 1486, 1490 and 1500, the see of Passau fell into dire straits, but the curia saw no reason for any mitigation. In 1513 Mainz elected Albrecht of Brandenburg archbishop, after a vacancy which had lasted since 1505, because he promised to maintain the benefice at his own cost. But the debts to the curia which he accepted on his installation were so great and led to spiritual huckstering on such a scale that the way was prepared for the indulgence controversy of 1517.

With the doggedness of an insatiable, crafty business mind, taxes and their ways of application were increased. Nothing was overlooked, and progressive delegation increased the number of those having a hand in the business. There is plenty of evidence of this. When Augustinus Marius, preacher in the cathedral at Regensburg, was nominated bishop of Freising, the Bavarian agent in Rome, Christopher von Schirnting, sent him an account of the demands of the 'money-hungry Roman curia'. These seemingly endless taxes rather spoiled the new bishop's joy at his elevation. The necessary clerical expenses were reckoned thus: costs of bulls and briefs and rights, of application to receive episcopal consecration, of application for a declined benefice, of application for permission to defer consecration beyond the canonical three month limit, of the briefs sent out in respect of these applications, of entry in the chamber register, as well as registration costs of the bulls, and cost of gratuities for searching in registers, and so on. There was no end to bureaucratic activity; and it remained quite unperturbed in face of the Lutheran storm which had already broken. When excommunication of Luther was being prepared in Rome, Luther's feudal superior, Frederick of Saxony, was still being dealt with according to the old methods.

The curia and the clergy were not alone to blame for this financial exploitation, of which we shall see more throughout the entire Church. Princes, humanist critics of the Church, town councils, all condoned this blatant exploitation of holy things, so long as the proceeds flowed into their own pockets. Maximilian's chaplain was provost of Nuremberg, of Mainz, and a prebendary of Trent and Bamberg. He is but one of countless examples. In this way princes rewarded their servants out of the benefices of the Church. Moreover, in these days, effective power of any kind could be bought quite openly. Everything had its price, even a man. The troopers, likewise, were involved in this. The sense of loyalty was seriously impaired by their mercenary readiness to shift allegiance to another flag. Another malady was the ease with which votes could be bought, whether in the consistory of cardinals or the senate of princes. Even a cardinal's hat could be bought.

From those days until now, the actual financial yield to Rome from the German bishoprics has been grossly exaggerated. The curia could not have subsisted on this alone, nor did the sums paid to the curia represent a threat to the German national budget. As we shall see, the territorial princes well knew how to protect their countries from too great exploitation. The sovereigns of England, France and Spain, for example, achieved this by preventing the export of currency and forbidding bequests to the churches. During the second half of the fifteenth century, moreover, the number of German offices filled by Rome greatly decreased – a plain consequence of the concordat with the princes. Even so, the yield that the curia gathered from Germany was very great. Most important, however, was the fact that the exaggerated estimate of this revenue actually predominated in Germany, and it could always adduce very important evidence in its own support. The fact which determined the process of history was this: if these dues were not paid, confirmation of the bishop's election was withheld. Now that the annate had become a prime scandal, and people were trying to remove it or limit its use, and as the justice of these attempts could not be disputed, it was very easy for the empire to begin to ask: "Are there not ways of dispensing with the confirmation of a bishop's election by the Holy See; might it not be confirmed by the appropriate archbishop?" Was it possible, indeed,

D

for a spiritual dignity to depend ultimately upon a monetary payment?

In all of this, much that was sub-Christian came to light. The basic problem is well illustrated in the figures of Sixtus IV, Innocent VIII and Alexander VI. Certainly these men are the plainest manifestation of the problem in a crude form. With their enormous sinful worldliness, however, attention is too easily fixed upon the immorality of a pope, his favourites, or the curia, in a narrow sense. This is not the most essential thing. In a society such as the Christian Church obviously immense importance is attached to the piety and sanctity of its members, its servants and its leaders. But equal, even greater, importance attaches to the correct or false structure, the correct or false structural design and edifice. For this reason the real problem which concerns us here, goes deeper with respect to such popes as Julius II or Leo X.

Pastor rejects the almost unconditional condemnation of Julius II as an utterly unpriestly man. Pastor asserts that whenever possible he assisted at mass, and frequently celebrated mass, and that he took a firm stand against simony. Pastor is right; but he is wrong also; for we cannot deny that under Julius II, too, with inner necessity even, politics, the world, and faction, prevailed in the curia. In contrast to Alexander VI, this belligerent pope was in real earnest about the Church, its unity and its reform. The fatal thing was that precisely with these most serious and conscientious concepts, politics, allied even with war as a means, could appear as decisive for the salvation of the Church, that interior, religious and moral reform seemed capable of realisation only by such means. The historical development of the papacy and the Church-state with its inescapable worldly-political obligations reveals the Church's fundamental dangers. These are far more significant than failures in the sphere of private morality.

When we turn to Leo X, in terms of this line of thought we are least likely to neglect the cultural–apologetic significance of his ecclesiastical patronage, which we still feel through the values created at that time. Both as a cardinal and then as pope, Leo was a man of high personal morality. This advantage, however, was not sufficient to effect a real removal of the abuses which so debilitated the Church. Immorality in the curia and the rest of the clergy, on a huge scale, as we know, was but the consequence of a false over-all relationship to secular affairs, to the law, to politics, and to possessions and pleasure. The extent to which this over-all development prevailed, even under Leo X, can be measured by the treatment he meted out to the Lutheran affair from the end of 1518 until the beginning of 1520 (see below, p. 244 f.), or simply by the manner in which his *possesso* was performed. Sacramental processions had become occasions of sheer ostentation by the pope and his court; and the pope, walking amidst nude statues of the gods, could read such inscriptions as these: 'Once Venus ruled (i.e. Alexander VI), then Mars (i.e. Julius II), now Pallas Athene wields the sceptre.'

The greatest danger for any organisation is not the obvious enemy but insidious disintegration. The disintegration of the Christian priesthood at that time did not come about merely through the vicious life of individuals here and there, but also, much more dangerously, through a manner of existence in which an un-Christian way of life was no longer recognised but accepted as normal. The Roman curia, the higher and lower clergy at the end of the fifteenth and the beginning of the sixteenth century unfortunately provide all too great a wealth of illustrations of every grade of decay, culminating in the condition which Adrian VI exposed in his very first consistorial address, using the words of St Bernard: 'So much has vice become the accepted thing, that those polluted no longer feel the stench.'

The great amount of more harmless secularisation that we have mentioned formed part of this danger. From sheer enjoyment of this world, this secularisation destroyed the sense of distinction between the sacred and the profane, between obligatory Christian faith and non-obligatory humanism.

It is not necessary for our purpose to study every aspect of these things in detail, and to discuss the long list of such abuses in pre-Reformation Rome. What we have said is sufficient. Other scandals of the Renaissance papacy are well known everywhere. The decisive thing is that the verdict proposed cannot be doubted, and that the state of affairs in the curia had become well known amongst all Christian nations as a result of a host of public and semi-public and private complaints, not least through the endless

chain of financial burdens or through personal on-the-spot observation (pilgrims, students, Hutten, Karlstadt, Luther). The history of the papacy on the one hand, that of the states and of the
Church on the other, provide a compelling proof of the correctness of the thesis put forward. Even Pastor's volumes on the history
of the popes, incontestable in this respect, contains it, especially
if we view the contents, not seriatim, but synthetically. Moreover,
in the comprehensive treatment of this ominous complex, 'abuses',
we shall discover how much sharper and more superlatively expressed are the verdicts pronounced on these things from sources
within the Church. Aleander, the most active man at Rome's disposal as the German Reformation was beginning, certainly the
most clear-sighted member of the curia at the time, in his dis-
patches to Rome, recognised dispensations, reservations and com-
positions, as unjustifiable innovations in view of the stipulations of
the Vienna concordat. For this reason a curb must be put upon
those who would never be satisfied with their endless benefices.

With perfect clarity he saw the danger of defection from the
Church which flowed from all this. The Luther affair became
linked with the thousand oppressive and arrogant tyrannous
actions of the curia. People were ready to subscribe to Luther's
heretical views for the sake of protesting against such injustices or
of being avenged for them.

Many a time Luther had vehemently castigated the fiscal
abuses in Rome. It was all too easy for him to do so. In justice we
must note that he did not exceed the statements of Alvaro Pelayo,
the member of the curia we already mentioned, when in 1518 he
summed things up at the conclusion of the explanation of his
thesis on indulgences: the authority of the Church had turned into
abuse, had become the servant of avarice and self-glorification,
and soon the whirlpool would engulf all in utter ruin.

Strongest proof of all of the terrible extent of corruption is the
fact that this spirit of Mammon did not vanish without putting up
any resistance, in face of Luther's threat to the very life of the
Church. We know, indeed, the tenacity with which the same evil
clung on until Trent, and even after Trent, in spite of the reform
inaugurated there. Right at the heart of the storm we observe how
Clement VII, exposed to various pressures, tried to profit by the
sale of cardinals' hats.

Had the curia produced no reaction to this corruption? We are aware of Paul II's categorical renunciation of Renaissance culture and of the pagan humanism of the Roman academy, the members of which lived off the curia. Here were the most important attempts at reform by the best of the Renaissance popes, Pius II; but not for nothing was he the one-time Aeneas Silvio de' Piccolomini. He was not the man to wage a colossal war in real earnest upon the corruption that had permeated the Church, and to carry it to a successful conclusion. Was there not sufficient sanctity about, with which to cover up the present black spots? Was it not still possible to disguise the manifest process of poisoning and the ceaselessly advancing disintegration of the Christian and priestly ideal?

This was possible, but only just. At all events the defection of the members of the Church to the ranks of these other leaders was bound to increase. Rome was seen as the hell that could not last much longer. A hundred times over the pope was described as Antichrist. And so, when, after bitter complaint 'by reason of the mighty sins and deceits of the second Julius and his predecessors' this same Julius was hailed by the imperial ambassador as the 'second God upon earth', this may have been but a turn of phrase; but in many passages Luther found dangerous and apposite copy for his massive polemic.

IV

Cast in the same mould as this papacy were most of the higher clergy – bishops, cathedral prebendaries and, above all, the college of cardinals from whom the pope was elected. We are compelled to say that this papacy was the fruit of a similarly aligned college of cardinals. Cause and effect are linked together and become endlessly interchangeable.

The Church had become enormously wealthy. In this context, the magnificent, extravagant store in many churches of gold and silver chalices and monstrances, of jewelled mass-vestments, was still harmless enough. It may be that all this was the expression of social insensitivity, but these treasures were offerings and had no part in sensual indulgence. To this day they represent valuable, often unique, cultural treasures. The real evil lay in the fact that the Church's income-producing property had grown beyond all reasonable proportions. In Germany at the end of the fifteenth century the Church owned approximately one-third of the land.

Amongst cathedral prebendaries and bishops the notion, and even more the ideal, of the priestly life had disappeared; amongst the bishops the notion of pastoral care had disappeared to such a degree that the whole idea had been exploded from within. The ideal by which the higher clergy in fact lived was that of the lord, possessing power that was a means of tyranny and the enjoyment of life. This went to such lengths that ecclesiastical and spiritual things were lamentably exploited to attain the meanest worldly and financial ends. Here again this basic outlook was infinitely more important and more dangerous than any particular example of a scandalous life. These prince-bishops were not simply priest-bishops who were also princes, dukes and counts. They were predominantly only the latter. How important was prayer in the life of this higher clergy? What did they know of the riches and truth of the religion of the Crucified, which they were supposed to represent so plainly? What part did the sacrifice of the mass play in this princely life? How much did they bother about the religious nourishment of the flock entrusted to them and for whose well-being the Good Shepherd would one day call them to account? There was scarcely any religious and pastoral link between bishop and people. In the end the last thing that interested them was to provide a supply of pastoral clergy. If forced to do so, they would even permit concubinage, on payment of a fee.

Perhaps the deepest cause of this unspirituality lay in the monopoly which, for the most part, the German nobility possessed of appointment to high prelatic posts. In an increasing measure the rich benefices in cathedral chapters and episcopal sees were being reserved for the younger sons of the nobility and even of the princes The decline of the knightly estate aggravated the demand for these privileges. This provided one of the few possibilities for the knight to provide for his children in a manner appropriate to their rank. This applied chiefly to seats in cathedral chapters and to aristocratic monasteries. To the princes, however, appointment to episcopal sees had become an important factor in political calculation. The emergence of the leading political powers – or those that took over the lead – in the history of the Reformation in Germany (electorate of Brandenburg), or of the Counter Reformation (Bavaria), is tied up with success in this matter. In a most scandalous manner, the most elementary requirements of vocation and education were sacrificed to politico-economic designs. Minors were frequently nominated. The dukes of Savoy regarded the see of Geneva as family property. Between 1450 and 1520 no fewer than five ducal princes were bishops of Geneva. Two of these were eight years old at the time of their nomination. At the outbreak of the Reformation eighteen bishoprics and archbishoprics in Germany were occupied by sons of princes.

This aristocratic monopoly was the chief reason for the distinction between the higher and lower clergy possessing such a totally different significance in these days from that which it now has: the gulf was almost impassable. In the late Middle Ages within the celebrated unity of the Church there was no clerical unity at all, least of all in Germany. For the two sorts of clergy the conditions of intellectual as of social and economic life, of rights and opportunities, even within the Church, were separated as though by an abyss. They lived in two separate worlds. In 1500 the cathedral chapter of Augsburg did everything in their power to prevent Maximilian installing his chancellor, Matthew Lang, a burgess, as their provost. Proof of the ability to joust was not only decisive as a qualification for a canon's stall, it was demanded. On the other hand, except in empty forms, the proper spiritual attitude was as a rule no longer set out as a condition.

In the most direct way this aristocratic monopoly had helped to prepare the way for the spread of the Reformation rejection of the Church. It was very easy to separate the people from these bishops. The Reformation storm broke upon the sons of princes and noblemen in the episcopal sees and in the cathedral chapters – i.e. at decisive points on the front – often having no vocation, and hence possessing no religious power of resistance, and, in addition, seriously involved in the territorial and political machinations of their elder brothers. Their minds were preoccupied with money, property and pleasure, with the prestige of their noble houses, and not with the care of souls. They listened apathetically to Luther's fervent sermons, or else they saw in these a possible way of gaining what they desired – to be less bound by morality and to augment their own material possessions.

This explains the despicable apostasy of so many bishops at the time of the Reformation. It explains, too, the dishonesty with which a convinced Protestantising prince like Duke Henry V of Mecklenburg was able to allow his seven-year-old son Magnus to be elected bishop of Schwerin, promising on oath to support, and protect the Catholic Church, and at the same time achieving Reformation secularisation.

From the purely administrative point of view the serious overlapping of the jurisdiction of bishoprics was a source of much friction, and a cause of weakening of the power of the Church and bishops. Jurisdiction over the possessions of the two Saxon lines was exercised not only by three indigenous bishops but also by the archbishop of Mainz and Prague, and the bishops of Würzburg and Bamberg, Halberstadt, Havelberg, Brandenburg and Lebus. Conditions were similar in Austria. In Switzerland, too, the same conditions provided a cause of the Reformation. The relative unity of the German confederacy was ecclesiastically divided up under Constance, Besançon and Lausanne.

The picture we have painted is not the exception but the rule. We see the contradiction of the religious, priestly, apostolic ideal of the clerical office, and a dangerous erosion of the Church from within. No organism can permanently survive such a violent contradiction of its own ideal. Unless a reaction sets in it must collapse. This had to happen all the more surely because this interior contradiction was bound to have a devastating effect upon the ecclesiastical power of the lower clergy and the laity. This was specially true when, in addition, people saw the obvious economic contrast – often intensified to the point of bitterness – to the good-living holders of episcopal or prebendary benefices, or when the faithful saw that they were being exposed to the harsh political power of their bishops. This sort of thing can be seen in its crassest form in the reaction of the bishops after the Peasants' Revolt.

In spite of this, once again it is not as though members of the burgess class could not have gained the profitable positions, and as though all of these prebendaries were living solely for pleasure.

Before as later, such benefices enabled even burgesses to pursue studies, and thereafter to serve the administration or continue study, as did the German, Nicholas Copernicus, who was a canon of Frauenburg in Ermland, or Eck in Ingolstadt, or Cochlaeus in Breslau.

Furthermore, it is not true that aristocratic monopoly caused none but the unworthy to reach the office of bishop or to accept the obligations of the rule in rich abbeys and convents. Amongst the monasteries who heroically persevered in the ancient faith we must count some, the members of which were all of noble birth. Dobhertin in Mecklenburg, about the painful decline of which during the years 1556–78 we have a specially detailed account, is an instructive example out of many.

Even so, what we have said does not exhaust the material. As in all parts of the Church, in Germany, too, we find zealous, pastorally minded bishops. There are many parallels to the mighty reforms which Berthold of Mainz successfully accomplished in his monasteries. When Archbishop William Warham released Erasmus from the residential obligation attached to the rectory of Aldington in Kent, he stressed that this was done quite contrary to custom and for very serious reasons. Bishop Matthew von Speyer (1464–68) was a stout advocate of genuine ecclesiastical reform. The various zealous bishops whom we shall encounter in the course of the Reformation in Germany, complete the picture. As we shall see, however, the completed picture still leaves much to be desired.

V

In their own way, the conditions amongst the lower clergy were in harmony with this model. The system of benefices and the multiplication of altar or mass-stipends resulted in an unhealthy increase in the number, and a debasing of the social condition, of the lower clergy. The amassing of benefices by one person, and the lack of zeal in pastoral care amongst these benefice-collectors, resulted in the colossal expansion of a system of badly paid, ignorant and socially inferior representatives. The result was the formation of a clerical proletariat of terrifying size and declining quality. In Breslau at the end of the fifteenth century two churches could count a total of 236 chaplains alone, priests whose sole job was to say daily mass. At the time of the visitation of St Gereon in Cologne in 1549 there were still thirty vicars to be found. In 1518 Zürich was content with ninety secular priests (and at the same time could boast over 200 confraternities). In 1526, that is at the height of the deliberate cold war on clerical privilege, Basel still possessed 200 priests. John Agricola reckoned the total number of clergy and nuns in Germany at 1,400,000. The true significance of this number is grasped only if we consider the size of the population of the cities in those days: only Munich and Cologne reached 40,000; some six others reached 20,000; Mainz, Regensburg and Würzburg had 6,000; Leipzig had 4,000. Up to onetwentieth of the city population were clerics, up to one-tenth if we include religious. Up to one-fifth of the benefices were supplied by vicars. The beneficiary himself naturally preferred to live in the city rather than in the country. In the collections of *Gravamina* complaints over these things are of daily occurrence. These were all the more in earnest as the worst qualified cleric regarded it as his natural due to claim those spiritual, legal and economic privileges that were beginning to lay such a burden upon the laity. Complaints were made that persons in minor orders were plying trades, wearing secular dress, using pastures and water, were even supporting a wife and children, and yet claiming clerical immunities and placing their worldly affairs before Church courts.

In order to perceive the colossal superstition in the popular piety of that time we must bear in mind that most of the resident or itinerant clergy scarcely surpassed the people in education, and were themselves full of superstition. On the other hand, they knew all too well how to 'deceive God and the world' on pilgrimages, at Stations, at saying mass, and by preaching indulgences, as Geiler and Murner decry. There is plenty of evidence of how mass was left unfinished before the canon, or finished off without any consecration as a *missa sicca* if they were dissatisfied with what was given at the offertory.

Here, too, the Reformation broke many chains, especially those of celibacy, long since loosened by a shocking increase in concubinage. The existent lack of religious power – only surpassed by crass theological ignorance – came to light, and now it became plain for how long many of these clerics had had no living spiritual link at all with the ruling ecclesiastical system, or even stood in revolutionary opposition to it.

VI

The religious orders shared in the general decline. The healthy ancient ordering of the monasteries themselves, as well as their relationship to episcopal and diocesan administration, was now upset with fatal arbitrariness as a result of the dangerous papal privileges we have already mentioned. As everywhere, here, too, the dangerous effects were felt of wealth and, in its train, aristocratic monopoly. All too frequently we meet with the rich, aristocratic abbot and the noble monk, possessing no vocation. The defection of monks and nuns was a common phenomenon in the fifteenth century. What many of these aristocratic 'nuns' got up to at any time, and especially at carnival time, was worldly and far from edifying, to say the least; often it was very much worse. The relations between the less strict groups of conventuals and the nuns in their pastoral care led to many scandals. The Begines earned the derisory title 'Barmaids to the Barefeet'.

John Indagine, dean of St Leonard's collegiate church at Frankfurt, accepted the verdict: the rage of the people against us is not entirely without reason. We are to blame if our infamies leave those of the gluttons and libertines far behind. In his *Enchiridion*, with ease and obvious acquaintance with the facts, Erasmus was able to castigate, not only the disappearance of the basic Christian virtue of love of one's neighbour, but also vocational envy and jealousy between religious orders.

The Cistercians had forgotten their great task of cultivation. Like so many others, now they saw life no longer as a task, but as the enjoyment of pleasure. Church and monastery buildings were allowed to dilapidate. There is no record of any work having been done on the Church at the monastery of Doberan during the last centuries of its life (it was dissolved in 1552). A similar decline can be seen from the fifteenth century onwards at Dargem. Amongst the Johannines and the Antonines in Mecklenburg, too, the decline was unmistakable. The life of prayer ceased to be regularly performed; in its place Mammon held sway, provoking discord and exciting the covetousness of the princes. The sister of Duke Magnus was known as the *impudicissma abbatissa* of the rich Clares at Ribnitz. The strict obligation of corporate prayer was discontinued and common property gave way to private property. Even many convents belonging to mendicant orders were no exception. In 1502 the cardinal legate, Raymond Peraudi affirmed that, as was well known, the Dominicans of five north German cities had abandoned the monastic life to which they had been vowed, to their own ruin and the creation of much scandal. In Rostock and Wismar we hear of *plurima scandala*. In 1517 Cardinal Cajetan had to prohibit arbitrary excursions and the possession of private property. In Rostock strife between the Dominicans and the Friars Minor was to blame for the refusal of the mayors to enlist their help in the battle against Lutheranism. They were left in no doubt that their quarrelsomeness had made their life 'stink to heaven'.

It is precisely such evidence from the predominantly agrarian region of north Germany that proves how general the decay was, for it was not restricted to the localities of genuine city culture, more typical of the south.

Here again the real evil was the decay of certain foundations of the life of the religious orders – dissolution of monastic community and the introduction of private property. Accounts of the state of the mendicant orders at the end of the fifteenth and the beginning of the sixteenth centuries, provided by reforming generals and visitors, are in full agreement with this. On a vast scale monks had obtained permission from Rome to live outside their monasteries. They lived outside on the most varied and tenuous pretexts. Even where monks lived together in many cases this no longer represented monastic community life. From the novitiate onwards enclosure was neglected; and in spite of the rules of the order, the novitiate itself was scarcely observed any more. Associations with the world remained or were renewed. The novices were exposed to alien, unspiritual and then – deriving from extreme humanism and the Reformation – to anti-Church influences. On the other hand, very often the laity had intimate dealings with the monasteries, took such an active part in their business affairs that it was easy for the notion to spread, that the monastic properties actually belonged to the citizens. This was a subtle device preparing the way, at least psychologically, for the secularisation that was to come.

The transition to private property was evident in the most diverse forms. Those who were living outside the monastery accepted secular benefices. Those still residing within the cloister retained their inherited properties, invested money with laymen, made use of the monastic garden for their own profit, sold or bequeathed their monastic cell and if they were professors, might even possess a private chapel and a servant.

Amongst the old religious orders the system of commendation in particular ultimately produced a devastating effect, for this system made the monastery thus 'commended' a mere economic asset in the hands of the new proprietor.

The conditions we have mentioned were most lamentable of all in certain city convents of the mendicant orders; for most of the pastoral care in the Church was entrusted to these. We can estimate the damage before and during the outbreak of the Reformation. We can guess the effect upon the people. It is not only from Erasmus, Hutten, the *Letters of Obscure Men*, and the rest of the flood of popular pamphlets that we learn how widespread was revulsion against, and mocking contempt of, monks and friars at the beginning of the sixteenth century; we learn of this also from irreproachable witnesses, loyal to the Church. One of the first companions of St Ignatius of Loyola was opposed to the founding of an order, 'because the very name was no longer acceptable to the people'. Morone expressed similar views in the forties of that century. In this we see the effects of the scandalous figure of the wandering friar, who, by his high connections, was able to gain the rank even of bishop, providing for his perpetual need for money by the simoniacal conferring of holy orders. Here, too, we see at work that indignation against all those tonsured clerics who throughout the whole year came to the parishes in an uninterrupted stream to collect alms. Alms indeed! They had a *right* to come – twice a year. The dates were fixed; the parish priest announced the collection on the previous Sunday. In addition there were alms-collectors for certain hospitals, and between times others as well who required, first of all, the permission of the mayor. These gradually became more and more obnoxious because there were so many Church collections as well for all manner of purposes outside the parish. The requirements of the parish worship itself were burden enough already. An offering was required for every conceivable thing: confession, Easter communion, extreme unction, even vigils and offices of the dead. When trying to understand the Reformation it is of the utmost importance to take note of the inflammatory complaints against these Church dues, and against ecclesiastical pomp, from the twenties of the sixteenth century onwards. That which then was loudly denounced as unjust coercion and commercialism, had long been the object of hatred.

It is not hard to understand how such widespread decay amongst the higher and lower clergy and in the religious houses made it very easy for a discontented laity to separate themselves from such an unspiritual clergy. These things must be kept in mind if we would arrive at a correct evaluation of the Reformation and its fearful indictments. Nor must we forget that for a long time persons loyal to the Church, true reformers indeed, had been describing these abuses in plain words, and had to some extent been proposing radical means for their correction. For example, tyranny and un-Christian injustice had long been recognised within the selfish, juridical and sophistical scholastic manipulation of spiritual privileges; and this assured unimagined success to Luther's mighty assault upon the Roman wall of the clerical state, although his rejection of a special priestly order was theologically unusually weak, even from a purely biblical angle. The centre of gravity had in fact been shifted from what was truly Christian to the periphera of mere clericalisation, which had often reached the extreme limits of externalism, materialism and secularisation. By all the laws of life and by the fundamental demands of Christianity, a reaction had to come. The injustice of common practice stood in the way of the very existence of the revolutionary critic. What the idea of the priestly office had come to be in practice, the falsification of the idea, now almost officially accepted, misled Luther into a denial of the priestly office itself.

On the other hand, we may ask: Is this picture not too one-sidedly unfavourable, drawn too much in black upon grey?

To reconstruct the life of a past age is always difficult, to reconstruct that of an age of ferment and transition and hence of violent contradictions is doubly difficult. Thus, frequently some harmless page in a chronicle seems to change the whole picture in favour of a much more orderly, even exemplary Church life. In fact, the picture is incomplete. Moralists and satirists are given to exaggeration. Chroniclers have a taste chiefly for the striking, not to say scandalous. Besides telling us those things we have observed, the same irreproachable castigators of human infirmity tell us also to beware of unjust generalisations. Wimpfeling was a severe critic. At the same time he protested that 'in the six Rhineland dioceses he knew of many, indeed countless, morally impeccable and learned prelates and clergy, of blameless vocation, full of piety, generosity, and solicitude for the poor'. The Reformation encountered religious fervour too. Without this, neither early Protestant devotional life nor Catholic reform would have been explicable. The amazingly significant religious value of popular piety at that time – of which we shall speak in a moment – presupposes a partially competent clergy both religious and secular. The sketch in Vol. II of the beginnings of the renewal of Catholicism will cite details and, in particular, provide an assessment of this value. The rigorous fasts observed in those days – no meat, no fat or cheese, no milk or eggs – extended to about 160 days in the year. If all too many readily sought a dispensation in return for a monetary offering, these penances were very often faithfully observed by the clergy. Heinrich Finke maintains indeed, that we must deny the real corruption of the clergy as far as the whole of Westphalia and Schleswig was concerned. There were even priests like H. von Pflummern of Biberach, who all his life refused to accept a benefice, and who said mass for the sick in the Biberach hospital without stipend for twenty-four years. It is true that all around him succumbed to the new doctrines, and he had to leave Biberach; but he went on serving the Church without interruption elsewhere. Amidst the general lamentation he refused to lose faith that God would save his Church.

Not only must we take note in the orders of considerable impulses towards reform in many monasteries (especially the progress of the Observantines who wished to return to a stricter interpretation of the rule of their order, and the union with reformed congregations), but must emphatically fit this into the complex of forces at work. The labours of the first half of the twentieth century have proved conclusively that in all of the mendicant orders there were still many houses wherein the monastic life flourished. In 1415 the Franciscan province of Saxony could number thirty-five reformed monasteries; and amongst the German Franciscans, moreover, there were those who zealously advocated reform, but who were equally opposed to the separation of the Observantines to form a separate section of the order (the Saxon provincial, Matthias Döring, d. 1469). Witnesses to the depth and power of the Franciscan Observantine movement are Bernardine of Sienna (d. 1444), a saint, his disciple, the mighty preacher, John Capestrano (d. 1456), the prominent Dietrich Kolde of Münster, and reformer of the Cologne province of the order, John Brügmann. In 1515 the town council of Wismar informed the pope that the Franciscans in their town led an honest, morally unimpeachable life, having no possessions of any kind, and enjoying the high regard of clergy and people. Amongst Dominican houses, those of Wismar and Rostock returned to a strict observance in 1468, that of Röbel in 1503; and it was the Dominicans in Mecklenburg itself, who displayed such powers of resistance at the Reformation. Like Bernardine of Sienna and John Capestrano, Professor John Nider (d. 1438), reformer of the upper German Dominican province, must be named as an outstanding individual figure who was closely bound up with the great events of the time. At the end of the fifteenth century the Bursfeld reformed Benedictine congregation numbered eighty-eight abbeys. While Bursfeld was carrying out a reform in the west and north of the empire, the Melker reform movement was at work in the same order in Austria and southern Germany. The Scots monastery in Vienna, the university of Vienna, and Tegernsee under its twenty-four-year-old abbot Caspar Ainsdorfer, all give evidence of the important religious impetus of this movement. Luther's Augustinian monastery at Erfurt adhered to the strict observance. His descriptions of his entry into the monastery, and his account of the years he spent there are incompatible with the assumption that there was a universal decline admitting of no exceptions. Luther tells us also that in his youth the clergy were not suspected of unchastity. In Magdeburg he himself had been profoundly impressed by the example of a model ascetic mendicant monk. The mighty fact of the rising orders of friars – with their female branches – was an important component of the religious life of the times. In 1460 the Windesheim reformed congregation of Augustine canons had no less than eighty-six male monasteries and sixteen female houses in the Netherlands and north Germany; in John Busch (d. 1480) they had an exemplary reformer, who reinvigorated the life in a great number of monasteries belonging to other orders as well. Names like that of the much mentioned John Capestrano, the towering figure of Savonarola in Italy, the fact that the south produced a host of saints, the single phenomenon – *The Imitation of Christ* by Thomas à Kempis on the lower Rhine, are all bright spots to lighten the gloom of the age.

If scandal was constantly being given by quarrels between the orders (as by the conflict of different scholastic parties in the universities), there is another side to the picture: the new type of friar became appreciated, in Rostock for example, alongside the older orders (admittedly experiencing almost absurd lack of understanding as well).

There may have been far too many monks whose god was their belly, and who were not nourished on the word of God; but at the beginning of the Reformation Charitas Pirkheimer, abbess of the Poor Clares in Nuremberg, vigorously denied the rumour that she and her community were ignorant of the pure word of God. 'We know the Old and New Testaments inside out, we read them day and night, in choir, at table, in Latin and in German, in community and privately as each one feels inclined. And so, we do not lack for the grace of God as it comes to us through the holy Gospels and St Paul. None the less, I lay more store upon living the gospel and showing its fruits than upon speaking much about it while failing to perform its works. But they say that we had never had it preached to us except dressed up in human pomp. I reply: we stick to the text of the holy Gospel and refuse to be driven away from it – dead or alive. If we must accept commentary upon it, I would far rather listen to that of the saints, to the doctrine that is guarded by the Christian Church, than to the commentary of an alien mind, such as is preached by those who are mere men and whose evangelical fruits are quite unlike the fruits and virtues of the saints, whom they reject.' This is evidence from the Reformation period. This brave abbess would scarcely have thought differently a few years earlier.

Before the Reformation the uncorrupted Carthusians had 230 monasteries and seventeen convents for women. The charterhouse in Trier produced the two great figures associated with the Rosary in its present form, and also John Rode (later a Benedictine, d. 1439) who provided the impulse for the foundation of the Burs-feld congregation, and who, like Henry Egher of Kalkar, prior of Cologne (d. 1408), became – indirectly, through the conversion of Gert Groot – the founder of the Brethren of the Common Life and of the Windesheim congregation. Lapses such as are found even in their ranks, remain exceptions that were unable to spoil the fine spirit which prevailed generally in these monasteries. It is undoubtedly most significant that in Mecklenburg, for example, not one Carthusian and not one member of the Brethren of the Common Life went over to the Reformation. The Brethren in Rostock, where their school was known as 'the German school', enjoyed such high esteem that in 1534 when the monasteries fell under fire the town council entreated them to continue their school. Even after the victory of the Reformation with its hostility to monasteries, the rector, Henry Pauli remained director of a college for philosophical lectures. These 'null brethren', as they were called, had maintained the spirit which their great humanist representatives had learned in the schools of the lower Rhine and expounded in Münster, Heidelberg and Schlettstadt – men like Agricola, von Langen (founder of the Münster educational sys-tem), Hegius, Dringenberg and Wimpfeling.

Everywhere it was greed for money that lay at the root of decay. Even so there were monks who, despising gain, were ready to sup-press a pilgrimage to some holy image, that was threatening an almost spontaneous genesis. Trithemius tells us of this.

In addition the reconstitution of religious orders in this period was of considerable importance. Most of these foundations con-cern Italy, but they affected Germany also. There were, for example, the 'humble brethren' (the *fratres minimi*) of St Francis of Paula (d. 1507), with their unusually severe rule. In the sixteenth century they could muster 450 monasteries.

In a sense Cardinal Nicholas of Cusa, whom we must name repeatedly when discussing this period, sums up the reforming powers of the fifteenth century. Nicholas of Cusa's hospital, en-dowed for thirty-three old men, still bears witness to the cardinal's Christian outlook. His great journey through Germany in 1451–52 as legate, accompanied by the saintly Dionysius von Rickel, presents the picture of a personally exemplary, indefatigable reformer, intent on truly religious affairs – synods, encyclical letters, visitations, public worship and sermons, the appointment of visitators. He was specially interested in promoting a healthy religious life amongst the people, and sought by all means to root out superstition and pious extravagances. This visitation manifested the reform movement at its peak, we might say. Moreover, it was by no means incidental to the general mental outlook of the time that Nicholas of Cusa had such close relations with normative courts in the curia. Admittedly he never achieved his chief aim, which was to reunite Germany really closely with Rome.

All of these things were by no means mere trifles; they were indeed important impulses towards Catholic restoration, and contributed to the formation of the period. It is all the more necessary to stress this strongly, because these things, being less obvious, are inclined to be overlooked or undervalued amidst the *chronique scandaleuse* of the period. Justice demands that we admit quite considerable exceptions to unrestrained generalisation.

In spite of these highly significant bright spots in the picture, the manifold decline, as we have described it, remains a simple fact. One of the most important reasons for this was that very few of the really creative forces of renewal survived into the second half of the fifteenth century, and that the reforming impulses did not reach out effectively beyond the sphere of the religious orders. It is true that the more frequent meetings of synods after the reforming councils was a fact of great importance; but since these reform councils the curia had become too suspicious. The higher clergy were a failure; and very little was done about the lower clergy.

It is therefore our serious judgment that indictment came, not simply from adversaries bent on ridiculing the Church but in an astonishing measure from the Church itself, even from the curia, very strongly from the Lateran Council which was concluded in the year when Luther nailed up his theses (Gianfrancesco della Mirandola to Leo X), and not least from Catholic Germany – Agricola, Wimpfeling, Geiler von Kayserberg, Sebastian Brant, Murner, Eck, the duke George of Saxony, the nuncio Aleander. Corroboration is to be found in the official depositions of the curia in Nuremberg in 1523, and in the reform memoranda of the cardinals in 1537. Pastor himself admits, concerning Gianfrancesco della Mirandola's address on the reformation of morals, that 'nothing makes us feel more sharply how much was needed at that time by way of reform, than the dismal picture drawn by this layman'.

We must go back also to the wealth of testimony, of curialists and saints, indeed, from the Avignon period, and to the radical analyses in the great mass of writings emanating from the various groups of representatives of the moderate conciliar idea: Gerson, Clémanges, D'Ailly, Dietrich of Niem. For the forces of disintegration that were then being denounced, in general went on developing mightily right up to the Reformation. In truth, 'the scandalous life in the ranks of the clergy aroused the hatred of the people for the clergy' (Wimpfeling). 'It is no longer the Holy Spirit, but the devil, who appoints those in authority in the Church; and he does so in return for money and favours, and through the bribery of the cardinals' (Geiler). The memorandum which Cardinal Lorenzo Campeggi produced in 1522 for Adrian VI, and his proposals for reform after the Nuremberg *Reichstag* in 1524, all fit perfectly into this picture.

The facts as described by these ecclesiastical witnesses completely confirm the invective of the sectaries, of the adogmatic humanists, and of Luther after he had completed his commentary on *Romans* in 1516. They are all the more incontestable since the situation described is the logical manifestation of the disintegration that had been developing over the previous 300 years, and of the reform of the Church which had been overdue for at least 200 years, but which had never been inaugurated.

The situation is one of astonishing incomprehensibility and yet of absolute fact. The fateful significance of the situation becomes even clearer when we discover that interest in dogma itself and in its clarification had become dangerously weakened even amongst the leaders of the Church. And the tension became all the greater because their own grandiose yet frivolous ecclesiastical self-consciousness prevented them from truly understanding and acting upon their own warnings concerning the coming judgment.

The actual decay in the ranks of the clergy and within the monasteries still does not provide a universal definition of where responsibility lay. In all of the great declines in spiritual life at this period, the most important factor by far was the wickedness of the curia. The members were weak because the head was sick. Through privileges, dispensations to monks – to individuals or to whole monasteries or even orders – through countless indulgences, and especially through exemptions and through concordats with regional rulers, by various means the chancelleries of the curia contributed to the decline in the discipline of the monasteries and of the clergy in general. And yet it was the curia also who supported the reform of the orders, the Observantine reform in particular. At the same time, however, the curia left such loopholes in the assurance of monastic rules, that in the end collapse was served much more effectively than improvement.

Blame must be laid also upon the aristocracy, who were more interested in their families than in vocation. This scandal had grown until it became condoned in the fatal custom of the institution of lay abbots, a practice which had been developing since the beginning of the Middle Ages. In the Reformation period the Augustinian hermit Hoffmeister, a zealous reformer, sought to find a partial exoneration of monasticism in this fact. 'The monks alone are not to blame for all the abuses. The landed gentry, the nobles, the king and the emperor who, from greed or some similar motive, force their children upon the monasteries, must share responsibility. The noblemen with whom we are saddled, against our will and their own, should from now on be maintained at some court, so as to leave our monasteries free for zealous young people. This would be one step in the direction of true piety.'

Another baneful influence was the interference of the secular arm in spiritual things, in the form of aristocratic privileges, of state or regional churches, or of patronage – spiritual as well as secular. Benefices were conferred from financial considerations; pastoral concern figured little or not at all. The princes who turned Protestant were merely carrying an old custom to its logical conclusion – alongside their Catholic rivals.

VII

The analyses we have made so far of religious life on the eve of the Reformation, have proved how useless empty slogans and one-sided praise or blame are. Like the period in general, religious life at that time displays an enigmatic complexity. The fifteenth century is the chaotic scene of a battle between two epochs. Its diversity can be partially explained only if we rigorously and stubbornly persist in using the phrase 'both . . . and . . . '. He who sees in this ever-fluctuating distribution of light and shade, and of light amongst the shadows, and vice versa, a weakness and unclarity of viewpoint, should not attempt to write history, certainly not of a period of such antitheses as fill the time of transition from the fifteenth to the sixteenth century.

The full difficulty of correctly describing the basic forces at work in this period only makes itself felt, however, when we try to draw a precise picture of popular piety within the Church. This indeed is where we find a deluge of antitheses, shading into sheer contradictions.

The laity's feeling for the Church was strained most of all by economic antagonism to the bishop and to clergy in general – beneficiaries and often the unscrupulous collectors of the taxes that fell due, large and small – and by the incredible worldliness of the clerical estate. Against the pope, as against the not uncommon foreign beneficiaries of endowments, was added national antipathy. There was a complex of discontent that was not limited to any particular time or place. It rested upon a centuries-old foundation of broad intellectual, religious and cultural history. Men's minds and hearts were full of opposition against, and demands of, Rome and very often of the clergy in general.

In spite of this, an astonishing flowering of popular piety within the Church can be discerned from the fifteenth century onwards, and most of all in the second half of the century. Foreign observers were struck by the fact that every village possessed a beautiful church, wherein priest and people showed a devout attitude during the frequent services. New buildings and extensions to churches were multiplied throughout the whole empire in such a way that there were few city, monastic, or cathedral churches, but presented a magnificent appearance.

The Church paid considerable attention to the religious education of the people. The greater part of the year, with its hundred or so Sundays and feast-days, and a hundred and sixty days of fasting or abstinence, fell in a special way under the aegis of the Church. The real advancement of popular devotion was effected by the object-lessons of daily life: mass, the administration of the sacraments (viaticum procession), blessings, processions, pictures, pious popular customs. Direct teaching was given through instruction at confession, and to some extent in schools, but chiefly at common prayer: the Our Father, the Ave Maria, the creed, the confession of sins and the ten commandments. The principal instrument of teaching religious truths was pictorial representation.

We observe also a fruitful elaboration of public worship with intensified popular religious instruction through more frequent and better sermons. A series of great preachers appear (Brant, Geiler von Kayserberg, Paul Wann from Passau, d. 1489). The city authorities were at pains to procure competent Lenten preachers by offering good stipends. The nobility insisted on their servants assisting regularly and devoutly at mass and sermon on Sundays. Geiler von Kayserberg held the opinion that a mass without a sermon did more harm than a sermon without mass. To neglect the sermon he accounted one of the worst of mortal sins, and the bad preacher or the parish priest who failed to provide a sermon, was damned out of hand.

The Sunday sermon was the most important of all preaching. This sermon gave instruction about the saints of the week, about feast-days and fast-days, was used to proclaim banns of marriage, to announce anniversaries and other commemorative masses, the distribution of charity, collections and indulgences. The sermon ended with prayer for the sick of the parish, and for all conditions of men, lay and clerical. It was one of the duties of the head of a family to listen attentively to, and note the contents of, the Sunday sermon, for to him and to his wife was entrusted the greater part of the religious education of their children (teaching them to recite and understand the ten commandments, the seven deadly sins, the Our Father, the creed). At the end of the sermon a hymn was sung. It was also the duty of parents to prepare their children for their first holy communion, which was not, as yet, a corporate parochial event.

As throughout the Middle Ages, the Church still used pictures in every way possible as an instrument of popular education. Windows, walls, doors and pillars of the churches, rood-screens and sacrament-houses, all the time presented the uneducated with an impressive story of the truths of faith. In the churches there were pictorial tablets containing typical summaries of the main groups of teaching, such as the commandments and the creed; and at home, too, men could hang up similar catechism tablets. People were confronted by a constant sermon in stone, wood and clay, upon the outer walls of their houses, on gravestones, wayside statues, upon their stones, in fine tapestries (the well-known Lenten 'hunger cloth'), and above all from the crucifix, the sign of our redemption that rose up around them everywhere, and from the eloquent statues of our Lady with her divine Infant, or receiving the dead body of our Lord from the cross. This constant sermon was comprehensive in substance and could be understood by all. After the invention of printing there was added a flood of pious engravings of subjects from the Old and New Testaments and from the lives of the saints, on virtues, vices, the sacraments, and on the art of dying (see below). Most certainly, throughout the whole of the year, throughout life indeed, all classes in society were presented on every side with a mighty preaching of salvation.

We find an almost fantastic wealth of endowments, and offerings of enormous value. There were endowments for altars, masses, sermons and pilgrimages, in favour of quite small groups, and in honour of a particular saint, chosen from a countless number, or in honour of some event in the life of our Lord or his blessed mother, or even in honour – and indeed for the exploitation – of some miraculous event, or relic with healing properties.

Above the host of saints, close to the group of 'holy helpers', was the triumphant figure of St Anne, the fanatical devotion to whom was a powerful expression of a high esteem for motherhood. And above St Anne stood our Lady. She was given the highest veneration of all. Everything was dedicated to her and bore her name – places, churches, altars, girls. The widespread custom of singing the *Salve Regina* on Saturday evenings arose as a means of extolling her fame. The devout soul of the people was as much expressed in fervent hymns to Mary and legends about her, as in the countless number of paintings and sculptures of the Madonna, some of them very beautiful. Many confraternities were formed in her honour, and many endowments made. In all of this period her praise was never silent.

The rosary was a unique means of advancing this devotion. A rosary was carried by young and old, and it was regarded as the sign of a Christian way of life. People held it in their hands as they died. It is to be found on many tombstones. Dürer bought one. Duke George of Saxony as a boy was urgently admonished by his mother, never to neglect his rosary.

The non-Catholic ought not to judge too hastily, the value of this repetitive prayer. Many souls are able to approach God, using only the most rudimentary forms of prayer; and for him to whom it is given, many apparently rudimentary forms become the road to deep contemplation. Moreover, at the heart of this form of prayer stands the life, passion and glorification of our Lord. The crucial point is our fundamental disposition. It is a fact that even the absence of critical judgment with regard to relics need not diminish the force of genuine, fervent piety. The Jesuit, Peter Faber, a man caught up in the new and creative Catholic piety of the mid-sixteenth century could shed tears of emotion in front of the relics exposed in Mainz.

Alongside the liturgy of the Church had developed an extra-ordinary blossoming of confraternities, closely associated with an intensified devotion to relics, and the collection of spiritual graces at home or on pilgrimage.

In addition, with the advent of printing, there began the energetic distribution of a most important edifying literature – old and new: versions of the Bible, commentaries on the mass, sermons for the home, spiritual writings on confession, on dying and various topics. Amongst certain groups the sermon in church was supplemented by lectures at home.

The total picture, then, is one of an almost confusing abundance of the most diverse expressions of Church piety, or at least, piety sanctioned by the Church. How must we characterise all of this? From the Christian point of view, what was its value?

To begin with: this confusing abundance is evidence of a striking agitation, all the more as the sense of sin, the striving for absolution, an almost agonised solicitude for salvation, penance, the thought of the departed suffering in purgatory, and the thought of one's death, all strongly characterise this piety, sometimes to the point of unbalance.

Agitation, however, is a disposition that is foreign to Catholic piety in general. For this reason people have often denied that late medieval popular piety in the Church was so characterised. Admittedly it was not the case that most of those who went to church in those days were perpetually in a state of anguish over their sins and in terror of the judgment. Such a view would be inconsistent with the vigorous everyday life of the time, and also with the Christian's spiritual life linked to the liturgy of the Church. But agitation was there, and it grew into anguish in such a fashion that anguish – along with many other emotions – became a basic factor of the period. The period was shaken in spirit – often sickly. Was not witch-hunting mania a disease? And the fear of becoming infected with syphilis, a fear which raged through Europe after 1495, brought severe spiritual disturbance in its train. The search for ever greater doses of divine grace, ceasing to make sense when indulgences began to be counted in millions of years, without doubt indicates an element of excited dissatisfaction. (In spite of all apostolic promises made when they were offered, earlier indulgences were constantly being revoked, and new plenary indulgences offered and acquired). The urge to go on pilgrimage, the *currendi libido*, often become truly epidemic. All of this opened up the way to the creation of a fanatical atmosphere that was able on occasion to run to extremes. The classic example of this is Hubmayer, chaplain at the pilgrimage church of Maria the Beautiful at Regensburg, and later an Anabaptist. To this movement also belong the endless number of confraternities for prayer and the acquisition of graces. These, all too frequently, were preoccupied with escaping hell-fire. This period sensed revolution pressing in upon all sides. It was, moreover, impossible for the mighty convulsions in the secular, political, ecclesiastical, papal and social spheres, and the radical activities of the great preachers of penance in this age of expectancy, not to produce an agitating effect upon the souls of men. How can we understand the epidemic, infectious surge of fanaticism amongst children in the fifties of the century apart from such an atmosphere of agitation (1455–59; and the children's pilgrimage to Mont-Saint-Michel, 1475)? And when it was announced that the Turks had reached the Rhine, popular credulity, which lived in expectation of a divine chastisement, saw this as a clear and dangerous threat which could not but leave its mark upon religious life. Very much the same mood is expressed by the countless numbers of ordinary pilgrims and the ever-increasing number of pilgrimages, especially as these very often were linked with expectation of the world's destruction.

The somewhat insubstantial character of such piety was demonstrated both by the craze for miracles and visions, which accompanied the enthusiasm for pilgrimages, and by the numerous restraining prohibitions and warnings issued by German synods and theologians during the whole of the fifteenth century. In the midst of attacks by the Reformers, Berthold Pirstinger was not afraid to admit and condemn the fact that in Regensberg people had turned Mary the Beautiful into an idol. Micheal Ostendorfer's woodcut of this pilgrimage clearly shows, in addition to orderly processions and prayers, many signs of a mental and physical excitement that went far beyond mere favour.

In conclusion, the enormous upsurge of prophecies, increasing until they became a public menace, and the blossoming of occult philosophy, underline the truth of our thesis. According to astrological calculation, people were expecting a second Flood in 1522 or 1524. John Lichtenberger with his multitude of prophecies could not be silenced; Joseph Grünbeck announced the change around of all social classes; after the outbreak of the Reformation bishop Berthold of Chiemsee (*Onus ecclesiae*) took up the tradition by combining all the Joachimite prophecies in a gloomy picture of the end of the world. In Paris, Agrippa von Nettesheim (d. 1535) founded his secret order for the discovery of the philosophers' stone. The hidden forces that surge through all things are the key which unlocks the riddle of being. Paracelsus (d. 1541), a pupil of Trithemius, lived and hovered in a world of utter unreason. A colossal resurgence of the thirst for knowledge took place, and with it, an eruption in all institutions, a revolution in opinions, presuppositions and imagery. The whole atmosphere surrounding Wilsnack – much disputed by the Church – and other alleged miracles of blood, is perfectly in harmony with this. Astrology was rampant throughout society. Good humanist churchmen, like the successful reforming Benedictine abbot, Trithemius (d. 1516), hailed it enthusiastically. It agitated popular groups; and even the educated were closely associated with the movement. Pierre d'Ailly (d. 1420), later a cardinal, wrote five tractates on astrology in a single year. Trithemius, too, believed in the connection, there-in expounded, between the heavenly bodies and human history. According to his muddled views, the course of history essentially depends upon the angel set over each planet for a period of time. His own period was governed by the angel of revolution who was to see the destruction of an old, and the establishment of a new, religion by 1525. We have already mentioned Reuchlin's venera-tion of the Jewish esoteric teaching which flourished in Italy. According to him there were secret powers hidden in the Hebrew alphabet. Aleander tells us that the imperial chancellor was far too well acquainted with language about constellations, and had desired a council because the stars of fate ranged themselves against every other solution of the problem.

There was a widespread superstitious belief in the efficacy of certain amulettes, especially as protection against spells, and 'by mere contact, against burning, shipwreck, storms and hailstones'. There was also the persistence of ancient half-heathen superstition in the prevalent personification of the forces of nature – in weather, in the fields, plants and animals; and there was belief in all manner of magical powers, cures for diseases in man and beast, protection against love-charms, and there was witch-mania, the focus of so much dispute between the Franciscans and the Dominicans, end-ing in the fearful business of the trial of witches. All of these things were bound to set the essentially much more robust spiritual consti-tution of our ancestors in dizzy vibration.

The general excitement of the decades preceding the Reforma-tion was, moreover, supported and augmented by sermons that were full of invective, quite unrestrained at times, and not entirely free from hatred. The agitation surrounding Savonarola's pulpit had minor parallels in German churches. The way was being pre-pared for the polemical preaching and the riotous disposition amongst the audience, that we find in the early Reformation.

It is in art that we find the most direct expression of these dangerous moods, extending from vague depression to a sense of death and fearful agitation in face of threatening uncertainty. Dürer, creator of *Melancholy* and of the engraving, *The Knight, Death, and the Devil*, drew inspiration for the arresting visions of his *Secret Revelation* (1489) from his own impulses. Tombstones are covered with sculptures depicting corruption. The creations of

Veit Stoss express violence in the figure, the face, and above all in the dishevelled garments or the loin-cloth, of the Crucified. Grüne-wald's Isenheim altar belongs to this genus in virtue both of the violent eruption of diabolical terror which it depicts, and of the violence done to the body of the Crucified, whose mighty limbs wage, as it were, a Vulcan-like battle against death, before they themselves convulse in death. The sorrow of the world is borne by the believing Adam, portrayed by Tilman Riemenschneider. The same burden is depicted in his *Scherenberg*, his *Knight of Schaumburg* and his *Kilian*.

This agitation, however, did not have its primary roots in an exaggerated sense of guilt. At least as potent a contributory factor was seething discontent with social and political conditions, a discontent which men felt in the very core of their being. The discharged troopers were a constant cause of uncertainty and hence of unrest, even in the periods between the many wars. In addition there was a large class of those who were constantly and restlessly on the move from place to place: students, merchants, the clerical proletariat. With good reason these have been called the 'shock troops of the revolution'. Likewise, discontent with the state of religion and of the Church was at work, and on the other hand, as we have already remarked, there was the expectation of the end of the world and of the new creation, which had been appearing since the time of Joachim of Floris. Here, then, in religion, are to be found the roots of this development; and that is where they remain.

One of the aspects of this faultily balanced religiosity was preoccupation with belief in the devil. This belief seems to have known no bounds. We find pacts with the devil, intercourse with the devil, the cult of the devil and witches' Sabbaths, all taken for granted as everyday things. Here we have indeed a thoroughgoing perversion of Christianity into diabolism. It is true that we must not unrestrictedly connect this tendency to see the incarnate presence of God everywhere with psychic agitation. The declining Middle Ages was filled also with laughter at the devil, laughter that was by no means that of despair, as liberalistic arrogance might suppose. Frequently it expressed the assured victory of the redeemed, and relish at the discomfiture of sly Satan outwitted. In the carving on choir stalls and in the rhymed proverbs of the time, this humour became a kind of harmless banter with the cloven-footed horned one. How self-assured is the aphorism of the knight in the abbey church of Doberan, who affirms that he will 'carouse in eternity with the Lord, while the devil thirsts for ever in hell'!

Amongst other things, the prophecies contained an element that was vitally important in further development. For centuries they had been proclaiming and calculating from the stars the coming mighty transformation of all existent order, especially the religious transformation of the Church, and also the social revolution affecting the nobles. In 1438 the socialistic-revolutionary and apocryphal *Reformation of the Emperor Sigismund* had appeared; and at about the same date the *Manifesto* of the Rhineland revolutionary. About 1440, in his *Net of Faith*, the peasant, Peter Cheltschizki had called for a total reorganisation of state and Church, declaring all use of force as in itself anti-Christian. Force had falsified Christianity within the Church. Only God and Christ, only complete love of neighbour and of enemy are of any value. Emperor, pope, nobility, burgesses, monks, universities and priests, all organizations, are bearers of power and of force, and so they must vanish. Every man can read about God's will in the Bible; and the worship of God is performed by each within his own heart. He has no need of any confession in order to be reconciled to God (Eder). The Thuringian Franciscan, John Hilten (d. *c.* 1500, a loyal Catholic) reckoned in 1485 that the papacy would collapse in 1514 or 1516. In 1524 Rome would be destroyed. In 1496 the woodcut of the ass-pope appeared, and in 1508 Grünbeck's book. Such promises, turning into expectations, were bound to foster unconscious and conscious breaking away from the Church.

Agitation on such a scale is unhealthy, at least it opens the door to disaster. Luther, however, and the second generation of Protestants, to whom Catholicism was a closed book, did not let matters rest with registering this censure. With unparalleled success, they accustomed the world to seeing this rich popular piety in the Church primarily, or even exclusively, as the *performing of works*, as a massive piece of human self-assurance, sheer externalism. Even Erasmus was one of the originators of this verdict, as a result of his unrestrained generalisations when he attacked current piety in the Church. According to him, in the Church one found nothing but threats of hell-fire, scruples, qualms of conscience, trivialities, Judaistic legal formalism and fear.

Undoubtedly externalism was to be found on a devastating scale. In many of the above-mentioned things it was blatantly obvious. There were the abuses associated with pilgrimages, the vast cult of saints, so often little more than the servant of self-interest. In the year 1500 the dukes of Mecklenburg settled Augustinian hermits to venerate the blood which flowed from Hosts in that town. Large quantities of spurious relics were distributed and venerated often with much superstition. The reckoning up of the spiritual favours collected and vaunted in churches and in confraternities frequently betrays that strictly religious bounds have been overstepped and all sorts of egoistic subordinate ends have assumed predominance. The most acute and most appalling example is the calamitous financial infection of indulgences and the crass mechanical view of their efficacy, especially within the kingdom of God beyond the grave – in purgatory. The instructions given by Cardinal Albrecht of Mainz to his commissioner of indulgences, and accepted by Tetzel as well, are immediately repulsive to any religious man. In a coldblooded commercial manner the indulgences were proclaimed according to an exact catalogue in the parish churches. Since the fourteenth century there had been countless indulgences in Rome. The fifteenth century saw a veritable inflation using astronomical figures. At that time, the plenary Roman indulgences included a host of bogus indulgences, which none the less as late as 1521 were carelessly attested by the papal vicar general, using the accustomed, assured, threatening and damning formulae. People must accept these with perfect faith; no true member of the true Church dare doubt their authenticity; anyone who did doubt sinned gravely. The solemn offering of extraordinary papal indulgences grew into a special evil. Besides this, on these occasions the great flood of people to the visiting confessor, in some measure forced him to perform his duties in the confessional hurriedly and superficially.

The widely displayed cultural potentialities of indulgences was much more than a mere accessory. This, too, enormously encouraged piety. Without the money put into circulation through indulgences, a whole host of magnificent churches and countless admirable hospitals would never have been built. The wealth of pictorial art within the churches likewise could scarcely have been produced but for the income from indulgences. None the less, a weighty suspicion of this dangerous entanglement with material things remains. Responsibility for this entanglement must be fully shared by the secular powers who, from economic considerations, were deeply involved in the increase of indulgences. In 1500 it was seriously proposed to cover the imperial budget by income from indulgences. This shows how deeply rooted the idea of indulgences was in the people; even more, it is proof of the serious perversion in practice of the real meaning of this spiritual grace. These things partly explain, too, the striking tension revealed in the behaviour of Frederick the Wise who, on the one hand, favoured Luther, on the other, energetically appealed to Rome for fresh indulgences, and held an indulgence celebration in Wittenberg in 1519 and 1520, which yielded a considerable income.

This development was not accepted in all parts of the Church without opposition. From the fourteenth century onwards, in many dioceses we see a battle being fought against the proliferating abuses of the system of indulgences. There were loud complaints against the huckstering methods of the indulgence-pedlars who were leading people astray; but these complaints accomplished very little. The evil spread everywhere because its roots remained untouched. The lure of money was too great. From non-papal indulgences at least, the local parish priest too received a share. Cathedral chapters, bishops – as in Würzburg in 1515, 1516 and 1517 – and parliament (1497, 1498, 1521), all opposed the preaching of indulgences, from perfectly religious and unselfish motives, what is more, but to no avail. The flood only increased. The Franciscan, Thomas Illyrius, knew that indulgences had increased on account of 'the greed of some prelates', that they had become utterly contemptuous. In his memorandum to Adrian VI, amongst other things, Eck complained of the unheard-of indulgence privileges of the Holy Ghost order who had gradually acquired for themselves a share in every possible indulgence (a million years and forty-two plenary indulgences).

As with indulgences so too the colossal multiplication of chaplains, masses, relics, confraternities and benedictions had run riot so as to become a danger. Protracted vigil at a death, anniversaries, multiplication of masses for the dead (including the 'overlapping masses'),[1] 'fixing up the soul' at interments, masses with double or several commemorations of the donor, and the whole array of hole-in-the-corner masses completely detached from the parochial system and said by quite ignorant clerics, all of these things displayed a semi-magical notion of the holy mysteries, and an isolation that was totally at variance with their deepest essence.

Nobles of high degree went in for collections of relics, and they were imitated on a smaller scale by the lesser nobility and wealthy burgesses. People went on pilgrimage to these relics. In Wittenberg they could pick up an indulgence of about two million years, in Halle one of forty million, by making an interesting tour, to the accompaniment of a few prayers.

The multiplication of feast-days, which Nicholas of Cusa considered to be the result of superstition rather than of true reverence of God, and the heightened esteem of sermons, did nothing to prevent these things, too, from coming to share in the general externalism. Quantity increased, but quality did not always do likewise. There were complaints about boisterous games taking place in church; so, too, sermons were often overloaded with buffoonery and profanity and colossal lack of critical sense, and all too infrequently did they preach Christ. For example, Oecolampadius was enraged by the *risus paschalis*. Even the titles of the sermons of Brant and Murner breathe little of the spirit of the gospel. Even when Christ does stand at the centre, all the trappings claim far too much attention. As distinguished a man as Geiler von Kayserberg could preach sixty-five sermons on the Passion in which he developed the comparison of Christ with gingerbread. Christ, our gingerbread, is compounded of the bean-meal of divinity, the old fruit of the body, and the wheat-meal of the soul, with the honey of compassion mixed in.

Nor was even the veneration of Mary, encouraged by the Franciscans and the Council of Basel, unaffected by this exaggeration. This applied to pilgrimages, to devotions and, sad to say, to theology as well, which did not remain free from dangerous hyperboles. To find this we do not have to search in some insignificant scholastic disputation, but simply to examine Occam's *Centilogium*, where we find such propositions as these. 'God the Father is the Virgin's

---

[1] *Schachtelämter*. See H. B. Meyer, *Luther und die Messe*, Paderborn 1965, pp. 97–8.

E

son. The Holy Spirit is the son of the blessed Virgin.' The same
applies to much of contemplative life. The level had sunk from
robust mystical spirituality to weird sensationalism, to 'fantastic
devotion and ultra-concrete imagination of faith'. Alan de Rupe
of Brittany, for example, a man who worked so hard to spread the
devotion of the rosary, at times practised and recommended meditations that were in very bad taste, not to say morally and religiously dangerous.

Besides the agitation of which we have already spoken, pilgrimages also displayed highly exaggerated forms of veneration of the
mother of God. We may recall, for example, that the events at
Niklashausen centred round visions and commands of Mary. Tens
of thousands, who for some time used to stream there day and
night, would throw their clothes into the chapel in honour of the
Queen of Heaven, and return home naked.

And the pilgrimages! All social classes took part. Credulity and
superstition could be seen here in extraordinary objectionable
forms. The travelling flaggelants were but a special exaggeration
of a pilgrimage-mania permeated with constant rumours of visions
and miracles of blood flowing from Hosts, that aroused moral tur-
pitude in the crowd and introduced all sorts of disorder into life.
Local exploiters like the regional rulers encouraged these urges,
not least on account of the votive offerings. In this way they hoped
to prevent Germans going on pilgrimage outside their own
country (scarcely any pilgrims came into Germany), and to keep
German money at home and set it circulating faster. In spite of
Cardinal Nicholas of Cusa, the archbishop of Magdeburg and the
appeal to the universities, the electoral prince of Brandenburg protected Wilsnack.

It is perfectly true that we must not make light of the hardships
and dangers to life itself which were part of going on pilgrimage.
These things were an expression of a genuine will to do penance.
'Nor does it matter,' affirmed the Westphalian Carthusian, Wer-
ner Rolevink, in 1478, 'if perchance some error should occur in
such things, provided it does not concern an essential article of
faith. As long as the people come with the devout intention of
honouring the one true God and his Son, our Lord Jesus Christ,
and his saints, and in the firm belief that their prayers will be
heard, then it is better to permit these things than to prohibit

them.' True enough; but this sort of theoretical judgment is of little help in face of the rank growth of late medieval practice. Alongside true belief there stood a colossal externalism. Faith and superstition all too frequently had become inextricably interwoven. The result was that faith was weakened rather than that superstition was ennobled.

Fervour in prayer and the depth of the rosary could not prevent much babbling. Geiler was aware of this. He warned people of such mechanical prayer: '. . . mutter, mutter, mutter, counting out prayers as though counting out money'. The magnificent concept of the communion of saints had been seriously damaged by too cut and dried notions. This came plainly to light in the traffic in indulgences of the time. For Erasmus it was a constant stumbling-block, to see people don a monkish habit on their death-bed, thinking that thereby they were more assured of eternal bliss, while other imagined that they would be safe from harm if they looked at an image of St Christopher in the morning. 'We kiss the saints' shoes and their dirty sweat-clothes, and we neglect to read their books, their most precious relics.' The value of many endowments in honour of the saints was lessened by their being made to serve some narrowly defined special purpose, thus encouraging the peripheralisation of Christian piety. To increase the social standing of the donating family was also one of the purposes of endowing chaplains, chapels and altars – a spiritual form of keeping up with the Joneses. This attitude was not strictly religious, but it did not entirely exclude the spirit of prayer and sacrifice.

All this wealth of devotion is made suspect from the Catholic angle by a single fact. Within the whole system the reception of holy communion played a very small part. Universally the power of this *opus operatum* above all others fell into the background of the spiritual economy. In general, people received only the strictly obligatory Easter communion after the likewise obligatory two confessions. (Communion was obligatory, moreover, on pain of imprisonment and corporal punishment.) And even then there was relatively great neglect of this minimum. There were repeated admonitions from synods that this once yearly communion must not be neglected. But these admonitions were in vain. In the second half of the fifteenth century the diocese of Eichstätt records 100 communions in one year, apart from the Easter communion, on only one occasion. Complaints about the state of the little-used ciborium and the sacred species reserved therein confirm this religious apathy.[2]

The picture is not sufficiently lightened by the plethora of masses, for the popular – and clerical – view of the efficacy of the mass was far too materialistic. People thought of little else than of how to exploit mass, to hear mass in order to gain temporal ends. Often enough their notion was plainly superstitious: the mass was magic charm. In addition, the economic function of the mass in the form of the stipend was greatly encouraged. There was a mass formulary of holy Job as protection against syphilis. Mass was said in order to recover stolen property; there were masses of sevens, thirteens and thirties, or series of masses numbering 5, 6, 7, 9, 13 or 30, supposed to guarantee liberation from evil; and, despite the Church's prohibition, there were even requiem masses designed to bring about the death of the living. This unhealthy multiplication of masses made use of very doubtful forms. A sevens mass for the dead, for example, had candles and offertory processions varying in number from three to nine, ten, twelve, seven, five and one – corresponding to the blessed Trinity, the nine choirs of angels, the twelve prophets and so on. We have already mentioned the scandal of the *missa sicca*. There were vexatious and dangerous associations of financial interest even within a notably interior religious life, as, for example, when the confessional manual or the priest in confession asked about the tithes or the pre-scribed offering at Christmas, Easter, Pentecost and the Assumption.

Similarly, the multitude of pious practices were substantially debased, so that, in spite of all the measures adopted by the Church, the religious education of the people remained superficial. It was superficial in the sense that the real spiritual riches of the gospel and the person of our Lord were not properly transmitted to the people, although in true Teutonic fashion a great deal of

---

[2] For a decade after 1479 the canon and parish priest, John Malitoris, gave holy communion daily (even thrice daily) to some women in his congregation. This seems to be an isolated case. Sectarian and Hussite influences were possibly operative. His zeal earned him an inquisition process at the instigation of the later author of the *Hammer of Witches*, the disagreeable Henry Institoris of the order of preachers. Daily communion was forbidden under threat of excommunication, as resting upon views that were akin to heresy. Infrequent communion was regarded as the correct thing.

moralistic piety was. Fundamental worship in Spirit and in truth revealed its power too little. A moralistic attitude which allowed dogma to recede, and gave unlimited scope to exhortations to improve one's moral life, characterised the sermons even of Geiler von Kayserberg, most popular preacher of the time. It was in line with this, too, that instruction by the pastoral clergy in the true celebration of the mass, of the canon and the consecration, should have been so inadequate.

We must never forget that the rising class who enjoyed education were a small minority. The vast number of people could neither read nor write. For this reason we must be on our guard against measuring the religious condition of the people simply by the wealth of popular piety to be found in edifying literature. The number of groups who really possessed Christianity, i.e. knew it as something which was alive and growing, was very small. It is not a case of equating Christianity with theology. As we have said, the whole atmosphere was still created by the Church, and that state of affairs was taken for granted. But it is most significant that the greater part of this pre-Reformation generation were predominantly Christians and churchmen, living from habit, from a habit moreover, that exhausted itself in keeping the outward precept, but never knew or lived by the interior spiritual treasure. The distinguished pastoral work of Eck in Ingoldstadt knew nothing, for example, of popular devotions in the vernacular, and religious education of the youth was likewise unheard of. Instead, the people participated in the choral office. This cannot be seen as sheer advantage for the Christian laity. It is a universal law of life, including religious life, that the mere possession of something without increase of the thing possessed, means diminution of strength. This process remains hidden for a long time; and then one day the loss is uncovered. In our own day this has become abundantly clear.

We now reach a further conclusion. Recently our attention has forcibly been drawn to the fact that piety in the medieval Church, even the late medieval Church, was nourished less on formal, theoretical teaching and learning – as in school – than on custom and habits of life, handed down from generation to generation. This custom had become so thoroughly mixed up with the daily, weekly, Sunday and feast-day rhythm, that the sacred – the commandments, prayers and hymns of the Church, the life and passion of our Lord, his mother, the saints, blessings and other ceremonies – presented itself, as it were, to men, attracting them, admonishing them, making demands. Life was more or less saturated with a host of religious traditions. In much, life had been built up entirely out of religious notions, and for the most part it was purely and simply pious and Christian, both in town and country.

It is very much worth while to draw attention to the life which pulsated within that abundance of popular piety. Religious energy lay hidden there; but in face of an evaluation that has recently emerged in folk-lore circles, we must affirm, that custom in itself is just as much subject to the requirements of the gospel as is any other expression which claims to be Christian. Custom can just as easily sink to a sub-Christian level, or lose its Christian substance, as can any aspect of the Christian's devotional life. Thus the overwhelmingly dominant role of the mass, for example, in the pre-Reformation era is no absolute proof of the universal Christian authenticity of devotional life at that time. The same holds true of the gay fulness of the life of the Church at that time, and of the casual approach to education for the priesthood. Fully recognising the primeval strength of the native soil, let us concede full value to all of these things. But the ultimate, sole value in Christianity is the greater interior justice of the gospel, the fulness of the mystery, the authenticity of the religion of the Crucified. Even the sturdy growth of religious custom having a Christian root can still run to externalism. No expression of religion and no religious substance are safe from this threat.

And for the rest, in which direction did this abundance, this power of popular piety within the Church move? It was not simply a case of 'the people having their faith and their ceremonies taken from them (by the Reformation)'. Without wanting to minimise the difficulty in making the thesis fit all the requirements of the context, let us affirm that in a remarkable degree the people, too, came out on the side of reform and renewal. That, to say the least, is no proof of the special health of what was specifically Catholic in the whole area we are discussing.

In spite of all these things there is the other side of the account. The deficiencies produced by externalism and crudity, by what was unhealthy, weak and sentimental, are by no means the whole story. The fable about Catholic work-righteousness that knew nothing of the Bible, of trust in the compassionate heavenly Father, of love and perfect contrition, or of true faith, but only the thunderings of the priests about the threat of hell, and the judge sitting upon the rainbow striking fear into all hearts, is a fable indeed, no matter in how many variants it is repeated.

Nor are we here concerned with the inadmissable attempt to paint over the unpleasant shadows; we desire, rather, simply to grasp the complicated reality as faithfully as possible, in all the interweavings of its various forces, and to avoid a one-sided judgment.

In fact, only crass rationalism is able to overlook the fulness of the constructive Christian content which is latent within that extraordinary multiplication of expressions of piety.

To begin with we must remember that the Church did not take the mighty assault of the sub-Christian, the pagan indeed, without putting up a fight. We have sufficiently stressed the guilt shared by practical theology and the higher and middle clergy for the abuses of the system of indulgences, and for other phenomena of decay. It is the part played by the clergy, above all, that can explain the riddle of the great revolution in the Church at the beginning of the sixteenth century; and certainly the worst thing of all about the abuses was that so many in the Church, leaders and led alike, put up with this sort of thing for so long, often accepting it as though it were good and Christian. The darkest thing that the late Middle Ages produced was the belief in witches, an evil which did not fully explode until the second half of the seventeenth century. The papal curia, with the fatal bull of Innocent VIII which gave official standing to the *Hammer of the Witches*, written by two Dominicans, popular theology and the practice of many ecclesiastical courts, all share blame for this.

At the same time, however, valuable reforming activity was going ahead. We have already mentioned the ecclesiastical reaction to the evil of indulgences. The fourteenth and fifteenth centuries provide a colossal outburst of synodal regulations against the hydra-headed superstition of soothsaying by lots or the observation of birds, magical invocations, lottery of the saints, magical incantations and astrology. Warnings were also issued against magical views of certain ecclesiastical blessings, especially those applicable to women, as, for example, that of the synod of Passau with respect to the cruciform immersion of the relic of St Blaise at the blessing of the St Blaise water in Mainz.

In describing corruption, we must not overlook the fact that in the bitter accusations the plain truth was not always declared. Very often people resorted to the 'fable convenue' and to the literary platitude; the complaint would be rhetorically strengthened, but the reality once again merely seen through the 'fable convenue'.

In reality, as well as the lamentable peripherisation we can see equally plainly an astonishing interiorisation, an emphasis on love and on trust in God, on a better interior intention to change one's heart, and on perfect contrition; we see, too, a real penitential earnestness and the preaching of Christ as our only salvation. The comprehensive researches of Franz Falk and Nicholas Paulus into sermons and the books on confession and dying, have produced the exact contrary to the usual affirmations about work-righteousness and servile fear of God, as far as this type of literature is concerned. It is far from superfluous if we recall once again the truly evangelical depths of *The Imitation of Christ* by Thomas à Kempis, a work that has exercised an unbelievably powerful influence ever since it was written, and also the gigantic editions of the pre-Reformation German Bible and of collections of sermons. (Between 1470 and 1520 there were a hundred editions of the Sunday Epistles and Gospels alone.) We would do well to heed at times the now old admonition of Kolde, that 'the writings of the Reformers can scarcely be used as a secondary source of Church doctrine and life'. There was a wealth of such edifying literature to supply all needs: there were numerous and varied prayer-books (*The Christian's Mirror*, *The Road to Heaven*, *The Gate of Heaven*, *The Soul's Comfort*, *The Garden of the Soul*), and booklets on confession, communion and marriage. The actual widespread use of these books proves what shall be explicitly confirmed, that this literature was not only printed but eagerly read also. After all, the practice of reading had now spread in some measure. Copied manuscripts had served but a few, but printing was big business; and books that did not sell were not reprinted.

Moreover, in spite of the reservations we have made, this piety was not confined to books. It was alive, too, in everyday family life.

We can find plenty to disprove the general thesis that the dubious multiplication of endowments or, even more, the externalism undoubtedly attached thereto and caused by it, had everywhere and exclusively set its mark upon piety. This fact is forced upon our attention by such families as the Pirkheimers and the Scheuerls. In his old age the father of the Pirkheimers became a Franciscan. Scheuerl heard mass daily with his family. These people lived by this edifying literature, and their requirements were mirrored in the Christian art of the period. Lanzkranna, the pre-Reformation provost of Vienna, portrayed Christian family life on Sunday. In this a genuine attention to the things of salvation – sermon, prayer, Christian doctrine and hymns – was combined with a healthy natural joy in living. The youth of Savonarola, St Thomas More and Eck, gives us a picture of a dignified, self-possessed and zealously nurtured pure Christian life closely attached to the Church. The more we examine the lives of solid citizens, the more we seem to uncover a continuous, healthy piety. How plainly, for example, do the filial words of Dürer depict his mother as a woman intent upon a life of piety within the Church, industrious, frequently visiting the church, holding edifying conversation about God, active in good works, determined to die a good death and to protect her children from sin.

It may be true that popular practice and even the practical theology of many theologians and preachers overstressed merit acquired by works, but there were others who spoke a very different language. Consider, for example, what we read in a late medieval prayer-book from Lübeck: 'Should a man die in mortal sin, even although he had previously converted every heathen, Turk, and drunkard, still all these good works would avail him nothing. A thousand times a thousand masses and vigils would be of no use to him. Even our Lady and the saints could not help him, supposing they were to intercede for him before God continually until the day of judgment.'

In such circles as these Christian life was taken very seriously indeed.

The same seriousness is to be found in a type of spiritual literature, said to be particularly characteristic of the period – that concerning *the art of dying*. A strong tone of solicitude, of shared responsibility, of love and a sense of the whole gravity of the 'great exodus' (L. Veit) pervades the well-known questions addressed to the dying. At the end comes the powerful prayer: 'O Lord, I interpose the death of our Lord Jesus Christ between me and thy judgment; O Lord, I interpose the death of our Lord Jesus Christ between me and my destruction; O Lord, I place the death of our Lord Jesus Christ between me and thy wrath. Lord into thy hands I commend my spirit.'

It is wrong to say that such thoughts were reserved as comfortable assurance for the final crisis. This would contradict the seriousness of the truths presented. The Church and pious custom saw to it that throughout their entire lives men were confronted with salutary thoughts about death. The great conception of the dance of death, of death, that is, who may make off with anyone at any time, was for ever being presented to men through plays, pictures and engravings. Besides this people were constantly being made aware of their implication in sickness and death through participation – sometimes obligatory – in viaticum processions, when the whole community was informed by the sound of the bell. The various confraternities which grew out of the desire to die a happy death, expressed this awareness in a specially marked way. These purely spiritual confraternities have been called 'sheer salvation insurance companies'; but if we consider the vast concept of the communion of saints, incomprehending rationalism, which clearly used the phrase 'insurance company' in a very debased sense, is deprived of its pretended cogency. To 'assure' the salvation of souls through the formation of spiritual and supernatural societies is a great and holy endeavour, an exalted form of striving for the certainty of salvation, something which one ought easily to appreciate. Such endeavour can, of course, become debased. Often, as we have seen, it did become debased; but it was far from being perpetually in that condition. And so it is as short-sighted as it is false, to point to a man like Jacob Heller, the great Frankfurt merchant, as being 'characteristic of the lifeless externalisation of a piety that had become senseless mumbo-jumbo', simply because in his will he had expressed this deeply Christian belief in the communion of saints, stipulating that 'after his death someone should make a pilgrimage to Rome and pray at the Scala Santa for the repose of his soul'.

In this context, too, even the practice of indulgences acquires a partial exoneration. The practice, fulfilling a living function within pastoral activity, greatly nourishes the communion of saints. After a viaticum procession, for example, the priest would announce in church: 'All who have accompanied the Blessed Sacrament are hereby granted 100 days indulgences; those who also carried lighted candles gain 200 days indulgence. . . . May Almighty God preserve this indulgence and all your other good works until the end, when you will have great need of them. And so I place your souls and bodies, and all that you possess, under the protection of God, Father, Son, and Holy Spirit, Amen.'

One point, that is of special importance to the history of the Reformation and to Protestants, may be stressed. This age, which saw a tremendous overgrowth of the cult of saints, by no means neglected the person of our Lord – not even in the realm of popular piety. Every expression of devotion in this period is full of the figure, the name, the image and the redemptive death of our Lord. The above-mentioned prayer for the dying provides particularly eloquent proof of this, as does the fact that in the midst of all of this veneration of our Lady and the saints we find the meditations of Thomas à Kempis, completely centred on Christ.

There is one manifestation, however, of the popular piety of those pre-Reformation days, which is still accessible to us, and which shows us that piety in all its purity. That is religious art, which in 1500 still unconditionally held the field. It is true that in its powerful individualism, in its Renaissance realism, in a certain bourgeois tendency, it displayed a weakening of the absolute demand of religion. At times a kind of secularisation seems to conquer. But individualism is still completely controlled by service to the liturgical community, as on the other side, the richness of these works of art derives from the communal labour of those in the workshops.

Consider the giants of that era: the one and only Dürer, Tilman Riemenschneider, Mathis Gothard Nidhart (Grünewald), Adam Krafft, Peter Vischer, Veit Stoss. These sweep away the legend of pre-Reformation work-righteousness, in so far as it claims to characterise the whole situation. It is absolutely true, that Dürer's roots were ultimately embedded in his religious potency; but it does not follow that Dürer was, in fact, a Protestant before Luther. The great religious themes of which he treats were there even before the Reformation, and were part of authentic, powerful popular piety within the Church. Before embarking on his journey to Holland with his wife in 1519 he commended himself to the fourteen holy helpers. He specially remarks that in Antwerp he bought a precious rosary. He describes enthusiastically the great procession which he watched there, and repeatedly he stresses the tremendous impression this made upon him. In his view, the man who on his death-bed receives holy communion, extreme unction, general absolution from punishment of guilt through papal authority, dies a Christian.

And what of Tilman Riemenschneider? What a wealth of true Catholic piety is contained in his three altars alone – the Assumption altar at Creglingen, with its rich religious individuality of the apostles, the large-scale composite triad of the Crucifixion altar at Dettwang and the impressive scene of the Blood altar in St James' at Rothenburg! It is the last named, perhaps, which provides the best glimpse into the curiously far-reaching polarity of pre-Reformation popular piety. The altar was endowed and constructed to house a bogus blood-relic, and thus belongs to the milieu of the exaggerated indulgence-traffic of the times; but it serves the central mystery of the Church – the holy mass. His portrayal of the action of the Last Supper, moreover, is full to the brim of the most genuine, the deepest, piety, perfectly in harmony with the Gospels. In the altar at Creglingen there are a few heads which seem to be on fire from within with human, yet saintly, devotion, in face of the wonder they are beholding. In his Adam on the southern door of our Lady's church at Würzburg, Riemenschneider accomplishes more than a work of genius in portraying the typical man: this man is on the march towards redemption, the primeval father of the coming Christendom. His pace hampered by the consciousness of tragic guilt, yet stirred by strong hope, already he believes like a Christian.

As late as 1524 this thoroughly German artist, whose son, with good reason, portrayed him on his tombstone with a rosary in his hand, left an endowment for masses. It is sheer fancy to suggest (Justus Bier) that any part of his work indicates a break with his former Catholic devotional attitude. If we project airy fantasies of today into the solid world of a Catholic Christian of the sixteenth century – as Felix Wilhelm Beielstein does – all serious discussion is at an end. Even in a novel, history can never become an exercise in sheer imagination, no matter how ingeniously it is handled or how much it is dressed up as deep insight.

Then there is Grünewald, the only German on a par with Michaelangelo – the greatest German artist of all time. And what was the inspiration behind this supreme miracle of revelation in colour? His art, so consummate in its power to arouse human emotion and excitement to the limit, and to display these things without reserve, never leaves the realm of piety. What depth is there too! The intense realisation of the apocalyptic, and the evoking of diabolical horror, are unusually instructive about the times. This in no way detracts from the straightforward belief of the man, which is perfectly in line with faith as interpreted by the Church. All this is true of the Madonna of Stuppach; it is patently obvious of the pietà at Aschaffenburg, and it speaks eloquently from every part of the altar at Isenheim, an altar created in honour of a saint, it is true, but the effect of which is to leave us with an enduring impression of the Crucified and Ascended.

Can we say that these are but isolated examples? We have only to wander through Frankish villages and towns to dispose of this objection completely. Think of Nuremberg, of St Sebald or St Lawrence. St Victor in Xanthia still has twenty-four carved altars; Ulm had even more, other churches had seventeen. These were altars, some of which took twelve, some twenty, some thirty years to build.

In addition, this art is evidence of the vast religious culture of the late Middle Ages. The masters and journeymen who executed so many altars, statues and pictures, must have had a good knowledge of the Bible, of the legends about saints, of the various phases of the liturgical year, must have been well instructed in the cardinal virtues and vices. The Madonna of Stuppach is full of allusions to the Song of Solomon. Our modern experience proves that this is no isolated example, for expert theology has to be consulted repeatedly, in order to interpret the language of these works of art. Frequently we stand helpless before enigmatic allusions, clearly meant to have an obvious meaning, or we face the task of identifying the figure of some saint or some whole scene in the scrolls on the capitals. But the men of that epoch were perfectly conversant with the saints, their attributes and their feast-days.

Already art was fast becoming the concern of particular, socially highly esteemed artistic circles, and of isolated artists. This development was parallel to the *learning-psychosis* of the Renaissance. In Germany, however, this tendency was not victorious. Most of the art in Germany was produced by artists who were firmly embedded in the people. It was art that emerged from the people themselves, from their artistic crafts. It was art that spoke to them and won their attention.

This richness was fully realised, however, only in the peak Christian performances of the period. To achieve a comprehensive and accurate description of the religious substance of the period, it is imperative that we take account of the saints it produced, of those men, that is, who lived completely in and for Jesus Christ.

Truly representative of these men is Nicholas von der Flüe (d. 1487).

All around him, too, the Church was falling to pieces. For thirty years Sachseln had to do without a parish priest. The person then appointed was obliged to go off to prison. Real decline, however, was often to be found in proximity to true clerical piety. Near by there lived a genuine priest who was able to show this peasant a way out of his anguish of prayer: the wounds of Jesus. From contemplation of the passion of our Lord, new and heroic piety came to this man. He discovered a perfectly calm piety of solitude, that found its completion and sacrificial power in the mass, wherein, as he tells us, the experience of the consecration filled him with an experience of inexpressible sweetness. He began to exercise a powerful effect only after he had withdrawn, with his wife's consent, from his heroic and loving wife and ten children to become a solitary hermit. His curious and simple speech had become a perfect echo of his complete, pure and humble oblation to his heavenly Father through Jesus Christ our Lord.

Without wishing in the least to minimize the extent to which corruption and externalisation had grown, the facts compel us quite simply to acknowledge – alongside the corruption, within it, and above it – perfect, healthy and unbroken Christianity, loyal to the Church. No formula is able to explain this inseparable intertwining, this abrupt juxtaposition of good and evil. The important thing is to be aware of the fact and see it as the expression and foreboding of a bitter struggle between two worlds. A few pages further on we will discuss which of these two factors takes precedence.

Most certainly, the possibility of the juxtaposition of such contradictory things and aspirations can arise only where the mighty tradition of a primeval power is defending itself with the sheer doggedness of health against attempts at destruction from within and without. But the grandiose significance of this can only be perceived by Christian theological reflection. For Christianity is the history of the Church which, in virtue of the Lord's promise, can never lose the Spirit of God. It is the history of the Church in which truth and holiness are assured in their objective inviolability.

The more we are in a position to stress all of this, the more are we thrown back once again for a solution of the riddle upon the real stone of offence. The interior brittleness of Church Catholicism at that time, which manifested itself so variously, was primarily the result of the one abuse and reaction to it. That abuse was in short the perversion amongst the clergy of the whole idea of religion, of the whole notion of what Christianity and the Church really are.

All of those loyal to the Church, from Eck until Canisius, were convinced that abuses amongst the clergy had brought about religious revolt. Machiavelli, too, affirms: 'We Italians have the Church and our priests to thank for our having become irreligious and wicked.' The same verdict applies to Germany, and it was reiterated a thousand times over, and expressly applied to the emergence of religious innovation: 'The Lutheran heresy arose on account of the malpractices of the Roman curia, and progressed on account of the degenerate life of the clergy' (Eck, 1523).

It must be admitted that the non-Catholic has to overcome serious difficulties if he wishes to grasp the Catholic values we have indicated, in their full depth. Catholic strength is primarily, although not exclusively, static. That which would kill purely personal and hence dynamic religious devotion takes far longer to kill a religion that lives essentially from more objective and superordinate ties. And for the pre-Reformation period, too, it was of decisive importance that many Catholics felt that the essentials of their religion remained self-evident. We might even say that they remained absolutely unshakeable.

It is precisely this specifically Catholic attitude that is unable to accept the much repeated Protestant fallacy that the multiplication of prayer-formulae, especially of rosaries, in itself constitutes a decay of Christian piety. It is only when one has had the opportunity of experiencing the use of such formulae as offerings to the heavenly Father, in deep devotion and under the guidance of the Church, that we understand how fruitfully the dangers that lurk here can be overcome.

This affirmation itself indicates a new tension within the same problem, for the inwardness we find in pre-Reformation piety bore, in a significant measure, a subjectivist colouring. It bore the mark of privacy, of the personal and also of the moralistic. This piety comprises the most intense striving for salvation by the individual soul. It is the prayer and endeavour of this soul that are central. The objective Church with its objective holiness was solidly affirmed, as were the sacraments and the holy sacrifice of the mass. None the less, the piety of that time to some extent diverted the individual – often considerably – from the objectivity of the liturgical–sacramental organism of the risen Lord and from the mediation of the special priesthood, thus leading him away from the realm of the great sacrificial community of prayer and sacraments. How did this come about? Because these powers for the most part had become obscured, and stultified in externalism; and because, in addition, the alienation of the laity in the Church had been prepared by one-sided clericalisation. The organism of the Church, consisting of necessity in the unity of the special sacramental priesthood and the general priesthood of all believers, was threatened.

In recent years it has been said that this moralistic – subjectivist attitude was a consequence of a basic defect in the early medieval evangelisation of the Teutonic peoples. It has been suggested that this work was too little based upon the genuine liturgical mysteries, that it failed to make the Teutons sufficiently familiar with the liturgical–sacramental system, but instead confined itself too much to creating a moral and didactic effect through prayers and Church discipline. With this as its starting-point the spiritual maturing of the Germanic people, and hence their advance towards the independence of individual personalities might well have remained insufficiently anchored in objectivity. In this sense, therefore, the possibility of the Reformation might be said to have been very early laid in the missionary methods of Teutonic missionaries amongst people of Teutonic and particularist make-up. Whereas, for the Latin mentality, life, with all its externalism and outward volatility, ultimately flowed from a superordinate political form – in the broad sense – finding therein an essential restraint and limit for its freedom, with the Teutonic mentality – so much more intense and more deeply personal – things were the exact reverse. In the realm of piety this meant, for example, that the Reformers found it easy to remove the kernel, that is the consecration, from the holy mass, without the people noticing what a decisive process was taking place.

The problem of the total Christian attitude is only to be solved by an integration of the objective redemptive event with the subjective disposition. Complete Christianity can be assured only through the consonance of these two elements. The integration must be of such a form, however, that the subjective human element does not outweigh the objective power of the objective event of the *Corpus Christi mysticum*. On the other hand, in accordance with our Lord's preaching, beginning with his first call to repentance, it is the improved interior righteousness of the new disposition within the conscience, that is decisive for man. If this latter obligation is accepted in isolation, the basic Protestant attitude arises. It is precisely the exaggeration, the one-sided isolation, of personal religious earnestness which constitutes the danger of heresy.

The classic illustration of this private and personal approach, still within the devotional aspiration of the Church before the Reformation, is provided by the new forms of devotion even then being created by Christianity loyal to the Church. There were the small, intimate discussion-groups and societies adapted to individual pastoral care, a new type of pious confraternity, especially the humanist and personal type of group practising the *devotio moderna*, an important manifestation of which was the society of Brethren of the Common Life, who were specially interested in pedagogy. Even here, where there was a most valuable intensification of late medieval piety, is revealed the disintegration of the objective and universal in favour of the peripheral and individual. Even here the formal attitude of late medieval sects exerts its influence.

Devotio moderna is, of course, *new devotion;* and the most important thing about it is that it felt itself to be new. It was a new feeling a new attitude, within the devotional life of the Church. The *devotio moderna* was an attempt to form the autonomy of the Christian within the Church out of the religious richness of Christianity and the life of the Church. It was an attempt, that is, to solve that fateful question, the correct answer to which had become – since the thirteenth century – the precondition of all perfect expression and perfect effectiveness of the Church. It was the beginning of an attempt to extend the concept of *Church* to cover *the whole Christian people.* People wanted to change the anomalous situation wherein the spiritually mature man was always the subject of clerical guidance, of clerical domination indeed, and stood in *no other* relation to the clergy. In this new movement we hear the voice of the responsible conscience. It was the mental attitude of moderate mysticism that was here setting itself in opposition to the too arid legalistic piety of contemporary pastoral usage, and, in some measure, of theology as well. A book such as *The Imitation of Christ,* with its prominent devotion to the Blessed Sacrament, is most certainly rooted within the Church. This book has no flavour of banal, non-committal optimism; instead, there is an explicit admission of sin, and a plain demand for the realisation of moral obligations in a genuine Christian life – for a moral life before God through Christ in the eucharist. At the same time, however, we must not overlook the element of moralism. Amongst the Augustinian canons of Windesheim and the Brethren of the Common Life, Christ as redeemer recedes a little, and appears more as the one who places the moral demands of the Father before sinners, and himself realises those demands.

To supplement the picture, the achievements of Christian art, too, must be set in their place, in these terms, within the interplay of forces. The intensification of devotion within the Church, which we have expounded, and which is manifested in works of art, by no means allows Christian artists to escape from the ranks of those who were preparing the way for a religious revolution. We must be quite clear on this point: a break with the Church's teaching would be much more easily accomplished, would affect a much wider circle, if the spiritual and intellectual climate of the times were fundamentally changing. The mighty eruption of the universally human and subjective into the ecclesiastical sphere through the staunch churchman, Michelangelo, is perhaps the clearest indication of this threatening danger. The same kind of assessment must be made, however, of the tendency to universal independence and hence to individualism in artistic experience and form, in Dürer, Riemenschneider, Grünewald and many others. Dürer manifests the problem in special depth. In no sense does strict dogma decamp; but the basic mystery to be solved is that concerning the wrestling of the individual as an individual – not primarily as a member of the Church, relying on the power of the Church – with the Holy and with revelation. Fra Angelico may have portrayed Bernard, Dominic and Francis as clear-cut individuals, but he could never have made them appear humanistic, strong-willed, autonomous personalities without any nimbus, as Dürer did with his four apostles.

The Renaissance points to the fundamental content of humanism: to the revolution from a theocentric to an anthropocentric view of life. In certain sectors of moral and intellectual life, humanist interiorisation might be accepted as a not unworthy representation of a good and Christian life; but it was, none the less, insufficiently affected by what was Christian, by Christ, by the redemptive and revelationary religion of the Crucified. There was a great danger that the Christian religion would be confused with morality. That would be to confuse the substance with the basic intellectual outlook which first gave its stamp to this substance.

The problem which here emerges in a particular form is one of the biggest of all the problems facing Church history. It is contained within the exact or inexact version of the vast early Christian concept of the *logos spermatikos*. It is no accident that a direct line runs from the monotheistic overemphasis of the second- and third-century apologists to the theological intellectual world of the humanists.

We do well carefully to distinguish between the concepts *religious* and *Christian*, and the concept *theological*. As in the state letters of the second Frederick in the thirteenth century, now, too, what was truly theological had largely become concerned with mere outer trappings, if not disguise, beneath which the kernel had vastly changed, had even disappeared.

As always in the history of the Church, it was not in those places where alienation from the Church and from Christianity had degenerated into open paganism that the greatest danger of undermining and hence of collapse appeared. At these points the fronts were clearly recognisable, and the Church, even as it then was, able to rally fairly quickly against the foe. As has already been said in another context, a greater danger lay in interior, creeping disintegration. This danger threatened where people mistook noble humanity in the midst of traditional forms of Christian and Church life for real Christ-Christianity, whereas in fact this looked for its models and strength to heathen antiquity.

In Germany this was obviously the predicament of the untheologically minded Willibald Pirkheimer, within a circle and environment that was unusually characteristic of the flourishing Reformation movement. He required of a true theologian, for example, prudence, education, scholarship, wisdom, practical experience, but forgot to demand piety. We see the devout Christian element much more strongly present in the theologically minded Erasmus; but this element itself gave rise to danger in the degree that other weaknesses, which we shall discover later, were also present. The occasional, largely justified, criticism of the Church of the time, proposed by these two men, in no way contradicts this assertion; for this very criticism was not provoked by knowledge of the true nature of the Church but by more outward symptoms.

We have established that pre-Reformation piety included elements both of externalism and of interior spirituality, elements that possessed value, and others that possessed none, elements that were Christian and some that were questionable. Even within interior spirituality we have observed the seeds of disintegration. Are we to rest content with observing this mere juxtaposition of elements? Might not one of these be found to dominate the picture?

This problem would appear to be soluble only if we disentangle our minds from a purely quantitative assessment of the abuses before us. Examples of decline can be matched by an equal number of examples of revival. The question at issue is rather the importance of the ecclesiastical organ in which the one or the other occurs. The second point at issue concerns the line of development.

The following consideration helps us to reach a solution of the problem. How, we may ask, was it possible for the obviously erroneous conviction, that in the papacy one had a means of buying heaven and of meriting it by human works alone, to become so completely and rapidly the almost universal view of even the first generation of Lutherans? Important factors in the production of the later legend were the confusion of memory and mind, and the hatred of Luther as he recalled past events; but this does not explain the first decade. Even Luther's extraordinary and early self-assurance in condemning all views opposed to his own is but an ancillary factor; by itself it does not provide an exhaustive explanation, for we may not assume that the voice of Luther, mighty as it was, could have utterly blinded all the protagonists of the new belief to the things that were going on around them, and which they themselves, jointly and severally, had accepted as Catholics for many years.

We are forced to conclude, therefore, that, in spite of the admitted presence of genuine spirituality, the general consciousness for the most part was impressed, not by this but by the externalism to be seen at the Roman curia, at the episcopal courts, the cathedral chapters and in popular piety. That is to say, in practice, the behaviour of many if not most Catholics gave the impression that heaven was to be bought by good works.

Anyone who makes a comprehensive and critical assessment of the general condition of the Church before the Reformation, is bound, in fact, to be struck primarily by the picture of dissolution.

Dissolution in the sense of an inward breaking away from the Church had reached an advanced stage. Every time the symptoms of the condition are rigorously examined we discover that dissolution had gone further than was formerly supposed. A different conclusion would be reached only by the semi-official and still widespread view that confuses true churchmanship with a correct confession of Church dogmas. It is true that so long as faithful adherence to the creeds survives, separation from the Church will not be accomplished. Such loyal adherence had, however, become seriously imperilled and greatly attenuated as a real possession of the faithful. It is simply false to equate the churchmanship of a man like the emperor Maximilian or Louis XII with the unshaken belief of the great figures of the high Middle Ages. Maximilian could – on account of the pope's alliance with his former Venetian enemies – violently attack the 'accursed priest, the pope' and the mighty sins and deceits daily committed by him and his predecessors. From this, in the context of the conciliar theory, it was but a step to the view that the papacy was capable of reform in its very essence; and no amount of correct profession of faith was going to help matters.

Nor is justice properly done to the burden of late medieval abuses by the proof, however thorough, that nowhere was there to be found any false dogma about the Church itself. The living function of an element has to be grasped within the totality of life. Unfortunately, however, it cannot be denied that in many cases the natural coarsening of popular piety was not sufficiently opposed but rather encouraged; and frequently this happened as a result of the all-oppressive curialism that surrounded the pope's plenitude of power. There is little indication that any control was exercised by the curia over the proliferation of legends connected with the expansionist tendency of the extra-primatial power of the papacy. Ample illustration of this is provided by the hoard of relics belonging to Frederick of Saxony (above, p. 121). These things represent crass materialism linked with deceptions, in practice all too readily capable of misleading the ordinary person into believing that this was how salvation is mediated to men. We must have a concrete picture of these things, must view these 17,000 shrines one by one and note all their fearfully materialistic implications; we must observe, too, that the devotion they demanded was represented as of a much higher order than the celebration of the holy mass itself. The traffic in indulgences plied by Albrecht of Mainz and Brandenburg leads us to similar conclusions.

All of this substantiates the conclusion which we reached earlier. The excellent basic views about true Christian piety, about love, perfect contrition, the removal of fear, trust in God and in Jesus, who is our only Redeemer, do not stand as simple counterbalance to dissolution and decay. These pure impulses were always eclipsed by blatantly external practice and its assiduous servants, the pamphleteers who turned out the practical canonistical manuals. It is indeed a pertinent observation, that 'from the severity of criticism, the amazing candour of complaint, and from the patience of those affected, we can deduce the large-scale acceptance of the establishment' (Eder). None the less, the awareness of faith that was expressed in this would have had to be formative in a genuinely Christian sense, if it was to be effective as a court of appeal. Does it not appear, however, that the countless severe complaints registered before the Reformation were bogged down, rather, in sheer hopelessness? Those who felt the Church's ruin most deeply and yet remained confident of victory, to some extent living by this confidence comprised a very tiny band.

VIII

Even if we make an exhaustive list of every single abuse, still we have not uncovered the most important thing of all. We must, rather, raise the details out of their isolation and understand how they all arise from an immensely broad foundation which was beginning more and more to embrace the whole world. Then we make the prime discovery: it is not the contents in themselves which are decisive but the basic formal attitude; not the state of affairs as they have come to be but the movement and its direction. On this subject we have already concluded, with indisputable correctness, that the mighty depth and stormy development of the Renaissance went far beyond the vigorous, autocratic independence of man expressed in Gothic and late Gothic culture, so that in the Renaissance, what was Christian progressively receded, and what was plainly un-Christian and pagan advanced. There now appeared on the scene, paganism, which saw man as the maker of his own laws. That many who fell victim to this pagan spirit remained Christians, does not disprove the fact that true Christian piety was no longer creatively present in them.

For Christianity the greatest danger did not lie in moral decline, serious as this was. As long as the foundations of faith remained intact, this weakness could be remedied. A greater danger lay in the preparation of fundamental dogmatic confusion, in a threat to the notion of revelation and of redemption. This is not to assert that the spirit of humanism had known no links at all with Christian dogma. Irreligious talk and conscious estrangement from dogmatic faith are by no means the same thing as life without belief. Luckily for the Church, in spite of the far-advanced break-away tendency, the deepest ties in life still remained attached to her. Had this not been so, the Renaissance and the Reformation would have swept the Church away.

With this qualification, however, it is true that the threat to faith was immense. The new feeling for classical antiquity, that is to say the deep positive relationship established with *pagan* antiquity, increased the danger that Christianity would lose its absolute claim upon men. The danger of relativism emerged both in the ethical and in the dogmatic sphere; and relativism is the real cancer, the truly disruptive factor, in the history of modern times. This mentality is expressed in the most contradictory forms. In the period under review we see it in the exaggeration of the idea of the state, which allowed fluctuating tendencies to determine political fidelity – Alexander VI and Machiavelli. The road led from occasional alliance between the curia and the Turks to decisive assistance of Protestantism by this same curia (see p. 244).

The chief infiltration of relativism came, however, through philosophy and theology. Nominalism and the subjective element in mysticism had already prepared the way. Above all, however, a certain undogmatic attitude had revealed itself in humanism from the start, that is since Petrarch, to the extent that here already was being expressed a conscious, sharp antagonism to scholasticism, that is to rational theology, in favour of an amateur theology of the philosopher who is now both poet and orator. This tendency was stressed further in the Platonic academy of Marsiglio Ficino at Florence through the recession of sacramental and ecclesiastical elements and the elaboration of an essential complex of Christian philosophy. In the mighty figure and colossal work of Desiderius Erasmus of Rotterdam (1466–1536) the development reached completion.

How difficult it is to describe Erasmus! There is a flatness about his life, especially his interior life. He is characterised by lack of definition; he stands for ever in twilight; and this is the ultimate meaning of his universal spiritual and intellectual endowment and attitude, which Huizinga, one of his most enthusiastic and competent admirers, formulated: people have been wrong to regard Erasmus 'as a psychological unity, for that is what he certainly is not. Ambivalence runs deep into his being. . . . His deep and most intense conviction is always this, that none of the competing views is able completely to express the truth.' Erasmus always uttered a sceptical 'Yes' and 'No', seeking, within the environment of a Christian, educated and peaceful ideal, a path that was burdened by no strain, and no decisive commitment. He was both unwilling and unable to draw ultimate conclusions. This led, not only to a tragic deficiency but to a weak and unsympathetic attitude that was also unusually dangerous; for Erasmus became a public force of the first magnitude. The abundance of his works, their many editions and his vast correspondence are all evidence of this.

In the midst of the mounting tumult of the epoch he it was – of all men – who remained a prisoner within his curious Utopia, right on until the thirties of the century; and he might have been the great reformer of the time – a reformer by his good advice. Erasmus represents the height of the Socratic fallacy – so fatal when the mastery of life is at stake – that the learned man is the good man, that education ensures moral improvement. He was utterly convinced that he would fail in face of the tumult. His vacillation from 1518 to 1520 – not tragic but certainly pathetic – his mean behaviour towards the dying Hutten, whom he disowned, his amazing lack of emotion when commenting on the criminal execution of his friend St Thomas More and of Archbishop Fisher (1535), show how right he was to consider himself unsuited for martyrdom. 'Not all,' he said, 'are strong enough to be martyrs; I fear that if trouble were to blow up I would follow Peter' (1521). Heroic Christianity was not his forte. He was able to justify himself, however. 'Christianity has known a host of martyrs, but only very few scholars.' It is true that in the call to a world-mission, uttered in 1535, the year before his death, he expressed the desire that God would give him the spirit of martyrdom; but this desire was sheer humanist world-weariness.

More than once, with true humanist flippancy, Erasmus flattered a man to his face, but despised him behind his back – Marius in person, for example, and More through Marius. At an early date he became suspicious of his friends. The flattery in which he indulged was almost shameless at times. For the merest gratuity (from Anna of Borselen) he denied his own deepest convictions concerning a purified Christian devotional life, and violated his own sense of good taste. He told Pope Leo X, to his face, that he was to other men as man is to the animals.

Erasmus placed all his trust in a safe middle way, as long as that way was allied to plenty of intellect. His ultimate goal was tranquillity and books. Of his own poetry he said: 'It never depicts any storm, or any torrent that bursts its banks, it never runs to any excess.'

This attitude explains the revolution in his relationship towards the times. In 1518 he was still preaching the advent of the golden age; but it was to come without violence and without political turmoil. He desired an individualistic and moral kingdom, produced through education indeed. With Erasmus – not with Luther – the destructive domination of the purely individual conscience appeared upon the scene of modern history.

Erasmus had never known the road to Damascus. He had a spontaneous aversion to the monastic life – where, however, he was much happier than he later admits, for in the cloister he was able to find that education which was all that he prized. The *devotio moderna*, however, had an immediate appeal for him. During his first stay in England (1491–1500) his interest was aroused in the 'theologians'; but there was no fight in him.

In the Reformation period Erasmus was epoch-making, as a theologian; but even here his intellectual attitude was moulded primarily, not by revelation but by education. Luther was quite the reverse. This education, encouraged by the friars, in England found its object and its framework in Colet – heir of the Platonic academy in Florence – and also in More and Fisher. This heritage comprised the later *Stoa* of Cicero, that is popular philosophical morality, the Synoptic Gospels, and a Platonic or Neo-Platonic interpretation of St Paul.

The humanistic pastoral manuals, which Erasmus began to write after his visit to England, are centred on one great objective: the purification of Christianity and the Church by means of a return to sources – both Christian and pagan. All was to depend upon the precise exposition of this programme.

The first contradiction emerges with the simultaneous mention of Stoic morality and St Paul. It becomes evident at once that it cannot be the specifically Pauline teaching on grace and redemption that is meant. The Stoic elements in the doctrine of our knowledge of God in *Romans* and in the sermon on the Areopagus are the window-dressing, to be backed up by the powerful pastoral personality of the determined apostle of the gentiles.

Erasmus recapitulates the questions of the second century apologists. His intellectual environment was very much the same as theirs. They were the first to try to mould Christianity into an elegant and serious humanism, reducing it to a few very simple truths: monotheism, virtue, eternal life.

The Enlightenment would one day draw the conclusions, omitting the Erasmian compromise with Church and revelation.

We must not be unjust to Erasmus. These Christian compromises were powerful realities. The affirmation of Christianity, of Jesus Christ, the Bible, the Church and the battle for the Church's purification, were genuine and basic. Frequently these things were all the more outwardly effective because of the genuine spiritual impulse behind them. Erasmus wanted to expel the paganism of the Italians from the liberal sciences and nourish these on Christ instead. With emphatic seriousness he demanded that new birth in Christ – so long overdue – should increase. In this way he achieved a real deepening of Christian life. We must remember with respect the colossal, strenuous, scientific work of the first editor of the Greek New Testament and of so many of the fathers, who was author also of the splendid moral tractates.

This achievement is even more positive than we can express here. This was the essential Erasmus. His battle against scholasticism was wrong, for he knew too little about scholasticism, and had come directly into contact only with its contemporary soulless extravagances. None the less he knew that St Thomas was the most careful of the modern scholastics, with whom none of the rest could compare.

He never ceased to express a most central concern both for theology and for reform in general, in his demand: 'Back to the sources!' As he said, the hearts of people are stirred far more by what rises directly from the heart at the source, than by what flows from secondary cisterns. Erasmus wanted the fresh taste of spring water. He possessed an instinctive feeling for what was original and not yet overgrown. He loved the apple that he plucked from the tree himself.

In this respect the publication of his Greek New Testament alone is of tremendous importance for the purification of Christianity. By this work, with a mighty impact, he once again placed the Bible at the centre of theological activity. He demanded that it be translated into all languages, be constantly kept at hand and read, that men accept what it actually says and refrain from theologising about it. Men in all professions, even artisans, should look upon it as their companion at work.

In his later days much of the frivolity of his witty youth departed; and as the increasingly victorious storm of the Lutheran revolution broke, his religious effort became greater.

It is impossible, however, to dispose of all objections. The deeply Christian and devout element was not the decisive element in Erasmus; and it does not indicate the real objective of Erasmus' effort and aspiration. He demanded that a non-specialist lay theology based upon holy scripture be made available to all, for their spiritual nourishment. But how seriously can we take his demand, when at the same time he demands, as a prerequisite, the calm learning of the three languages of holy scripture – Latin, Greek and Hebrew? The religious value of his work is undermined by the dedication attached to the first edition. This matches the postscript written by Oecolampadius, which smacks of the highbrow humanist time-server and not at all of the spirit of the New Testament. Consider, too, the 'methodus' in the same edition. Even in the expositions possessing the greatest religious fervour and the most directly evangelical tone our suspicion is aroused. We read fine phrases behind which there is no will to realise what they advocate in real life.

Consider, too, his moral sermons on and criticism of scholasticism, monks and the Church. His criticism is so derisive, destructive, so smug, and so ambiguous. Firm intention of moral improvement and unconditional religious commitment are lacking. And the witty mockery, unsupported by an inflexible demand, was the very thing that earned Erasmus the fame he enjoyed all his life. His kind of Christianity was a matter of education. Baptism was the initial expression of the Christian philosophy. Whoever has a pure heart and teaches by his pure life is a Christian.

It is refreshing when we hear Erasmus joining in the biblical affirmation that nothing is stronger than truth. It all sounds very suspicious, however, when this truth of Christianity is sought in a utopian morality of renewal and a good natural endowment. True, he contrasts the wisdom of Christ with human argumentation, but again he is suspect, for he specially attacks the scholastics, or 'Stoics', as he derisively names them, whereas he makes no complaint against humanist wit and wisdom.

There is no doubt at all that Erasmus wanted to remain true to the traditional Church. 'Neither death nor life will separate me from the fellowship of the Catholic Church' (1522). But he said also: 'I have never fallen away from the Catholic Church. I know that in this Church, which you Lutherans call the pope's Church, there are many things that I do not like; but I see similar things in your communities. A man finds it easier to put up with an evil to which he is accustomed; and so I will suffer this Church until I find a better, and this Church will have to suffer me until I myself improve. He fares not too badly who steers a middle course between two different evils.' What pathetic ambiguity, moral and theological! The hard core of the ecclesiastical system is removed and the whole thing reduced to cowardly mediocrity. By his very evasion of clear decisions and essential commitment Erasmus did harm to Christianity.

We shall see how this attitude was normative for the 'churchmanship' of the humanist princes. For that very reason this is the point at which the far-reaching question arises: how can we explain why saints like More and Fisher, men like John Colet, Wimpfeling, Sadolet, Vives, Cardinal Cajetan and Pope Adrian VI not only on occasion praised this 'reinstator of theology' (Cardinal Albrecht of Mainz) – as they might have Eck and Gropper – but remained his firm friend until death?

In the end of the day Erasmus remained in the Church. His discussions with and against Luther on the subject of man's free will even became one of the decisive intellectual elucidations of the history of the Reformation. But how did he remain in the Church?

As a half-Catholic. He made no *effort* to remain within the old
Church, but remained suspended in the middle, wavering and
undecided. He remained faithful to the old Church 'having first
done it great harm, and he renounced the Reformation and in
some degree humanism as well, having first advanced both of
these movements considerably' (Huizinga).

Erasmus accepted the Church – just as on occasion he accepted
the sacrament of penance – piously, out of respect for tradition,
but not as really obligatory, not as something instituted by Christ
(or the apostles).

This brings us to the historically critical point in the significance of Erasmus. That is Erasmus' basic attitude – his vagueness.
In theology, however, vagueness means to be a-dogmatic or undogmatic. In theology Erasmus was a born relativist.

To maintain or to reject the faith of the Church is a serious
matter, a final issue, for those, that is, for whom it is an issue. If
such an one, forced to make a decision, reaches the decision to
maintain the faith, then he is bound to have done with all trivial
side issues. And no such man would speak as Erasmus spoke:
'I could have been one of the chorus-masters in Luther's
Church.'

F. X. Funk once disputed Janssen's unsatisfactory verdict on
Erasmus. He was right; but he said: 'I find the *Enchiridion of the
Christian Knight* so Christian that I would not have the faintest
reason for denying its authorship by one of the fathers, had I discovered it ascribed to his name.' This is a typical unsatisfactory
question with regard to the eternally indeterminate Erasmus. In
order to be a genuine Christian theologian it is not enough merely
to say nothing directly anti-Catholic. Correctness is not truth.

Erasmus' impertinent acrobatics with scriptural texts – as in the
Moria – cannot be regarded as the work of a genuinely devout
person. And this jesting with holy things was no passing mood but
an expression of his essential nature. He was incapable of taking
the most serious thing of all seriously. He failed to perceive the
limits of human powers, and so learn reverence. Having first
immeasurably exaggerated human powers, he fell to mockery,
even contradicting his own admonition to deal reverently with
holy things.

Erasmus had very little comprehension of defined and obligatory dogma. He still believed in the holy eucharist, but was at
pains to avoid any more precise definition of our Lord's bodily
presence. He had no interest in dogma, as his death – without
receiving the sacraments – once again proves. His opinion was that
there are many definitions that 'can be left unknown or undecided
without danger to a man's soul. . . . The chief thing in our religion
is peace and harmony. This can be attained only if we define as
few points as possible and leave each man to his own judgment on
many things. Many controversial points are now to be put to the
ecumenical council. It would be much better to defer this sort of
question until the time when all parables and riddles will be past
and we behold God face to face.'

Erasmus, the scientific philologist, was a lover of allegorical
interpretation. This served him well in turning revealed religion
into something non-binding, or in relegating it to the realm of
natural reality.

Erasmus was a product of the *devotio moderna,* which he had
learned from the friars in Herzogenbusch and in the monastery of
the Augustinian canons (Steyn or Gouda). But he was no perfect
representative of the *devotio moderna.* He adhered to only a part of
it, to that part which differentiated it from the traditional piety of
the Church. Erasmus developed the *devotio moderna* in a one-sided
manner. For the most part, he allowed the sacramental devotion
of the Church, as expression of the religion of revelation and redemption, and which was accepted as an essential part of the
devotio moderna, to wither away. He may not have so completely
equated education with Christianity as did the Erfurt humanists,
but he was with them on this point. He preserved the fulness of the
faith out of the Synoptists and St Paul rather better than they did,
and he had portrayed and made effective this greater religious
fulness in an unimaginably richer intellectual world. His simplification of Christianity did not suffer from the same weak flatness
and poverty of the Erfurt circle. But no matter how much we stress
this, the essential fact remains: Erasmus was non-dogmatic and a
relativist. This means that he placed Christianity in danger of its
life, and all the more as his intellectual influence extended.

Here is a deep self contradiction: by his mighty action in producing the Greek New Testament, with purifying power he

brought the world and the Church in contact with the basic fact of redemption through Jesus Christ, and at the same time, out of this religion, out of the Christianity of the Crucified, he constructed a humanist, 'human' morality based on man's natural capacities and on education.

Only a very rigid rationalist would describe Erasmus simply as a non-Christian or as anti-Christian. One would have to be motivated by a strong antipathy against him, or else possess very little discrimination, to fail to see the great significance of his Christian effort. But it is just as impossible to understand the essential man if we fail to place a large equestion-mark against this very judgment. This sounds paradoxical: it is a paradox. And that alone is why it fits Erasmus. He is utter vagueness. He is everlastingly evasive. This is true even of the last decade of his life when, after the break with Luther, little more was at stake. We are compelled to describe this as the unrestrained effort to achieve independence (Huizinga). At the same time, however, it is the all-out effort of cowardice, at least of indecision. Erasmus' statements against paganism have to be set against others in the *Colloquies* and against the great *Adagia*. The comparison discloses that the note of the *Jupiter optimus maximus* sounds much louder than that of the *Jesus Christus Redemptor mundi*, in spite of what the antipagan statements suggest. What did 'Redeemer' really mean to Erasmus, the representative of rationalist morality? Because indecision and lukewarmness so much marked his essential being, it is hard to accept the antipagan zeal of his latter years as the expression of a genuine change of heart in God's sight.

It is true that nothing could be better for Christianity, which worships the Father in Spirit and in truth, than the spiritualisation that Erasmus sought to implant in it. And this was never more true than at the time when the externalism in theory and in practice of the Avignon system so damagingly set about its work of debasing and devouring the substance of Christianity. None the less, Erasmus constituted a threat to Christianity and the Church. He personified the inadmissible attempt to accomplish, in a radical fashion, the coming of age of the Christian people, the laity in particular, and to make human reason and will the measure of Christianity in many respects. Erasmus represented the threat to dogma by relativism, to the kingdom of grace and redemption by ennobled stoic morality. It is short-sighted to observe the great value of his allegorising, that is his essentially volatile interpretation, of Christianity, and not to notice these radical errors which we have pointed out.

An adequate interpretation of Erasmus requires this definitive presupposition: one must believe in the necessity of a dogmatically fixed religion. To the extent that the evil of its dissolution is greatest if the dissolution is accompanied by perfect intelligence, knowledge, moderation, tranquillity and ethical formation, then our sentence upon Erasmus must be crushing indeed.

There were two other ideas which encouraged Erasmus to destroy dogma. He explained Christianity as fundamentally identical with all true religion. This was possible only on an undogmatic view of Christianity. It is not superfluous, on this point, to recall certain constructions in contemporary *Utopias* (even that of Thomas More) and ideas of Nicholas of Cusa. Cusa was no relativist, either in theory or in practice. All the same, his ideas about harmony amongst religions and about the underlying unity of all religions in the adoration of God were able to confuse people for an indefinite period. In many ways the eighteenth century seemed to be anticipated. In addition, Erasmus proposed a kind of scriptural principle: the Bible, as interpreted by scholars, ought in the end to be the norm of Christian belief. It is true, the Church and its teaching authority were to be retained; but where was the obligation to accept this authority? Quite emphatically, Erasmus demanded the unity of the Church; but the biblical principle – as we may call it – was bound to militate against this unity. The Catholic concept of the Church, which sees the faith of the individual as growing out of the Church, had not yet been destroyed, but was severely attacked. The subjectivism that urges on towards heresy was basically affirmed.

It is quite inadmissible to collect a handful of polemical statements of Erasmus against the official piety of the Church and, from these, to conclude that he was opposed to the Church. In order to understand this man in some degree, and to avoid doing him injustice, we must be able to make the most refined distinctions; we must possess sufficient mental flexibility to follow a very tenuous line that is still truly Christian, and yet see that this same line is inimical to the very heart of Christianity.

F

In face of this colossal threat to her life the Church remained silent; or rather, she fêted this disturber of her dogma.

It is true that in 1526, eight years after the Leipzig disputation, the Sorbonne condemned several of Erasmus' statements as heretical; and in 1529 the unfortunate French translator, De Berquin, was burned. In 1528 the Spanish inquisition took an interest in Erasmus. The reform memorandum of the official cardinals' commissions of 1537 recommended that the *Colloquies* be kept out of the schools. Pighius, and even Erasmus' friend Ambrosius Pelargus (1531), were strong in their criticism of this work. Some time later the *Colloquies*, the *Moria* and other isolated writings were all put on the *Index*. St Ignatius banned Erasmus' lectures. There were many who blamed him for the Lutheran revolution. 'He laid the egg, Luther and Zwingli hatched it'; 'Either Luther is Erasmian or Erasmus Lutheran'; 'Along with the Lutherans he has destroyed true (Christian) philosophy' (Eck, 1540).

On the other hand, in 1525 this same Eck had regarded Erasmus as an orthodox Catholic. Cardinal Ximenes wanted to have him brought to Spain. Adrian VI remained his faithful protector, and had previously attempted to have a professorial chair given to Erasmus immediately on his arrival in Louvain. Archduke George of Saxony offered him a similar post. Leo X accepted the dedication of the New Testament and had Sadolet send warm compliments. We have already mentioned the fact that More, Fisher, John Colet and Sadolet remained his friends. At all events, no official curial action was taken against him. Even a man like Stanislaus Hosius, later bishop of Ermland and papal delegate at the Council of Trent, had no qualms about Erasmus; and this attitude was not confined to his youth, when he was all intent on visiting the world-prodigy (1529). All his life he preserved his affection for Erasmus. In his own diocese he replaced the strictly orthodox catechism of Filippo Archiato by that of Erasmus.

Most certainly it casts serious doubts upon our modern judgment to find so many eminent contemporaries, who knew him intimately or, like Leo, knew him through high recommendation, speaking so highly of him. But we appeal to facts, and these would have to be discredited. On the contrary, we believe that we can confirm the facts even more strongly.

In 1518 and 1519 Erasmus had spoken of the papacy to John

Lang in the most equivocal terms. In 1518 he maintained: 'Every-one approves Luther's theses. I can see that the monarchy of the Roman pope, in its present form, is the curse of Christianity . . . ; but I do not know if it is expedient to touch this abscess openly. This would be a matter for the princes. I am only afraid that they are hand in glove with the pope in order to share the spoils.'

On 15 January, 1521 the pope expressed his delight to Erasmus, that all suspicion of Erasmus' orthodoxy with regard to the holy see, which had arisen from reports and from some of his writings, was now dispelled, so that the pope was once again able to grant him the recognition which had been temporarily withdrawn. No one, it seemed, was so fitted to carry out the work required at that time, as Erasmus.

The last affirmation is disturbing. It shows in a flash both the threatening carelessness and the theological confusion in the Church. From this angle the Reformation acquires new, positive significance for the Church. Erasmus represented the threat of dogmatic dissolution within the Church. Luther called men to a profession of faith. He shook people awake.

There was only one man on the Catholic side who in some measure recognised in time the danger embodied by Erasmus. This was the papal nuncio, Aleander, himself a humanist of some standing. At an earlier date he had spent a few weeks in Erasmus' company at Naples. In Louvain he had intervened on behalf of the renowned humanist and forbidden his being attacked in ser-mons. But at Worms in 1521 he began to see things more clearly. 'God forbid that we see fresh papal briefs to Erasmus couched in the same tone as that printed at the beginning of his New Testa-ment and containing an approving explanation by the pope of a work in which he expresses views on confession, indulgences, excommunication, divorce, papal authority, etc., which Luther has simply to take over. But the poison of Erasmus works even more dangerously. . . . ' This may well have been written from personal irritation with Erasmus, but the general verdict stands. The most dangerous doctrines are not always evident.

Erasmus at length came into contact with Luther. But Catholics did not see the true Erasmus even in this controversy. They ap-plauded his book on free will, because it contradicted Luther; but they failed to see that the primary aim of the book was to propose an optimistic morality that left little room for grace, sin and redemption.

Theological confusion within Catholic theology was one of the specially important preconditions which precipitated a revolution in the Church. It is one of the keys which to some extent unlocks the riddle of the colossal apostasy.

This confusion reigned not merely amongst the real professionals in this subject, amongst the theologians or those who ought to have been competent, the bishops, but in the broad double section of society of those who exerted a very powerful influence upon the course of events, either in their capacity as moulders of public opinion – then becoming of immense importance – or in their capacity as the wielders of princely power.

Within this twofold circle theological confusion was expressed at its worst in the view of Luther's movement as almost nothing more than a disciplinary affair. Because many, without the slightest hesitation, judged that Rome was unjustly damaging Germany, financially and politically, and because hatred of Rome had reached enormous proportions – as Aleander clearly proved in 1521 – they lightly cast off the Catholic doctrine guarded by the pope. The new doctrine was used consciously and, even more, unconsciously, to attain the fervently desired end: the overthrow of the power of the pope.

Theological confusion revealed itself even more profoundly, however, amongst the guardians of the doctrine of the Church. We have seen this in the case of Erasmus and the way he was treated by the Church. We shall meet the same factor again with respect to the youthful Luther, the indulgence-controversy of 1517, the Leipzig disputation of 1519, and right down throughout the entire course of the history of the Reformation. Why was it that the un-Catholicism of the Lutheran innovation was not seen somewhat more clearly?

Things could not have been otherwise. The whole age, the nations and all classes of society, had fallen into chaotic confusion. Nothing seemed sure any more, and there was little that could still be clearly recognised. It was not just one or two unimportant or interesting intellectual exercises which Luther set for theology: the issue at stake was how to grasp afresh the whole meaning of

Christianity, the purpose of man and his place in the process of redemption.

The darkness became all the more ominous because Catholics suffered from the illusion that Catholic doctrine had long since been settled on the disputed points. Few theologians were exempt from this illusion. In the polemic of the day – as we shall see – most of them used the *unanimis consensus* of the Church as an argument, whereas, in fact, on important questions only a more or less hazy opinion was the substitute for sure knowledge. The deliberations at Trent are proof of this.

But it was theological confusion that made possible the rooting of obviously heretical views in Catholic soil; only through this confusion was the Reformation able to thrive.

SIX

National Churches

National Churches were a phenomenon which accompanied the rise of the princes. It was a necessary concomitant. The medieval Church-world structure of society and the priestly militant structure of the state did not permit the two spheres to remain neatly separate. It was no accident, but in the logic of things, that the notion of the independent, autonomous state, put forward in the interest of the princes by their jurists, should militate against the representatives of the Church, in order to gain as much as it could for itself from their rights. This process had been going on since the early Middle Ages. A classic example is provided by the struggle of Philip IV to establish a Gallican Church and a French papacy.

In Germany this development led to the formation of territorial Churches. As soon as the princes tried to expand and centralise their power, they could not ignore the most important power-complex in their realms – the Church, characterised by spiritual and spiritual-temporal jurisdiction, episcopal jurisdiction and vast property. Their attempt to hold all the power within their territories in their own hands, could not stop short at the wealthy monasteries and at the considerable export of regular and extra-ordinary taxes to Rome. The theory of the inviolable, sacred property of the Church had long since lost much of its certainty. Certainty waned all the more as the blatant worldliness of so many clerics became more and more apparent in their life, business and the rights they claimed.

The same thing was true of the mightily flourishing cities. The close proximity and intertwining of secular and spiritual within the close confines of their walls seemed to demand the intervention of the council even more directly.

In both municipal and state life, however, out of these conditions there arose, automatically, interventions even in purely ecclesiastical affairs. At the beginning of the sixteenth century, in many regions and in the cities of Switzerland, even, as in those of Germany, people had grown accustomed to this. The tendency was obvious: the pope, the bishops, the abbots, the generals of religious orders, must be ousted.

Quite obviously the territorial princes of Germany had the same intrinsic 'right' to interfere in the temporal property of the Church as had the sovereigns of England, Spain and France: more, indeed, because the greater part of the property of the episcopal sees and of the Church comprised former royal property. Thus, what had finally been accomplished or confirmed for the western monarchies through concordats with the holy see (Spain, 1482; France, 1516; England had isolated herself in 1343 and 1366), i.e. almost unlimited domination over the material power of the Church (and what influence that gave over the sphere of religion and the Church), could not be so illegal in Germany. And so a similar result was reached in Germany, in particular by the application of a series of ancient rights, such as that of patronage and bailiwick. The secular arm had never been a merely passive servant of the Church, but had always been a participant in some way. Now, in a sense, it wanted to become the owner.

In Germany, too, the curia helped on the course of events, and here again, by means of all sorts of concessions which they made to the princes towards the end of the conciliar era and after it, in their struggle to rise into the ascendancy in power-politics. In Germany as in France the representatives of Pope Eugene IV as well as the representatives of the Council of Basel strove to gain recognition for their masters. Both parties offered privileges. The pope won, in Germany, not least through the diplomacy of Aeneas Silvio de' Piccolomini, later to become Pope Pius II, who by bribery won over a section of the power-hungry, schismatic electors for the emperor and the pope. The outcome was the princes' concordat of 1447, with its vast financial concessions, and in 1448 the Vienna concordat of Pope Nicholas V with the emperor Frederick III. This concordat negotiated the transfer of considerable spiritual rights, which Eugene IV had granted to the emperor in 1445 (right of nomination to six bishoprics, 100 benefices in his hereditary lands, right of visitation of monasteries of the country). In the years that followed, according to the political climate at the time, these agreements were continued, now here, now there, without any real interruption, in the form of reciprocally dispensed privileges – right of presentation to bishoprics, the right to control the finances of the Church concerning change of incumbence, the right to approve or forbid indulgence collections and the like. Such concessions from the curia may well have had religious and moral motives – the reform of the monasteries in general, or the more effective prosecution of that reform; but their chief purpose was to be found in Church politics. They were an instrument in the secular warfare against the independence of the bishops and in the secular securing of papal claims on benefices. Frequently they were a purely political business, as with certain agreements between Charles V and Clement VII in 1528 and 1533.

The development had its most material foundations in the ecclesiastical and ecclesiastico-economic reserves of the territories, and was greatly encouraged by these foundations. Other operative factors were the need of reform in the monasteries and amongst the clergy, the pastoral impotence and failure of bishops and abbots in face of religious decline, and the particular religious and moral interest of the Christian authorities in the required reforms. In addition there were the pleas of the lower clergy for protection against the reforms initiated by the bishops, and the pleas of the lay subjects for protection against the arbitrariness of clerical exemptions, of clerical egotism in manupulating tax exemption and of clerical jurisdiction.

As we can see, there were opportunities for genuine religious zeal as well as for economic exploitation. Often the two are found together, as, for example, with Emperor Maximilian, who was deeply concerned with the reform of the Church and of morals and the relevant detailed proposals, or Duke George of Saxony, or the Bavarian dukes at the time of the Reformation.

When it was a case of the protection of subjects against clerical exploitation, the secular government were in fact the only body in a position to intervene; for they alone possessed the power to do so – along with the Church. In the common needs of life as it had now come to be, the distinction of rights, duties and enjoyment, that is the legal and economic privilege of the clergy, had long ceased to be consonant with a sense of justice, and so the intervention of the secular power in the Church's sphere of influence acquired a certain justification. Likewise, in face of the obvious need of reform of clergy and monasteries – a reform that was not, apparently, to be initiated by the clergy themselves – a reforming zeal amongst highly orthodox princes, loyal to the Church, had produced in these princes a sense of obligation to strike at the root of the abuse of clerical privilege, just as the self-interest of others saw in the same circumstances an attractive excuse for feathering their own nests, to the disadvantage of the Church. In the later Reformation period how often we hear the cry 'Reform!' when it is secularisation, complete or partial, that is the real aim.

We must take good note of this if later we are to judge fairly the appropriations of the Lutheran princes.

The most powerful instrument of governmental control of the life and property of the monasteries was visitation. From the second half of the fifteenth century until the sixteenth century (i.e. before the Reformation) these visitations became countless. There were governmental visitations carried out in the name of the Roman central authorities, or with their approval; frequently the princes were give a certain opportunity of interference through being invited by ecclesiastical visitators to co-operate in superintendence so that possible abuses might be reported. Others appeared upon the scene on their own responsibility. Cases are known where no enquiry or approval by Rome can be proved, and others where none resulted, and there was an encroachment by secular power that was not legalised by canon law. Nevertheless, in the fifteenth century and at the beginning of the sixteenth century many monasteries were reformed in this manner, frequently by the use of force, necessary in order to overcome the resistance of the occupants of the monasteries to healthy reforms.

In Mecklenburg in 1452 the princes had gained such influence that a knight of whom they did not approve was unable to become prior of the commandery of the Knights of St John in Eixen. In 1467 Ribnitz was visited at the instigation of the dukes, Wismar in 1468, in presence of the dukes. The same thing took place with the 'Nullbrüder' at Rostock in 1475, although there was no question of degeneracy there. In 1485 Duke Magnus caused every collegiate church and monastery in his territory to be visited. In 1493 the dukes laid much increased taxes upon the above-mentioned commandery in Eixen. The suit concerning this matter was not wound up until 1514, and then in favour of the dukes. The dukes presented candidates for the commandery who were not even members of the order. The resistance of the order led to strife and violence and in the end, during the Reformation, to a process in the imperial high court in 1534–69, when no legal decision was reached. The commandery of St John at Mirow was forcibly secularised. This was possible because interference was justified in this case by proved religious degeneration. With the Antonines, interference in their rights and property went the length of giving away their chapel and real estate.

The real aim of the secular authorities was far-reaching. It is formulated in the saying of Charles the Bold, that he intended to be the sole emperor and pope in his own land. As early as the fourteenth century Duke Rudolph of Austria had tried to achieve the same absolutism. In his land he wanted to be pope, archbishop, bishop, archdeacon and dean. By the multiplication of extraordinary privileges, and by the autocratic extension of his rights, the ecclesiastico-political power of the duke of Cleves became so great that the proverb arose: 'In his own lands, the duke of Cleves is pope', and the proverb seemed almost to confer legality upon the situation. In Hessia people had long since become accustomed to autocratic disposal of Church property. In Baden the margrave reformed a whole series of monasteries – autocratically in many cases. Even the duke George of Saxony, loyal churchman that he was, called himself pope, emperor and German master, in his own lands. His rule was absolute. He knew how to make use of the visitation of churches and monasteries so as to extend his control of presentation to benefices far beyond what was already allowed him by curial consent. We have already heard of the dukes of Savoy who regarded the see of Geneva as their household property. The dukes of Tyrol looked upon their bishops as court chaplains. When

Nicholas of Cusa wanted to introduce reforms in his diocese of Brixen, he ran into the violent opposition of Duke Siegmund.

The efforts of the territorial princes to extend their power over the sphere of the Church formed part of the general line of development, and, because of the various causes which we have explained, was not too difficult a task. It is worth noting however, that here too, the curia lightened the task. Amongst many other things blame must be attached to the curial style, with its rhetorical and superlative formulations, which did not always set out the 'ecclesiastical' rights granted, with the required precision.

The territorial princes achieved their ecclesiastico-political aim. Episcopal dispensations required approval by the territorial overlord; the tax-exemption of the clergy was abrogated; public worship as well as monastic discipline was supervised; the secular authority had to approve Church taxes and collections that were prescribed by Rome. Some pilgrimages were forbidden, others inaugurated. The princes succeeded in great measure in becoming lords of the Church and of the churches within their lands.

Only on one important point did the attempt fail. They were unable to break the dominance of clerical jurisdiction; and this was the very thing that constituted such a stone of offence; for ecclesiastical courts were able, not only to summon all clerics before these courts in every legal issue but to try virtually every legal issue in these courts. According to law, every mixed case, and every appeal whatever, could be tried in these courts.

Here, too, the reaction had always been noteworthy. Opponents of the system made use of a legal device that had known considerable success in France. 'Appeal on account of abuse' made it possible to turn from a clerical court to a secular court. And people became increasingly practised in preventing legal processes from slipping off to Rome.

The whole course of Reformation history was powerfully affected by this development, both in respect of the innovators and in respect of those who remained loyal to the Church. In the process, Rome saw the necessity of making concessions to the Catholic powers, that is to the Catholic princes. For their part these princes exploited the embarrassment of the curia, sometimes from noble, sometimes from selfish, motives. The reform proposals which Eck was to lay before the pope in 1523 and later, suggested a series of measures against religious innovation, that were bound directly to bring about a considerable strengthening of the territorial Church system in Bavaria.

Meanwhile a now Protestant territorial Church system had emerged. In this the whole tragedy of the system became evident. Since the thirteenth century the curia had been playing a decisive part in the erection of territorial Churches. Many concessions to the princes were occasioned by the Avignon exile and the papal schism, by political calculation and religious–ecclesiastical reforming zeal. In spite of its many services to the Church, the territorial system in the end remained the real counterpart to the Church; and now it revealed itself in real earnest as the downright opponent of the Church. In the national and territorial Church system the papacy had itself bred its deadly enemy; for – apart from all opposition from within Catholicism, then and later – the territorial princes led the Reformation to victory, not least by reason of the territorial Church system as this had been evolving up to that time, mightily assisted by the policy of the curia. Without this territorial Church system, springing from Catholic roots, Luther might indeed have appeared, but the Reformation could never have won the day.

No one would still want to deny that the possibilities of a revolution in the Church had become unusually great. The failure of those really holding responsibility had been proved on all sides, in a manner that we rarely find in history. The opposition had infiltrated all classes of society and was loudly expressed in many forms. There was a universal expectancy of a coming revolution, even within the Church. The storm broke as soon as the man appeared who knew how to unleash the forces of the age. Martin Luther stepped on to the stage. He seized at the challenge of religious new birth. 'The Reformation came like the fulfilment of a long overdue self-liberation' (Eder).

BOOK TWO

The New Epoch:
The Reformation in Germany

PART ONE

The New Religious Pattern

ONE

Laying the Foundation: Luther's Youth

I

In great measure the German Reformation is Martin Luther. Luther, that is to say, forms a great part of German history during the Reformation period. His importance demands, therefore, that any historical study of the period provide a thorough, detailed exposition of Luther.

Martin Luther expressed very few views to which we do not find parallels in earlier theologians and reformers. None the less Luther is something new – an original phenomenon of creative quality and power. He is a proof of the great mystery of all life, that the whole is essentially more than the sum of all the parts, in this case, than the sum of all of the separate ideas. Luther was certainly also the spark that lit the heap of powder that had long been piling up – but he is much more.

It seems easy to describe this man. His day-to-day life, outward and inward, is exposed to the clear light of day, as it were, in a great mass of his own sayings, and a colossal number of reports concerning him. His interior life, as we have said, was not exempt, for the amazing richness of his literary works – few of which should be described as 'books' – is one great confession of his agitated soul.

However, Luther's unique intellectual and spiritual endowment, the transformation of nature which he underwent, his unrestrained impetus of will and of feeling in love and hate, his tendency to emotion and experience, added to his very early self-consciousness and resultant sense of mission on the largest scale, his revelling in paradoxes allied to a perceptible deficiency in theological and conceptual precision, his sometimes complete massing together of feeling and experience on the occasion of sudden oppressive sorrow or suddenly liberating fresh insight, and finally his utterly amazing eloquence, which became more and more vivid as its assault upon mind and ear climbed relentlessly towards its climax, flooding the reader or hearer with elemental power, all of these things, on the one hand, led Luther of necessity to those exaggerated superlatives which fill his works from beginning to end, and on the other, opened the way to far-reaching vacillations that develop into plain contradiction.

All of these circumstances, the reality of which is still to be established, show how difficult it must be to pick out from Luther's statements, from time to time, the thing that was decisive for him, when seen as a whole.

The older Luther became, the less fitted was his mind – and even less his emotions – to reproduce faithfully what he had experienced and believed in his Catholic days. After long interior preparation his mind rapidly changed, and in his imagination popery became constructed as one great evil. We have to see, to feel, the prophetic impulse through which he identified the essence of Catholicism with the corrupt condition of the Church at the time. Clear or even calm tones are hardly ever heard in all his thousand mentions of the pope's Church. His attitude to the papacy had turned to one-sided hatred. He lived and moved and had his being in this hatred. His judgments proceeded from it; he talked, wrote and acted in terms of it every day. At the beginning of the parliament of Augsburg in 1530 he seemed to show some appreciation, but this did not last.

How could Luther have described his own past but from this point of view? It had been his own papistical period. He, too, had been involved in these things. And so he perpetrated objective falsification through the power of deep conviction.

Having taken full account of these facts, we see how cautious we must be in our evaluation of Luther's retrospective judgments, even the most renowned of all – the preface to the first volume of his collected works of 1545, which contains the magnificent dramatic description of his reformation experience in the tower.

Luther's works are full of such reminiscences – consider for example his literary utterances, the table talk with his close adherents in particular. It is these very reminiscences, animated by seething fury against the papacy and Catholicism in general, and perpetuated by Melanchthon and others of the first generation, that have created the notorious Luther legend, through which Protestants down to very recent times – until Otto Scheel, in fact – saw the Catholicism of those days.

It was from this first Luther legend that Reformed polemic, as well as the Catholic reaction to it, acquired its churlish tone throughout the centuries; and for the same cause, for 400 years right down to the present day, historical study of the Reformation has been largely unable, on either side, to arrive at accepted conclusions. Here as everywhere, bilateral confessionalism, i.e. a one-sided attitude of antagonism, has proved its fundamental fruitlessness.

As today we are on the verge of discovering the more or less objective substance of the Reformation, so also both sides are experiencing a purification of zeal and a deepening of faith that enables them to reach some agreement in their view of Luther. We have daily proof, however, that not all who are competent are in fact playing their part in this work.

On the other hand, it is not only rigidity of belief – preconceived sympathy for the hero of the Reformation or hatred of the disrupter of Church unity and a condemned arch-heretic – that must bear the blame for the split in the interpretation of Luther. Proof of this is supplied by the variety of interpretation put forward by Protestants, who are not all of one mind in an enthusiastic estimate of Luther, but represent a great wealth of mutually contradictory views of the Reformer.

Luther is an ocean of powers, impulses, perceptions and experiences. His eloquent power of imagery is incomparable, as is his power of pathos. The richness of his utterances is almost entirely the result of *ad hoc* decisions arising out of totally different situations, the utterances of one subjectively inclined and insufficiently controlled by a system. He himself saw and admitted the Vulcan-like quality of his work. He maintained that he was not one of the allegedly great minds, who are able to exhaust the meaning of scripture at one glance, without having toiled, resisted temptation and gained experience, who are in fact nonentities: in contrast to these, he had developed through writing and teaching.

Thus it was and still is exceedingly difficult to gain a review of the whole subject, and to avoid the basic error in the analysis of Luther, an error into which he himself fell when interpreting the New Testament revelation, and through which alone he became a heretic: the error, that is, of making an arbitrary selection from a comprehensive content, and declaring that to be the whole thing. And it was and still is easy to pick one thing out from the mass of his utterances, and overlook another, and so to construct, very close to the real live person, a most impressive and powerful Luther. The most recent effort along these lines was made by Thiel. It is immensely hard, however, by contrast, to make a balanced survey of the whole richness of his genius, and, from that review, to explicate his truly decisive quality, without falling into the trap of making a harmonious selection pleasing to one's own taste.

Fundamentally, Luther worked entirely from experience. Self-confidence, sense of mission, arrogance, peremptoriness, strength of will – all at the level of genius – all compelled the situation of the moment to take on, for him, the character of crisis. Thus the unsurpassable superlatives, which are used as though unique, vary with the object of the different experiences. Exclusive superlatives like 'never', 'nothing', 'all', etc., because for him such a common-place of polemical propaganda, that they flow from his pen at times completely and obviously misplaced.

People have, none the less, made a valiant effort to see Luther as a systematiser. Luther did not think of himself in that light. He thought that his own books, stimulated by outward events that were governed by absolutely no regular order, formed a rather coarse and disordered chaos. They were, he said in 1545, 'much too wordy, and becoming wordier – nothing but a forest, a chaos of words'; and in 1530 that they were: 'sword, fire and earthquake; stormy and bellicose; the work of a rude forester breaking new ground'. His most systematic work was his book on the non-free will, written in 1525. He never successfully completed his plans (*c.* 1530) for a complete dogmatic treatise on justification.

Even the admirable analyses of Karl Holl have not put a stop to attempts to see Luther as a systematiser. Anyone who wants to do this must first dry him out in a retort; and that is the very thing most vigorously resisted by this full-blooded son of the Thuringian soil. It is true that now we are far more skilled in such cold-blooded operations than men were in the days of Melanchthon, and a far greater richness is left intact. Nevertheless the result is essentially the same – Luther's explosive power and life force are reduced.

If we accept Holl's definition of a systematiser as 'a man who is capable of viewing mighty configurations of ideas as a whole', then indeed we can say without hesitation that Luther was such a man; for his whole strength, which was also his weakness, consisted in his ability to focus all of the many and deep problems of the doctrine of redemption at a single point – as we shall see presently. We used the term 'viewing'. This is most appropriate in respect of Luther's intellectual and spiritual works. We could express the situation negatively also: in his conceptual thinking, Luther lacked any element of intellectualism. At all events, such a quality did not in the least affect the dominance and intensity of his intuitive and emotional primary experience. Obviously we must not judge what is characteristic and unusual in Luther from those passages in which the new religious sentiment, the very ambiguous, living religious testimony, is still overlaid by the old terminology, those passages, that is, wherein Luther still seems to be speaking the language of nominalist scholasticism, whereas this language is no longer a true vehicle for his thought. The efficacy of Luther's thought lay precisely in its not being pure thought, but belonging most emphatically to the domain of the heart, the feelings, the soul. Whoever doubts the experiential character of Luther's fundamental utterances will never be able to do him justice. This applies also to that document which still had such a clearly scholastic ring about it – the first dissertation on the psalms. Even these apparently speculative expositions, elaborated according to the fourfold sense of scripture, are moulded in substance by a psychological experience. The scholastic categories are mere scaffolding that Luther had not yet discarded.

As a rule, however, one gives the word 'systematiser' a rather wider connotation. We expect a systematiser not only to have a vision of the whole context but also to define every detail clearly, to be able to elaborate the context, to express the interrelation and superordination of the parts, and to resolve whatever tensions there may be. Luther did not do these things; and it was necessary that these capacities should be lacking, for his power could never have existed alongside systematisation. He had to break through all boundaries.

But his words were not spent in a thin flow of idle rhetoric. On the contrary, he possessed, too, a quite unusual power of concentration. He felt the irresistible need to reduce everything to a few basic doctrines, to a single point. This power and this need he possessed, however, not as a disciplined thinker but as a *doctor hyperbolicus*. He knew the scholastic distinctions, but had no time for them. His theological concepts, much as he tried in his early days to define them sharply, are blatantly ambiguous. They display the manysidedness of new life.

Those who deny these things might care to answer this question: how else could it have been possible for Luther, using largely the same words, to link his central experience – which turned the fear of hell into his gate of paradise – to such different concepts as that of man's atonement (to Staupitz, 1518), and the justice of God? He was able to do this because he did not think theologically, but felt and preached in a religious and prophetic manner.

The intermingling and the ambiguity of his theological concepts is most apparent when we try to define and distinguish the important complex of concepts comprising the *iudicium Dei*, the *iustitia Dei*, *iustificatio*, *timor Dei* and *assurance of salvation*. There are passages which demand and require this. But there are also significant passages where the concepts intermingle. Then everything coalesces: fear of God, anxiety about election, humility, self-abasement and faith, justice – human and divine. On this basis alone it became possible for a single word to alter the whole face of the Bible for him, whether for good (the account of 1545) or for ill (on Ps 77:55; 1513–15).

In great measure German mysticism, with its more spiritual but less defined terminology, helped Luther to clothe his religious experience in words. The fact that Luther was so fond of replacing the abstract formulae of late scholasticism with the wealth of words and images provided by New Testament preaching, is one explanation of the mystery of his profoundly Christian effectiveness. But he neglected far too much to make precise definitions and distinctions. Instead, he indulged in amplification and emotive utterance.

Luther is the antithesis of correct measure. He represents absence of measure and formlessness. Just as his monastic controversies, in spite of all allusive, even fundamental, theological and scholastic concepts, were indeed in great measure a chaotic emergence of life, drawing from this their endless fresh power, and thus resisting all external influences, so this power manifested itself as a tempestuous stream that scarcely acknowledged any banks. Luther produced formulae that abhorred measured tones as weakness, that knew no systematic construction, that were unable to grasp exterior objective values calmly and clearly; but the effectiveness of these formulae lay precisely in the immoderation of this turbulent stream.

All this was an expression of Luther's nature: subjective, sentimental, eruptive, the spontaneous expression of the spiritual collision taking place at that time.

Not only did Luther love superlatives: he raised them to the level of paradox. He loved the paradox – more than this, it was the life's blood of his theology. There is nothing astonishing about this statement: it touches the foundation of Luther's disposition. His love of paradox is not an overflow from an accidental mood, not even simply his basic mental and spiritual attitude. It is part and parcel of the core of his theology, of his *theologia crucis*, i.e. of a theology in which contradiction itself appears as the very sign of truth. The accursed criminal on the gallows, forsaken by God, is the Son of God.

In understanding Luther it is of prime importance that we make this quite clear, and do not block the way of access to the underlying depths by a too hasty refutation. The contradiction of paradox became Luther's form of creative expression. He took full advantage of this, for in the paradox lay inexhaustible depths of dark creativity; it provided a multitude of lines of thought and justified them all. But he had to carry the burden of the paradox as well: oppressive inner contradiction on the one hand, as well as the watering down and the coarsening of his ideas by mutually opposed followers and imitators, some of whom ended up by destroying what was best in the substance of his thought. Out of the fulness of Luther later ages have separated out a series of decisive or practical formulae in terms of which they have represented his ideas and doctrines of faith in schoolmasterly fashion, with more or less feeling and enthusiasm for this great man of God; and in this way they have made their own lives fruitful. Formally, the same process has been at work in Catholic theology, especially since the Reformation, during which period, with the help of defensive and rational propositional scholasticism, catechesis and edifying literature have transformed the fulness of religious prophetic preaching into a dry intellectual presentation of concepts. One of the judgments, if not the chief judgment, this makes possible, allowing us to go beyond customary superficial comment, is that his religious and theological ideas contain contradiction – consciously, deliberately and in logical consequence of his basic attitude. With Luther the Catholic synthesis of the organic *complexio oppositorum* was supplanted by a harsh contradiction, in the sense of sheer impossibility. Its richness is not the fruitful unity in tension of Yes and Yes, but the oppressive juxtaposition and intermingling of Yes and No. Sinner – just man: both are real and remain simultaneously within a single soul and persist emphatically right to the bitter end. This juxtaposition is not achieved, however, through a higher synthesis or through irenic harmonisation but through a stubborn 'at the same time'. The interior contradiction holds no terror for Luther. Indeed, the divine mysteries of the cross are necessarily a stumbling-block to human reason. Their truth is illumined by their impossibility. Luther comes very close to the *credo quia absurdum*. In his doctrine of election and in the presentation of his redemptive faith he revels in this very kind of contradiction. A thing is absolute certainty, because it is faith. But the certainty of election consists in the sinner's uncertainty whether – intrinsically a sinner now and always – he can give up sin, that is avoid being forced into destruction, and be one of the elect.

'In the Epistle to the Romans St Paul wishes to destroy all the wisdom and righteousness of the earthly man, and, in place of it, to stress and exalt sin. How such contradictions will work out, and with what reason they are entitled to exist, we will see in the life to come. But here we must insist that this is just – for faith is addressed to the incomprehensible' (*Lecture on Romans*, 1515–16).

The model, the foundation and justification of these tense paradoxes, lies in the God-man, Jesus Christ, and in his life; and Christians in their turn are true copies of him. His very first lectures on the psalms illustrated the fundamental law of paradox: 'Hence Christ is at once accursed and blessed, at once living and dead, at once suffering and triumphant, so that in him all evil may be consumed and through him all good be offered.'

II

Martin Luther was born in Eisleben on 10 November, 1483, of peasant stock, amongst whom it was customary for the youngest son to inherit the farm. In spite of Scheel's untiring research we are unable to reconstruct the exact milieu of his ancestral home. We find things there for which we no longer have exactly corresponding expressions; and there are gaps that we cannot fill. We know that Luther's mother herself went into the wood to gather fuel, and that on one occasion, on account of a nut, she whipped young Martin until she drew blood. Obviously they were poor. On the other hand, Luther's father was not always a simple miner but became an independent shareholder in a small mining company. What economic status does this presuppose? Luther's father would have worked in this business himself; but that did not signify poverty. At all events Luther's father, the eldest and hence first to have to leave the family nest, had gradually climbed back into the social niveau of the well-to-do middle peasantry. Otherwise he could scarcely have allowed his son to study; and certainly he could not have made such a show on the occasion of his son's first mass.

Luther's youth was not, therefore, unduly hard. He received a strict education, such as millions do, without any danger to their souls, but which may leave a permanent mark on one or two of more sensitive fibre. This need have nothing to do with mental illness. It is most probable that Luther's sensitive and unusual spiritual disposition carried traces of youthful impressions all through life. His scruples of conscience, his anxiety over sin and his fear of judgment, in short, his central experience of anguish, so deeply mark his spiritual countenance, that we may well account these a burden inherited from his own youth, considering his unusually robust mental health in other respects.

What made up the religious capital of Luther's parental home? All we know is that within the context of normal Catholic faith and life, belief in the devil and in witches was strongly stressed. The value of late scholastic edifying literature and of the Catholic liturgy provide us with no directly applicable yardstick. All depended upon the energy and the fulness with which these values were mediated by parents, teacher and priest. If the dominant spirit was that of a narrow, rule of thumb Christianity of accepted custom, in which the commandments and prohibitions and the thought of hell were diligently placed before people's minds, then in spite of all spirituality, the edifying books, the riches of evangelical preaching and of the liturgy were all of no avail. The fear of hell remained dominant.

It may well be that the boy's heart was addressed more personally for the first time during the brief visit of the Brethren to his school in Magdeburg. (We know how later, after the aridity of scholasticism, his spirit warmed spontaneously to Tauler and to 'the Frankfurter'.) It was in Magdeburg, too, that he received, probably for the first time, an impression of heroic piety, in the saintly Prince of Anhalt who went through the streets as a mendicant monk.

Luther becomes truly comprehensible for us only at the point where he bound his life directly to what is religious – and this is a highly symbolic fact. This was at Erfurt, a university city of many religious houses, and later to become the centre of pagan German humanism. From the summer semester of 1501 he had been attending the university. In January 1505 he completed his doctorate in philosophy and then made his dramatic appearance.

Obeying his father's wish he had begun to study law. He was considered a lively and merry fellow who could sing well to the lute. At the same time he was a serious young man whom the boisterous set of young humanists called 'the philosopher'. Luther was interested in humanism and studied it – although not that of the second decade – but there is no evidence that he was in close contact with the spirit that prevailed amongst that set. However the matter stood, in 1505 something seems to have gone wrong, and halfway through the semester he went on vacation. On his return journey from home, then at Mansfeld, he was overtaken by a storm at Stotternheim. Lightning struck close to him and he cried out: 'Help me, St Anne, and I will become a monk!'

There was nothing strange in a peasant's son like Luther invoking St Anne in those days. But why this sudden vow? To say that the religious life was something very close to medieval man is no explanation of why a cheerful student of jurisprudence should so suddenly change the course of his life. It would be sounder to assume that the thought of the religious life had in some way or other been in Luther's mind for some time.

It is true that even on this point the question cannot be finally settled, no matter how neatly we reconstruct the situation to our own satisfaction. There is no apodeictic proof that his vow in the thunderstorm (his 'fright from heaven') was merely the sudden ending of a long-prepared sequence of thoughts, and that it was not the inexplicable eruption of a sudden movement of the will. Luther once said that he entered the cloister because he despaired of himself. We are quite unable to define exactly the kind and intensity of the anguish and the sadness of his student days, and even less to point precisely to the time of their appearance. On the other hand, in view of the unquestionable, very deep depression symptoms in Luther, the monk and young priest, we cannot by any means rule out as impossible an unpremeditated, sudden decision. Admittedly the decision to enter religion makes more sense if it was prepared for by a fairly long period of intensive self-scrutiny against the background of his fear of judgment.

No one doubts that it was a serious motive which drove Luther into the monastery; but people also say that some spiritual compulsion kept him there. If this phrase is to retain its meaning, there are grave objections to this view. Let us admit that Luther made that vow in the storm at Stotternheim while in a state of terror, half unconsciously, half involuntarily, in a panic. What then? Unfortunately we may not assert that someone did not keep him in the monastery. The awaking of the religious vocation very often extended to a too insistent persuasion to accept the grace that was offered. It is certain, however, that Staupitz, the serious-minded vicar of the order, who played such an important part in

Luther's life, and other spiritual directors, would never have kept Luther in the monastery on the strength of a forced vow. Those we have in mind were not like the monks of Erasmus' malicious skit, who morally softened up the talented student for entry into the monastery, and then kept him there against his will. The distinguished Augustinian monastery which Luther entered had so many postulants that it had no need of trying to catch vocations.

Not until later did Luther affirm that his vow was elicited under duress. His first monastic period shows no signs that his new vocation had been taken up under some spiritual compulsion that was morally forced. Like everyone in his position at that time Luther knew perfectly well that a forced vow was not binding. He need not even have applied for a dispensation from it, although people still talk of this. Luther made a sudden decision to enter a monastery, but, in accordance with his tough will and his intense religious earnestness, that decision was whole-hearted.

Luther's years spent in the monastery are a demonstration of the limits of Ranke's demand that history recount things as they really happened. It is true that essentials are represented by outwardly visible and unambiguous signs, whether these be persons or ideas; but the essentials also lie beneath the visible and recountable surface, and must therefore be disclosed through reflection. The supreme power behind the Reformation was Martin Luther; and clearly the most decisive influence upon him – the inexhaustible power-centre as he began to preach and act in public – were those silent years spent in the monastery, years about which we know relatively little. Those years of Luther's spiritual struggle within the monastery – years we cannot recount – are more important for the history of the Reformation than all that follows, and which we cannot fail to see and which provides a story that can be told over and over again. And so to understand the history of Germany in the Reformation period it is essential for us to examine with special care those years of Luther's retiral before and after ordination.

The spiritual picture adds up to this:

He was utterly thrown upon himself – struggling, without any secondary objective, for salvation – alone with his own conscience in the sight of God – driven on until in danger of spiritual annihilation.

These monastic years (including the years as a student of theology) were Luther's great creative burden. He was mercilessly compressed into himself. This created so much spiritual substance that a life in face of the world could live upon it (distinctly as an antagonist to the world). This led to the word of this pressed out soul arousing such an echo deep within the conscience; and the theological foundation of this word often could not be provided until after it had been tried out.

On 17 July 1505 Luther entered the monastery. In the same year Hutten abandoned the religious life.

The monastery of the discalced eremite Augustinians in Erfurt, which Luther chose out of the eight monasteries in that town, followed the strict observance. It was not wealthy and no one there lived in luxury. What Luther said later (*To the Christian Nobility,* 1520) applied quite well to his own monastery. 'Ten or more ought to be joined together to form one that is properly provided for.' This statement corrects Luther's later untenable complaints about the idiotic self-mortifications – especially hunger and cold – which took place there, and also balances the thesis of the universal degeneracy of the monasteries.

Almost half of the seventy brethren were priests. Luther spent about two months as a postulant and then was accepted for the year's novitiate, the prior saying the following prayer over him: 'May God who has begun the good work in you bring it to completion.' . . . 'Accept O Lord, this servant of thy grace, and grant that by thy help he may persevere in thy Church and merit eternal life, through Jesus Christ our Lord . . ., and that he may be preserved by the holiness which you pour upon him . . .' In spite of the 'may merit', the motto above Luther's monastic life was not work-righteousness but renunciation of his own works and abandonment to the power of God. It was the opposite of what he later affirmed. Certainly theory and practice are not quite the same thing; but such a serious deviation from the rule in a strict monastery would have to be proved. The sheer exaggeration of Luther's accusations, however, is their own complete refutation.

Having been officially accepted, but before he was allowed to take vows of chastity, poverty and obedience to a spiritual superior, Luther heard such serious words as these from the mouth of the representative of the Church: 'You have experienced the rigours of our order; for you have lived amongst us in all things as one of ourselves. . . . And now you must choose one of two things: either to leave us, or to renounce this world utterly, and consecrate and offer yourself totally, first to God, then to our order. . . . And I add: after you have thus offered yourself you may not shake off the yoke of obedience for any reason.'

Luther committed himself for ever: 'I, brother Martin, make my profession and promise obedience to almighty God and the blessed Mary, ever virgin, and to you, brother Winand, prior of this monastery, in the name and in the place of the prior general of the order of the brothers eremite of St Augustine the bishop, and of his lawful successors, and I promise to live all the days of my life without possessions and in chastity, according to the rule of this same St Augustine.'

The prior concluded: 'Almighty and eternal God, thy servant Martin is on fire with burning love for you. To you he vows steadfastness within this community, and bows his head to your yoke. Pour forth your grace upon him so that on the day of judgment he may be set at your right hand, and rejoice that he has perfected that which he vowed. Almighty and eternal God, who, under the patronage of our father Augustine, has united a mighty army of sons within your holy Church to oppose the invisible foe, enkindle in our brother, who has just now bowed his neck to fight under the discipline of so great a father, the love of the Holy Spirit, so that he may give you knightly service in the obedience, poverty, and chastity, which he has now vowed, and that he may hasten along this life's road, receiving at last by your gift the crown of eternal reward, having completely triumphed over the world with all its pomp. We beseech you O Lord Jesus Christ to number your servant amongst your flock, as he desires to confess you, denying himself and following no other shepherd than you, refusing to listen to the voice of strangers, but hearing only you who said: "Who would serve me, shall follow me." O Holy Spirit, who has revealed yourself as Lord and God, we ask for the boundless grace of your fervour; and we entreat you, who blow where you will, to fill this your servant with fervent devotion, to edify him with your wisdom, to guide him by your providence, to keep him in your grace, and to instruct him by your unction. May he glow with such fervour that in all tribulation and fear he may be revived by your unfailing consolation, that, grounded in brotherly love and in accordance with true humility and obedience, he may joyfully persevere, and accomplish that which he has vowed – trusting in thy grace. Grant to this thy servant steadfast perseverance and perfect victory at the end. Through Jesus Christ our Lord. Amen.'

'Later on Luther abandoned the monastic life. As a result of his monastic life he became a heretic. He ought never, therefore, to have been allowed to enter a monastery: he had no vocation.' A flat argument indeed! Luther took his monastic life in real earnest, so much so, that his serious-minded superiors never once thought that he was an unsuitable candidate. On the contrary, the legend that Luther was an unruly and disturbing influence in the monastery, where he fitted in only against his will, is utterly without foundation. Besides this, such an unreliable member of the community would never have been specially chosen for studies and the office of professor. Until 1517 Luther's behaviour in the monastery remained all it should have been, whether as an ordinary monk or as the vicar of the order, who successfully led others in the discipline of the order.

There can be no question of anyone in the Erfurt monastery, or of Luther in particular, having been able to practise asceticism in a manner injurious to health. There certainly were cases in those days of novices suffering direct injury to health as a result of the kind of food and of too little sleep. We know this from, for example, the non-heretical ex-Dominican, Peter Sylvius, whom 'the superiors were reluctant to release, but encouraged in his profession'. Thereafter he again suffered 'agonising distress and torment on account of his own weakness, too little sleep, wearisome choral office, and hunger'. But there is no proof that such things affected Luther. In his monastery the practice of asceticism, in spite of its reality, was marked by obvious discretion. In addition, during the years 1505–10 and later Luther was in general perfectly robust. His later assertions concerning the pathogenic mortifications in the monastery were simply untrue.

The most important factor influencing Luther's world-historical development, in his early monastic years, was his getting to know the Bible. The zealous study of the Bible was a strict obligation amongst the Augustinians. Each novice was presented with a copy of the whole text of holy scripture. This was the beginning of a marriage relationship between a man and the book of books, a relationship infrequently found in such intensity anywhere else. It was thus that Luther laid the foundation of his astonishing familiarity with the text of the Bible. Only a few years later, in his sermons and lectures, in open polemic as well as in his own interior private struggles, the whole wealth of scripture was effortlessly at his command, and the very style of scripture merged with his own. Luther was particularly attached to the psalter; next came Romans, then Galatians – 'my epistle, the one in which I have put my trust, my Kate von Bora'.

It would appear that all the harvest which Luther had laid up in store, lay dormant until he took up his theological professorship. But this was a creative dormancy. After his journey to Rome, in Wittenberg the private and public utilisation of these things began to appear – arousing immediate astonishment.

A year later Luther was ordained priest and offered the holy sacrifice for the first time. Undoubtedly he did this with great fervour – probably with supreme fervour, as reported by Fr Nathin, who described him to the nuns under his charge as a new St Paul.

Unfortunately it is precisely in this sacred action, so important in the life of a priest, that we encounter Luther's striking spiritual and nervous excitement, and this is a little disturbing. He himself has described the occasion in such a way that there can be no doubt of its reality. It was such a powerful experience that Luther could scarcely go through with the celebration of mass.[1] The occasion of this was said to have been the thought of the nearness

[1] This strong emotion attached to another occasion, when (perhaps at the conventual mass) the gospel passage about the possessed was read, and Luther shouted out: 'I am the man!', and collapsed. Luther's father, who was present at Luther's first mass, contributed a second discord to the celebration. He maintained a genuine peasant coolness towards the monastic life and said he hoped that the alleged heavenly voice in the thunderstorm at Stotternheim had not been a diabolical apparition. He was not convinced of his son's vocation.

of the terrible divine majesty, invoked in the canon of the mass as the true and living God.

Sad to say, there is not the slightest suspicion that Luther took the sacred words lightly or only half in earnest. He entered into their significance with his whole soul, his whole mind and with all his strength. He made the words and their meaning come fully alive and fresh for himself.

This already shows us something of the greatest importance concerning a man like Luther. It was not the whole of the text he was reading which affected him, but only that part of it which corresponded with and appealed to his strong but one-sided disposition, and to his interior tension of the moment. Luther had a tendency towards ruminative, self-tormenting intensity. At that time for him the thought of the majesty of God was more immediate than the thought of God's infinite mercy. And so he read right past the sublimely comforting words with which the canon begins: 'Most merciful Father'. True, this is but an episode, a detail; but it has a symbolic significance for Luther's whole cast of mind and development. Luther did not react to the whole content of the sacred text of revelation but only, with the greatest intensity, to specific parts.

In spite of this selectivity, however, one thing affected Luther at this time, and indeed always in some degree, with the power of a primeval force. That was the profound interior, specifically religious, sense of God as the wholly other – the *majesty*. 'Something unspeakably great remains, something which raises the eyes of frail man to God: this is the divine majesty – the earth trembles, for the majesty of God is terrible.' Later on, in defiant mood, Luther frequently blotted out the thought of this *tremendum*. In this we shall discover a new side to his nature. But we have once and for all encountered the great central point in his life, that will never disappear: God's incomparable greatness beside which man can be nothing, nothing of any ultimate significance. God alone – nothing of man. This is Luther's whole programme.

The incident at Luther's first mass reveals a considerable psychological instability in Luther at that time. This, added to his scrupulosity, has earned him the reputation of mental illness. These things are not, it is true, particularly strong indications of psychological robustness; but, on the other hand, we have to take account of Luther's colossal industry and output then and later. Very little experience of the spiritual life or of spiritual direction is required for us to understand how quite serious attacks of depression at a particular point can affect someone otherwise perfectly robust in mind. With Luther, however, these symptoms were the outflow of a deeply rooted, subjectivistic, scrupulosity. 'We lived under the delusion that unless we were perfectly pure and sinless like the saints in heaven, we could not pray and would not be heard.'

All that we know about Luther, including his early monastic years, clearly proves that he grew, not by reason and calm certainty but through feeling and excitement. His development did not originate in knowledge but in religious feelings and their corresponding interior experiences. In his growth, the primary thing for Luther was his own experience. All the rest of exterior life, teachers and doctrines, even the Bible, were things merely added on to this basic primary experience. As we have said, Luther sought with all his strength, for God alone, and to become completely subject to him. When God has completely revealed himself to him in the words of the Bible, he will then become subject to the word. This is his basic attitude. His work itself proves this, and the farewell letter of Staupnitz, his former Catholic teacher, corroborates this by its exaggerated statement: 'You have led us back from the pigs' mash to the fields of life.'

And yet, from the very start, this subjection is something utterly different from the simple abandonment of the straightforward Christian. From its beginning it is an appropriation by the seeker, the wrestler, the fighter, by the giant, Luther. This is the all-important fact: he who desires to surrender himself without reserve to God's word has never been a hearer in the full sense of the word. We shall see that this fact overshadowed Luther's path until the very end. Down to his very roots, Luther was cast in a subjectivistic mould.

When in later days Luther spoke about his monastic period, the idea of terror at the prospect of the judgment to come always appears – quaking terror allied to the fervent hope of finding grace in the eyes of this God through liberation from an unusually oppressive sense of sin.

In this struggle Luther made use at first of the means laid to his hand through the monastic discipline commissioned by the Church: prayer, mortification and, above all, confession. As he admitted later, confession saved him from despair. On the other hand, he complained bitterly that it had not calmed his terrible agony, not even when he increased its frequency; nor yet did he find peace after he had been directed by his novice master, then by his spiritual director, and then by the excellent Staupitz, along the road that was to become his own – the road of redemption by the wounds of Christ, which for us are the righteousness of God. Perhaps nowhere else do we see so clearly Luther's utter inability to accept a decisive thing objectively, as in this central concern of his painfully struggling, stricken soul. He was so much the slave, not just of his own ideas but of his own way of thinking, that he could never understand what others were saying to him. Thus for years he failed to see the liberating meaning of Rm 1:17; and then he discovered it afresh for himself, but with a meaning that went too far and turned heretical.

This was one of the laws of his development and one of the secrets of his strength. Always and everywhere, he had to bear the burden of the search, the struggle, the discovery, alone. This was an unimaginably painful struggle. At that time he was following the mystery of the cross. Staupitz was right, psychologically and theologically, when he said to the struggling Luther: 'You do not know whether such trials are good and necessary for you, otherwise you would produce no good.'

What was the manner of thinking which thus prevented him from finding what so many others did find? It is rather naïve, in view of the mighty ascetic and saintly figures of the medieval Church, simply to assert that Luther took it all more seriously than they did, and hence demonstrated the impotence of the Church's means of salvation. Luther's obstacle was rather that he misconceived the nature of sin and the state of sin, and also the process of liberation from it. His conception was false from the Catholic viewpoint, and, in respect of the process of liberation from sin, false from the viewpoint of the later Reformers too. Luther understood neither of these things as realities that are accessible in their essence to faith alone, but conceived them as psychological data, grasped by human experience, by psychological perception and

G

feeling. From absolution he demanded a transformation of being which made demonstrably palpable his improvement, his sanctity. In addition, at an early date he was already defining as sin every concupiscent tendency towards sin. Because, as is obvious, no amount of absolution could make him feel liberated from this, he felt that he had not been freed from his sins. He could not bring himself to hear and to accept in faith the Church's declaration: 'Thy sins are forgiven.' He misinterpreted the sacrament of penance as a 'work' of his own doing; and in like manner to some extent he exerted himself to propitiate God by mortifications. Luther struggled and worried away at these misunderstandings without any result. And this, too, makes his later fearfully exaggerated attack upon alleged Catholic work-righteousness much more understandable. The Reformer's deep-rooted hatred can be very largely attributed to the exhausting torment with which the self-created phantom assailed his life in the monastery; but later he was to identify this phantom with Catholic doctrine.

When from scholasticism he learned that the goodness of works depends upon God's infused grace this threw him into fresh anguish; for once again he did not believe this with simplicity, but demanded of himself – in the name of the divine tyrant and jailer – that he fulfil the law in love. And he never told himself that God's grace would perform all that was necessary for him, if he were only to put his whole trust in it.

His confessor told him: 'You are a fool! God is not raging at you: you are raging at him.' He was right; but Luther was unable to grasp the redemptive meaning of the remark.

This behaviour reveals a further element, which likewise was to regulate his total development. For him the realm of the objective event of the Church lies completely on the periphera of interest. All attention is focused on one's private experience of salvation. The concept of the Church as an organism from which the individual Christian draws his very first breath of faith, the notion that the judgment and action of the Church are the pre-condition of the truth of the religious and theological judgment, and of the holiness of the actions, of the individual Christian, had far too limited a reality for Luther throughout his entire life. That is to say, in addition to his psychological make-up there were also basic theological attitudes which characterised Luther as a radical subjectivist.

The first dissertation on the psalms (1513–15) enumerated the basic principle that all that is affirmed literally of our Lord Jesus Christ is to be understood allegorically of his Church, for the Church is like him in all things. It might be objected that as all of the psalms are interpreted as speaking of Christ, the Church too becomes a chief theme in Luther's first dissertations. But this conclusion is invalid, because the basic principle is insufficiently utilised and the Church's sense of faith is but little invoked as a corrective of the immediate insights gained from private study of scripture. The conclusion is even less valid in respect of the bitter years of monastic struggle. The first dissertation upon the psalms was written after a liberating revolution had already occurred.

Were I concerned merely to expound my views, not caring whether or not they are accepted as undiscussible by Protestants, I could be content with what has been said so far. But today exposition of the history of the Reformation has plainly become a matter of vital interest within the ecumenical problem. We may be permitted, therefore, to dwell a little longer upon these things.

Luther said an enormous number of things which are evidence that his struggle was that of a humble listener; and other statements, in which he ceaselessly demands faith, are the very core of his teaching. Very early on he commented on Augustine's *Confessions*: 'Be a humble reader. Do not judge in haste, for it is hard to get to the bottom of the matter.' There is a warning in the first dissertation on the psalms: 'To treat everything with doubt, and to go after novel doctrine is the greatest temptation of the Lord. Therefore beware, O man! Learn rather to judge humbly, so that you do not become an innovator and transgress the bounds set by your fathers. . . . For God has not set down the spirit of the law upon written pages, but in the men set in authority over us, so that we can receive it from their mouths. If this were not so, what could be easier for the devil than to lead astray him who wants to be his own teacher in scripture . . .? *One falsely interpreted word can twist the meaning of the whole of scripture.*' The italic is Luther's.

This restriction, which sounds rather like a warning to himself, very soon significantly lost its force for Luther. Undiminished, however, remained his determination to place himself under the judgment of God every moment of his life.

But let us note: it is not mental attitude and intentions that are decisive in a man's constitution, but his being. There can be no doubt that Luther always wanted to bow to the law and judgment of God. But was he successful? Was it not the case that Martin Luther's mighty human impulses turbulently broke in upon his desire to do what God demanded, allowing his personal idiosyncrasy to assert itself? We will judge these things later when we attempt to elaborate Luther's personality in terms of his whole life. We shall find that in fact his own ego invaded the area of his zeal for the honour of God.

This process began very early: it was based upon the structure of Luther's personality.

Before we can follow out the climax of the struggle of the monastic period, thus completing the framework within which Luther's reformation revolution was accomplished, we must first briefly note the outward course of his life. External events provided considerable stimulus for his inner growth.

In 1508 Luther left Erfurt and entered the monastery of the eremite Augustinians and also the university of Wittenberg. This university, with St Paul for its patron, was new in the full sense of that word. It had been founded in 1502, a year after Luther had begun his own academic life. A year before Luther entered the university, it received papal approval (1507). It was a university without a tradition, in a poverty-stricken, economically insignificant, peasant, petit bourgeois, little town of two thousand souls, situated 'on the fringe of the civilised world'. In 1521 Cochlaeus spoke contemptuously of this university that existed outside the sphere of culture – '. . . nothing of any importance can come out of that'. The very opposite was the truth. This absence of tradition was of the utmost importance, for it opened the door to all manner of opportunities for the spirit of independence, and it alone provided the possibility of an unrestricted following, such as a revolutionary required. For an emergent heretic of Luther's colossal independence, it was a paradise, although he was quite unaware of the fact. In keeping with the whole outlook of the period, the basic conception of the statutes was utterly orthodox, as was the high esteem accorded in the statutes to St Paul, St Augustine and to the inerrancy of holy scripture.

It was in this university, then, that Luther applied himself to the study of theology, and also, as teacher, to the exposition of Aristotle's moral philosophy. He was twenty-five years old. His religious world, founded upon the Bible, encountered the scholastic and Occamist superstructure. The independence of the budding teacher at once sensed the non-Christian element in Aristotle. More precisely, the problem of the relationship between religion or theology and philosophy became very acute for him. As Erasmus and other innovators had felt long ago, he too regarded the imperious infiltration of philosophy into theology as a threat to religion. Luther's fideism had begun, and his effective renunciation of 'the whore reason' – not of reason itself but of its primacy within Christian preaching and theology. He solved the problem of our knowledge of God in the negative sense: to comprehend God is to diminish God. God cannot be known. Natural knowledge of God is a lie, because in it man makes himself the measure of God. God is the wholly other. The mystery of God can be unveiled for us only by God himself. 'Against its will, reason must confess that God is too great for it.'

On this point Luther's viewpoint was still only conditionally linked with opposition to scholasticism. It was first and foremost an expression of his all-embracing, utterly unshaken belief in God, and, as we shall see, of his Occamism. For Luther, God was absolutely self-evident. But man dare not presume to try to define God's nature more exactly. There is a proof of God's existence, but it is not conclusive. A year later he was to feel even more acutely the lack of respect in controversial and logic-chopping theology. He denounced the very thing that was later to be denounced in him in a slightly different form – speaking with profanity about holy things. 'When disputing and praying we theologians use the holy name of God with such irreverence, we dispute with such impudence about the Trinity, about formal and real distinctions. . . . This is arrogance; and it worries the theologian as little as a cobbler is worried by the way he treats his leather.' And so Luther's concept of God turns to the *Deus absconditus* and to his secret and, for us, unsearchable judgment: 'At all events, let every presumptuous mouth be stopped, lest someone hastily provide God with a rule according to which he must judge wherever he punishes some sin or other.'

As we see, this is a logical development. The experiential demands the irrational. There can never be too much of the incomprehensible about God. We have already seen that there were essential foundations which predisposed Luther to speak in paradoxes, to formulate a theology of the cross, to teach the arbitrary predestination of man for hell.

In the following year, 1509, this antiphilosopher, back again in Erfurt as a *sententiarius*, reached the end of his development in all essentials. This does not mean that now Luther had banished all conceptual thinking from theology. In 1514, when preaching about the Word that had become flesh, he followed highly philosophical and abstract processes of thought concerning the eternal thought of God, concerning the absolute intelligence that is the essence of God, a living movement in God, is God himself. To provide an explanation by analogy he relies upon Aristotle's doctrine of motion. But Aristotle would have understood his statements as little as the theologians. They have to be applied correctly.

Such statements are the infrequent residue of his earlier academic capital; they never constitute the core of his thought.

In his avoidance of ratiocinative thought he was greatly assisted by St Augustine, who on the other hand played a decisive role in the interpretation and working out of Luther's struggle to be free from sin, for justification, for free will, and his struggles over original sin.

We know how far removed St Augustine's knowledge of God is from discursive and systematic argument. For him, God is an immediately given, colossal reality, and yet, both St Augustine the philosopher and St Augustine the worshipper are constantly aware of the unknowability of his majesty. On the other hand, St Augustine strongly stressed the impotence of the will and the reality of sin, of that sin which enslaves even the righteous. In certain later statements these ideas, along with that of God's free predestination of man, appear finally in such an exaggerated form, that Luther is able to deduce from them that St Augustine acknowledged a totally depraved will in man, and the persistence of original sin. And this was precisely what Luther believed to be demanded and proved by his own psychological experience.

In addition to the Bible, Aristotle and Augustine, there was finally another complex of decisive factors, which we have already mentioned. In those years between ordination and his becoming a doctor of theology (1507–13) Luther was nourished by scholasticism in what was then its *modern* form – Occamist nominalism, as watered down by Gabriel Biel. We will reserve discussion of the highly important effect of this world of ideas upon Luther until later when the context is more appropriate.

In 1510–11 Luther travelled to Rome on behalf of his order. We can affirm that at this time his conscious attachment to the whole ecclesiastical institution had in no way been weakened. Luther saw nothing of the Rome and Italy of Julius II's Renaissance; and certainly he enjoyed none of it. It was winter, and in the dirty streets the new Renaissance palaces made no great impression. Luther was staying in the monastery of Santa Maria del Popolo. There is no evidence that he was in any way moved by the marvellous world of Renaissance art that spoke to him from this newly-built church. Luther was blind to these things. He was seeking the God of grace. His interests made him look for the holy Rome. The special opportunities of acquiring grace that were localised in this city were for him, as for every Christian, obvious realities and the most desirable goals. There were the special faculties of absolution possessed by many of the confessors, the opportunities of gaining indulgences at so many relics, churches and altars, standing upon ground hallowed by the blood of martyrs, not least the Scala Santa which the Saviour himself was supposed to have sprinkled with his own blood.

Luther's expectations were disappointed. Frequent general confession disclosed to him the ignorance of the Roman confessors. In the manner of saying mass he encountered a criminal flippancy. Later he said: 'Like a fool, I took onions to Rome, and brought back garlic.' The context which would reveal the precise meaning of this remark is lacking, for his sayings belonging to this period all come from later years. But this much is clear: here was a serious-minded religious, who already had gone through such intense inward struggles, in the Rome of Alexander VI and Julius II, in the Rome of the *mirabilia* with its large-scale piety of people and clergy; here was the northern German in a strange, more light-hearted and volatile Italy. A certain cooling of attachment to the mother of Churches could very easily be the result. Above all, this could sooner or later provide encouragement for a process of breaking away from the Church, if that process had already received an energetic impulse from another quarter.

It is true, we must admit, that at that time no sort of essential crack appeared in Luther's Catholic conviction. Years later he was preaching perfectly correctly about the pope and his power and the need of these things in the Church as the only fortress against schism. Much later still, now a Reformer, he confirmed it in coarse and bald imagery: at that time he was still willing to look upon the face of the pope.

It is instructive that in Rome at that time Luther's allegiance to the Church suffered no weakening: for Luther had already spent a year lecturing on the *Sentences* of Peter the Lombard; and he had read Augustine critically. With what independence, too, he had rejected the philosophers, including the master of them all – Aristotle. That is to say, at this time the critic in Luther was able to get on perfectly well with ecclesiastical practice. Criticism was at work, but concerned itself only with theological or philosophico-theological theory. This provides valuable elucidation of Luther and his development; it strongly supports the thesis that he was moving towards a reformed and heretical position without base ulterior motives.

Luther had gone to Rome as the opponent of a vast reform plan for the order, proposed by the vicar, John Staupitz. On his return he transferred his support to Staupitz. This change of view was the first of many that were to take place in the course of his life. There was his attitude to the peasants, to the congregation and to the princes in the new formation of Christian life, and to external Church discipline. There is some reason in asking whether this first change of view was a real breach or not. The lack of sources of evidence prevents us from reaching any very sure conclusion. It is important, however, to note that there is no compelling reason which makes a breach with tradition the only explanation. The fact that Luther went to Rome to oppose Staupitz' plan is a good testimonial to his zeal, for he believed that this was the only way to fight for the strict observance. The fact that, after he had returned and taken part in general consultation under Staupitz' leadership, he offered Staupitz his support may well be traced to the fact that now he could see how this plan would not lead to a diminution of religious zeal, as he had probably feared, but rather to its assurance.

There are many passages and all sorts of formulations in which Luther states that it was Staupitz who provided the decisive stimulus which led him to discover the gospel. Unfortunately, once again information about the substance of this stimulus is not clear. We may well affirm, however, that Staupitz' style of spiritual direction seems to have been undoubtedly characterised by a certain calm superiority that was free from the constrictions of scholastic theology and religious bullying. It was not just any kind of spiritualised style, but a deeply Christian and religious style, which had to maintain its composure in face of Luther's qualms of conscience and anxiety over sin. It had to reveal its strength, that is, in face of a psychological disposition into which a primeval religious value erupted, the predisposition towards the Holy, that is to say, Luther's mighty, congenital sensitivity for the utter evil of sin. Staupitz' calm and reasoned advice to Luther – to turn away from too excessive efforts of his own, from ruminating on his own condition or about his election, from private disputation with himself or with others about these things, and simply to turn to God and to Jesus, to objective redemption, that is to grace – was nothing other than the sound Catholic theology of the *doctor gratiae*, St Thomas Aquinas, so little known by Luther. Staupitz handled the scrupulous Luther correctly, both from the psychological and from the theological point of view. He was simply to look upon the wounds of Christ crucified. Then election would already be at work. From that place shines the predestination of God. 'Go, believe, take hold on Christ!' The only trouble was that Luther was incapable of accepting this objectively.

No sooner had Luther returned from Rome than he was transferred to Wittenberg. In 1513 he took his doctorate in theology and became professor of exegesis in place of Staupitz. He was to devote the rest of his life to this work. First he lectured on the psalms (1513–15), then on Romans. And now at last we have come to the point where, thanks to a wealth of contemporary documents (these two lecture series), we can directly follow his development for ourselves. By the time Luther took up his post as professor of exegesis and quickly became the focal point in the university, the centre of attraction for hundreds then thousands of students, he had already abandoned the Catholic foundation and taken a decisive step towards the new viewpoint which we called the reformed. In that short space of time between the conclusion of his journey to Rome and his assuming the professorship at Wittenberg some revolution seems to have taken place in his interior life. Now we must describe the development that had its origin in that experience.

First of all we must again make perfectly clear that it was not the hammering out of a new doctrine which gave Luther's development its importance in world history. The importance lies rather in the fact that he won an inward battle of annihilation. Luther had constantly, by some means or other, been able to arrive at theological discoveries, approximating to those we described as reformed. Many theologians before his time had reached similar conclusions. Without his interior struggle, however, and the power released in him alone, Luther would never have become the Reformer. It was only the mysterious combination of the reforming personality with the theological discoveries arising from it, that produced the possibility of a world-wide influence.

The first thing we are taught about Luther's cast of mind by his earliest theological notes (1508–10), contained in marginal comments on Augustine and Peter the Lombard, is this: from the very start, here was an unusually critically perceptive mind which made judgment with great independence and self-confidence. The few times when Luther puts forward his view more cautiously – even allowing for the *determinatio ecclesiae* – are exceptions. As a rule he formulates his judgment with noticeable, even striking, overstress. This is expressed in his sharp rejection of the non-Christian Aristotle, of all philosophy indeed, which he sees as a mere playing with words of no use at all when dealing with the things of God. Man's knowledge is little better than that of the beasts. For Luther, following Hilary, the only theory of any use in knowledge of God is God's word. This was a concept he failed completely to find amongst the professional contemporary subtle theological agnostics. Luther's strong self-will has already become apparent, as has the one exterior thing that moved and convinced him – that which is credible in itself, the word of holy scripture that is to be believed without question.

On the other hand, we see his perfectly calm religious conviction that by faith in his incarnation Christ is our life, our justification and our resurrection. His commentary on Rm. 1 : 17 (1515–16) is substantially identical with this affirmation.

Luther found himself still in the middle of the development that would not end until his reformation revolution. For a while he went on using many Catholic formulae as though they were self-evident, not seeing that they ran counter to the new direction in which he was moving.

In the sphere of the natural sciences such extraordinary independence as Luther displayed from an early date is always of the greatest value. And it can be valuable, too, in the sphere of the scientific penetration of revelation. But there is always one indispensable condition that, in accordance with the inviolability of revelation, it be essentially supplemented by the attitude of the listener. This was the very thing that Luther lacked. The profound humility before the unknown God which lay behind his arrogant rejection of Aristotle, and the less often mentioned reservations mean little when set against hasty reliance on one's own opinion, a reliance that all too soon led to an almost perverse, unrestrained criticism of the doctrines of faith. We see very little evidence that Luther felt permanently bound by his own stipulation that all care be taken to ensure that the traditional deposit of faith be not endangered.

From the days of his youth, Luther's concept of the unknown God had been that of the wrathful judge. The doctrines of Occam now turned him into the God of caprice; for the basic thing in the Occamist concept of God is that God is and must be absolutely free from every possible norm or definition conceivable or expressible by man. This freedom amounts to utter caprice. This means that God calls one act good and another bad, commands one to be done and forbids the other, because of 'interior reasons'; he could have made things quite the opposite. This is full-blown nominalism, which makes the sacraments mere outward signs, and grace a mere gracious designation of the favoured soul. It goes further and says that in the sheer arbitrariness of his sovereignty God predestines this man to heaven, and that man to hell.

Seen from this angle, Occamism is the grandiose but undisciplined exaggeration of the concept of the *wholly other*. It is un-disciplined because one-sided and full of contradiction.

The philosophical expression of these Occamist views is the renowned proposition of the double truth – an emanation from the idea of the wholly other, i.e. of the radical separation of the divine from the natural. The two orders are so sharply separated that it is impossible for the powers of nature, for reason, to claim any right to deal validly with the divine in any way whatever. Truth concerning the divine is imparted solely by God's own revelation to man. It may well be that man's reason will lead to conclusions that contradict the truths of faith.

We can see how this system gives systematic recognition to contradiction. No further proof is required to make obvious the close relationship between this and the basic views of Luther the anti-philosopher, who much later admitted that he was of Occam's school. We think of Luther's doctrine of non-sanctifying grace, of merely imputed justification, of the sacrament as nothing more than preaching – not as an *opus operatum*.

And now, contradiction: this same Occamism which set the natural man at such a distance from God, at the same time leaving him at the mercy of God's utter caprice, deduces from the Bible the summary obligation for man to obey the commandments of God. And this – so Occam asserts – man is able to do by the power of his own will; for if he does what is required of him, God will not withhold the necessary grace. This is surely a fantastic exaltation of human power to the point of practical Pelagianism.

The Occamist system is radically uncatholic. It is easy to see what a colossal burden it was bound to lay upon the over-anxious Luther, struggling to feel free from sin.

In what way was it uncatholic? (*a*) The system bears no existential relationship to truth; (*b*) it makes grace virtually a superfluous accessory.

How did it burden Luther? It told him that if he did all that was required of him God would not refuse him grace, that is justification. But in spite of all his efforts still he could not find a sense of being free from sin. Only one conclusion was possible: the fault was in himself; he had not done all that was required of him.

Immediately, at this very point began the greatest danger for Luther's scrupulous and unstable psychological state. Occamism taught that, in accord with God's good pleasure, men were also predestined to eternal damnation. Statements from Augustine and from Romans were adduced in support. Luther was overwhelmed by the waves of despair: was he numbered amongst the damned? This was no rhetorical question. It has to be placed in the context of the extraordinary, insatiable desire of a radically religious heart for the presence of God, for justification. But this heart remained tightly enclosed in the grip of a scrupulous consciousness of sin.

Luther has described for us his terrible fear of hell with unusual vividness. While allowing for traces of his tendency to use superlatives, for the influence of the German mystics, for allusions to St Paul, and for mild unhealthiness, we must admit that his descriptions have the ring of inward truth about them. 'I know a man who maintains that he has frequently suffered these torments of hell. They lasted but a very short time, but the pains were so great and hellish that no tongue can speak of them, no pen can describe them and no one who has not experienced them can believe they are what they are. If these pains were to run their full course, were to last half an hour or even a tenth of an hour, a man would be utterly destroyed; all his bones would be burnt to ashes. God appears in terrible wrath and with him the whole of creation. There is no escape, no consolation, neither inward nor outward; everything accuses you. A man stammers out: "I am cast away from the light of Thy countenance", and dares not even pray: "Lord cast me not away in Thy displeasure". In such a moment – incredible as it sounds – the soul no longer believes that it can ever be heard at all. All it knows is that punishment has not yet run its full course. And yet punishment is eternal and you cannot imagine it in temporal terms. All that remains is the sheer cry for help and terrible groaning, but the soul does not know from whence aid will come. In this state the soul is stretched out with Christ – all its bones are numbered. There is no spot that is not filled with the height of bitterness, terror, anguish and sadness. And all of these will last for ever. . . . It is to be overwhelmed in an eternity of unbearable, inconsolable terror' (1518).[2]

---

[2] Indirect confirmation of this is provided by Luther's exposition of Christ's abandonment by God on the cross. 'If you are not so moved as already to be burning in hell and damned and dying, then you cannot worthily utter such words.' 'No one can understand another in holy scripture if he does not possess the same spirit.' See also below, p. 200 f.

Seen from the point of view of the schools of the high Middle Ages, this Occamism was no system but its denial. It was a question but no answer. On account of the contradictions we have mentioned, it was indeed an unanswerable question. Luther had discovered and felt this insoluble problem, had experienced it in all its soul-destroying mercilessness, and had formulated it. Then he broke everything up by detaching Occamism from theology and trying to conceive its separate concept purely from revelation, thus rejecting Occamism from this side. This meant (*a*) that Luther traced back the *concept* of God to the reality of the biblical Father of Jesus Christ, messenger of the good news; and (*b*) that he distorted the other elements in Occamism by denying the power of the human will.

Occamism with its overstress on the will is the classic formulation of that which Luther designated *work-righteousness*, and which he asserted was Catholic doctrine. We do well to note that Luther was not thinking merely of the well-known abuses and extravagances of Church life. Nor had he in mind the exaggerated affirmations of boorish polemics. This was Luther's own conviction about Catholic teaching.

We would be hard put to it to understand Luther's inner despair and agony over sin in connection with our redemption in terms of justification by faith, if we do not assume that he was enslaved by Pelagianism through a curious concatenation of misunderstandings and interior experiences. According to this view, man was obliged truly to earn for himself a righteousness in God's sight by the performance of works in the fullest sense of the word. We can avoid this conclusion only if we assume that Luther was completely pathological or that his mighty and impressive descriptions of the soul's workings were sheer phantasy.

And we cannot simply contradict this conclusion by those pre-Reformation assertions that clearly prove how Luther knew that Catholic doctrine did not support this kind of Pelagianism. In such questions, which decide a crisis in the life of such a one-sided and experientially advancing personality as Luther, the whole issue centres upon interior knowing, upon being possessed by one's knowledge. From the very beginning of his first dissertation Luther had underlined the distinction between knowing and possessing. Not for nothing is he the type of those minds that can read over certain statements in utter and dangerous blindness, even although they repeat them often in word and in writing.

That this must have been the case with Luther seems to be confirmed by later texts. From the Coburg Luther sent out his admonition to the clergy of the old Church. In spirit he approached the Catholic estates of the realm and urged them to heed at last his voice and his doctrine. To gain their ear he pointed out the abuses, which he had corrected, in practice and doctrine. We must assume that in such a case it pained Luther greatly to have to obstruct the full effect of his own words; but his conviction compelled him. And so in the *Admonition*, in the section *On Penance*, he wrote: 'We have been taught that we must make satisfaction by good works for our sins, even those against God.' 'But if we say that we must make satisfaction for our sins, are we not simply denying the Christian faith?' 'What can any soul do, however, except fall into utter despair, if it has no other consolation in sin but its own works? There is no denying these things. We have the manuals in front of us, and these say nothing about faith . . . , but plenty about our own empty works.'

Did Luther really assert these things?

It was possible only because Luther himself had gone so far astray in his own mind in pursuing a struggle of the utmost scrupulosity and stubbornness. Luther's fight against work-righteousness was a fight against his own deepest pre-Reformation concept. Before his breakaway he himself was vehemently committed to achieving justification by works.

Luther's misinterpretation of Catholic teaching is seen in its most sensational and exaggerated form in his attitude to the Catholic assertion that good works are good only if performed from the love that is infused by God himself. For Luther this was no amelioration of his condition but its aggravation. Now he had to perform good works in a spirit of perfect, infused, love; and his strength simply did not reach that far. What a terrible tyrant is God!

Luther found himself in this condition as early as 1508. We may not presume, indeed, that then or later Luther lived constantly in this state of unbearable tension. What we see here are the extreme climaxes which acted as the levers and explosives leading up to the Reformation revolution. Obviously, Luther's spiritual and intellectual life was not made up of nothing but these violent elements.

We are now able to recognise the basic error of the view which made Luther's struggle so hopeless for him. He wanted to be assured experientially of his being in a state of grace. He had to know it, better, to *feel* it. In his pre-Reformation period, not to know if one were in a state of grace was the same as not to be in that state.

No one could affirm that this is the Catholic view. Within himself Luther wrestled and overthrew a Catholicism that was not Catholic.

We are not justified in refuting this conclusion by pointing to the Catholic attitude of so many Occamists of Luther's time and before it, especially the views of his own Catholic and Occamist teachers, Jodokus Trutvetter and Bartholomew von Usingen, who made a lasting impression upon him, despite his later complaints. These Occamists simply enjoyed the fruits of a happy illogicality. Occam was fundamentally uncatholic in temperament. Gabriel Biel (d. 1495) put him back on the rails, ecclesiastically; but Luther was more logical than his predecessors.

On a wider view this means that in a very significant way when we consider Luther's heretical development we come up against the influence of the late medieval theology of the Church. It is true that the point of contact is the above-mentioned erroneous presupposition of Luther concerning sin and the experience of justification; but there was also an essential fertilisation from Church theology.

We are bound, moreover, to observe, that Luther's urge for self-assurance of justification, for an interior sense of certainty, that he was free from sin, had been prepared for by the style of late medieval piety. This piety was all too ignorant of the objective organism of the mystical body of Christ, of the elementary fact that primarily it is the life of this organism which animates the Christian with supernatural life, and that the Christian's participation in that life only comes about secondarily. Already individualism had won part of its fateful victory. This was the road followed out to the end by Luther's experiential and extremist nature – he could accept no partial solution. The end lay in utter one-sidedness.

His revolution largely consisted in his discovering the ancient Catholic truth that man must *believe* in the forgiveness of sins as in salvation generally. He overlaid this discovery with uncatholic concepts which led to his break away; and these concepts were retained thereafter. The Lutheran revolution left us with the notion of concupiscence regarded as sin, and of the enslavement of the corrupt will.

The longing for an emotional experience was so much part of Luther's fundamental disposition that the Reformation revolution was never able to get rid of it. Luther did say: 'He who seeks peace through inner experience and feeling seems indeed to be tempting God as though he would have peace in act and not through faith.' But in his annotations on Tauler he stresses *sapientia experimentalis* over against *doctrinalis*. Even later he still did not know of a perfectly simple, objective, accepting faith. He always linked the mysterious process whereby the sinner becomes endowed with faith directly with emotional experience and with the *taking hold of* faith, of election. And if he could not accomplish this *taking hold of* faith he fell into the reverse experience of condemnation. The soul that has fallen into despair 'knows not whether it is damned or blessed, it imagines, indeed, that it is already damned and is falling into the pit of hell. But this experience is the beginning of bliss; for the fear of the Lord is the beginning of wisdom. This is true contrition and humility of spirit, the sacrifice most pleasing of all to God. Then, as they say in the schools, grace is infused. But at the time a man knows nothing at all of his jurisdiction, but thinks that the wrath of God is being poured out upon him.'

These considerations and conclusions have brought us close enough to the complicated mechanism of the Reformation revolution to allow us attempt to construct a picture of that revolution.

Unfortunately we cannot reconstruct the process chronologically and objectively with absolute clarity. Luther's recollections contain all sorts of transpositions, some of them serious in effect. These recollections have made it quite difficult for us to understand his Reformation breakaway. He has tended to coalesce the process too much in a single and definitive act. In reality the revolution proceeded by several breakaways, each of which was separated from the others by its own special and extensive preparation. And so, frequently, the colossal relief of the break is distorted by and merges with unhappy rebounds of despair. The picture is well known to observers of spiritual crisis. With Luther everything is so much more sharply defined, so much more intelligible, in proportion as his spiritual advance from time to time was more experiential and more individual. The deeper and more exaggerated and agonising his experience of judgment and of sin, the more violently he threw himself upon the liberating light, the more powerfully did he experience from time to time an isolated solution as liberation. Luther's contemporary accounts are insufficient. Besides this, in them the concepts of sin, original sin, the righteousness of God, the assurance of salvation and of faith – so normative in understanding the revolution – are not so much clearly thought out as made relevant to life. Correspondingly, Luther's theological terminology displays significant variations.

We are already aware of most of the fundamental theses which express Luther's interior development away from the Church. Reason must abscond from the sphere of Christian belief; concupiscence can never be overcome; man is always sinful, and in the process of salvation his powers remain absolutely nothing; meritorious actions are thus excluded; God's action alone remains.

This means that a radical separation has been effected between nature and grace, between natural goodness and redemptive grace. Luther acutely felt the essential difference between the two entities. It was not merely, as Erasmus affirmed, that the practices of the ceremonial law provided a Judaistic legal righteousness, but so was the actual fulfilment of the decalogue. These become Christian only through faith within the pure and complete scope of the free gift of God's grace.

The most powerful, or at least the most evident, levers in this development were the concept of God's righteousness, and the concept of justification by faith.

We are repeatedly forced to stress this fact: Luther's development, in the most comprehensive degree imaginable, was a highly personal process. It was worked out as though in solitary confinement. He quoted scholastic literature, but in reality scarcely noticed what he read there. These were mere words. For years he read vital statements, from the Bible itself, he even learned them by heart, without seeing what he read. He was aware only of himself, or, as in 1515–16, he read his own thoughts into the texts before his eyes.[3]

We know also the content of this experiential situation: it is circumscribed by the majesty of God, over against which stands the sense of helplessness of sinful man, whose whole being only makes sense if he is accepted by God. His being is thus destroyed at its core if this link with God is threatened. And it is threatened by the very majesty of God himself, i.e. by the concept of God as expounded in a widespread theology and popular form of Christianity. This concept of God had become one-sidedly dissociated from the true form of gospel. Luther was oppressed by *the Godhead* and the *judge*. He possessed no lively sense of the concept of God given us chiefly by Jesus himself, the concept of God as Father – our Father. The attitude taught and demanded by Jesus is indeed that of the utterly worthless servant of God, and yet it contains nothing whatever of the terrified uncertainty of Luther. This was significant, and fatal. The fact that the hyper-religious Luther did not proceed from the gospels but began his struggle one-sidedly from St Paul's and St Augustine's theology of sin, was bound to reap its proper reward. He ought rather to have looked out of himself and followed the Lord's guidance from the wholeness of the pages of the gospels. His reckless personal struggle reveals the limits and the dangers of his worth.

Before Luther had found decisive deliverance from this situation of the distracted struggling sinner before the majesty of God

[3] I would like to make clear that this is not meant to contain any suggestion of the reproach of bad faith. It is true that this does provide considerable opportunity for criticism of Luther. God's revelation to man in the Old and the New Testaments, as Luther himself recognised, is not a theological doctrinal system. In its all-embracing scope it is the living proclamation of God, uttered from diverse points of view and to the most varied concrete circumstances. It is so all-embracing that virtually every situation of mankind is accounted for. Such an all-embracing message cannot be purely conserved by any one man. Thrown upon his own resources, he is bound to be one-sidedly selective. Only an organism which, like the revelation of God's Word himself, is also a work of God, is able to conserve this all-embracing treasure. That organism is the Church. Luther, however, paid no real heed to this custodian. And so did not conserve the whole extent of revelation evenly but reacted to it individualistically.

through an interior revolution, he had already received an important if weak impulse towards deliverance from Staupitz and other
spiritual directors who tried, by the simple application of Catholic
doctrine, to direct him away from his own exaggerated, tense
efforts at appropriating the grace of God, to God's own freely
bestowed gracious assistance, presented to us in Christ crucified
(see above, p. 193).

In the end it was the word of the Bible that tipped the scales.

Instead of helping him on, the study of the Bible, significantly,
only laid a heavier burden upon this work-righteous fearer of the
majesty of God. In the end, however, it was the Bible that enabled
him to break loose. He himself has described the process as con-
densed in the famous incident in the tower of his monastery at
Wittenberg.

'I was driven on by a stubborn urge to understand Paul of the
Epistle to the Romans. It was not a lack of fervour that had hitherto hindered me, but a single word in the first chapter: "For in it
(the gospel) the righteousness of God is revealed" (Rm. 1 : 17); for
I hated the phrase "righteousness of God". Following the usage
and exposition of all the doctors I had been taught to understand
this phrase philosophically in terms of the so called formal or
active righteousness in virtue of which God is righteous in himself
and hence punishes sinners and the unrighteous.

'I felt that despite my exemplary life as a monk, in God's sight
I was a sinner with a most uneasy conscience, and that I dared not
rely upon being reconciled with him through my works of satisfaction. Thus I did not love this righteous God who punished sinners:
I hated him. With silent, if not blasphemous, yet colossal mur-
murings, I became terrified of God. Was it not enough for poor
sinners and those for ever damned through original sin to be
burdened with all manner of misery by reason of the ten commandments; did God have to pile up new terrors of his righteousness
and wrath through the gospel itself! Thus I raved on with wild and
distracted mind. And in my distress I kept hammering away at
this passage in St Paul, fervently longing to discover his meaning.

'I grovelled night and day until, by the mercy of God, I began
to pay heed to the context where I read: "the righteous lives by
faith". Then I began to understand the "righteousness of God" in
such a way that the righteous lives by the gift of God, that is by

faith. And I understood that this was the meaning: the gospel reveals the passive righteousness of God through which the merciful God justifies us through faith, as it is written: "the righteous lives by faith".

'Then I felt as if new born and having entered through the doors leading into the highest heaven. All at once I saw the whole of scripture in a new light.

'I ran over scripture in my mind and made the same discovery concerning other phrases like "the work of God", i.e. what God has effected in us, "the power of God", i.e. that by which he strengthens us, "the wisdom of God", i.e. by which he makes us wise, "the strength of God", "the salvation of God", "the honour of God".

'And behold! As my hatred of the phrase "the righteousness of God" had formerly been great, so great now was my love of this the sweetest of all phrases. This passage in St Paul became for me the very gate of heaven.'

In this way, with great power of dramatic condensation, the elderly Luther of 1545 looked back and described his early experience. There are comments on Psalm 71 which Luther made in 1514 and which illuminate this retrospectively described experience. These comments lack Luther's lively eloquence as exemplified in the above passage, which displays Luther's amazing and lavish use of the biblical material that came without effort to his mind.

Point of departure and fundamental thesis are one and the same statement: 'In scripture the judgment of man is that which is contrary to the judgment of God. In its chief (tropological) sense the "judgment of God" is that by which he condemns whatever comes from man himself – the entire old man with all his deeds.' Luther specially adds: 'even our righteousness (Is 64:6)'. 'He alone is justified who regards himself as cast away and worthy of damnation. He who has died is justified (Rm. 6:7). This is the meaning of the phrase "the judgment of God" as of "the righteousness of God" or "the power of God" or "the wisdom of God" – i.e. that through which we become wise, strong, righteous and humble, become justified. . . .

'There are some exquisitely sweet petitions like these in the psalms: "Vindicate me O God!" (42:1); "Arise, O God, and judge the earth!" (81:8); "He comes to judge the earth" (95:13).

"Judgment" is always used in the sense of "judge me O Lord",
i.e. give me true humility and the death of the carnal man, the
condemnation of my ego, so that I may be saved by you in the
Spirit . . . In a prophetic sense, however, the words take on a fearful meaning, full of dread, for then they point to the last judgment.

'And yet it is an astonishing thing that grace or the law of grace
(which is the same thing, viz. the gospel) is at once judgment and
justification. The reason for this is undoubtedly because it judges
and justifies him who believes in it. In this sense every word of God
is judgment.

'And then, he judges in a threefold sense: he condemns the
works of the flesh and of the world. He shows that what is wordly
in us is rejected by God and worthy of damnation. And so, whoever is attached to him by faith, becomes despicable and worthless
to himself – a nonentity and worthy of damnation. Hence, mortification and crucifying of the flesh and the renunciation of all worldly things are judgments of God – judgments which by his judgment, i.e. by the gospel and his grace, he effects in his own. In this
way justification results. For he who regards himself as lacking
justification . . . , receives grace from God . . . ; for this reason the
gospel is called the judgment of God, because it stands opposed
to the judgment of man. It condemns what man affirms, and
affirms what man condemns. This judgment is presented to us in
the cross of Christ. In this way: as he died, an outcast of the people,
so we must bear the same judgment along with him, must be
crucified in spirit and die, as the apostle explains in Rm. 6:4 f and
8:10 f.

'He who wishes to gain deep understanding of St Paul and the
other holy scriptures must take these expressions in the tropological sense explained above: "truth", "wisdom", "power", "salvation", "righteousness", must be understood in the sense that
through these things God makes us strong, saves us, makes us
righteous and wise. . . .'

There can be no doubt that in all this Luther was dealing with
the material which had been his most frequent and constant study.
For him, as is obvious, the *righteousness of God* had become the great
central point of theology, and all his religious interest centred
upon it. We have an almost immediate experience of his own
reverence, for in the end he is writing both words in large letters.

It is quite incorrect to suggest that the dissertation on the psalms was the direct echo of the experience in the tower, described by Luther in 1545. It is true that we can trace the substantial progress of the young lecturer – a progress of which he himself was aware. But there is no hint of an immediately preceding fresh discovery, in these expositions, which follow the strictly scholastic scheme of the multiple sense of scripture, and other scholastic distinctions. There is no trace of a very recently quaking and despairing seeker. Nor is there any suggestion of a prayer with which, shattered, Luther clinched this overwhelming discovery. What Luther expresses here must have been the result of a longish period of elaboration. Neither then nor at the time of recording the experience did it remotely possess the conclusive significance of a Reformation revolution, which Luther described in 1545 as a rejection of the opinion of 'all the doctors'. This clearly demonstrates the ambiguity of the text.

None the less, the unusual impressiveness of the backward glance of 1545 makes it impossible for us to assume that it does not correspond to something essential in the Reformation revolt as there portrayed. This essential element must first of all – in accordance with Luther's whole style – be far from conceptually clear and defined thought, and close to a living type of experience. In the second place in spite of this it must be intellectually and theologically fulfilled in a manner that is not purely concerned with religious sensitivity. Both of these aspects are applicable to the description of an interior revolution, which Luther addressed to Staupitz in 1518 (i.e. the preface to the exposition of the theses on indulgences) and which he retrospectively attaches to the period in the Wittenberg monastery (certainly the phase before he became a professor of exegesis). The revolution here described is supposed to have been occasioned by the theological concept of *paenitentia*, i.e. penance; and Luther made the liberating discovery that it ought to be conceived as *metanoia*, a change of heart. This description agrees, down to the smallest psychological detail, with the reminiscence of 1545. And yet this account was twenty-eight years closer to the actual events.

It is not true that Luther's interpretation of the righteousness of God as the grace by which we are justified was a completely new discovery. His assertion on this point in the preface of 1545 is false. All of the medieval exegetes had put forward this interpretation; and Luther must have read this the moment he began to study that passage in Romans, which so disturbed him. The trouble was that he had not really taken in what he read. To begin with he was simply prevented by his different style of religious and mental structure from breaking free of the notion of punitive justice. Thus he made a fresh discovery of the saving justice of God. At least it was new to him.

His discovery was more than this, otherwise it would have remained strictly Catholic. It was new in the much more all-embracing sense of Reformation heresy. Luther did not understand this new interpretation in the same sense as the medieval Catholic exegetes, who saw it in terms of a total Catholic attitude. Luther's view included the annihilation of the power of man's will and the establishment of man as sheer sin.

Luther's passive righteousness of God is the gospel. The gospel, therefore, is not the preaching of the wrath of God but of his compassionate mercy. Luther's experience in the tower laid the foundations of his theology of consolation and of that sharply stressed contrast between the gospel and the law, which we accept as something characteristic of Luther.

Luther's theology of consolation had nothing whatever in common with a superficial certainty of salvation, once and for all provided by faith. It has to be conceded that Luther's terminology is unclear and is patent of a dangerous quietistic interpretation of certainty. This, however, is not consonant with Luther's real meaning. For him, certainty of salvation is and remains bound up with uncertainty. His programme is to be found in his first thesis on indulgences: the Christian's whole life must be repentance. 'When you go to confession you dare not think that you are going to shake off a burden in order to live at ease.' That is to say: Luther's theology of consolation cannot be severed from his theology of the cross. It was only his imitators who tore the two apart, or rather suppressed his profound theology of the cross. Thereby they rendered Luther's inheritance powerless for his Evangelical successors, and made his refutation by Catholics a mere schoolboy's exercise. For the real Luther – despite serious vacillations – the two live in closest partnership. And it is only the two together that reveal the

full meaning of his views on the righteousness of God. The whole of
scripture is about a single thing: Christ crucified, the Son of God,
who himself was abandoned by God on the cross; who suffered
the pains of hell for us and so redeemed us. But this horrific act of
the crucifixion of God reveals not only God's mercy but also the
fact, that this compassionate intention was necessary, that God's
wrath was and is upon us all, and that we shall all be liberated by
his righteousness that is disclosed in the gospel, that is in Christ.
In this way Luther linked Rm. 1 : 17 with Rm 1 : 18.

In the course of his life Luther drew enormous power from these
two thoughts; and we ought not to show contempt and assert that
'all devout medieval souls showed a natural reluctance to look
upon the horrible portrayal of God upon the gallows'. Such a statement makes no sense when we think of great medieval figures like
St Bernard of Clairvaux, St Francis of Assisi, St Bonaventure,
St Thomas, Seuse and of the abundance of portrayals of the
Passion.

In itself the transition from *active* to *passive* righteousness has
nothing to do with subjectivism. The first dissertation on the
psalms, which in part already operates with the new concept, provides a genuine case of the opposite. Luther no longer merely feels,
he sees. He sees Jesus Christ standing like a man before him. And
yet we cannot fail to observe the grandiose way in which here the
subject, man, moves into the centre of the process of redemption –
even if only as recipient. With amazing fullness, the communica-
tion of redemption to man is made the whole purpose of the text
of New Testament revelation. It is the mighty God-man synthesis
of the New Testament. The transition was made, however, by
Luther, the one-sided subjectivist. Immediately the synthesis lost
something in favour of one-sidedness and subjectivism. It did so
through the enlargement Luther gave to the concept of sinfulness,
and through the dogma of free predestination even to hell.

The essentially experiential element in Lutheran theology as
classically represented in the different phases of the Reformation
break-through was decisively completed through presentation in
theological concepts. This is directly applicable to the struggle in
the monastery, and applicable with certain reservations to the
subsequent elaboration. This is not contradicted by the fact that

Luther's theology, even in the first dissertation on the psalms and in the commentary on Romans, is fructified by the mystery of God incarnate in Jesus Christ. Luther made all of the psalms apply to Christ. If it is true in a most fruitful sense that the theology of both works, in its exposition of justification by the concepts of the righteousness of God, etc., presupposes that Christology is its true theme (E. Seeberg), these concepts are no less the object with which Luther is grappling. That which in the dissertation on the psalms is deduced from Christ and the humiliation of the God-head in his incarnation, concerning the fundamental meaning of life and of faith, is not the first phase in the emerging Luther. That phase lies earlier, clearly centred upon the justificatory action of the sinful and highly scrupulous man, Luther. And for the other phase, those concepts are not derived from the historical, brighter and less tense picture of Jesus provided by the synoptists. The Christ who stands at the centre of Luther's theology is the risen and exalted Lord of St Paul, the Lord who has been sacrificed. Even in this early period, therefore, his language, in spite of great urgency, does not bear the stamp of that concrete picturesqueness which Luther began to use with such mastery from about 1520 onwards, and which later he could claim as his own.

In its first form the experience in the tower must be placed not later than 1512; but the transition already effected in this, required time for its complete explication.

A first achievement in the direction of the Reformed, or no longer Catholic, viewpoint came with the great commentary on Romans in 1515–16. The introductory sentence, which we have already quoted, formulates the whole theme with unrestrained boldness and genuinely Lutheran paradox: 'In Romans Paul teaches the reality of sin in us, and the sole righteousness of Christ.'

What is, according to Luther, the real nature of sin? It lies in the attempt, in any way and in whatever degree, to give what is human a place in the process of redemption. Corrupt concupis-cence is an approximate explanation that does not keep solely to what is essential, nor truly accentuate it. At an early date Luther affirmed this in a Quietistic sense. It is unfair to God if a person desires and seeks the righteousness of Christ. Through the sin of our first parents the whole of human nature has become opposed

to God. It is capable only of sin. (In the Heidelberg disputation of
1518 he had already clearly expressed this idea: 'It can be proved
that man's works, no matter how good they are or seem to be, are
yet mortal sins . . . The works of the righteous are sin. How much
more those of the unrighteous! Man's works are works of the law;
and, according to Galatians 3, are accursed. This curse is not laid
upon venial sins, and so man's works must be mortally sinful.'
Again he says: 'The works of God performed through men do not
become meritorious simply because they are not simultaneously
sins.')

Most important of all, however, the commentary on Romans
presupposes unconditional predestination. 'God gives grace only
to those he chooses. He does not will to give it to all, but reserves
it for a selection drawn from their midst.' If God punishes, he does
not, then, punish in the same way, even if the sin is the same.

Luther spoke somewhat equivocally about the mystery of predestination. In his commentary on Romans he affirms that it is not
such an abyss as people imagine, but for the elect is of exquisite
sweetness. To the wisdom of this world, however, it is certainly
bitter. To the weak he commends the wounds of Christ for comfort, and only of the strong does he demand that they come to
terms with the idea of predestination to hell, for God himself lays
this burden, this trial, only upon a few strong Christians. But in the
same commentary he also gives serious warning: he would not
treat of this subject were he not compelled to by the necessary
structure of the commentary. For this is the most powerful wine
and the strongest meat.

At all events Luther ventured out upon vast depths. His expositions were carried out in a spirit of deep humility before the distant majesty of God, without whose will nothing can exist – not
even hell. And his will sustains all things, even a wicked action.
Luther states quite simply: God wills evil, otherwise it would not
exist, but he does not love it.

Unfortunately this does no more than split up the original difficulty; it does not solve it. How can God's righteousness be vindi-
cated if man is unable in any way or in any degree to take a stand
for or against God? This is the point which Luther, with his rejection of theologising, would have had to take very seriously. His
simple affirmation of man's free predestination to heaven or to

hell, in the context of his profound exposition of Romans 9, remains peculiarly impressive. But when he begins to prove his affirmation and enunciate contradictions, he refutes himself. It is far from satisfactory to take refuge in the statement already quoted: 'How to reconcile these contradictions, in what sense they can properly exist, will be seen in the world to come. Here, however, we can only insist in faith that it is true – for faith is directed to the incomprehensible'. Luther, in fact, forgot the Gospels in which the co-operation and the rewarding of the servant are so obviously expressed. He did this in order to ignore reason and remain firmly upon his own ground.

None the less, this need not prevent us from perceiving the seriousness of these thoughts and their consequences. It would be petty not to recognize the bold grandeur and unusual power of the attitude of faith; and we cannot dispose of the passivity of the will, the perfect renunciation of one's own knowledge and will, which Luther demands, merely by labelling his attitude 'eccentric'. In their very exaggeration – almost reaching contradiction – they bear the unmistakable mark of the power of the gospel. 'He who does not deny himself, not having learnt to lose himself in the will of God and submit to it, will for ever be asking why God wills this or that, and will never find an answer. And this is only right; for this foolish worldly wisdom exalts itself against God and judges his will as though it were something of little value, whereas it ought to place itself under his judgment. Hence the apostle curtly destroys all its reasons with a single word. . . . Who are you, O man, who wants to dispute with God? And then he gives the clear explanation: Does the potter not have power over the clay? God so wills and therefore it is not unjust; for all belongs to him as the clay to the potter'.

The commentary on Romans also contains the phrase: 'Grace bestows new being', but it no longer has an infused transformation in mind, rather a new personal and juridical relationship of man – still a sinner – to God. God's grace is nothing other than his mercy – his merciful acceptance of the sinner.

For the rest this commentary – already Luther's official severe criticism of abuses in the Church, in his capacity as a professor of theology – is characterised by the utmost independence of the Church and the clergy, and even more, of the pope. It is significant that, conversely, a certain leaning towards the secular powers is expressed.

The last clearly defined move in the intra-theological development before his official clash with the Church was Luther's attainment of the certainty of salvation. What did this mean, how could it be reconciled with predestination, and, on the other hand, how could it avoid turning into Quietism?

Indeed, certainty of salvation forms the core of the verdict: 'by faith alone'. Just as this formula was misinterpreted and debased in an antinomian sense, so, too, the formula concerning personal certainty of salvation was misinterpreted and debased by far the greater part of Luther's supporters. Luther himself was not blameless – for it was a consequence of the inner contradiction contained in his paradoxes – but it was contrary to the mighty demand which he made along with it. The slogan: 'By faith alone' was not intended to encourage a morally lax life; just as little was certainty of salvation intended to cripple the religious effort of the Christian. Later on Luther was to reproach many Lutherans, in the person of Agricola, with having excluded the law, thus turning the new doctrine into a preaching of carnal certainty. For Luther himself certainty of salvation brought with it no spiritual indolence, for temptations never cease all through life. If they do that is a sure sign of condemnation.

As we have said, Luther's doctrine of the certainty of salvation is a peak in his paradoxical thinking. In this doctrine the Yes and the No are not merely blatantly juxtaposed, but each becomes the sole guarantee of the other. Here, if anywhere, Luther's doctrine arrives at the *credo quia absurdum*. For it is not just any sort of mild certainty of salvation that Luther demands but one that is absolutely free of all vacillation. Equally, however, any certainty that one is no longer in danger of hell is a most devilish temptation. The chief aim of Antichrist – in Luther's view the focus of all that is opposed to God – is to produce in men the sense of final security. 'According to the judgment and the experience of every devout soul, the greatest temptation of all is to be aware of no temptation' (Psalms, 1512–13). 'If you are looking for a sign of grace, and want to know if Christ dwells in you, then no sign will be given you except the sign of the prophet Jonas. If you have spent three days

in hell, that is the sign that Christ is with you and you with him. . . .
But the man who is sure is not in the least safe' (Psalms, 1512–13).
'Even if we are thoroughly assured that we have surrendered to
Christ in faith, yet we are not certain that we believe all of his
words. And so, even such believing surrender remains uncertain'
(Romans, 1515–16).

Luther remained true to these views, even if in practice they
became somewhat suppressed in favour of a more rough and ready
direction of the people and of his preachers. At the start of his
second great battle (against fanatics), he used the notion of temptation to test their election: 'To test your spirit, ask yourself whether
you have experienced the anguish of heart and divine rebirth,
which can carry you through death and hell. The cross is the one
guarantee, the only reliable touchstone' (1522).

Thus, certainty of salvation is closely bound up with uncertainty.
To this we must add a mighty daily contradiction in Luther. This
was his unbounded reliance upon the sole truth of his own interpretation of scripture. According to his teaching this was a matter
of life or death, justification or damanation. And so from this point
contradiction took a detour back to the problem just solved.

Between these large-scale expositions there spreads out the
further, more tranquil growth of Luther the theologian. During
these years he was intellectually constantly on the move. He assimilated fructifying elements from many sides, even when he rejected these elements or gave them his own one-sided interpetation.
We can detect this clearly in, say, the exuberance with which he
greeted the *Theologia Deutsch*, a fifteenth-century German mystical
tractate rediscovered by himself. In this work he found what he
failed to find in scholastic quibbling over non-essentials: a religious
theology, free from all professional, philosophical apparatus,
and speaking straight to the heart. Moreover, it was written in
German – of more value than all the theologians who wrote in
Latin.

It was this very non-philosophical approach which led him and
others so close to the Bible (see above, pp. 182, 189f.). Luther's evolution from Catholicism to his fundamental Reformed convictions
cannot be understood apart from his special relationship to holy
scripture. Later (1518) when he wanted to open up the way to the

Bible for his friend Spalatin, to begin with he pointed out that here was something 'completely different'. That is to say one could not understand it by ordinary means, with philosophical categories. These were in fact the very things which prevented the dialecticians from grasping the meaning of as much as a single chapter. They were the slaves of Aristotle and of Porphyry.

Luther cut right through this false attitude. A too scholastic intellectual gymnastics had made sterile the whole richness, depth, variety and life of the gospel. These masters of disputation were incapable of reading the word 'grace' in St Paul without immediately fitting it out with a precise definition. In 1510–11 Luther bemoaned: 'There are many things that we could easily understand ... had not philosophy given birth to so many conceptual monsters.' He swept these away and tried to re-read the Bible in a quite naïve way, to recapture its lively colour and fresh accent. 'One must read the Bible as though it had been written yesterday' (1521 to Dolmetsch). It has to be experienced. Luther achieved this, and acquired an extraordinary relationship to it. He knew it inside out. This provided his theological structure and his polemics with an amazing sense of ease and superiority. According to his grasp of the Bible, the Bible supplied all his needs with absolute sureness. It did not do this always by giving a clear and permanent interpretation. It produced, rather, a sense of extraordinary authority. To this end Luther had recoined the expression 'the word', endowing it with tremendous majesty. *The word* is the mighty power that interprets life, and directs it according to the will of God. Luther tells us that in face of the right word of scripture his most serious temptations vanished – temptations which he could never otherwise have withstood for a minute, let alone vanquish.

Simply to refute Luther's false assertion that the papists scarcely ever read the Bible, is to give no indication of the real place of the Bible in Luther's Christianity. The whole question is: how was it read? It was undoubtedly read in a Catholic way, that is in terms of a system. Long since, however, the Bible had ceased to be presented in the context of a theology filled out by faith, prayer, sanctity and all the treasures of revelation, and was now presented through an arid and confusing system of propositions. Year in, year out, clergy and people read or heard on Sundays only the never-changing sequence of short excerpts from scripture; and in the universities, in spite of the customary cursory reading, study of the Bible was sustained very largely by this same fragmentary spirit. It was Luther's mighty and fateful achievement once again to penetrate the infinitely differentiated world of biblical expressions and images, the uniqueness of the Bible in all its variety of local colour and of authorship. Luther enabled men once again directly to encounter the fullness of biblical revelation, as though a scholastic system of dogmatics had never existed; and he was able to turn these lectures into a lifelong task of burning fervour. Luther discovered the Bible; and it was a fateful discovery because Luther separated this eminently Catholic act from the Church, rejecting its authoritative, living, teaching office. For none could this living, fruitful, personal penetration have been more dangerous than for the one-sided Luther. The psychological attribute he could least do without was his independence. In theological matters this expressed itself in a quite extraordinary independence of tradition. He isolated the Bible. He read it by itself, that is severed from the organism to which it belongs, from the Church.

It is highly significant that the point at which Luther struck up his lifelong association with the Bible did not lie in the New Testament. It was not the accounts of the gospels that first moved him, and from which he sought light to illuminate the dark night of his soul. It was the psalter, those theological–poetical books with their intensely experiential portrayal of a man struggling for and with God, with the majesty of God, which is truth, righteousness and judgment. Next in his preference came St Paul's theology of sin, grace and redemption.

In many points, Luther's fundamental development before his public appearance has always been variously described. There is one point, however, upon which all must agree. If Luther's struggle within the monastery is to make any sense at all, it demonstrates that Luther had grown away from the Church without realising it or wishing it. In his search for the God of grace he found himself outside the Church before he knew that he was outside. His breach with the Church was in no way motivated by any preconceived revolutionary programme or any base impulse or desire.

Irrefutable proof of this is the consciousness of sin with which Luther constantly struggled.

It is true that this concept of the consciousness of sin and its application to Luther suffers the fate of many much used and often heard phrases. It is too hastily interpreted and set alongside the verdicts to which one has long been accustomed. In this way we will never get near the reality that was Luther. Thus we are unable to understand him or his role in the development of the Church; nor can we dispose of him. Once again we have to see that the formula enjoys its full meaning. 'The consciousness of sin' sometimes did have a weakened sense for Luther – a certain anxiety, an emotional disturbance before God. But this was not its real meaning. In his expositions of justification and election and Christ's abandonment on the cross we find his true portrayal of the reality of sin. It is something monstrous, so limitless that its cure required no less than the marvel of God hanging on the cross, an accursed criminal. Luther falsely exaggerated the power of sin's dominion by seeing nothing but sin in man. But with what earnestness he treats the subject, even when he is so unfair to the 'hypocrites' by his extravagant absolutism and his unrestrained, spiteful and arrogant fulmination against them, which for his own part leads him dangerously near the vice of self-righteousness. As few men have done, Luther experienced the monstrosity of sin in all its destructive immensity. The consciousness of the reality of evil in the world became the centre of his thinking. In this way he made the mistake of suppressing part of the voice of God in revelation and in nature – of which man is a part – and had reached a false solution to his problem; but it would be scientifically incorrect, as it would be unchristian, because of his dogmatic errors to refuse to recognise his tremendous power. He screwed up all of the commandments of God in the gospel to the pitch of a demand for perfection, thus driving men all too easily if not into despair, at least into laxity. But what a demand! Luther may have persisted in his hatred and calumny of all who disagreed with him, but we are obliged to remember that in reaching his theological solution he proceeded with the same fearful and fearless ruthlessness towards himself.

In the end of the day everyone has to grasp this fact. If in Luther we find a false interpretation of revelation this resulted, not

H

from laxity and lack of depth but from an exaggerated seriousness and too much zeal, allied, of course, to his own obstinacy. The unspoken sufferings of his particular way of development drove him into a false one-sidedness; but this one-sidedness was characterised, not by levity but by an intensified seriousness and interior power.

This one-sidedness may not have been ignoble, but it was fatal, as all one-sidedness is fatal, until its core is removed. Luther's later development proves this fact; and the effect of his teaching upon his congregations partly proves it. The proof was completed by the eighteenth-century recoil of Protestantism into the opposite of what Luther desired.

Let me now clearly define the method that I am rejecting. I refute the opinion that a heretic can only be made if he is a man of little intellectual and religious depth. It is a poor interpretation of history which says that a superficial mind lacking religious depth was sufficient to deal the colossal blows which rent the Church. It would be a serious indictment of holy Church if this were true. No, nothing short of the uncovering of the Church's own deepest treasures, but in a one-sided and hence objectively false presentation, could have inflicted such wounds.

TWO

The Beginnings of Lutheranism

I. PUBLIC EMERGENCE: 1517

The year 1517 saw the Turks conquer Egypt, and the end of the fifth Lateran Council. This council was thoroughly papal, but it heard loud complaints against the evil state of the Church in head and members. At the council on 23 May took place the great creation of cardinals which was to give the Church the particular composition with which it was to face the Reformation. Election was governed by personal, family, economic and political motives. The scene was dominated by the Renaissance princes of the Church. Beside them stood a few influential representatives of the coming Catholic reform: Adrian of Utrecht – Charles V's tutor – the great Dominican theologian, Cajetan, and Campeggio the diplomat. In that year Cochlaeus who, after Eck was to be the most powerful Catholic theological protagonist in the German Church's defensive war against Luther, was ordained priest in Rome, and began to write. Cardinal Ximenes, reformer of Church and state, who prepared the way for the coming Catholicism of the Counter Reformation in Spain, died. His sovereign, Charles I of Spain unambiguously registered his application to his grandfather Maximilian for the office of holy Roman emperor. Hutten published Lorenzo Valla's proof that the Donation of Constantine – one of the foundations of medieval papal power – was a forgery.

Part two of the *Letters of Obscure Men* appeared, heightening national feeling and greatly intensifying the urge to revolution. In Mainz the *Reichstag* echoed with complaints against abuses in Church and state, and revealed anxiety at the rise of the common people and the knights. The duke of Gueldres openly waged a war of pillage throughout the whole of Holland. In Louvain Erasmus was enjoying the height of his fame. In 1516 he had produced his edition of the Greek New Testament. 'People are in expectation of something great, and all eyes are being turned more and more towards Erasmus: he will be the man' (Huizinga). In that year Hans Sachs proclaimed a new era; and in a letter to Leo X Erasmus announced the dawn of the golden age.

But it was left to Luther to uncover the true face of the age. In March of that year he had completed his commentary on Galatians. In September in a disputation he launched a strong attack upon scholasticism. Then on 30 October the lightning struck; at the age of thirty-four Martin Luther, already the undisputed leader of the new university of Wittenberg, published there his ninety-five theses on the efficacy of indulgences.

In 1505 Pope Julius II (d. 1513) had begun the rebuilding of St Peter's in Rome, under the direction of Bramantes. In the Middle Ages it had been common practice to finance public works, especially the building of churches, by the issuing of indulgences. Following this custom, Pope Julius II proclaimed a jubilee indulgence in 1507, to raise funds for this new project. The indulgence was renewed by his successor Leo X. To gain this indulgence the usual conditions had to be fulfilled: the performance of some good work, in this case, as often, the giving of alms. In addition, the preachers of the indulgence were given special powers in administering the sacrament of penance. By these powers they were able to absolve in confession those who sought a certificate of absolution from sins normally reserved to the pope. This relieved them of the necessity of travelling to Rome. It was necessary also to pay a prescribed sum of money which was adjusted to the economic and social status of the penitent. It was taken for granted that absolution from these, as from any sins, required genuine repentance also; and indeed, this condition was explicitly demanded in every certificate of indulgence.

A just verdict upon the whole indulgence controversy of 1517, and hence an intelligent interpretation of the existent problems, depends upon an intelligent distinction between theory and practice, or better, between pure theology, on the one hand, and the popular practice of the Church, on the other. We include in the Church's practice, however, that debased form of theology which prevailed in the formulae and in the whole style of the curial and episcopal chancelleries, and in the majority of pulpits.

All through the later Middle Ages the antithesis of these two factors developed until, on the eve of the Reformation, it had become a basic feature of the whole theological situation. The correct theological theoretical exposition of the distinction between mortal and venial sins was less important than the casuistic and juridical discussion of questions about man's dues in the sight of God. Men were more interested to know how far they could go in a particular case without falling into sin, or what they had to do to be rid of some sin, or to help the holy souls, or to avoid the pains of purgatory themselves. The central thought of the worthless servant, still alive obviously in theological circles – although misinterpreted by Occamism – the servant who was still worthless even after he had performed all his duties, was utterly suppressed, for practice was too strongly guided by those other categories which have been mentioned.

Nor can we speak about indulgences if we do not know what they are. Many have forgotten this simple fact. If we are to take up complaint against the abuses of the system of indulgences, we must know where the substance ends and the accretions begin. A good example had already been set by vigorous contemporary opponents of these abuses – Wimpfeling, Archbishop Fisher of Rochester, Cochlaeus, Ulrich Kraft (professor of law then parish priest in Ulm 1501–16), the Dominican, Peter of Luxemburg who preached: 'He who would gain an indulgence must be in a state of faith and of love'.

An indulgence is the remission of the temporal punishment due to sin, never of the guilt of sin itself. This remission is worked out either on earth or in purgatory. It depends upon the idea of vicarious satisfaction. One of its essential presuppositions is, therefore, that of the Church as the mystical body of the Lord with Christ as head, of the communion of saints.

The application of indulgences to the faithful departed presented special problems, and, according to the common theological view at the beginning of the sixteenth century, was effected only by way of intercession, not by an act of papal jurisdiction. Very few theologians (e.g. two very different men, Eck and the Dominican John Faber) supported the view that there could be an unconditionally certain application. The view found its supporters rather amongst those who held the more rough and ready practical theory of the chancelleries, and amongst the preachers of indulgences. We should note, however, that even this theory cannot be summarily rejected out of hand.

According to the view held in those days, that which was able to bring aid to the souls in purgatory was nothing other than the condition laid down for every indulgence, that is the performance of some good deed, in the end some kind of sacrifice or prayer performed by one member of the mystical body, and which, according to St Paul, is able to benefit other members. An obvious presupposition is that the mystical body, the Church, is the appointed organ whereby the Lord himself exercises his care. That is to say, the Church, within the framework of its priestly power of the keys, is able to apply the abundant merits of Christ and his saints. In the last analysis the sale of certificates of indulgence (not of absolution) was such a sacrifice. In itself this sale was by no means 'the extreme of materialisation, for the departed has no share in the process through some form of contrition or sacrifice'. The article in the apostles' creed about the communion of saints completely contradicts such materialism. To be logical, objections like that just quoted would have to attack this article itself.

The case of the sale of certificates of absolution is simpler. Because such a thing obviously does not in any way make easier or replace unavoidable repentance, it is nothing but the granting of a privilege by the pope or his representative, for which one must pay a tax.

In reality neither indulgences nor even less, remission of sins, were being sold by the Church.

In itself the performance of some material action in return for spiritual grace was perfectly legitimate. It is true that this was a departure from early Christian practice and ideas. But it was no Roman invention. It was in line, rather, with a Celtic and Teutonic attitude, as is demonstrated by the evolution of western medieval penitential discipline. It represented a coarsening of Christian ideals, but not their denial. The danger of denial first emerged when indulgences began to threaten real moral and Christian earnestness.

This came about. There were two principal causes. First: the mitigation of strict ancient Christian penitential practice through indulgences led, like every mitigation, to the demand for ever greater privileges. The curia gave in to these demands; and thus arose the second cause: indulgences moved from the sphere of the simple performance of some monetary sacrifice, and led to a fatal development of curial fiscalism, to unchristian secularisation. Both of these elements in turn were closely linked with specifically late medieval piety, to the extent that this was connected with pilgrimages and relics. The immoderate multiplication of indulgences and the fiscal function they were made to serve, allied with the dangerous externalisation of late medieval piety, largely emptied the profound idea behind indulgences of all religions content, in many cases turning it into something quite unchristian.

For the present a single indication of what is meant will suffice. A result of the colossal spread of indulgences was that the notion of punishment to be paid by penance completely dominated the Christian mind at that time. No matter how legitimately this notion can be integrated in theology, the centre of gravity was in fact pushed well out on to the periphera. The more correct theological stress on repentance and love, set forth in the edifying literature of the times, was severely suppressed. Life and theory went two different ways.

Danger became reality when correct, reticent theology was ousted in practice by the rough and ready theory of the chancelleries and the indulgence preachers. At the close of the Middle Ages the extravagances of indulgences merge with excessive curialism, one-sidedly aimed at temporal power.

These abuses had indeed reached dangerous proportions. It is true that the theory of indulgences has always remained correct. The tendencies mentioned provide no justification at all for the assertion that Catholic theology in those days developed some sort of extra sacrament of indulgence. Any such seriously meant assertion rests upon utter confusion.

At no time did the Church ever promise remission without contrition or repentance. During the schism of the west there were dissolute deceivers who did promise such a thing. They did this in the same way as they forged papal bulls and sold them – as swindlers. They did it in crass defiance of all the Church's teaching. And it is illuminating to see that such swindling was possible within the milieu of the unscrupulous fiscalism of Boniface IX and his like. Anything beyond that, however, by way of earlier rumour or recent statement rests upon ignorance or distortion such as may be found in low works like the *Pfaffenspiegel* and other anti-Christian manuals of freemasons and communists. In spite of his petty scholastic style, the painstakingly exact proofs of Nicholas Paulus are absolutely correct. This applies also to the arguments put forward from the Catholic side in the indulgence controversy of 1517.

This, however, is far from concluding the verdict. Now we are only beginning to form a true evaluation. The question turns not upon the correct interpretation of the words, viewed abstractly, but upon the interpretation actually put upon those words, and upon the direction in which they developed with dialectical necessity. Even the theories of Tetzel can be proved correct; but the practice he represented and which the Church approved had become largely unchristian. It is impossible to prove that his extreme view, that an indulgence can be applied with certainty to a particular soul, in every case contradicts Christian doctrine, and so is essentially false. But if it is suggested that this application is possible by a sinner having no repentance, that someone in a state of enmity with God, merely by paying the money, can interfere in the secret judgments of the divine majesty, this is the reversal of all that is Christian; and anyone with the least Christian sensitivity is at once aware of danger. The minimising of repentance, which blatantly appeared in the gaining of an indulgence on behalf of a departed soul, gave its stamp to the rest of the practice of the professional indulgence pedlars, no matter how correct the theory underlying that practice. The goal of those who commissioned such preachers was business. To gain their ends they offered to the public – in perfectly good faith – a gloriously easier way to assurance of salvation.

The ambiguous terminology in use for indulgence material was well suited to such purposes. This had evolved in association with the tendency to ever more abundant granting of indulgences and its fiscal exploitation since the time of Boniface IX. The deliberate reticence of Cardinal Nicholas of Cusa over the preaching of the jubilee indulgence of 1450 made little impression. The desired unctuous exaggeration of the advertised indulgence graces won the day. Complete remission of all punishment and guilt was perfectly in order, for repentance and confession were presupposed. But it was so easy for it to seem that the remission of sins was included in the gaining of the indulgence, especially if the preaching of indulgences laid stress upon the sale of the indulgence rather than upon the need for penitence. When the jubilee indulgence was preached as 'the greatest grace and reconciliation of the human race with God', the result depended entirely upon whether or not the preaching and the hearing was done in a spirit of Christian penitence. The people in those days were as little educated theologically as they are today, and as little accustomed to logical hair-splitting. They saw things in broad outline, and the danger of coarsening of ideas was very real. As can be shown, in Germany at the beginning of the sixteenth century there existed a perfectly correct exposition of the doctrine of indulgences, appreciated by a few educated people; but this was no match for the more magnificent and noisy competition of the preaching of indulgences to the accompaniment of bell-ringing, solemn processions, erection of crosses, papal bulls and innumerable extravagant sermons.

The full disintegrating power of the abuse of indulgences was revealed in that affair which became the occasion of Luther's first public appearance.

In 1513 the twenty-three-year-old Albrecht of Brandenburg, youngest brother of the prince elector Joachim, was elected archbishop of the important diocese of Magdeburg by the cathedral chapter. (Albrecht's predecessor had been a Saxon, who also occupied the see of Mainz.) It was an old tradition that the same young man be installed as administrator of the collegiate church in Halberstadt. Finally, in 1514, Albrecht was elected by the cathedral chapter of Mainz to be archbishop of this diocese also, and prince elector. He had undertaken to support the collegiate prebend at his own expense. We have already learned how Mainz was in need of cutting down its expenditure. Within the space of ten years the archepiscopal see had thrice fallen vacant, and each time the confirmation dues to Rome for the see and the pallium had amounted to 14,000 ducats.

Now Albrecht had to apply to the pope not only for confirmation of his election to Mainz but also for permission to occupy this see while retaining that of Magdeburg and the administration of Halberstadt. Such an accumulation of benefices was unheard of, in Germany at least, and was in fact forbidden by canon law. But Leo X was not going to be hindered too much by canon law when political and financial advantage was at stake. With his decisive connivance the ambassadors from Brandenburg were granted confirmation on payment of an additional 10,000 ducats. Moreover it was the curia who made this proposal acceptable to the ambassadors, for they suggested a method by which Albrecht might raise all or part of the sum to be paid. They would make over to the archbishop of Mainz the sale of the St Peter's indulgence (see above, p. 220) in the archdiocese of Mainz and in the Brandenburg territories, allowing him a half share in the proceeds. The contract was perfect; a deal was made with the Fuggers who, in return for a share in the income from the indulgence, advanced the archbishop 29,000 Rhenish guilders – and the whole shameful business was complete.

That this let loose the Reformation storm is highly symbolic and an expression of historical retribution, for all the corruption in the Church of that time had its chief cause in the fiscalism of the curia, which was rotten with simony. In the case just mentioned, the curia, contrary to canon law, in return for cash, and in the hope of gaining political advantage, were allowing a young, worldly man to hold an irresponsible accumulation of benefices. In so doing they turned indulgences into a means of exchange in big business. The executive organ of this business carried on between the custodian of the merits won by Christ's blood and a worldly prince of the Church was a bank. Corruption could scarcely have been more blatantly expressed. We are struck with amazement to discover that Catholic theologians are still so hide-bound by formalism that they can discuss whether or not this affair was simony according to the strict letter of canon law. Even to raise such a question is to create religious confusion. Anyone can see that the whole affair is utterly at war with the Spirit of Christ.

As a result of various delays, it turned out that the preaching of the indulgence, taken over by the prince elector of Mainz, did not start until the beginning of 1517. For the most part the monetary yield was little enough.

The indulgence preachers of the elector of Mainz based their sermons upon his *instructio summaria.*

This short guide provides an exact illustration of what has just been said about the abuses of the indulgence system. Its theory can be justified; but the tendency has to be sharply rejected, for, by the use of pious formulae, it was rapidly turning the indulgence sermon into sheer commercial advertising. Money, which was of secondary importance, became the central thing; the atmosphere of the sale-room prevailed everywhere; there were pompous and solemn openings, and then bargain clearances at the end.

The Dominican, Tetzel, subcommissar general of the archbishop of Mainz, faithfully followed out the spirit of this instruction. There is no doubt that he taught:

> As soon as your money clinks in the bowl
> Out of purgatory jumps the soul.

Admittedly it is also certain that he never claimed that an indulgence could expiate future sins. This calumny was first set going by Luther in his pamphlet *Against Hans Worst* in 1541.

Tetzel was very well paid; but he cannot be charged with any serious misdemeanours. He was not one of those indulgence preachers of whom Eck complained that they paid their mistresses with certificates of indulgence and confession. But he was one of those, pilloried by Emser, for whom repentance and contrition had become eclipsed by money. In fact, for the sake of financial gain he stressed in a dangerous way the mitigation of the demands of the gospel of redemption.

In 1516 Aleander gave the warning that many people in Germany were merely waiting for the right man to show them how to defy Rome. Obviously when Luther heard of the traffic in indulgences he would be goaded to the limit.

When preaching in Jüterborg, Tetzel was inundated with people from the neighbouring town of Wittenberg in the electorate of Saxony where, because of political and fiscal enmity with

Brandenburg, the indulgence was not permitted to be preached. Luther came up against the matter in the confessional. He got to know about the *instructio summaria*. What a contrast he saw to the terrible struggle against sin and hell, which he had endured in the monastery, when he summoned all his strength to escape from the wrath of God. Tetzel lived in a world where a simple monetary transaction could buy 'unheard of and abundant graces'. We must carefully reflect on the tension between these two worlds before we are able correctly to assess the part played in Luther's development by opposition to the preaching of indulgences – an opposition not so important in itself.

It is impossible to understand the true nature of Luther's battles, of his theses and his answers in the period between 1516 and 1519, unless we are thoroughly conversant with the mighty formative process which Luther had passed through in the preceding decade. In method and substance Luther had moved far away from the establishment. However we assess him, he had constructed a new world. He had discovered this world in the greatest possible isolation from the disturbing and interfering public. In 1517, when he encountered indulgences, that is a scholastic theory expounded and actualised in an explicitly curialist and secular form, he was meeting a completely strange world. He had opposed it in theory, but he had never known its authentic existence. His theses on indulgences and the appended refutation by Eck are proof of this: 'this is Aristotelian science, not theology'.

Luther's reaction was to produce his well-known ninety-five theses in Latin 'on the power of indulgences'. Following the custom of the age, he fixed these to the door of the castle chapel, and challenged the scholars to a disputation. Without any dramatic design on Luther's part this took place on 31 October, the vigil of the patronal feast of the collegiate church of All Saints in Wittenberg, in which the prince elector kept his famous collection of relics, to which an indulgence of a million years was attached. Luther's aim was not to reach the common people, otherwise he would have written his theses in German. At the same time his aim was not simply to pose prudent questions. When producing these theses Luther was animated even more strongly by the conscious mood in which he had addressed his disputation theses against scholasticism in September of the same year. 'I do not want anyone to think that I want to whisper these things in a corner, even if they do despise our university'. The most we can say is that here and there they were perhaps deliberately exaggerated and to that extent 'somewhat obscure and enigmatic, as is the custom'. For this reason Luther tried later, in a letter, to keep himself in good standing with the pope.

For Luther, however, superlatives and exaggeration were not exceptions but his normal mode of thought and speech. It is true that he was still unwilling to condemn indulgences out of hand (thesis 71). In 1518 (sermon on *Indulgence and Grace*) he allows some justification to indulgences: '. . . therefore we ought not to object to indulgences, nor yet ought we to recommend them to anyone'. None the less the theses were a real attack; and not just upon the abuses of indulgence preaching. The attack was already levelled at the heart of the power which offered the indulgence.

In his last autobiographical sketch of 1545 Luther did not want to admit this; but he contradicts himself. His reminiscence allows no reality to the earlier reservations in the theses; he gives the impression simply that he had trampled on indulgences. On 1 November 1527 he celebrated the jubilee with 'a really special drink'. If, as he maintained in 1545, his only concern had been to uphold the true opinion of the pope on indulgences against the hucksters, he would hardly have been able to let loose such a diatribe against the wealth of the pope, nor ask why the pope did not simply empty purgatory on the spot. Without realising it. Luther admits this himself in his reminiscence. He asserts that until the Leipzig disputation of 1519 he had been guided by the authority of the pope. At the same time he says that even at that time (1517–19) he no longer acknowledged the divine right of the pope.

Dr John Eck, the theologian from Ingolstadt, who entered the arena as soon as Luther made his public appearance, was perfectly correct in seeing the attack upon the papacy as the quintessence of the indulgence theses. Although the fear of economic damage to the curia might be the first sign of sensitivity to Luther's enmity, his attack was clearly directed against the essential structure of the visible Church, especially against the pope (theses 25 and 27). From various angles a one-sided tendency towards the general priesthood was adumbrated (theses 37 and 90).

Once again the mainspring of criticism was the overstressed

separation of the divine from the allegedly purely human, a separation which we must take as Luther's central conception, and which we shall prove to be decisive for the whole process of the Reformation. In this case it appears principally as the abrupt exclusion of the power of the keys from the other-worldly sphere (theses 5, 6, 8, 20, 21, 22, 34, 38). The papal canon is applicable only to the living, and does not reach beyond the grave. It is not the pope but God, who remits sin. The pope simply declares that God has remitted it (theses 10, 11, 13).

When Luther complains (theses 81 ff.) that the indulgence pedlars make it very difficult for a competent theologian to defend the authority of the pope against the telling objections of the laity, his arguments do not thereby become any less damaging. Luther's eager desire for attack is all too evident. All too gladly does he appeal to the disaffection of the laity. He smells out the possibilities lurking in this situation. If these rambling objections of the laity were to be suppressed by force and not resolved in a reasonable way, then such action would give the Church and the pope over as a prey to ridicule (thesis 90). The voice of absolute authority had had its day; the laity were on the verge of revolution: Luther became their prophet.

In reality the theses, at the deepest level, were aimed at the people. Luther states this forcibly and unambiguously in his letter to Albrecht of Mainz in December 1517. His aim, he says, is pastoral. He is affected 'not so much by the shouting of the indulgence preachers – which I have not heard – as by the false notion which the simple, poor, coarse people create out of it. They believe that having bought a certificate of indulgence their eternal bliss is assured. . . . But no man can be assured of his salvation by the action of any bishop, for he is not assured thereof even by the infused grace of God. The apostle demands that we work out our salvation in fear and trembling. . . . Why then are the people being relieved of fear and given assurance by these false fables and promises of forgiveness? . . . For it is asserted that by the grace of indulgence men are being reconciled to God'.

That is to say: the theses on indulgences are an expression of Luther's theory of the uncertainty of salvation, of his theology of the cross (theses 1, 63, 64, 68). This is most clearly expressed in the great prelude to the theses: 'When our Lord Jesus Christ said "Do penance", he wanted us to make our whole life a penance.[1] And so the Christian life is not peace, peace, but the cross and yet again the cross. It is a walking with Christ through suffering, death and hell. Thus the Christian puts his trust more in reaching heaven through many trials than through easy security' (theses 1, and 92–5). It is the 'wholesome pain which it is more just for man to choose than reject' (sermon on the indulgences, 1518). Comfort is death, hardship salvation (theses 63 f.). Comfort and ease are embodied in the indiscriminately dispensed and highly over-rated indulgences. By these the majority of the people are deceived. They learn 'to fear punishment rather than sin'.

To sum up: the dangerous accessory which had been blown up into the essential thing was peevishly rejected in its lesser significance, and instead, true penitence, love, God's word and God's grace were placed at the centre (theses 53, 55, 62).

We have already seen how Luther's theological development towards the Reformation revolution was decisively advanced by a fundamentally non-Catholic Occamism, which had taken root within the Church. Now we discover that the foundation too of the public Reformer was decisively occasioned by a non-Catholic realisation of Catholic principles, by the fiscalised practice of indulgence. Both stimuli had a continuous effect upon him. The resultant was his unhappy confusion of extreme scholastic views and false practices in the Church with the Church itself and its genuine doctrine. And this confusion decisively influenced Luther's entire life's work.

All that we have so far heard about the indulgence theses might well have remained within the realm of theology and its controversies. It only became epoch making because Luther went beyond theological circles, and raised an echo throughout the nation. That is to say: the world-historical situation, especially in Germany, was such that the cry of this monk harmonised with what part of the nation were consciously expecting, and the bulk of the nation were sullenly and inarticulately expecting. They expected that this call would set off a cataclysmic, European, popular movement,

---

[1] This is simply good Catholic doctrine. Thomas à Kempis had introduced his *Imitation of Christ* with the thought: 'Whoever desires to understand and take delight in the words of Christ must strive to conform his whole life to Him,'

especially in Germany, a movement that would press on towards the light. In short, they expected the interests of this monk, through the spiritual sensitivity and power that mark a great historical moment, without more ado to become the interest of great sections of the people. The nation's response turned Luther into a Reformer.

In an almost enigmatic way the theses raged through Germany. How much more comprehensive was the external form of the excitement, how much more directly did interest touch existence, than did the heavy-going controversies of Erasmus with the theologians and the whole allegedly antiquated system of piety! Even Luther himself seems to have felt some displeasure at the unexpected commotion. Was he being led into some evil temptation? Humility struggled with a sense of mission: 'If you want to start something up with me, then do it yourself, and preserve me from letting my own wisdom take over.'

It was not the fault of theology and of dogma if to some extent the nation replied in an elementary way to this theological document. This was caused, rather by the oppression laid upon Germany by the intensification of 'papal power in secular affairs', and by curial fiscalism. Without the *Gravamina of the German nation* the nation would not have answered that first call of Luther's, Luther would not have become a reformer, and the Reformation itself would not have happened.

Luther himself was not untouched by these developments. His indulgence theses were not the work merely of a pastor but were composed by a demagogue and popular orator, who instinctively sensed an ally in the discontent of the nation, and who from the start reckoned with this factor. It is not important for us to know the part played here by knowledge and calculation. What is essential, however, is to note that Luther was already consciously speaking in some sort of alliance with the anti-Roman agitation of the nation. Even more important, perhaps, was the fact that with his religious discontent Luther had sounded a wholly German note. The seething unrest which was proposed by the first thesis as the general scheme of the whole Christian life, and which declared war to the death upon lazy security, gave imperious expression to German longings. This too commanded attention.

This encounter of Luther with the nation was only the begin-

ning. The Latin tongue in which the theses were written symbo-
lises this fact. None the less, this foundation was the start of an uninterrupted growth leading to the climax of the drama in 1520 and
1521.

The immediate, like the remote, effects of the indulgence theses,
the theological and politico-ecclesiastical discussion which now
began concerning Luther, the emergence and first advance,
that is, of what we call 'the Reformation', was entirely dependent
upon the widespread vagueness of the theology of the age, vagueness, indeed, in the mind of the Church. As we have seen, this
vagueness was both expression and consequence of the general
confusion of the Church, as presented in the western schism – in
Avignon – in the whole late medieval political and intra-ecclesi-
astical battle against the papacy, centring on the conciliar idea,
in the contradictions of Occamism and, on the other hand, by the
shocking disintegration of the Christian and priestly ideal in the
worldliness of the curia and the clergy.

The Reformation is incomprehensible apart from this theological vagueness. Without it, the radical ideas expressed by Luther
in 1517 would have encountered a general repulse from theologians and the decisive majority of public authorities, and would
have died away before even taking root. As things were, vagueness as to the import of the Lutheran ideas confused the best
Catholic minds – laity, clergy, monks, theologians and even canon
lawyers – until the late twenties and thirties, even into the forties,
as the religious controversies show. Here is the point at which we
become acutely aware of the vast distinction between post-Tri-
dentine and pre-Tridentine Catholicism, and, again, of the importance of practical theology and the practice of the curia in
contrast to genuine theology.

The controversy over indulgence was itself in great measure an
expression of this uncertainty and confusion. The papal curia felt
this when in 1518, after the fruitless hearing of Luther by Cajetan
(see below), a special decree was issued elevating Cajetan's view
into the official teaching of the Church.

Unfortunately the Church did not react uniformly with such
decision. It was too much at the mercy of the humanists, whom we
have recognised as specially effective upholders and propagators

of that vagueness (the a-dogmatic Erasmus is an outstanding example). These were men whose interest lay not in genuinely religious questions but in education, in the flourishing of culture, for they regarded themselves as the vehicles and transmitters of these things. And so, not even the decisive years of the Reformation were able to awaken them – not even in Germany. Thus, too, they were strong in praise of Leo X, himself a great advocate of humanism. His fatal lack of interest in dogmatic subjects were praised by the humanists as the innate gentleness and meekness of the representative of the gentle Christ, qualities which were to be unfairly cited against Luther by self-seeking monkish controversialists.

Even professional and specialist theology, however, must bear considerable blame for this prevailing vagueness. Occamism in philosophy and theology, as in the sphere of Church politics, amounted in the end to dissolution, to the acceptance of caprice, of relativism. In addition it inclined dangerously towards individualism. The notion of the objective Church had become unusually weak in Occamism. Occamism, like German Thomism, at that time lacked any real intellectual and religious power. Both were bedevilled by the well-known emptiness of unimportant logic chopping, by sheer aridity. It is utterly erroneous to think that theological clarity and certainty can for ever be preserved in rarified formulae. Such devices may well be of use in excluding positive errors; they are negatively correct; but theological clarity denotes truth, and truth is a fulness. This fulness of truth alone has power; and the very things that were absent in those days were this fulness of theological truth and the accompanying power of theology.

The full import of theological vagueness was not exhausted with the field of theory. The unsatisfactory function of the idea of the Church within theology was an expression of a like defect in the practical mind of the Church, and in turn it reacted upon that mind. The sense of Christian unity had been decisively weakened by a mighty centrifugal movement. The nations, and even more, their leaders, were much more acutely aware of the interests of France, or Spain, or Germany, as the case might be, than of the interests of the universal Church.

The core of this theological vagueness was undoubtedly uncertainty about the manner and extent of the papal primacy. The unbounded and often foolish exaggeration of temporal, specifically medieval papal sovereignty and its equation by the curialists – although vaguely defined – with the primacy of jurisdiction in the Church, offered an easy target to those who were attacking papal power. Justified criticism of curialism spilled over on to the primacy of jurisdiction. Through the conciliar theory and its various formulations embracing the whole of Christendom, presented before, during, and at the great reform councils, this criticism in the end became a universal concern. Quite apart from Wycliffe's teaching and the Bohemian revolution, for a considerable part of the Christian conscience the Roman primacy had become the most controversial issue in the world. This meant that the Catholic ideal, the notion of something inviolable, had been obscured in an essential point, had been attacked in its essence.

Before we can weigh this up in all its gravity we must first clearly realise the colossal extent to which the battle against curialism was regarded as justified and necessary – whether curialism was seen in its worldly and fiscalised form, or its constant arbitrary defiance of law, which seemed to make uncertain all that was stable.

An element in this practical aspect of theological vagueness was provided by the theological apathy of those powers to whom was entrusted the actual ecclesiastical rule of a territory. If the theologically apathetic and juridically minded counsellors of a spiritual or lay prince regarded the papal curia almost as the economic enemy of their land, the temptation became great for them to give *a priori* recognition and support to the emerging theological opposition to the papacy.

Finally we have to adduce a certain universal intellectual indecision that was effective far beyond the theological sphere. This was an expression of the searching spirit of the age, of the psychologising attitude, of the radical desire for freedom and equality. It was the age which produced the *Utopia*, whose author was canonised; but in More's *Utopia* suicide of the incurably sick is praised, as is the absolute equality of all religions, as a means of ensuring religious peace.

On p. 156 we have already spoken of the almost fatal significance of theological vagueness for the eruption of the Reformation. The history of the Reformation provides actual proof of this, step by step. (Not least, the fatal errors of the popes become intelligible, and in decisive points, partially justified, when seen from this angle.) Let us note in passing one or two illuminating examples.

Perhaps the crudest of all particular cases was that the Leipzig disputation was able to take place at all, even after Luther's indulgence theses and all of his devastating utterances. Amongst the questions discussed was whether or not salvation could be attained without any co-operation from the human will; again, the celebrated thirteenth thesis claimed that the primacy of the pope rested merely on inconclusive decrees dated between 1100 and 1500. The naïve remark of the loyal Catholic Duke George of Saxony to Luther in 1519 reveals a great deal. He said that it was immaterial whether the power of the pope rested upon divine or human law: he was still the pope. Theological vagueness had reached such a state that people could declare the prime issue to be of no importance.

In 1518 the bishop of Brandenburg requested Luther to withhold his indulgence manifesto, although its entire contents were good Catholic doctrine. In the end he permitted its printing, including the important resolutions to the indulgence theses.

In 1530 the theologian, Cochlaeus, reviewing the period around 1519, wrote that then the Catholics had enthusiastically accepted Luther's doctrine without the slightest hesitation or suspicion. At that time Cochlaeus had been first and foremost a humanist, able to write to Luther, in true Erasmian style, telling him that he should 'leave learning, religion, and the state in peace'. (Note that he puts learning in first place.) In fact, the two Franciscans, Quiñones and Glapion (imperial confessor), judged Luther very favourably as late as 1520. It was only the *Babylonian Captivity* that shook their trust. The same can be said of John Faber of Augsburg, who was particularly optimistic in his assessment of Luther.

After 1518 Frederick the Wise commended Luther as destroyer of indulgences; but in 1520, when Luther's attack had been in progress for two and a half years, he presented his much augmented treasury of papally indulgenced relics to the faithful with renewed vigour. At the same time he once again encouraged Luther to compose a book of sermons for the feast days.

In the discussion with Luther in Worms in 1521, after the celebrated hearing at the *Reichstag*, there was no mention of the authority of the pope, but merely of the authority of the Church and of the councils. In his address Vehus even named amongst the works that were of value to the Church, the sermon on good works and on twofold justification, and yet both are clear testimony to his Reformed view of justification by faith.

When Eck, in his capacity as apostolic nuncio, ordered the university of Vienna to take proceedings against Luther in terms of the *Litterae Apostolicae*, and to burn his writings, the university, with the exception of the theological faculty, raised a protest. Certainly the university made it quite plain that they would support no heresy. In spite of this, their refusal to act can be taken as their support of Luther. They cited from the proceedings at Worms only those things that were not unfavourable to Luther, and also the fact that Paris still had not condemned him.

As late as 1530, after the publication of Melanchthon's Augsburg Confession, there were still a few loyal Catholic bishops in Augsburg who were perfectly satisfied with its contents. Even although at that time Cochlaeus, like Eck and Fabri, was dogmatically clear-sighted, ten years later controversy and the longing to reach a reconciliation had conditioned him so that he would have accepted a declaration of the innovators that they subscribed to no other deviations from the Church's teaching than were contained in the Augsburg Confession. In 1532 the papal legates Campeggio and Aleander were informed in Regensburg that even the curia had been impressed by the Augsburg Confession.

Luther himself had experienced this theological vagueness in his own soul, for, until the Reformation revolution, his own theological development had proceeded by means of Occamism. And now in literary polemics he was repeatedly encountering the same thing. Although decidedly Lutheran in its exaggeration, Luther's reply to the papal nuncio, Vergerio, in 1535, had a bitter taste for Catholics: '*We* do not need a council, but your poor people do, for you do not know what you believe.'

This sort of extensive and deep theological vagueness obviously had the most serious consequences for the mind of the age. For a long time the nation were not nearly so aware of having fallen into enemy camps as we now are inclined to suppose. As yet people could not be labelled simply 'Catholic' or 'Lutheran'. In its beginnings and right down into the forties of the century Reformation history was not a straightforward battle between two clearly marked separate entities. Even as the division became ever clearer, for a long time the schism was still not felt to be decisive and irreparable. In the concrete situation for a long time the individual did not know to which group he belonged, or where the boundary ran between this and that doctrine and way of life. Just as Luther had grown away from the Church unintentionally, and for many years preached his doctrine as genuine Catholic doctrine, so for a very long time many of his contemporaries did not see his doctrine as radically separated from genuine Catholicism, but as its pure presentation, which the clergy were still free to accept, if only they would allow themselves to be 'reformed'. As yet the term 'reform' was no badge of heresy. For long enough the composition of the parties varied quite considerably. What was the Lutheran doctrine? It was still evolving. Even although at an early date it became dogmatically sharply differentiated from the old teaching of the Church, this was not realised. It is true that already many decisive writings of Luther were available, but even the extraordinary number who read them made up but a tiny section of the nation. A concise, official programme still had to be derived from Luther's works: a new confession of faith had to be written. The application of the new doctrines would first have to be sought in the practices of daily life and in public worship; and this was still a long way off. How manifold were the interests that appealed to the newly discovered gospel; and how various the corresponding doctrinal views! Moreover, the civil authorities took a hand in the reshaping of things; and what was it that motivated them? What were the beliefs of Philip of Hesse, when he threw in his lot with the innovators, what those of the Saxon electors, and later, of the electors of Brandenburg, Nuremberg and Strassburg?

Conversely: what did Catholic profession mean? Trent was still in the future. The late scholastic development, as we have seen, embraced strange contradictions within itself. How were uneducated and theologically ignorant chaplains to find their way in this labyrinth? What is more, these same chaplains had no sense whatever of any kind of independence, for they were all appointed by one or more patrons, and regarded themselves as the mere protégés of these men. These clergy, especially at the start of the second decade of the century, were in no position to distinguish between the old religion and the new, or to teach according to the one or the other – in so far as they taught anything at all on their own initiative. Most decisive of all, they were in no position at all to see the essential difference between the Catholic doctrine of the holy sacrifice of the mass and Luther's doctrines; and they certainly could not defend the Catholic doctrine against Luther's attack.

II. LUTHER AS INTERPRETER AND MOTIVE POWER OF THE AGE: THE REFORMER IN THE MAKING

The fate of a new idea depends utterly upon its ability to create a body for itself, by which it is sustained and spread. The initial voice must attract an audience, and this in turn must provide new voices who take up the preaching of the message. The leader must have his loyal henchmen in battle.

Luther found and formed such a circle, first of all in the lecture room, then amongst his colleagues in the university of Wittenberg, then within his order.

His whole inner theological revolution had already been accompanied by the deep conviction that theology was in need of re-formation in the sense of being infused with new life. This side of his interior revolution had been guided and fulfilled by the Bible, St Augustine and the mystics. Even in Luther's earliest declarations we can discern how violently he rejected the emptiness of theological activity, how he refused to accept formulae without examination, how he was quick to sense accretion, and able to get back to the heart of things. In exegesis he desired to get behind the commentators to the text and context of the Bible; and in Church history he desired to break through legend and falsehood and arrive at facts. The state of all of these things hurt him – 'offended him', he said. He read the sources. As well as Augustine he read Jerome, whom he placed as far behind Augustine as Erasmus placed him in front of Augustine. Although he perceptibly moved more and more away from Erasmus, because he knew that ignorance amongst the regular and secular clergy must be opposed and new decisive truths uncovered, he made common cause with Erasmus, whom he hailed as a confederate.

His progress, in sharp distinction to the humanists, did not arise in intellectual zeal or genius (1518), in 'dead intellectual', philosophical knowledge, as had happened in almost all thinkers after Augustine (1516), but was closely allied to the concern of the struggling Christian. Bible study must always begin with prayer; when he declared the meaning of scripture to Spalatin, it was God who inspired him, 'for none is teacher of the divine words but the author of the word himself'.

This was the spirit which moulded the lectures that soon made him the centre of attraction in the university. What stimulus it gave him to see how he was making breach after breach in the former management of the university! 'By the power of God our theology and St Augustine grow and rule in our university. The students no longer make sense of the expositions of the *Sentences*. It is the Bible and St Augustine who now attract the audiences.' A revolution had taken place which drove a wedge between the spirit of the youth and the declining old teachers. Luther's hope was that true Christian theology, that had not been understood by the masters, would become a household possession amongst the youth. His theology was simply what Christ had taught him, and – 'why has he not taught me to speak otherwise?'

How tensely they waited to see if the university would be remodelled according to the proposals set before the elector. 'What an opportunity to reform all of the universities and do away with universal barbarism!'

The sense of intellectual eruption was so strong in this very year – 1518 – that it persisted even in face of the threatened Roman process. The summons to Rome implied a serious threat. It was a matter of life and death. None the less, on 1 September 1518, Luther informed Staupitz that he remained completely unconcerned in mind and heart. The trials which assailed him were of quite another kind. His self-assurance was extraordinary: enthusiastically he tells of the mounting prestige of Wittenberg, which was developing its own brand of theology, clearly corresponding to a notable public need. In the middle of his report he expresses enthusiasm for the chair of Greek. 'We are all enthusiastic about learning Greek.' And then he becomes fearful on account of his assurance: 'Pray for me,' he concludes, 'lest in this temptation I find too much joy and confidence.'

We must be clear as to the significance of the emergence of a

Lutheran university in Wittenberg. The importance lay in the future, with the youth and their immense creative powers. In this place an important source of power was being formed, from which very soon a ceaseless flow would emerge of those who had fallen under Luther's spell, the prophets of the new anti-Catholic theories; and these men would carry the message into the whole empire and beyond. By 1521 Cochlaeus had become aware of the magnitude of this danger. He wrote to Aleander to say that the peace of the Church could be assured only if the whole Wittenberg nest was destroyed. From then on the suppression of Wittenberg remained part of his programme – and of Eck's.

The circle around Luther widened out beyond the limits of schools and orders. This was of prime importance. We must guard against calling all of these supporters 'Lutheran' in the dogmatic sense. Precisely in this field do we see theological vagueness at work, harmful to the Church, favourable to innovation.

Trying to assess the new spirit at the time of the Reuchlin controversy, Pirkheimer had mentioned in one breath Erasmus, Reuchlin, Mutian as well as Eck, Cochlaeus, Murner, Emser and Oecolampadius. As one amongst many he had named Luther also. The general intellectual situation was still quite confused. Hardly anyone realised the true significance of Luther. Even Mutian only knew him as the one-time musician and philosopher from Erfurt who wanted to restore 'true piety' (*recta pietas*). All around, public opinion was with him and his attitude – far beyond the circle of those who were ready to go with him all the way. It was this wider circle that made Luther a really popular figure. And it was the humanists who were the decisive factor in the construction of this wider public. They were the propagandists of the age, until the preachers took over. All sympathies were with the reckless and inspiring prophet of a deepened Christianity and castigator of a degenerate Church, who seemed at last to be blazing the trail to true renewal. In Luther all the liveliest interests and fervent hopes of national and Church life seemed to be so assured, that the dogmatic rupture involved in his criticism and protest was easily overlooked. People applauded the protester and religious reformer, and failed to see the revolutionary. How hard it must have been for a man like Cochlaeus to keep his head when tossed back and fore between the different aspects of Luther.

Luther's further theological development was linked first of all with the indulgence controversy. The true germ of development grew of itself out of the ninety-five theses, becoming clearer and clearer. That is to say: the issue was that of the power of the pope, of the authentic teaching office. The whole idea of the Church was under examination. Luther could not find a lawful basis for this Church in scripture. There was nothing new in that; but he failed to find it in scripture as he interpreted scripture. In so far as he understood scripture he felt himself bound by scripture as by the voice of God. This, then, is the explosive point: he, an individual, claimed the right to determine the content of scripture.

The inner dynamic as well as the tragedy of this development lay in the fact that official theology and official places in Rome made insufficient distinction between the clear and essential substance of faith and peripheral things; that the scope of spiritual power was insufficiently defined. It was not so much a question of whether or not there was another source of revelation outside scripture, but rather of the assertion that things were being preached in Rome that were contrary to scripture.

The year 1518 was like the clearing of long choked sluices. Luther was already partially aware of the nature of the battle upon which he had entered. Even after allowances have been made for a certain amount of rhetoric, his statements still display considerable trust in God: 'I am still saddled with this body of nothingness, weakened by many and constant trials. If you do away with it I am but an hour or two poorer in terms of this life. All I need is my kindly Redeemer, Jesus Christ. I will praise him as long as I live. I am unconcerned either about fame or shame, and neither of these will stand in my way. God will see' (to Staupitz, 1518). Tetzel's replies to the theses appeared and were burned by Luther's students in Wittenberg. The Dominicans were preaching against the new heresy. Eck's *Obelisci* on the indulgence theses aroused Luther's anger. Indeed, Eck condemned the theses without having properly understood them. Was there no theologian alive besides Eck? 'In all of his hotchpotch there is no theology at all, nothing of the Bible, that is. It is all scientific whimsicality, sheer dreaming and presumption. I admit that it is all true – if one accepts the theories of the schoolmen. But I deny what Eck affirms. He drowns in the wisdom of the schools, and smells of

Aristotle . . . ' Luther clung to an utterly different mode of thought. In May the Augustinians held their general chapter in Heidelberg, and it was Luther's task to dispute on sin, grace and the absence of free will. As we have seen, he completely ruled out all trace of goodness in human action (p. 211). Once again he rejected Aristotle in favour of a more lively and affective surrender of the will, as advocated by Plato and Pythagoras.

It was in the year 1518 also that the hearing of Luther by Cardinal Thomas Vio de Cajetano took place. Cajetan had come as papal legate to the *Reichstag* at Augsburg.

Seeing his large-scale monetary schemes endangered by Luther's opposition to indulgences, the archbishop of Mainz reported to Rome. His report would seem to have been made without undue haste and without personal rancour. In February Leo X still regarded the squabble as a small matter. He ordered the new general of the Augustinians to call his subject, brother Martin, to order. In June a process was initiated against Luther on suspicion of heresy; and in July he was summoned to appear at Rome within sixty days.

On 7 August Luther received the summons. The very next day he went to his friend Spalatin (George Burkhard of Spalt, 1485–1545), the most influential clerical secretary to the elector Frederick of Saxony. He examined the possibility of keeping the case within the country.

Meanwhile a radical advance had taken place in Rome. In August, Maximilian and the *Reichstag* had requested the pope to initiate proceedings against Luther. Through some anonymous influence, Luther was declared an heretic after a secret and summary process. As a result, a brief dated 23 August was sent to Cajetan, directing him to treat Luther as an heretic, to take him in custody, to excommunicate all of his supporters and interdict his place of residence. The elector was commanded to hand Luther over.

There was nothing astonishing about this behaviour. Indeed, it was only to be expected. There were quite enough reasons. Luther had preached revolutionary sermons on the impotence of the bann of excommunication. He declared that it was a purely human invention, and, like the whole claim the pope made to secular power, originated in hell. It was all part of the general corruption of the Church; and Luther now proceeded to expound the nature of the Church in a totally different fashion. 'If you are unlawfully excommunicated, you ought not to give in. If, as a result, you die without the sacraments, good for you! Count yourself blessed – you will receive the crown of life.' This was, in fact, an ancient Catholic idea. Lazarus Spengler exaggerates greatly when he says that excommunication 'sends a man straight to everlasting damnation'. It is true, however, that the language of the curial chancelleries with all its deliberate vagueness certainly encouraged this frightful concept. In the context of revolutionary ideas in the Church and by the tone in which it was expressed, Luther's declaration was nothing but Catholic in its effect.

And yet an astonishing thing did happen. A mighty revolt took place. The process in Rome was suspended. The elector, who had complied with Luther's suggestion, carried out his design: the case was kept in Germany. More than this – Cajetan was ordered to give Luther a fatherly hearing and let him return unmolested to Wittenberg. This illogicality was fraught with serious consequences. The theological vagueness of the age, and the disruptive caprice, which Paul III's reforming cardinals had once declared to be the real root in the curia of all evil, now appeared in all its stark reality. This time the consequences were to threaten the life of the Church.

What, then, had happened? A new Roman king had to be elected while the ruling emperor was still alive. The pope opposed Charles I of Spain, Maximilian's nominee. Thus he became the natural ally of the elector of Saxony, who in addition was prepared to ask the *Reichstag* to approve the Turkish tax.

Now we come to that point in the development which was able to decide whether or not the Reformation would actually take place. To this extent it was one of the most important moments in the whole of Church history and of German history.

Rome at that time was much less capable than Germany of making even an approximate forecast of the devastating consequences which would result from the dragging out of a process against a German monk. Unfortunately this incapacity in no way lessened the damage to the Church which actually resulted from this delay. Nor was the damage lessened by the fact that this delay had its origin in a secularisation of the Church's administration, long since censured by holy servants of the Church. It was common-place for most of the Renaissance popes to subordinate the interests of the Church and religion to those of the world. But now, right in the middle of the radical attack, the whole fatal immensity of this shift of the centre of gravity disclosed itself.

Cajetan's fatherly consultation with Luther in Augsburg came to nothing. Luther had refused to recant. In spite of this refusal and Luther's appeal to the pope, after his being better informed of the case, in spite of his flight from Augsburg, even in spite of his appeal to a council, the process against Luther remained at a standstill (as far as its effect was concerned) from November 1518 until September 1520. Not until the latter date did Eck enter Germany with the bull of excommunication. It is true that after the imperial election in September 1519, the proceedings were set going once again in Rome; but nothing really happened until the sessions of May 1520. Not until June 1520 was the bull of excommunication, *Exsurge*, issued.

There had been a delay of almost two years, a delay for which the pope must personally share the blame. Certainly after the hearing in Augsburg, the papal decree on indulgences appeared, putting Luther in the wrong; and Cajetan demanded that Frederick hand Luther over. At the end of 1518 the curia sent the Saxon papal chamberlain, Miltiz, to Germany, to see to the hand-ing over of Luther. This, however, was a secondary commission. His other objective was more important and very much at logger-heads with the first. He had to win over the electors by conferring temporal favours. This activity of Miltiz – still going on in 1519–20 – was important because it showed how an issue of the utmost importance for the Church could fall into the hands of a conceited, second-rate curial official, and could be misused as a means of satisfying the vanity and avarice of a little upstart. In October 1519 the new papal legate Jerome Aleander once again demanded the surrender of Luther to the pope by the electors, and that they initiate the customary proceedings against the writings and ad-herents of an heretic. Neither of these things was set about with any vigour.

It is true that exaggerated Roman self-consciousness blinded men to the colossal danger. Sheer physical distance made understanding of the manifold and confused happenings in Germany difficult. But how can this excuse the guide of the Church, the responsible teacher of its inviolable truth, the representative of quite unambiguous anti-heretical canon law? The declaring of someone an heretic is certainly not liable to modulation.

The total result was this: the curia allowed the man who had already been declared a notorious heretic – although not publicly – two years in which to establish his cause amongst the public. This two-year respite was decisive, for nothing so favours the growth of an idea as time for undisturbed taking root.

This principle was operative here in a high degree, because in these two years national, religious, humanist and political forces grouped themselves mightily around Luther, and for the first time turned his activity into a threat to the existence of the Church. The early years, 1517–21, when Luther was still in the full flush of his religious output and zeal, when he fired popular imagination with his celebrated 'No' at Worms, when the Reformation was taking root largely as a religious and anticurial movement, facing no planned and efficient threat to its growth – these years by themselves were decisive for the Reformation.

It has been truly said that perhaps nothing would seem to justify Luther so much as the curia's deferring his energetic suppression in favour of the passing Italian political interests of the papal state (Stadelmann).

And so, Luther was ordered to appear at Augsburg. He was there from 7 October until 20–21 October.

Four hearings took place before the cardinal. According to Luther these became drawn out into conferences and disputations; and they were supplemented by several letters from Luther to the cardinal.

These hearings once again made it clear that Luther rejected the theological idea of the Church as something objectively given and objectively efficacious, and that he exclusively stressed the idea of personal faith. Luther, however, proceeding from an attack upon externalism and materialism, only saw contradictions, when in fact only the power of synthesis would have made a true judgment possible. Abuse would have had to be rejected and personal faith extolled, without falling into the trap of ultimate subjectivism.

That which Cajetan meant by 'Church', and that which he demanded in the name of the Church, were significantly more than Protestant representations allowed. The issue was not just that of the hierarchical concept of power, but fundamentally of the sacramental objectivity of the Church.

Luther's conferences with Cajetan were his first direct contact with the official Roman curia. The primary fact was that in Luther's eyes the cardinal was identified with the scholastic theology for which Luther had long since lost all respect, and which, encouraged by an almost unbounded sense of his own *biblical* superiority, he suspected and despised as totally opposed to Christian doctrine. In this frame of mind he now disposed of the cardinal. Writing from Augsburg to Wittenberg he said that the cardinal had absolutely no understanding of his theology. That was true, for in the cardinal's eyes Luther destroyed the Church, and in Luther's eyes the sophistries by which the cardinal meant to honour the Church, were a denial of Christ.

It was at Augsburg that Luther's breach with the curia first became public. His appeal to the pope when better informed – repeated at Augsburg on 16 October – was already a protest against the pope. With an inner logic there followed at once (after his secret flight) an appeal from the pope to a council (28 November).

The most significant thing is undoubtedly the colossal impudence of Luther's tone in Augsburg, his unbounded independence in face of the papal decrees. He charged them with the distortion of scripture, just as he condemned the cardinal for denying Christianity. All these things were but the words of men, and of that he had no fear whatever. In particular, the theory of the pope's superiority over a council was sheer pernicious adulation. In the first conference with Miltiz – in the same year – he opposed the pope as his equal, as though both of them were engaged in a dispute about the Bible: 'The pope will acknowledge no judge, neither will I bow to his judgment.' Soon after (1519) he testified to Miltiz that he suspected that in Augsburg the cardinal was trying to lead him away from the Christian faith. It is not surprising that afterwards Luther was not sure if Cajetan was a Catholic Christian at all.

The key question is about to be asked: is the Roman Church

Christian? In theory the dogmatic breach with the Church had long since been made. It was realised in fact, through Luther's meeting with the cardinal. Luther now faced the consequences for the Church of his fundamental convictions.

As with the indulgence theses all subsequent separate events grew far beyond their planned intention, by a kind of hidden infection. The hearing before Cajetan in Augsburg became an expression and encouragement of resistance to Rome. Luther gave a German expression to accumulated anti-Roman feeling. The fact that pure theology could appear as a side issue caused the hearing and Luther's defiance to become a lever for the German–Lutheran rising. Luther was not alone before Cajetan. He was surrounded by a great wave of deep sympathy, and this was already preparing the way for dogmatic revolt. It prepared for this without, for the most part, suspecting what the consequences would be. Indeed, considering the theological and politico-ecclesiastical evolution of the two preceding centuries, no one was able to guess the consequences. Just as Luther had grown away from the Church without meaning to do so, finding himself outside her dogma before he knew it, so the Reformation happened before it was recognised as a change of faith, and because it was not recognised as such.

The year 1518 already brings us to the end of the antipapal line which Luther had begun with his attack, in the indulgence theses, on the papal power of the keys. It had continued in the resolutions attached to the theses, in his defiance of excommunication, and through his appeal to the pope better informed. In his discussion with Cajetan the threatening necessity of breaking with the Roman Church had already appeared. And now, in December 1518, Luther felt that 'the whole affair had not really begun'. For the first time we hear the slogan that was to make the breach even wider: the pope appeared in the role of Antichrist. Thesis thirteen of the Leipzig disputation, which decided the breach, was to be no more than the historical garment clothing this thought.

These years reached their climax in 1519 with the disputation between Karlstadt, Luther and Eck, during the days of the imperial election in June–July. This interrupted that period of comparative calm in the struggle, marked by Miltiz, the gift of the golden rose to Frederick the Wise, and Luther's moderate 'Instruction upon some articles proposed by his patrons' (1519). The disputation set the fire alight. The affair was now advertised throughout the whole intellectual world, and this time there was one straight issue: the papacy or not?

In his commentary on the indulgence theses Luther had spoken of a time when, as under Gregory I (590–604), Rome had not been set over all Churches, at least not over those of Greece. In his published report of his transactions with Cardinal Cajetan in Augsburg he had supported the same statement with the assertion that the Bible could produce no proof of Rome's supremacy over the Church. Meanwhile Eck, who, after the indulgence theses, had guessed that Luther would become the radical opponent of the pope, had chanced to meet Luther's colleague Andreas Bodenstein from Karlstadt. With Luther's partial consent a disputation was arranged. When Eck published his theses, the twelfth – later the thirteenth – was directed against Luther: 'We deny that the Roman Church before the time of Sylvester (314–35) was not set over the other Churches. On the contrary we recognise the occupant of the see of Peter in every age as the successor of Peter and the universal disciple of Christ.'

Nowadays the details dealt with in this disputation are of interest mainly to the history of theology. They erupt, however, into history at large in two ways. The disputation made evident important forces in the battle of the Reformation, and forced Luther to draw epoch-making conclusions.

The forces were revealed in the personalities taking part, and not only in the actual disputants but also in the humanist–theological public who followed the disputation in tense expectancy, and who afterwards expressed their views in a wealth of animated signed and anonymous writings. The Leipzig disputation represented a further, decisive step by Luther into public life. This disputation exerted its influence beyond the schools and became a matter of wide ecclesiastical and intellectual interest. The reason was very simple. Out of the overlaying debris of trivialities questions were once again being raised that affected the deepest things in man. What is man's place in the process of redemption? Does he play his part in this, as Eck affirmed, or is his will utterly powerless, as Karlstadt affirmed? Is man active or passive, that is,

I

in the process of redemption? In this process does he stand directly before his God, as Luther said, or is the papacy a mediator for man, by divine law, as the Church and Eck, its representative, would have it? Although Luther and Karlstadt may claim their share in the purely theological work of this disputation, in the end we are faced with a clash between the religious and the theological–speculative attitude.

Andreas Bodenstein of Karlstadt had studied with the Dominicans in Cologne, and since 1507 had been introducing their method at Wittenberg. Luther and he thus came from two opposite philosophical and theological schools. A journey to Rome in 1514 had had a much stronger anticurial effect upon Karlstadt than upon Luther. Luther had taken his doctorate in theology under Karlstadt.

Within the circle of Luther's collaborators, Karlstadt was the important type of the mediocre teacher. He arrived at originality only late in life, he vacillated quite a bit, until finally he despaired of the work of his youth and of his more recent years, and decided that theology was nonsensical and superfluous. He was the type, however, that, despite ambition, always preserves honourable intentions.

Dr John Eck, the precocious child who at eleven knew the scriptures almost by heart, was the type of scholar who has a colossal memory. He was the typical master with considerable ambition. He mastered the whole science of his time, especially theology, with unerring, almost playful, ease. He knew the available sources and all theses and their possible solutions. He was second to none in drawing distinctions. All these things, however, were possessed or done intellectualistically: he never gave himself to the subject. His ease was not that of the genius but of the highly gifted master. He knew everything – that was taken for granted. But for him there were no burning problems; nor was there in him any kind of painful, interior, creative disturbance.

Eck was a man with a loud voice, a master in the art of disputation, which was used as a means of establishing the world championship in learning – rather like the crowning of a bard in the cultural sphere. He had won fame in the most important universities – even in Italy. Now it would be a feather in his cap if he could unseat him who, alongside Erasmus, was perhaps the most celebrated man of his time. This would bring him all the more renown as the issues at stake were so basic.

Eck achieved his end. In the disputation he did overthrow Luther. The majority admitted this; even Luther admitted it in a half-hearted way. (It is true that Luther's statements vary a great deal. In one of his writings attacking the Church humanists like Duke George and Jerome Emser, his report of the disputation is an excess of pride.) Eck knew more than Luther, not to mention the stammering Karlstadt with his laborious textbook quotations.

All the same, Eck was deceiving himself. As far as he was concerned the Leipzig disputation was not a responsible performance. It generated no religious power. His letters dated at that time betray a painful lack of any religious or moral commitment, and reveal overweening ambition. And to indulge this fully, Eck perpetrated a petty, useless deceit, and allowed himself to be aided by Karlstadt. Because he initiated no religious impetus his words remained lifeless. They served merely the purpose of correct formulation; the audience took nothing permanent and living away.

From Luther's angle things were quite the opposite. He knew less than Eck did, and he kept repeating himself; but his whole personality was fighting for an intrinsically decisive experience. The old words he quoted were new because he had painfully and laboriously rediscovered them for himself. The Leipzig disputation became a mighty proof of the impotence of dead rectitude in the face of living totality, even when it undertook such an impossible task as corroborating thesis thirteen.

This thirteenth thesis of Luther's in turn shows how Luther viewed everything to do with the papacy in the Church from the periphera. Luther was able to prepare his thesis only because by the papacy he understood chiefly the plenitude of secular power, although his thesis covered much more, viz. the primacy of jurisdiction.

The battle over this thirteenth thesis resulted in the struggle moving out into the wider fields of Church and world history; thus the Leipzig disputation of 1519 must be counted as one of the decisive moments in the Reformation.

Before the disputation even Luther had no clear view of his goal: 'God is drawing me and I follow without resisting.' He said also: '. . . the disputation concerns only the scholars . . .' At the disputation Luther's attitude then displayed a curious mixture of erratic, bold advance with a fearful hesitation at the thought of the consequences. Now he was becoming aware of what hitherto had been hidden – that he had to choose between his own theory of redemption, which he had always assumed to be identical with the teaching of the Church, and the primacy of the pope. It was Eck who forced a decision upon him. Luther's view was that no Christian is bound to believe anything that is not found in scripture. Indeed, to believe any such thing is forbidden. This raised the problem of Huss and the Hussites whom Luther abhorred. There could never be any justification for schism from the Roman Church. Admittedly, amongst the articles proposed by Huss and condemned by the Council of Constance there were some that were most Christian. Eck now had Luther in a cleft stick: Luther immediately argued against the councils in a form that could cost him his reputation in Germany. He attacked Constance, the pride of Germany, the council at which the Germans had saved the unity of the Church. And so he was a Hussite after all. If the Council of Constance – an ecumenical council – condemned Christian propositions, had it erred?

And so Luther was caught: he admitted that even councils can err.

Luther had gone much further than simply to deny the divine right of the papacy. He radically attacked the Catholic concept of the Church.

Once again the theological confusion of the times was shockingly revealed. Before the disputation the universities of Paris and Erfurt had agreed to act as arbiters. They would decide who had won. That is to say, people thought that it was a case of a purely scholastic opinion being proposed against the hitherto *opinio communis*. In fact we find that contemporary literature did view the disputation in that light. But the judges pronounced no judgment. This expressed the fact that the disputation had exploded the idea of the validity of scholastic comment. There was no longer any common ground from which to judge. Who was the victor? We are still asking this question, for it is an improper question. The fact that none of the theological faculties unequivocally condemned Luther, that not even Eck's own university, Ingolstadt, dared to judge, shows the confused intellectual leaderlessness of the Church party, and the vagueness of their position. In 1521 the theological faculty at Vienna were still appealing to the silence of Paris in order to avoid committing themselves to a decision.

The absence of a verdict from the universities produced an appropriate substitute – a deluge of statements from both sides, from participants and others, of tractates and anonymous pamphlets. The decisive theme had been announced, and Luther had given a revolutionary answer. Still, people did not see clearly, but the age instinctively sensed that something critical was happening.

And now Luther's own development became completely dominated by the admissions made during the Leipzig disputation, that pope and council can err and had erred. Hitherto he had measured his assertions against the standard of the Church in a very casual way, but now he plainly rejected the Church. As a result he denied the visibility of the Church, and, correspondingly, cut himself off from tradition as a binding force in matters of faith. So, too, he cut himself off from the fathers, Augustine specially included. In this way the whole life and history of Christendom was disorientated and called in question. The house, in which till now Christendom had dwelt, no longer existed. He had to build life up again from the start; and his programme for this venture was set out in the great Reform writings of 1520.

In the year 1520 Luther really and truly broke victoriously through to the nation.

In spite of the colossal controversy going on around him since 1519, he was still far from being the central figure of the age. In 1519 it was Erasmus who was able to herald the coming golden age – albeit for the last time. Luther, on the other hand, as a genuine public force stood alone, in spite of the humanist circles who supported him and even greeted him with jubilation. But in 1520 Luther became the master of a huge section of the nation, while simultaneously the Church's official decision and the active sector of its theological propagandists went against him.

The course of events is characterised on the one hand by the Roman process, on the other by his personal advance displayed in the great manifestos of 1520.

All of these writings converge on one theological point: faith is the whole of Christian life; thus there is no special, but only the universal, priesthood. A fundamental principle of medieval society, the division into spiritual and secular, was gone. A multitude of consequences issued on all sides.

This was much more than a theological statement. The line of argument followed at Leipzig was moving on. The manifestos of 1520 were of world historical importance precisely because they were of more than mere technical theological interest. Luther now stood right at the centre of the universal, surging life of the people, a people in a state of elemental excitement in search of something new. He was now the sustainer, as he had been the instigator, of that mighty universal ferment that was destroying the old world and ushering in a new one, in pain and tumult. He was no longer in a monastic cell, nor yet in a study, but out in a world that was changing, that *he* was changing.

For this reason, after the Leipzig disputation Luther wrote increasingly in German. He felt himself more and more cut off from the professional theologians, and he began to address himself to the laity. In harmony with this, his style became intimate and spiritual rather than technical. In line with this development, too, was the outward form – concise and handy. His works could be bought by all for a few pence. A similar change came over Catholic counter propaganda. Those who still wrote heavy tomes were living in the past.

Luther's manifestos of 1520, both in content and in form, represent his historically most important utterances as a Reformer. They were the purest as they were the most effective expression of his views. They still have these qualities today. They were of the utmost importance in fanning the blazing brand into a German national conflagration.

It was only later on that Luther took up a stand on many quite central questions – the fanatics, the peasants, Zwingli in 1529, or those enshrined in his later Christological statements, which undoubtedly represent his most profound contribution to theology. But all of these questions fit in only accidentally to the framework laid down in 1520. In forcefulness of expression or direct connection with the revolution in process, they come nowhere near the manifestos. Moreover, with the exception of the legendary reminiscences of the *Table Talk*, which provides a caricature of his Catholic period, they did not permeate the general mind of Protestantism. Besides the catechism and the songs, the thing that really exercised a universal effect was the manifestos of 1520. (The Bible cannot be included in this context.)

The contents of these documents were important indeed; but we must note, too, that they were effortlessly composed and poured out, as though by some subjective necessity, packed full of ideas and images and gripping appeal; that they bore within themselves the sign of a call to rise to the fatal opportunities of the hour; that they exactly fitted the appointed time.

We must not interpret the word 'manifesto' as though Luther had proceeded in a theoretical and constructive way. These manifestos were, rather, professions that were born directly of dialogue with the times. But the fact that Luther fastened with such assurance upon essential points, thus creating a real programme, is proof of the inner logic of his now heretically based development.

There are three documents which appeared within the space of three short months – from mid-August to mid-November. (a) *To the Christian Nobility of the German Nation*, concerning the raising of the Christian level. (b) *On the Babylonian Captivity of the Church* (in Latin). (c) *On the Freedom of the Christian Man*.

(a) The title of the first document is instructive. The national theme is clearly incorporated, and no limit is set to the improvement contemplated. It was to be all embracing.

Its prime object, therefore, was not so much to demand that the nobility reform their own ranks, as to call upon them to improve the state of Christendom, which was in such a bad way. Because the clerical estate are so useless, the laity themselves must play the part of physician. The enormous advance of the lay element from the thirteenth century onwards, its increasing involvement in ecclesiastical affairs, and its competition with the one-sidedly clericalised Church, which was simultaneously developing in precise parallel and antagonism, now reached its climax. The laity gathered up all their hatred and rage against Rome in order, with revolutionary voice, to proclaim their own rights within the Church. Since Wycliffe's time there was nothing new in stressing these rights. What was new was that the colossal revolt against Rome of many Germans, who were more Catholic in mind than inclined to heresy, saw this variously interpreted lay self-help as the only way out of the situation.

The intellectual situation was very much as it had been during the western schism after the nineties of the fourteenth century, when the endless, universally admitted distress of the times had caused the idea of emergency law and self-help to assert itself in face of the failures of the curia. The only difference was that then a host of well-meant proposals, varying greatly in pertinence, had been all mixed up together; but there had never been a leader to make them effective. Now the greater part of Germany acknowledged an absolute leader and incomparable spokesman – Luther. In great measure this was because so many failed to see that a breach in faith was involved, and because nearly everybody was intent, with every justification, on attacking unspeakable abuses, especially the abuse of papal power. For whatever reason, they accepted Luther as leader. For his part he used this position mightily to advance his cause.

Luther placed the whole issue on the simplest possible basis; and in face of the colossal opposition that there was to Rome, the formula he chose was inevitably attractive: the priesthood of all believers. 'All Christians possess a truly spiritual status and amongst them there is no distinction save that of function. This arises because we possess one baptism, one faith, one gospel, and are equal as Christians. Anyone who has emerged from the waters of baptism may pride himself on already being ordained priest, bishop or pope, although not everyone may be suited to exercise such an office. Therefore let every congregation elect a devout citizen to be their priest.' No lengthy explanation was needed, to show how indefinite the concept of priest had now become, and how necessary it was that it should remain vague.

Here at last was a radical solution to the problem of the coming of age, the declaring responsible, of the members of the Church. The air was filled with a host of demands for independence in all spheres of life – social, intellectual (humanist) and religious. Luther's call was like the conceding at last of a long-deprived right.

This book shows how fatal had been the effect of the one-sided administration of the Church in favour of the clergy. And it had not even been done lawfully. Seen from the angle of the innovators, the whole Reformation can appropriately be described as a protest against this clericalism – a protest of the ordinary Christian against clerical exploitation. This exploitation extended beyond the fiscal sphere. Luther, the shaker of foundations, was much more deeply gripped by the idea that the ordinary Christian had been defrauded of his rights as a Christian. Since the thirteenth century at least, the active enlistment of the laity in the work of the hierarchical apostolate as a fruit of the Church's educational programme, had been overdue amongst the now autonomous nations. But Avignon and the Renaissance, i.e. the mighty secularisation of the papal secular power, had interrupted the line of development providentially set in motion by Francis of Assisi, himself a layman, with his third order. Instead, development had been diverted into aristocratic egoism. Scarcely a trace was left of the spiritual, strictly churchmanlike freedom with regard to excommunication and interdict, that had still been known in the twelfth century, and expressed by such people as St Hildegard. The Reformation saw itself as a revolt against ecclesiastical oppression.

This verdict is not invalidated by pointing to the increased and obviously freely given support which the Church enjoyed during and after the Reformation. Loyalty to the Church at that time does not cancel criticism.

From the fundamental conviction that there are not two distinct ranks within Christendom but only one, it followed that the precedence of Rome could no longer continue. Rome can claim neither the sole right to interpret scripture correctly, nor to call an ecumenical council. These rights belong rather to every Christian. We must take good note of this declaration if we would understand the impetus and the inevitability with which the laity called out for a German council at the next *Reichstag*. The structure of the Church had become a human organisation. The radical declericalisation of the notion of the Church on the one hand, and its democratisation on the other, were accomplished. Because the rulers of the Church now were seen to have mere human authority, for the most part they were subjected to deadly attack.

And now, juridically, economically and in religion, the idea of national autonomy pressed into the foreground. Just as people ought to have a large measure of economic autarchy (away with luxury, expensive foreign groceries, the immoral merchant class and the ravages of interest!), so every country ought to have its own special type of law. (What a fearful dissolution of the empire was thereby legitimated!) Most important of all, at the head of the German Church there ought to be a German archbishop with his own ecclesiastical court, in which the pope has no voice at all. Annates ought to be retained by the princes in the country, as in France.

If we go through the complaints and demands which Luther listed as an agenda for a coming council we repeatedly encounter disarming lack of understanding of historically evolved forms. The picture of Roman abuses in life and in administrative practice and legal prescriptions is built up in a one-sided fashion. His vivid descriptions of these things, as though that was all there was to the papacy, makes bitter reading. We will meet Luther's lack of refinement again. The Reformer's limitations are most clearly seen in his unbridled extravagance of statement.

First of all we must see quite clearly the significance of these reproaches for the growth of the Reformed attitude. The whole of Germany was full of the mood expressed in the German *Gravamina*. The fury of this document was once again clearly formulated. Was such fury not justified? We recall that there had been countless complaints from loyal Churchmen. Karl von Bodmann summed it up: 'In Germany we are all of one mind, as far as such complaints are concerned – from the emperor down to the last beggar.' We are justified, therefore, in saying that in broad outline Luther's picture of unholy Roman fiscalism was perfectly correct.

And yet on the other hand, how terrible for Catholic ears is the crass climax of all this uproar, the statement that this rage and all of these castigating speeches find their justification in the conviction that the regiment of Rome is diabolical, leading eternal souls into everlasting destruction.

In passing verdict upon Luther, however, everything depends upon this question: what was his fundamental conviction and to what extent did he hold fast to it? If we say (above, p. 248) that he believed with all his heart that the pope was Antichrist, that no words were too violent to reject him, then Luther's appallingly destructive exaggerations appear as the logical one-sidedness of the true revolutionary who is blind to the redeeming features of the opposition. He sees nothing but abuses. Were he to see the ten per cent that is good the impact of his condemnation, which is not something for theologians but for the masses, would die away. Luther the revolutionary was utterly the slave of his own viewpoint He completely identified his cause with God's. It is true that he said his work and teaching would gain strength from persecution, and all he feared was that this would not happen. But that was only one side. His confidence urged him on to endless affirmations; and arrogance showed its ugly head. When he was thinking over his later *Babylonian Captivity* he wrote to Spalatin saying that he would 'stir up the Roman generation of vipers in quite a different way'.

His call went through the land in a veritable storm. We can no longer appreciate fully what it meant that within a few days four thousand copies were sold and edition upon edition followed. 'For the first time in German intellectual history the views of one man dominated the minds of the nation' (G. Wolf). Conversely, Luther became more and more aware that the nation were waiting for him to speak to them, and that he was called to lead the people.

(*b*) Close on the heels of this first manifesto came another, written in Latin, and aimed at a smaller circle – *On the Babylonian Captivity of the Church*. Of all that Luther wrote it is his most radical theological attack. The Church, he affirmed, was being held prisoner by the hitherto accepted sacramental doctrine. His attack was directed, not just at the seven sacraments but at the traditional concept of the sacraments, at the objectivity of the divine life present in the Church's liturgy. Thus Christianity became swallowed up in a religion of feeling at the very point where it was supposed to be fully protected against such subjectivity. The mysterious centre, which, by the law of growth, could have restored the unity of the Church in face of the heretical views of individuals or groups, had been challenged. The most fatal thing for the Catholic Church at the time of the Reformation was not the battle against the pope but the draining away of the objective source of power, the emptying of the authentic mystery.

At this point, as at so many others, we see clearly that the root of the fundamental Reformed attitude was Luther's individualistic, singular and personal way of thinking. It is the fact that he thought radically and experienced things only in terms of his personal conscience, never in terms of the living, objectively existent fellowship of the Church. The theological arguments with which he attacked the Church's views of the eucharist and the Church's withholding of the chalice is in line with this basic attitude. There is never a hint that the Church founded by Christ is the steward of revelation, that revelation, besides being found in scripture, must of necessity be expressed in the life of the Church, so that it is not enough to look for this life merely in the externals which were rightly being challenged.

On no account, however, may we overlook the way in which Luther appeared firmly to link even this protest with the simple, inescapable words of the gospel, and the power which he thereby put in the hands of the Christians of his own confession. And even if on this point he allowed himself latitude in terms of his very personal approach on the whole he seems to be significantly tied to the word of God. Undoubtedly this not only gave his battle most prospect of success and his heresy most appearance of justification but also made it a mighty and inescapable protest against externalism in the administration of the treasures of revelation.

More than this: in his denial of the objectivity of the sacraments Luther did not go the whole way. He left that to Zwingli and the fanatics. This was a fortunate circumstance for Christianity. As in Marburg in 1529, so here he held fast to 'This is my body.'

In addition, infant baptism remained the objective presupposition of the possibility of redemption. All baptised persons, that is, still formed a unity. Together with the real presence of our Lord in the Lord's Supper, this is the point at which a new sacramental fellowship in Christ may one day be able to restore the unity of the Church.

This confession of a limited objective power (of an *opus operatum*) would seem to be based upon an unusually weak theological foundation. Even here Luther's subjectivism powerfully makes itself felt. 'Believe, and you have already enjoyed.' The faith of the recipient is what effects the real presence of Christ, for the substance of the bread and the wine remain unaffected, without transubstantiation.

The full import is obvious. The specific sacramental office of the priesthood is done away with, without a word being said about it. It has simply become superfluous. Spiritualism wins the day. A special priestly office is of value at most as a pedagogical and pastoral function, requiring a special knowledge of scripture, to enable its holders to preach the word.

The section on matrimony is particularly instructive concerning Luther's theological and polemic technique. It reveals his tendency to simplify. He speaks of the subtle impediments to marriage, and asks that the subject be examined calmly and without prejudice, in the light of faith and natural prudence. Then, alongside the complicated regulations, he places the simple sentence of scripture: 'What God has joined let not man separate.'[2] Many of the regulations challenged seem so impossible that a casual word is enough to call their validity in question, so that they appear questionable to the readers, most of whom never pause to ask what justification one has for designating all of these regulations, without reservation, as sheer human arbitrariness. It is certain that here as elsewhere the weakness of Luther's theology consists in his failure to think in terms of the reality of the Church. He thinks entirely in terms of his own singular, individual personality, reading the Bible entirely on his own and constructing all things upon his own interpretation of it. This is the fundamental weakness of all heresy. But how many of his readers were able and wanted to put these preliminary questions, considering the immediate legitimacy of his criticism?

It amounts to this: Luther's sharp criticism arose again and again out of religious considerations, whether he was appealing to the freedom Christ brings, or fulminating against human multiplication of the occasions of sin and hence of sins, as a result of the proliferation of precepts.

In contrast to all this he laid claim to his freedom as to something that must never be lost. But how dangerous was the form in which he expressed this – an irresistible allurement to the subjective caprice of all antinomians! 'As I see it, there may have been holy and pious men who stipulated these impediments to marriage. But why should the sanctity of others burden my freedom? Why should I be restricted by the zeal of other men? Let him who wishes be as holy and as zealous as he likes, he will not rob me of my freedom.'

This document continues further in the same direction – the

[2] This is the place, too, where he expounds his revolutionary thesis of the lawfulness of clerical marriage.

battle against man's self-justification (especially that of monks) which had already been started in the ninety-five theses. Spiritual treasures and the kingdom of heaven belong to all good Christians without distinction. And so there is no question of monks being able (as Luther affirms), by repeated monastic baptisms, to divert all righteousness to themselves, leaving nothing over for ordinary baptised Christians.

All that is required to refute the radicalism of these complaints is to refer to the current theological views and the operative canonical prescriptions that were known to Luther. On the other hand we must not overlook the fact that the curia did not hold fast enough to those views, and that Luther even exploited this kind of self-refutation (as in the *Admonition* of 1530, *To my beloved Germans* in 1531, and elsewhere). Simoniacal sale of graces had become a widespread practice within the curia. All of the more recent studies, which show that the actual sums stated in the past have been considerably exaggerated, as has been the extent to which German benefices were exploited, cannot contradict the official statements of, say, the reform memorandum of the cardinals appointed by the pope in 1537, or of the personal recommendations of Cardinal Contarini in 1538 concerning reform of the benefice system. These documents explicitly state that curial practice ought to be independent of the extravagances of servile curial officials who inflate the power of the pope until it becomes the arbitrary sale of benefices, crowning their unchristian theory with the unheard of assertion that a pope cannot possibly commit simony. Contarini stresses particularly that 'these simoniacal abuses have destroyed the freedom of Christians and provoked books like *The Babylonian Captivity*.'

(c) *On the Freedom of the Christian Man* is Luther's most pious writing[3] Again it was written in German and was of special importance in expanding the circle of his adherents. It affected the whole of Christendom, even his opponents, by its sensitive simplicity and warm piety. It is here that Luther is closest to the Catholic atmosphere. The pamphlet became a Reformation pamphlet only in virtue of the one-sided views which had been expressed in its two

---

[3] Obviously this judgment sharply distinguishes between the book itself and the prefatory letter to Pope Leo X.

precursors. One of its basic views is that of the priesthood of all believers, already expressed in the letter to the nobility. With extraordinary evangelical depth and a fervour that came close to the people, Luther preached free surrender to the heavenly Father and the free Christian service of our brother that arises from that surrender.

There is a new element, too. With a tremendous feeling for the world and language of the synoptists he presents the gospel of Christ and forgiveness through faith in him. Frequently justification is portrayed in a thoroughly Catholic manner as something actual, just as the doctrine of the necessity of good works for the disciplining of one's own body and the advancement of Christian corporate life is affirmed.

Christian freedom, as Luther had already taught in *The Babylonian Captivity*, is not some precious extra but the quintessence of the redeemed man. 'Christians' is but another name for the people who enjoy Christian freedom, who stand in contrast to the people who are slaves of the law. It is true that it is only when we come to polemics against the multitude of Roman regulations and the resultant multiplication of possibilities of sin and the danger of legalistic piety, that this concept becomes so sharply accentuated. We must be on our guard, however, against understanding it only in the light of this polemic. It is essentially positive in its application and a consequence of the dogma of justification: by faith alone man is completely freed.

Of all Luther's writings this pamphlet is the one that comes nearest to Christian and religious humanism. It is true that Luther's writings probably contain none that is more calculated to sadden Catholics; for here we see most clearly what the quite extraordinary religious power Luther possessed could have accomplished by way of reform within the Church.

In view of such writing it is hard to come back to the Luther who so recklessly, unrestrainedly and destructively reviled the Roman Church in the same pamphlet (speaking of the 'stinking murderer's lair in Rome'). It is prefaced by a letter to the pope ('to the most holy father in God, Leo X, pope of Rome, every blessing in our Lord Jesus Christ'), which, in its humble solicitations, is strangely removed from these and other radical outbursts against the pope, made at the same time. We are at once disarmed by the immoderation, and confused by the contradiction, and both tend to incriminate Luther. And yet we must not hastily condemn him of deceit. No deceiver would ever have placed such contradictions so close together. Luther was in a ferment, in a transformation of being. He still bore the past in himself, and he saw only a confused image of himself.

Most certainly this work was also an attempt to destroy the legality of excommunication at its root, and so to exorcise the danger – 'A Christian man is free master of all things and subject to none' – and it is all too evident that in face of the imminent threat to his life, Luther was trying to preserve moderation. But it is very plain that this moderation was not calculation but the attempt to reach a harmonious synthesis, and that the very threat to his life neither provoked special coarseness in Luther nor turned his freedom into timidity.

It was in this inexhaustibly fruitful year, 1520, too, that Luther produced the sermon on good works. It preceded the pamphlets and was part of a series of pastoral and religious writings. Luther himself thought very highly of it, and it was his most popular presentation of his theology of faith, of his spiritual concept of the Church as a spiritual fellowship of souls in one faith, recognised through baptism, the eucharist and the gospel, and of his theology of sin, which exaggerated the reality of sin as much as it denied the possibility of sin in believers.

But there were other ways in which Luther was driven on. His historically inadequate conception of papal primacy, which he had made his own in the course of preparing for the Leipzig disputation, received a mighty reinforcement in the year 1520. Luther read von Hutten's edition of Lorenzo Valla's work on the donation of Constantine. This was a mighty thrust – the foundation of papal power a colossal swindle! Indeed, this was an invalid inference; but again it acquired probability from the excesses and vagueness of curialism, which confused the secular power of the papacy with the essence of primacy.

If, then, the power of the pope was founded upon a lie, he must be Antichrist. During the same year Luther read the writings of Huss, the heretic who had been burned, and in these he recognised his own doctrine.

Meanwhile the great blow from Rome had been struck. While at work on *The Babylonian Captivity* Luther learned for sure that Eck had entered Germany bringing a bull against him. This was the bull *Exsurge Domine* dated 15 June. It did not as yet pronounce excommunication upon Luther, but merely threatened: 'Arise, O God, plead thy cause; remember how the impious scoff at thee all day!' (Ps 74:22). It went on solemnly to call upon SS Peter and Paul, the whole host of the saints, and all the Church to arise against 'the boar from the forest' (Ps 80:13) who ravages the vineyard of Peter, despises the Church's interpretation of scripture, but who, like all heretics, from self-seeking and to flatter the people twists scripture to his own mind. The new ideas proposed by Luther had long since been condemned by the Church, especially with reference to Huss. Out of defiance, Luther clung to these ideas, although the pope tried to instruct him through Cajetan and offered him a safe conduct and free journey to Rome so that there he might have his error unambiguously cleared up.[4] Stressed as specially important was the peculiar relationship of affection which the holy see had with Germany, to whom the pope had presented the imperial crown of Rome, and who, for her part, had always been protector of the Church.

From Luther's doctrines the bull selected perfectly correctly those (cf. below, p. 321 n.) which made his breach most obvious, those, that is, in which he denied the power of the Church and of the priest. In all, forty-one articles were rejected and in part declared heretical. Whoever persisted in these doctrines fell under the greater bann with all its far-reaching spiritual and temporal penalties. Luther and his followers were adjured to return to the Church. They were given sixty days' grace. Should this time pass and no revocation be forthcoming they would be regarded as notorious heretics and have to bear all the resultant penalties imposed in canon law.

Luther's followers were not named individually. It was left to Eck, who, in his office as papal legate, brought the bull to Germany, to append the names according to his own judgment. Amongst others he fixed upon Karlstadt, the humanist Pirkheimer, Spengler the town clerk of Nuremberg, and an aristocratic canon

---

[4] Luther doubted the truth of this offer. No trace exists, however, that his doubts were founded.

of Augsburg Bernard Adelmann of Adelmannsfelden. At this point all sorts of intrigues began to play their part. Because it was known that Eck had had a hand in framing the text of the bull, many saw in it an expression of personal enmity, and this did nothing to augment its impact. On the contrary, considering the solemn promulgation of the bull it must have damaged the prestige of the Roman curia even more.

The effect of the bull not only lagged far behind cherished expectations; it had no effect at all. Otherwise how could the subsequent hearing of Luther at Worms and the indolent behaviour of the German bishops in so serious a case have been possible. The reception given to the bull revealed once again how much the prestige of papal decisions had already declined. Even in loyal Church circles the bull was not looked upon as an irrevocable decision. Once again the conciliar idea with its democratising and dogmatically corrosive overtones was at work.

Luther flared up in the most defiant revolt. Now the bull proved to him that the pope was Antichrist. Prierias, whose *Answer* had been edited by Luther, who supplied also a foreword, commentary and conclusion, had noted this already: 'If they teach thus publicly in Rome, then by this writing I, too, will publicly declare that Antichrist himself sits in the temple of God.' In the authority of his baptism as a child of God and heir of Christ he set himself against pope and cardinals, and ordered them to do penance and correct these devilish blasphemies quickly. 'If you do not, then I damn you in the name of Christ our Lord whom you persecute.'

On 10 December Luther provided this attitude with an outward, revolutionary form. Before the Else gate of Wittenberg he burned the papal code, works of scholastic theology and the bull of excommunication.

This action made a deep impression. The call to the Christian nobility had already begun to effect a clarification and schism amongst Luther's former followers. Many now began to recognise, besides the protester, Luther the dogmatic revolutionary, and the devastating extent of his alarm call, as well as the anti-Church core of his doctrines. *The Babylonian Captivity* hastened the process. A whole series of authors like Erasmus, the Dominican, John Faber of Augsburg, and the Franciscans, Quiñones and John

Glapion, have expressed the horror that this pamphlet aroused in many Catholics who hitherto, although with some reservations, had enthusiastically supported Luther, and explained how after that pamphlet it became impossible to think of reaching a settlement of the dispute.

Staupitz, the superior of Luther's order, was specially involved in Luther's fate. To a certain extent he had exercised pastoral care over this tormented young monk; and it was he who had been installed as professor of scripture at Wittenberg. He appreciated Luther's opposition to scholasticism and the over-externalised Church. But he was a Catholic, and had to put up with the process of development. He saw the dangers, too. The tumult had already reached such a height, and Luther's theses were so radical, that he dispensed Luther from obedience to the order. This was a relief to the order and its vicar capitular, Staupitz. For Luther, too, it was a liberation, the psychological effect of which cannot be over-estimated.

The excommunication and Luther's action in burning the edict brought even greater catastrophe. The humanists parted company with him. A man like Cochlaeus – humanist and theologian – hitherto well-disposed towards Luther, now became his opponent. The work of theological defence gathered momentum, and the different camps became defined. This is perfectly understandable, for the burning of the bull of excommunication was a revolutionary action, even in a social sense. It was a crude declaration that the theological and ecclesiastical battle already implied an attack upon the foundations of the past order of life. The action had immediate political repercussions. The imperial court had already agreed that Luther be permitted to appear at the next *Reichstag;* now this permission was withdrawn.

III. THE REACTION OF THE TIMES

Until 1521, that is until the imperial legal attitude was made absolutely clear, the whole Reformation movement remained somewhat obscure and undefined. For this reason analyses of the years 1518–20, in so far as they attempt to uncover underlying forces, can only claim to be provisional orientations. They cannot pass final judgment. None the less they are indispensable if the

uncommonly varied, highly fluid, living pattern is to be made evident, from which the history of the Reformation proper drew its
impetus.

The new disposition of power had already been illustrated by
Luther's stay in Augsburg in 1518. Luther was a mendicant monk,
one of that despised and hated class who formed a chief target in
the attack upon the Church. At the same time he was already one
of the best known and most admired men in Germany. Even the
celebrated Peutinger had invited him to dinner. On his journey to
Heidelberg an aristocratic gentleman, Bishop Lorenz von Bibra of
Würzburg, granted him a lengthy interview and was deeply
impressed by Luther. 'Do not let them take this devout man, Doctor Martin, away from you. They do him an injustice,' he wrote
to the elector Frederick. In Heidelberg the disputation won for
him the support of two prominent intellects, Martin Butzer, a
Dominican, and John Brenz (d. 1570), the later Reformer of
Würtemberg. Both of these men played an important part in the
progress of his work. In the same year, at Luther's instigation,
Nicholas of Amsdorf studied St Paul and St Augustine. In this man
Luther won one of his dearest friends, who went with him to Leipzig for the disputation, and to Worms in 1521, without a safe conduct, and who was one of the few who knew of Luther's stay at the
Wartburg. He was an inflexible Lutheran, a typical controversialist, like Flaccius Illyricus, full of impatience, and a great heresy
hunter. Agricola (John Schneider of Eisleben) himself came forward as an advocate of Lutheran views, and it was he who first
published Luther's exposition of the Lord's Prayer at the beginning
of 1518.

There was a mind of totally different stamp, too. One of the
audience at the Leipzig disputation in 1519 was Müntzer who
became preacher in Zwickau in 1520. He was one of the leading
figures amongst the fanatics, of whom we shall hear more.

The same year saw a Wittenberg student, Hector Pomer,
installed as provost of St Lawrence in Nuremberg. The young
man, Nesen, a pupil of Erasmus became city schoolmaster in
Frankfort-on-Maine, a city he was to lead into the Protestant camp.
Urban Rhegius was called to do battle against the innovators in
Augsburg, where, in 1518, Luther had won a following; but this

was only to set a thief to catch a thief, for Rhegius had already become secretly attached to Luther's viewpoint.

At the university of Wittenberg as well as Luther there was Karlstadt who went with him to Leipzig and who was soon to adopt radical opinions himself. As we know already, Luther had well and truly become the focus of attention at Wittenberg. For years Wittenberg had had its own special brand of theology. In 1518 in the preface to his edition of the *Theologia deutsch* Luther was compelled to ward off suspicion cast upon this theology. People were saying that they acted as 'if there never had been people before, or anywhere else'.

From the end of August 1518 onwards Melanchthon was a resident professor in Wittenberg. He was a mere twenty-one-years old, a scholar of classical languages whom Erasmus admired, and one of the chief figures of the Reformation. He was even more than that.

To these we must add that zealous and important follower, Luther's friend in the Erfurt Augustinian monastery – Lang.

It is evident already that the forces which allied themselves most closely to Luther, were anything but strictly homogeneous. There was already a wealth of differing personalities. This variety corresponded to the schismatic tendency already contained in Luther's basic principles. It is particularly important to note the Butzer– Melanchthon, humanist axis, which paved the way for a link with Zwingli and the later relativist attitude of Acontius, and hence prepared the way to dissolution.

In Augsburg the humanists, even the celebrated ones, had canvassed for Luther. It was from their circles that the Reformer enlisted the broad front of support which joined in his battle against Rome, scholasticism and monasticism, and was required also as a positive force in achieving a purified Christianity, such as they thought they would find with Luther. And after they had encountered the objectionable Eck, promulgator of the bull of excommunication (to the bishoprics in electoral Saxony after September 1520, to the university of Wittenberg on 3 October), they showed much more active support for the outlaw. Here, too, the types vary greatly: Cochlaeus, Erasmus – Pirkheimer, Hutten, Melanchthon. We will have to return to this when we come to discuss the alignment of forces after Worms and the sojourn in the Wartburg.

The Bavarian and Austrian nobles declared for Luther very early on. All of the princes, spiritual and secular, however, adopted a very hesitant and cautious attitude.

There was a most significant fact about the band of active followers who were forming around Luther – they were young and opposed the older generation who upheld tradition. It was in the nature of things that such a classification should be accepted only *parte potiori*. None the less the fact is illuminating. H. Schoffler has shown, although with some exaggeration, the amazing consequences for the history of the Reformation which arose from the old idea of 'youth versus tradition'.

There is another important detail that ought not to be overlooked. At Augsburg, high-level politics seemed desirous of taking a hand in the Luther affair. The indications are slight, but none the less the French ambassador presented his compliments to Luther. Nor was this so slight a thing as its effects at the time might have suggested. It was all in harmony with the emergent great line of France's development towards political Protestantism, a line that was to exert a decisive influence upon the whole course of the Reformation. A starting-point for the political application and exploitation of the whole affair was now at hand. This was in fact embodied in a man – Luther's feudal superior, Elector Frederick. Since 1501 the elector Frederick of Saxony had made it his business to prevent Church revenues from his lands being taken off to Rome. In the end he had used this revenue to found his university. Political opposition to the Brandenburg cardinal in Mainz, as well as financial interests, caused him to refuse to have the jubilee indulgence preached within his principality. It is easy to understand how he would be sympathetic towards Luther's attacks. Luther was already to some extent enjoying electoral protection.

As we have seen, in the fifteenth century Germany, in contrast to the western monarchies, had very imperfectly come to a sense of national individuality. In a most tragic manner, the Reformation repaired this deficiency. It is true that the English ambassador at the time of the preparation for the imperial election could report the presence of an unusually powerful anti-French German patriotism; and, following Ranke, we may interpret the election of Charles of Spain as an explicit expression of German national sentiment; but it was the Reformation that first gave real impetus to German national consciousness. Unfortunately, it immediately split Germany from top to bottom.

When analysing this national consciousness and its growth a whole series of important questions must be distinguished. To begin with we must avoid the misconception that Luther was *consciously* a political, national leader. He worked for his own Germans, he felt for the well-being and the sorrows of Germany, and he expressed these things forcibly. He acclaimed, strengthened and exploited, the anti-Roman feeling of the nation. The exuberance with which he applauded the theology of Tauler and the 'Frankfurter', written in German, 'which contains more solid stuff than the solely approved Latin works of all the scholastic doctors', clearly shows how conscious he was of being a German. Throughout the centuries his translation of the Bible was one of the most powerful unifying forces in the nation. None the less he was and remained first and last a preacher of the Word, which was for all men equally, and transcended absolutely all that was human or national. He was an evangelist and a prophet. There was good reason for his national consciousness being so strongly negative, viz. anti-Roman.

During the deciding years of the Reformation there was a whole phalanx of forces, from Hutten to Sickingen, who tried to draw Luther directly into the politico-revolutionary liquidation of the 'parsons'. He refused to be drawn into this. At the end of 1518 he came very near to shifting his field of operation from Germany to France.

Obviously we must not seek explanations for this withdrawal in the bitter words that Luther often found himself compelled to utter concerning the Germans: that they refused to listen to the new gospel, or that the Germans were full of moral defects. 'Each land must have its own devil. Our German devil is a wineskin and must be called Tipple, for he is so thirsty and merry, and no amount of wine or beer seems to satisfy him. This eternal thirst will remain the plague of Germany until the day of judgment. Drink remains a great idol amongst us Germans, and has the same effect as the sea and dropsy.' Luther plainly spoke as a German pastor to Germans, and such passages as these are balanced by others like his significant: 'With us Germans, Yes is Yes and No is No.'

Further, we must radically separate the question of the arousing of the nation in these days, from the electoral and princely leaders of the states. Most of them, because of their pathetic egoism, were ready at a moment to hand over the empire from the Habsburgs to the French for a few thousand gulden. Their territorial self-interest made almost impossible any notion of making a sacrifice for the good of the whole.

Ever since the Council of Constance – to trace the causes back no further – the battle for a reform of the German Church had been fraught with national considerations, as was the case also in the western Churches outside Germany. As with the rest of Europe, in Germany the process was carried out as an essentially antipapal or anti-Roman struggle. Germany, as we have seen, appeared in exaggerated form as the object of Roman financial exploitation. The complaints made at the same time concerning the infringement of her honour, her laws and her freedom, were impressive but less well founded.

The whole range of German *Gravamina* since the fifties, egoistic as they may have been in detail, egoistic as they were still conceived in the specially important *Reichstag* of 1521, all relentlessly augmented the feeling that Rome was the enemy, and the oppressor of the Germans above all. In those decades of emerging capitalism, the territorial principalities and territorial Churches, most circles including the nationally minded clergy (cf. Archbishop Berthold v. Henneberg of Mainz and Cochlaeus) felt that it was wrong and in part impossible for Germany to be financially so dependent on a foreign power. When the committe of the *Reichstag* at Mainz, in the year of Luther's indulgence theses, complained that the country's wealth was leaking away to foreign countries, to Rome in particular where new impositions were being devised daily, they were merely harping upon an old theme. The complaints against the financial exploitation of Germany by Rome may have been exaggerated, but the hard core remained, and even the unjustified exaggerations had their effect.

Instead of voting the Turkish tax to the emperor and the pope, the Augsburg *Reichstag* of 1518 complained bitterly of earlier non-customary or illegally increased monetary demands by Rome, of infringement of German rights and the granting of German benefices to foreigners. These ideas were then well and truly impressed upon the mind of the entire people through the various diets of the estates and principalities in 1519.

Humanism, within and outside the Church, gave added impulse to this ferment. The national interest of humanism had remained within the sphere of education, in contrast to the nationally more active Italian humanist movement. It first began to emerge from this sphere with the emergence of anti-Roman feeling. The climax at which the development through Hutten made contact with the Reformation movement was provided by part two of the *Letters of Obscure Men*. The chief contributor to these was Hutten, hater of Rome, humanist and nationalist. Europe was now dominated by Erasmian satire, but in its characteristic non-committal form. The *Letters of Obscure Men*, however, had become a loud national challenge. They were a much more direct summons to the Reformation rising, inseparable from national sentiment, than was Erasmus, who, for his part, as forerunner of the religious revolution, was intellectually infinitely more important.

To some extent Hutten, too, was spokesman of the contentious and discontented German knights who were led to their ruin not by him, however, but by Sickingen (below, p. 360). Because of this connection, like Sickingen, he was the representative of a dying age. He, however, abandoned the dying age with the utmost resolution, and threw in his lot with the new. In 1518 he still had the idea that a crusade would canalise the chaotic forces raging in the nation; but in the following year anti-Roman feeling completely won the day. In February his first satirical dialogue appeared, aimed right at the Romanists. In 1520 he joined the ranks of German authors, beginning to write in German and translate his Latin works into German. He tried to make contact with the masses. His first anti-Church collection of dialogues appeared, and once again this laid all of the blame for every evil, for financial burdens, for corrupt religion, and for the political impotence of Germany, at the door of Rome. German freedom could only be won by a fight against Rome, against the clergy in general. It was by this way – not a religious road – that he joined forces with Luther. 'You have got me for a helper, by whatever means ... ' With God, who was also one of the party, he would free his long enslaved fatherland. The title design on his *Conversation Piece* of 1521 is symbolic. Beside the title is Luther on the one side and Hutten on the other. Beneath the picture is the defiant resolution, applying his usual device (*Alea iacta est*) to the special situation: '*Perrumpendum est tandem, perrumpendum est:* now we've had enough! now we shall break through!' The appended saying and the picture that fills the remainder of the title-page permits no misunderstanding whatever: 'I hate the Church of the evildoers.' We can see how knights and troopers fulminated against the pope, the cardinals, the bishops and the whole clerical estate. In fact, there was threat of total revolution. 'Everyone is behind Hutten and Sickingen, who now alone rules as king in Germany' (Aleander reporting to Rome). In autumn 1520 – not till then – Hutten left the court of the cardinal of Mainz, and Sickingen's Ebernburg became the centre of a solid group of Lutheran sympathisers (in the sense we have explained).

Hutten was the first man to stimulate creatively a German national consciousness. It is true that we must use the word 'creatively' in a restricted sense if we are to avoid misunderstanding Hutten as greater than he really was. However much we value his destructive work and overlook the damaging quality of his obscenity, he remains the type whose energies are unco-ordinated, whose disturbing passion lacks any genuine, clear and fruitful programme, whose unrest does not move along the straight rails of lucid thought and clear objective. The fact that he turned his rage more and more one-sidedly against papal Rome caused the supporters of the Reformation greatly to over-estimate his power and the purity of his ideal. He did an enormous amount to arouse German self-consciousness. Even so, he was the very one above all others, who burdened this consciousness at its foundation with a negative accent, an anti-Roman sentiment, and thus did it much harm.

We ought not so readily to overlook the colossal one-sidedness of his anti-Roman assertions. That he declaimed so impressively and without any restraint against the threat to German freedom from the curia, who, it seemed, were strangling any possibility of remonstrance, is no proof of the legitimacy of his diatribe. And that his cause, supported by Luther's Reformation and despite his own failure, was ultimately victorious, can decisively influence the judgment on this man only of those who are deceived by historical relativism.

Hutten's writings show us one of the most important weapons of that period – pamphleteering. This was at its height between 1518 and 1525. When the Peasants' War came to an end it lost one of its necessary stimuli. In the late Middle Ages such writings, anonymous or signed, had vastly increased. All that was in need of reform was dealt with and ridiculed in these pamphlets; all discontent was menacingly voiced. In a thousand ways, the *Gravamina* as well as apocalyptic prophecies, were spread amongst the people by these pamphlets. They sprang up in huge numbers in a popular, lighter, antischolastic vein, expressing a kind of layman's theology, giving voice to the demands of the peasants and simple folk, and, indeed, of every class in society. And this all proved that the masses were beginning to have a voice. That is not to say that the uneducated had become authors. The authors of the pamphlets were more or less educated; but they knew the people, they spoke for the broad masses, and these in turn spoke through them. Corresponding to a general development of the times, these proclamations at the same time urged on towards radicalism. Their sayings (and woodcuts) circulated in uneducated circles. To this extent opportunities for the growth of revolutionary ideas in turn spread even amongst the illiterate.

Extending far beyond this pamphlet literature, arising from many sources, including the *Reichstag* and humanist letter writing and book producing circles, a highly important force was now forming – *public opinion*. Hutten used this instrument brilliantly.

Luther took up the pamphlet form with instinctive sureness and masterfully developed and exploited it. It is true, as we shall see, that thereby he also did spiritual harm to his cause. At first, however, this instrument undoubtedly greatly speeded up his victory. What a contrast strikes us when we place side by side his polemical writings and those of his opponents! We contrast him with Prieras, Hoogestraeten and Alfeld. His tone, his intellectual agility, made even the weakest argument victorious over against the too dry correctness and dreariness of the scholars of the old Church.

The contents of the pamphlets of the Reformation period ran parallel to the course of the general struggle. At first and most powerfully they attacked Roman and clerical avarice. Slowly

Luther's religious ideas were taken up, but, apart from the more striking formulae, little use was made of them. In certain districts like Westphalia, besides social demands the only things stressed were practical religious topics – the form of public worship, the cup for the laity and marriage of the clergy.

This public opinion, expressed also from the pulpits, gradually began to dominate Germany, feeling itself to be something German for the very reason that it was anti-Roman. What Ranke said of the diverse political, humanist and explicitly ecclesiastical reform movements operating in the Germany of 1519–20 is true: 'There is an inner link between these tendencies. People wanted an end to Roman influence.' Nor can we suppose that this frame of mind was confined to the intellectually radical circle around Hutten or the religious, ecclesiastical revolutionaries around Luther. There is no exaggeration in Aleander's view that in 1520 the whole of Germany was anti-Roman.

Moreover, in Rome people had become so insensitive to the whole situation that in March 1521 Giulio Medici, cardinal secretary of state, was able to describe the German attitude as 'bestial ingratitude'. In Rome they did not recognise the depth of German anti-Roman sentiment, of anti-Roman hatred, indeed. One Roman, however, on the German scene felt it deeply, and reported the situation to Rome clearly and a hundred times over. This was Jerome Aleander. He had himself been mobbed, and had first-hand acquaintance with the anonymous *Litany of Vices*. He called Germany simply 'anti-Italian'. The attitude of the Germans was so hostile to everything Roman that the papal legates, himself and Carracioli, were in danger of their lives. The princes petitioned the emperor to liberate them from the tyranny of Rome, and made use of the occasion to vent all of their venom upon the curia. 'The whole world, most of all the greatest powers in the world are hostile to the curia.' Aleander said that after Luther's heresy had been recognised many indeed forsook him; but everything was outweighed by 'the hatred which burned in them against Rome', and which caused even those supporters of the emperor who opposed Luther's heresy, passionately to resolve to get the better of the pope. Many in fact supported Luther without sharing his views. They did this 'simply to defy Rome and take control of German Church property on the pretexts provided by Luther'.

In truth, the power of this anticurial mood derived very largely from self-interest. Not just in 1521 but a full decade later, when the dreadful situation had become abundantly obvious, this same avaricious self-seeking outweighed all other considerations even with those princes who remained in the Church. Indeed this motive never disappeared at all. After the emperor's long absence and a great advance of the religious innovation, in 1530 the *Reichstag* at last seems to have come to a decision: the protest of the states and the cities would be forcibly suppressed. On the other side the Turks were threatening. The Catholic majority (principally the spiritual estates, whom the others followed) made use of this situation to declare that they would sanction the Turkish tax only if the papal bull, which Ferdinand had acknowledged in Germany and Austria, was rescinded; for they 'did not want to be subjects of the pope at all in this sense'.

We have already noted the reasons Aleander adduced for this revulsion against Rome: the illegal innovations made by the curia. This was the cause of the primacy of the pope becoming a disputed question. It was entirely in harmony with this mood that even such a loyal prince as Emperor Charles V, paying heed to Aleander's report, felt it most desirable to produce a thorough justification of the edict directed against Luther at Worms, 'on account of his people, so that they would not think that he had been too quick to carry out the pope's orders'.

Are we justified in describing this anti-Roman feeling as German national consciousness? It is certainly necessary first of all to bear firmly in mind that this national sentiment was strongly negative, and an impulse of the second order, something antipathetic. And we must take fully into consideration the egoism of the German princes, which simultaneously inclined so strongly and unscrupulously towards France.

But the awakening sense of nationhood was an affair for the nation, not the princes. Princes and subjects were far from forming a unity. Territories and people passed easily from one dynasty to another. The power and position of the princes was still very much a purely dynastic affair, concerning private possession and enjoyment. The real unity that was on its way was prepared for, and encouraged by, impact with the centrifugal impulses of the princes. To be perfectly accurate – even this princely egoism,

that wanted to keep the Church's revenues in the country instead of trickling off to Rome, strengthened the German sense of
solidarity.

Admittedly we find the decisive answer only at the point where
German anti-Roman tension expressed itself most sharply, and
where the highly important question arises of the relation between
national consciousness and Reformation. That point is represented
by Luther, and, possibly, Hutten.

In general we might say that in them anti-Roman sentiment
arose from such a contradiction within their being, that it became
far more than a merely negative force: it became a nation-building
creative power. At Augsburg Duke William of Bavaria admitted to
Contarini: 'Luther would not merely have been favoured by the
whole of Germany, he would have been adored, had he stuck to
his original position and not got entangled in obviously heretical
beliefs.' This corroborates Aleander's report.

This, then, was Germany's attitude to Luther, according to the
judgment of a loyal Catholic. Was he the nation's hero, as so
many claim without the slightest qualification, or was he not?

The gravity of this question for Germany cannot be exaggerated.
It affects all Germans deeply, for it signifies nothing less than the
question whether and how far the affirmation of the Lutheran
Reformation was the business of every German, whether and how
far Charles' outlawing of Luther in 1521 was un-German.

It is of paramount importance, in settling all that is contained
in these questions, first of all to decide whether the mighty agitation that shook the whole nation as a result of Luther and his
teaching indicated a unified will. History's answer to this is a 'flat
'No'. There was a multitude of divergent impulses; and there was
an emphatic and persistent loyalty to the old Church.

It is unhistorical to see the initial and long-lasting general anti-
Roman agitation, of which Luther was the most powerful exponent, as signifying general agreement with all that Luther now
means to us. On the contrary, we have to distinguish sharply
between the battle against Roman encroachments and various
abuses in the Church, and dogmatic belief. The example of Duke
George of Saxony, the utterly loyal Catholic, who introduced the
Gravamina against Rome at the *Reichstag* of Worms in 1521, is

sufficient to illustrate this distinction. His attitude was representative of a large section of all sorts of clergy, and laity, and of the
bishops and theologians.

Nor is it true that national awakening was to be found only
amongst those who attacked the Church. No one has yet refuted
Janssen, who showed that there were strong positive national
impulses arising precisely from German humanism within the old
Church. The staunchly Catholic Cochlaeus is a most important
representative of this attitude in the Reformation period. The
vastness of the task, of the possibilities, and of the danger, facing
the nation were increasing; and all that Cochlaeus had to say
about it was said within the framework of the concept of the
empire. He desired to see the empire once again become the
reality it had been in the vanished period of national greatness.
For him the Roman pope and the Roman emperor together were
the guarantee of German greatness. Despite a certain inner un-
reality, the conception he worked out in 1523 was a grand one: he
marked out the sweep of German history from Charlemagne and
Hadrian I to Charles V and Hadrian VI, demanding that these
two be as creative a pair as were the first two. They would have to
be great to resist the threat to German greatness that was Martin
Luther.

This Catholic national consciousness, too, had its negative
aspect; and this was undoubtedly decisive. Here, too, hatred
helped to provide the real impetus and favoured the growth of the
national idea. Further, there is no doubt that here more than just
the general national consciousness was being expressed, and that
Cochlaeus, for his part, was exploiting the special fertilisation of
this awakening by the Reformation. However, his hatred was not
directed against a foreigner, as was Luther's. The total object was
Germany. To this extent his national attitude was more positive
and less burdened by a dangerous spirit of enmity.

In spite of this we are forced to come back to that other basic
fact: a deep common German antipathy to Rome did exist, and
had become a most lively and clamant concern of the nation. It
was this antipathy that applauded Luther at first, before his heresy
became evident. In this sense *the nation* did indeed rise up. *Germany*,
in the sense in which we have heard Duke William of Bavaria
speak of it, or as Hutten conceived it in 1520, would not tolerate

Luther's being handed over to Rome. According to Aleander, in these early decisive years, when the dogmatic issue of Luther had not yet been separated from the matter of a generally awaited Catholic Church reform, the active section of the nation including many supporters of the Church in fact stood by Luther. *The nation* was behind Luther, critic of Rome, regarded as a reformer within the old Church.

The reception – or rather the rejection – of the bull of excommunication provides an impressive illustration of the situation. It is an historical fact of first rank, that in the middle of a politically peaceful country, not at war with the pope, a bull as important as this, a bull concerning the foundations of Church and state, could not be displayed, as regulations required, except on the doors of the merest handful of churches. This shows how closely tied up with Luther's cause were even those ecclesiastical figures who obviously would not subscribe to his doctrines. This was no issue merely for the theological schools; it concerned life, and its full dogmatic import had not yet penetrated the mind of the nation.

If, then, during those decisive years of the Reformation, Luther enjoyed such strong support from *all Germans* – at least in the sense indicated – was there not a possibility of the whole nation following him as an ecclesiastical revolutionary? Was the possibility of national unity not, in fact, destroyed by the emperor's outlawing Luther?

It was the territorial rulers who called the political tune in every sense. These territorial princes were far from united, either amongst themselves or as a force against the emperor. On the contrary, their political egoism was essentially unlimited and particularist. It would have been a Utopian dream to suppose – *per impossibile* – that had the emperor espoused Luther's cause all of the princes would have followed suit. This most certainly would not have been the case with the Bavarian dukes, with Joachim I of Brandenburg, and Duke George of Saxony. The contradiction (political and religious) we have here, like that between the emperor and the Protestant territorial princes, would have obstructed the Reformed unity of the nation. Besides this, we would first have to prove that the overwhelming majority of clerical prince electors and prince bishops were prepared to break faith with the Church. Such proof cannot be produced.

To speak in more concrete terms: at that time could anyone have even dreamed of the possibility of a Lutheran emperor? Who might he have been? Charles, Francis I or some German prince? For Charles, Germany in any case was only part of the total picture. Quite apart from his religious alignment, there was an inevitable political antagonism between his universalist tendencies, which he dared not give up, and the demands of the German estates. For his part, however, a Lutheran unity was impossible politically, on account of Spain and Italy. Under Francis of France as emperor the probability of an alliance with Protestantism would have been even less, on account of French nationalist considerations. Any German prince other than a Habsburg, however, would have had to reckon with the sharpest opposition of the Habsburgs, and in turn religious antagonism had become used and encouraged in the service of political antagonism.

Finally we have to ask a question which goes to the very root of things – the religious question. Despite much religious confusion the Catholic Church and her teaching were still inviolable and living enough to make the idea of any unity of the nation in opposition to the Church unthinkable. (The uniform accomplishment of the Reformation in England and the Scandinavian countries is no counter-proof; for in these countries there was no question of a popular movement. Moreover, the political structure of the slightly unified empire was utterly different.)

If, then, a great number of German princes, cities and people, regarded it as a sacred thing to hold fast to the old Church, can we say that it was desirable that they should do violence to their faith for the sake of confessional unity, for the sake of that confessional innovation that was destroying the hitherto existent unity? Such hypothetical discussions about the unchangeable past are always dangerous; but once started up, have to be carried on to the bitter end.

In the end our answer to the whole problem has, in the nature of things, to be given from the standpoint of a fundamentally religious and Christian view. We have to admit that much is to be gained by treating the question from the same fundamental standpoint as Luther did. For Luther, was the concept 'nation' a prime value in the absolute sense, or can what is highest be found only in supernature? Luther had no doubts; he unhesitatingly affirmed

K

the latter. Precisely from his standpoint, the problem can only be solved by examining the justification of his dogmatic views. If we reject these views, we have to reject Luther himself.

There is another problem, not exactly identical with the one we have just discussed. Did the Reformation movement, as a heretical system of doctrine, take root in the bulk of the nation? We will find that to some extent the problem can be dealt with exhaustively only if we consider it case by case over a longish period of time. It allows of no complete solution, for there is no means of ascertaining without any doubt the free resolution of the masses We shall, therefore, merely provide a few necessary indications to show more exactly the religious situation of the people about 1518–20.

From the Catholic side we have frequently appealed to the rigid Catholic life of faith in explanation of the strength of the Church in face of the Reformation storm. But our analysis of late medieval popular piety has shown what deep rents were to be found here. A host of incidents from the Reformation and the Counter-Reformation show in addition how many circles were saved to the old faith by the Reformation law of the princes. (For a filling out of this fact by the opposition, see p. 407.)

Conversely, the first years of the Reformation allow of no doubt that even the heretical Luther and Hutten, who joined forces with him in rebelling against the pope, appealed immediately to the people and carried them with them. Again it is Aleander who corroborates both things for us, but who sees correctly that Luther's utterance went much deeper.

Above all, Luther himself sensed how great masses of the people were religiously oppressed and were ready to follow him. He felt that 'the people were longing to hear the voice of the Good Shepherd, Christ, and were clamouring like the disciples with amazing zeal for the holy scriptures' (early 1518). Solicitude for real people had been his chief concern in writing the indulgence theses. To prevent the movement from running along a wrong track he published the short sermon *Indulgence and Grace* in 1518. This sermon actually ousted the theses. His *Instruction on Diverse Articles* of 1519 sought to achieve a similar restriction. Still, however, as we would expect, he underrated the Church: 'The law of God ought to be honoured above that of the Church, as gold and precious stones are treasured more than wood and straw.'

The mere fact of Luther's colossal literary output, running into vast editions, is proof that there was a popular movement afoot. The problem none the less very soon becomes much more complicated, especially at the moment when the estates of the empire in Worms began to take sides for and against Luther, and again when the unrest set going rose independently to a tumult in Wittenberg, Zwickau, Allstedt and then in the Peasants' War.

Nor may we overlook the extraordinary ignorance of religious matters amongst the masses in those days. The lack of any regular religious instruction of children, the lack of primary education for most people, so that they were unable to use the available religious literature, the religious lukewarmness of the lower clergy, and their astonishing ignorance of the Church's basic doctrines, all of these things could have but one result. Thorough proof of the facts is provided by Protestant visitations of the twenties, and by the experience of all Catholic reformers.

IV. CATHOLIC POWERS

What part did the power of the old Church play in this struggle, and how powerful was it? What was the mind of Catholics? Did they see the danger? Did they close their ranks? Was their resistance timely, energetic and directed by a unified plan? Was there a Catholic front at all?

These questions introduce the whole great theme of Catholic reform in the sixteenth century. I will reserve until the second volume an exhaustive description of the things connected with this. Meantime the situation was overwhelmingly dominated by the eruption and advance of religious innovation; and it is this that concerns us at the moment.

We are concerned primarily with clarifying the state of mind of Catholicism in relation to the questions just formulated.

There was one valuable Catholic asset, the existence of which can be demonstrated, but which appeared seldom in individual cases. This was the continuing common Catholic faith with its prayer and sacraments in the accepted usage of everyday life, in cities, monasteries, villages, until, either freely or under coercion, they went over to the new beliefs. The essential objectivity of Catholic values, the objective holiness of the Church, the *opus operatum* of her sacraments, resulted in this Catholicism possessing great importance within the total disposition of forces in Germany at that time, however badly it was weakened by the countless abuses we have been discussing.

But there was no such thing as an entity which we could call *the* Catholicism of the time – a unified and uniformly directed militant community. Here, too, the fearful disintegration of the notion of Christianity and the Church since the late Middle Ages, had had a centrifugal and confusing effect on a large scale. There can be no doubt that at first Luther's rebellion had a religious purpose. The curia and many bishops, however, were far from religiously orientated, to judge by their outward actions. Even the army of Church humanists were activated by the most diverse motives. Theology had very largely become imprisoned within scholastic controversies that were taken far too seriously, and had been split by the radical dispute between nominalism and realism. Out of this there arose a second not very encouraging characteristic – disunity in the interpretation of the situation and hence in the reaction to it. This meant an undoubted diminution of strength. And in the third place: on all sides, but most decisively within the Roman curia, there was a fatal underestimation of the danger.

Throughout the late Middle Ages the self-assurance of the Roman curia had evolved in a strangely confused fashion. It would appear that in face of increasing attack, the papacy had gone from strength to strength. Throughout the whole of the fifteenth century, however, the centuries' old demands for reform had resounded in Rome, coming both anonymously and officially from Germany. France and Germany had even tried to call a separatist council at Pisa. The papal Lateran Council had listened to the most severe judgments on the situation, and the most ominous threats for the future. 'Many were of the opinion that things were going badly for the Church, because its head was preoccupied with amusement, music, the chase and foolery, instead of wisely considering the distress of the flock and weeping over its unhappy condition. The salt of the earth had lost its savour, and all that one could do was to throw it out and tread it under foot.' But no calamity happened. Savonarola was disposed of by Alexander VI. Julius II proscribed the threatening schism and raised the political power of the papacy to heights as yet unknown. And now the son of Lorenzo Medici the Magnificent, a cardinal at fourteen years of age, was set upon the throne of the world at the age of thirty-seven.

This sort of progress in the secularisation of Christianity, of priestly and ecclesiastical ideals, this distortion of the pastoral office into a right to possess pleasure and power, the widespread suppression of the serious notion of the *Ecclesia crucis* had inevitably led to the irresponsible exaggeration of the curial sense of power. On the other hand, a realistic assessment of the danger threatening within, and now from Luther without, was almost impossible. The curia over-estimated their own, and underestimated the hostile, power.

We may not cite the gloomy prognostications, emanating from curial circles, as a contraction of these things. At least they decide nothing. We must wait almost a decade, until the sack of Rome in 1527, before such clamant threats against the curia are heeded and made a guide for action. For the time being people were utterly incapable of seeing what was going on. The decisive proof of this is the way in which Luther's case was handled, the way in which politics militated against religion, and then defeated it. It was bad enough if, for political reasons, the imperial interest tried to exploit the Lutheran cause, but that at least was the action of a political, secular power. No such excuse can be made for the representative of Christ, all the less so when we think of how the fiscal benefice traffic of the curia kept up its ridiculous and trivial calculations, to the detriment of Christian interests, and right at the height of the decisive storm, as Aleander's despatches from Worms tell us.

Cajetan's report of his interview with Luther reached Leo on about 19 October 1518, when he was at Corneto. He was able to work up scarcely any interest. In both consistories held there at that time the Luther case was scarcely mentioned. The days were taken up with hunting and the theatre.

This is perfectly in harmony with the way in which on 3 February, Leo X had given the newly designated general of the Augustine Eremites the task of getting Luther to give up his views. It was all done so casually. Even the command to make haste need not deceive us: 'Do not delay, for the evil increases every day.' This same imperturbability is to be found also in Leo's mandates to Aleander in Worms. No doubt he was superficially motivated by a new, unaccustomed solicitude, on account of heresy in Germany. Unfortunately there is no evidence that this stirring in any way went beyond the text of the much repeated curial formulae and Bible quotations ('desiring not the death of the sinner', 'leaving many sheep to go and seek one that was lost', 'more joy over one repentant sinner' . . .) and signified any genuine awareness of the evil and its causes. The silencing of Luther seemed easy of accomplishment; after that all would return to normal. 'We will receive this same Martin graciously like a dear son and load him with honours.' The same spirit is revealed in the superficial pictorial language of the lines added in his own hand by Leo X to his brief to Charles V on 25 February 1521. The pope was unaware of any really serious danger to the Church. The addition shows his interest in the emperor's intervention, that is in a matter of power politics – no more. 'Charles is to take up sword and shield . . . so that after the uprooting of the weeds, the wheat will thrive, and after the fog is dispelled the sun will once again shine with peaceful brightness upon Germany . . . '

We have no desire to overlook the indications that individuals and some isolated groups in Rome itself and in the curia saw the perilous condition of the Church before Luther's time, now saw it threatened by him, and spoke up about these things. These groups, however, did not dictate the official line. Moreover, many of the powerful warnings were only half believed by the very people who uttered them. As we have said, the multiplication of complaints did not signify a corresponding increase in insight. Such complaints were too commonplace to make an impression any longer. During the ninth session of the Lateran Council Antonio Pucci might threaten: 'If at this council we do not regain our good name, which is almost lost, and our health, which is sickly and in dire danger, then there is no way out, no flight, no more hope'; but what was the use of this sort of thing if no one was willing to give up the profits derived from the abuses?

We must concede the point, that the curialists were far from the scene of battle. The mighty popular rising that was welling up in Germany could not be detected in Rome. In Rome, apart from the official political angle, the whole affair could be viewed more academically. All the more so because even in Germany this stage was not quite past. There can be no doubt at all that Eck's labours at the Leipzig disputation revealed this academic attitude. Eck was aware of an attack upon dogma; but was this a danger to the world-wide Church? Amongst true Erasmians this irresponsibility lasted even longer. At the end of 1519 Erasmus still found no time to read Luther's writings. At Worms, as Luther's opponent, in 1521 Cochlaeus was still at this stage, and in 1523 he expressed the same conviction in print.

There is no mystery about this. In the Rome of the Medicis, with its many embassies, its law-suits against mutinous cardinals, its theatres, painters, sculptors, architects, where the masterpieces of Raphael and many others were everyday things, where there was daily excitement over the discovery of ancient treasures and priceless manuscripts, how could the complaints of a solitary monk in a distant land set off even the slightest reverberation?

This difficulty, this very impossibility of Luther's breaking into the richly charged political and cultural atmosphere of the centre from which the curia ruled the whole earth *was* the evil, and proclaimed the guilt.

True – the inability of the curia to recognise Luther's Christian earnestness and hence to see the danger threatening the Church's life, was of a certain benefit to the Church. Loyalty to the Church, even where that loyalty was only superficially Christian, where it appeared to be no more than an attachment to power, thus remained unbroken and unshaken on a large scale. In those decisive first years not a trace of wavering disturbed the self-confidence of the curia.

That, however, is no Christian assessment. A Christian assessment would have to state that this failure to understand the danger did not arise from a great purity and fullness of Christian life. There was a lie at its root, something which was bound to erode the substance of Christianity.

What they saw, then, in Rome, was Luther's attack upon papal power; but it was seen in too one-sided a way. Too little heed was paid to the significant religious kernel of his attack. And so the defence set in motion by the curia lacked the necessary commitment with body and soul to that which would have been felt as the decisive battle. Such commitment could only arise when religious 'possession', and religious heroism recognised the foe, and threw itself against him, all or nothing. It was the Jesuits who accomplished this great feat; but the Church still had thirty years to wait to see it.

It was Aleander at the *Reichstag* at Worms in 1521 who painted a vivid picture of this attitude in all its variously conditioned intrinsic confusion. We can describe this now without any fear that thereby we will reproduce the situation inexactly. Aleander was undoubtedly one of those cardinals who saw the threatening danger most clearly. In his reports to Rome he stressed this strongly, and occasionally he had prodded the politically hesitant imperial side. The issue had absolutely no parallel with which it could be compared. 'The danger is so great that if our dear emperor shows the slightest tendency to yield, the whole of Germany will secede from the see of Rome.' 'Things could become very bad indeed. . . . The heretical wound has deteriorated in the worst way possible, so that all despair of its immediate healing.' 'If the imperial party do not proceed energetically against Luther, such a fire will soon be burning that all the water in the sea of Flanders will not put it out.' 'Rome's underestimation of the Lutheran affair is highly dangerous, for the very reason that to make fun of Luther and not to take the matter seriously is dangerously embittering the Germans.'

Aleander himself occasionally underestimated the danger. He, too, suffered from the fundamental Roman disease. His report was cast in political and diplomatic terms. 'The curia might be a bit more discreet with reservations and pluralities, and especially in the matter of German courtesans – until this storm is past.' Even he had not recognised the real power of this outburst. He saw only the externals, and so, dangerously underestimated it. He did see, it is true, that 'practically all of the clergy with the exception of the parish priests sympathise with the new doctrines', but he did not understand that even those clergy who had been well endowed by the curia still welcomed the idea of an anti-Roman council. He was full of astonishment because 'monks of orders other than Luther's showed such enthusiasm for Luther's cause'. He would have liked to 'overthrow monk with monk'. He repeatedly advised the method of calling trouble-makers to order by offering them privileges or benefices. One must speak soft words, promise the earth, cardinals' hats and so on. Perhaps we might overlook the bribing of imperial officials by the papal nuncio. But he tried to use the same method to influence people with Lutheran views, people like Doctor Burchard: 'a man with something of a passion for innovation, whom the Lutherans desire to win over, and whom I am asking to think things over'. This method was tried with Capito. He was made provost of St Thomas' in Strasburg, and from then on he worked for the Reformation until his death in 1541. Admittedly Aleander said: 'By this bait we may not have made him one of us, but at least he will do less harm to the Catholic cause, for the provostship will occupy his interest.' All this went on in spite of the fact that Aleander was compelled to report that the opposition saw through this method, and that this 'most terrible and dangerous calumny' brought the people's hatred upon the papacy, and their contempt upon the imperial mandate, just as much as if it had been downright bribery.

What petty methods these were, considering the deep causes of the storm! What blindness to the religious problem! And at the curia, too, they had a very inflated notion of the efficacy of external actions such as the burning of heretical books. According to Aleander, Rome really imagined that it could 'strangle the Lutheran rising by this sort of action, and rest in security. Otherwise I cannot understand how people can for so long completely neglect their own honour and advantage, can ignore, indeed, a matter of life and death for Christianity and the papacy.' On occasion, however, Aleander was equally short-sighted. This becomes most evident (even grotesque) with regard to the finally perfected Edict of Worms against Luther. The issue was settled – so he thought – by this one juridical act. 'Luther's whole reputation is now gone. No one talks about him any more, except perhaps a few raving villains, who only stay with him for the loot.' The curia took the very same line: the grateful acknowledgment of the papal vice-chancellor to Aleander on 6 June 1521 could not be more extravagant in its over-evaluation of this edict.

This continued to be the attitude of the curia throughout the whole of the Reformation period.

There is endless documentation for this. Petty and inappropriate means, and diplomatic procrastination were constantly used. This makes sense, perhaps, when we consider that in 1524 the curia were still so badly informed as to believe that only Saxony was on Luther's side. In the consultation between Clement VII and the cardinals at the beginning of May 1524 there was very little seriousness, mixed with pomposity and hide-and-seek. Having heard a few reports they resolved: 'not to reject the idea of a general council out of hand; one should, however, note the obstacles arising from the state of war, but at the same time have negotiations in prospect. Concerning the complaints: they would promise to adhere to the prescriptions of the Lateran council and ... would consult further.'

The most important feature was the absence of religious depth.

Aleander himself shrank from grappling with religious objectives. Not only 'does excommunication no longer make any impression upon the Germans', even 'the appeal to faith, religion or the soul's salvation achieves as little, as do blessings and curses, for here the whole world is lukewarm in faith and jeers at it'. Whatever could be described as the power of faith in Aleander's own attitude and activity is beside the point: 'I do not seek my own advantage, but that of Christ, as he alone can testify.' For him, God's help is necessary in face of Hutten's attack. 'In this affair God will one day show that he is the greater.' Once or twice he gives a thought to the danger to men's souls.

Occasionally his perception went a bit deeper. He stated that the Lutheran movement could be overcome only by positive Catholic growth – as well as through the pending ecclesiastical court. This implied a long-term programme – improvement of the priesthood, and a consequent overcoming of the terrible hatred of the laity for the corrupt clergy; positive pastoral work; a thorough literary apologetic that was free from coarseness and over-simplification. Once he touched on another decisive point: one might hope, with God's help, to be victorious yet 'if in Rome we work hard to accomplish a transformation pleasing to God'. He even went so far as plainly to admit the Church's guilt. These things, however, were not his leading theme. This accuracy lacked driving power; it remained a mere formality. Meanwhile, what of the threatening danger? 'On account of our sins this accursed sect may be with us yet a while.'

In the light of the gospel and of all religious manifestation in the history of the Church from the very beginning it would seem that the work Aleander was doing for the Church against heresy would have required the support of an organised campaign of prayer, to obtain God's protection. (This remark may strike official historical research as curious – a proof of how far we have departed from the religious examination of Church history.) There is virtually no trace of a genuine prayer-life about the Aleander of the *Reichstag* at Worms. He mentions how 'yesterday and today (Holy Thursday and Good Friday) he had spent a little time with God and his conscience'. In view of the predominance of his totally different interests we need not take this statement as an indication of modest humility.

In their Christian and ecclesiastical context these things must be much more strongly stressed than has been customary in the past. A permanent victory could have come only from something substantial, not from tactical and diplomatic moves. The Reformation storm in the decisive early years was, for the most part, a battle over substantial things. In so far as the attitude described characterised the Catholic establishment, the Church was bound to be defeated. Deliverance came from other hidden depths.

When the rumour spread round Worms that Luther had been murdered on his homeward journey, and passions ran so high that the papal representatives appeared to be in danger of their lives, Aleander himself certified his readiness to fulfil his duty even to the death; for, he said, 'let the Lord's will be done; it is his cause we defend'. Undoubtedly his intention was serious. He had in mind the unwavering fulfilment of his duties in the service of the Roman Church. This went hand in hand with a correct but shallow and uncreative piety, unhallowed by any heroic virtue. This is the very image that is typical of the whole effort that was put forward by Catholics at that time to combat the innovation. This was specially true, as we shall see, of the literary effort.

What does a review of German Catholicism tell us about the condition of the Catholic mind?

We shall see strength as well as awareness of the danger varying greatly as the years go by. Twelve years later, in 1532, things seemed so desperate, that people were inclined to seize at help from whatever quarter. Better to have married or secretly married priests than none at all. A few years later still (11 March 1538) that most energetic bishop, Augustine Marius wrote in disgust: 'I have given up all hope of the troubles of the times and of the Church ever being repaired or the sects overcome, no matter how much the popes bestir themselves, even if they call a council' – which will not happen in any case.

Here, then, is one of the characteristics, if not *the* characteristic of the active section of German Catholics: in contrast to the attitude south of the Alps, in Germany there was an acute awareness of the danger. Aleander's description of the situation was essentially correct, if perhaps a little too sharply accentuated. 'Mortal terror has seized everyone.'

> The shepherd has been struck down,
> The lambs are scattered,
> The pope has been chased out. (Murner, 1522)

Amongst those actually engaged in the fray, the sense of danger was to increase until it became fear that the empire might be taken away from the Germans, and until, in face of the irremediability and apathy of Catholics, Cochlaeus and the young John Hoffmeister (born 1509/10) demonstrated the essentially greater devotion there was on the Protestant side.

Let us consider first of all the prince bishops. These men were no leaders. In the early years it was their silence and apathy that produced all the essential problems. Their behaviour over the bull of excommunication makes this obvious. We know the type of nobleman's or prince's son who was entrusted with episcopal power. His main feature was religious spinelessness, to say the least, and often we discern duplicity of a much worse kind. These men neither saw any danger nor made any effort to see it; and they were not prepared to give generous and consistent support, even by supplying material things, to those who were ready to battle against the storm. A capable bishop like Gabriel von Eichstätt (and we will come across several such men) might honestly recognise Lutheranism as a divine chastisement, a punishment for the inactivity of the bishops; but he was compelled to write: 'In Augsburg I have said these things to several bishops, but it makes no impression, it does not touch their hearts.'

They preferred to leave the work to their advisers. The canker was apparent during the early years of the Reformation in the way in which many bishops – even Albrecht of Mainz – had assistants who sympathised with the Lutheran cause, who were straightforward Lutherans or became so. This is the parallel to the incomprehensible state of affairs bemoaned by Aleander, that even within the curia there was a pro-Lutheran party, who were quick to inform the German Lutherans of all that was going on in Rome. The bull of excommunication was printed in Germany even before its publications.

As the bishops, so were the cathedral chapters – 'the fat canons devoid of piety', as Eck called them. With them we find the same ignorance, indolence and worse; and, correspondingly, a meagre supply of any spirit of sacrifice or loyalty.

The picture is completed by the religious and secular clergy who, vacillating or already decided, supported Luther. We have heard what Aleander had to say: ' . . . practically all of the clergy, with the exception of the parish priests, sympathise with the new doctrines.' 'Amongst the scholars there are many enlightened and upright men who take less offence at Luther's writings the more honestly and deeply they are attached to evangelical truth. We see how by his blameless life he commends himself to all, and that everyone, whose judgment is incorruptible, wishes him well. All admit that they have been improved by this man's writings.' Thus wrote the Dominican John Faber from Augsburg in 1520.

The printed word was undoubtedly one of the most characteristic expressions of the sixteenth century. This was true of the Catholic side too. Their literary performance, to which we will return later, will give us the most exact insight into the character, the strength as well as the weakness, of the Catholic effort, as it was throughout the entire Reformation period.

In the forefront during the earliest years we meet two men, well known to us already, whose work is typical of the Catholic mind. Both had already badly undermined their own authority by their unfortunate and unintelligent entry into the controversy with Luther. These men were Prierias and Van Hoogstraeten – both Dominicans.

At this particular point it is worth remarking that to play down the polemical value of these men is not to deny their scholarship or the value of their other theological work. In this respect we will have to supply certain corrections. It was, however, a real embarrassment to the Church that these men, of all people, were amongst those first opponents of Luther who in great measure had lost the sympathy of the learned world through their part in the Reuchlin affair. In addition, Prierias' pamphlets made it all too easy for the budding Reformer to dispose of the whole thing. As we have said, Luther published them himself. Immediately, the importance of fresh, inspired energy, over against lifeless tractates, became obvious. Prierias' first pamphlet is an exact expression of the irresponsible self-assurance of the curia. It was a courageous attack, but lacked foundation. Prierias' co-religionist, John Faber of Augsburg was right when he demanded that people read Luther's writings before denouncing him as an heretic or even contradicting him.

John Eck was a man of totally different stamp. We already have some idea of what he was like from the Leipzig disputation. He, too, had plenty of self-assurance. In Germany he was the faithful representative of the papal curia, in good things as well as in bad. In every respect, however, his performance reached the level of greatness, although not, indeed, from the start.

Eck's tireless counter efforts and the ruthless manner in which he went about his work during the early decisive years contributed greatly to taking the theological controversy right out of the atmosphere of the schools. This was critical in turning the Reformation into a living issue in public life. However much egoism and greed for glory played their part in Eck, it was he who compelled Luther to disclose the uncatholic foundation of his thought. By so doing he made it clear to the public that ultimate values were at stake; it was not just a non-committal dispute over things of more or less interest.

We must, indeed, ask whether Eck's ruthless sharpness was not too little blessed by religious power and a sense of responsibility, and whether, as a result of this effect, it did not unnecessarily urge Luther on. The question arises not least with regard to Eck's manner of promulgating the bull of excommunication. It would repay us to consider whether it would not have been better to have shown more solicitude for the peace of the Church. After all that has been said, quite obviously we do not mean that relativist indifferentism or apathy should have been indulged. But could not the bitter complaints – treated with such superiority and not the slightest attempt at understanding – have been dealt with a little more cautiously? Ought not Luther to have been given a brotherly warning before being declared a heretic? Today we know that there was no prospect of success; but at the time no one could have known; and so this does not excuse them.

Of more practical use to the Church was John Cochlaeus, although he was no intellectual match for the Ingolstadt professor of theology. Cochlaeus was parish priest of Frankfurt, later a canon of Breslau, and the only man in the Catholic phalanx to see the Reformation through to the end. He died in 1552.

Cochlaeus' milieu was the strongly anti-Roman Nuremberg Pirkheimer circle. Even in his Cologne days, besides scholastic theologians (including Ortwin to whom were addressed the *Letters of Obscure Men*) he numbered specially amongst his acquaintances, humanists, one of whom was Hutten. He had not chosen theological study from an interior sense of calling, as Eck had done, nor even out of love for the Church. Like so many others he was interested in a benefice.

Something deeply spiritual happened to him, however. In contrast to Eck he experienced an interior transformation. A crisis came in Frankfurt in 1520. Until then he had been well disposed towards Luther. Now he parted company with him. He was the first humanist of any eminence who turned towards the Church and openly opposed Luther. Instantly the hue and cry of unbridled and calumnious polemic was raised against him.

Cochlaeus was by no means blind to what was of positive value in Luther. In 1537 he attributed Catholic values to the Reformer as he was in 1518–20. This makes his becoming an anti-Lutheran appear all the stranger. He, the humanist from the cultural revolutionary circle of Pirkheimer, would find it enormously difficult to break with Luther, who had been joyfully acclaimed as the German Reformer, antagonist of the pope's Church and its doctrines. What, then, had moved him to make his decision? Foolish rumours about what had started Luther off. 'The affair was not started in the name of God, and so it will not proceed in his name either.' He heard also that the Augustinian was fighting the Dominican, Tetzel, because his order had been entrusted with preaching the indulgence. Even in 1549 Cochlaeus still dared to repeat: 'Luther's silence in the face of such a charge so completely revolted me that thereafter I suspected and abhorred all that he did.' And so upon such empty accidents was based the emergence of one of the chief forces in the old Church that was fighting for its life.

Obviously there were other deep contributory causes; but if thus we may not exclude Catholic faith from Cochlaeus, in the end, in true Erasmian manner, what led him to oppose Luther was his interest in the learning that was about to blossom, and his fear of Luther's irresponsibility and provocation of unrest. It was not merely incidental that the work of this most faithful Catholic champion was based at first upon no genuine or significant religious foundation.

And so the polemic against the new doctrines was bound to suffer from these false presuppositions. From the start they made light of it: there was nothing new in Luther other than his gift of invective – he had set the whole German Church in a blaze merely to be revenged on one man, Eck. In his commentary on Luther, Cochlaeus fixed the Catholic image of Luther for the centuries to come. He prided himself that this work had put an end to the false opinion about Luther hitherto current amongst Catholics, that is to 'the gross error that Luther had been a good, devout and saintly man, more versed than anyone in holy scripture'. Moreover, in this work by using a rough axe upon a rough trunk he took over the worst coarseness of Lutheran polemic: 'Luther is a child of the devil, possessed by the devil, full of falsehood and vainglory. His revolt was caused by monkish envy of the Dominican, Tetzel; he lusts after wine and women, is without conscience, and approves any means to gain his end. He thinks only of himself. He perpetrated the act of nailing up the theses for forty-two gulden – the sum he required to buy a new cowl. He is a liar and a hypocrite, cowardly and quarrelsome. There is no drop of German blood in him. . . .'

The anti-Catholic authors of later times made hay of such aberrations as these. Today we are able to see more accurately and hence more deeply.

There is more to Cochlaeus, however, than these unpardonable lapses in judgment. 'There can be no doubt of his desire to serve the truth, of his subjective conviction that he honestly tried to arrive at the truth about Luther, in spite of all his errors and false conclusions and hatred.' Even more – his life was a life of sacrifice, for the Church and for his fatherland also. His horribly thin polemic was constantly paid for by great effort. Over and over again it was his enormous, active, laborious and costly attention, which advanced the literary theological work of Catholics and brought it to public notice. He threw in his weight on every possible literary front. Above all, all his life, at great material sacrifice, he had built and maintained printing presses, until they fell into the hands of Lutheran authorities or were sold; then he built new ones. He declined a lucrative post in Rome so that he could carry on the work of controversial theology in Germany.

Aleander himself had recognised the need to mobilise Catholic intellectual resources, and had pleaded for an improved polemical theological effort. He had demanded that the pope foster this literary defence, and Bible study. In so doing, as a humanist he had correctly realised that correctness of doctrine was not everything: writers were needed as well. Rome's reaction was bad. Cochlaeus, who did such an enormous amount for Rome, and did it so selflessly, had to pay three hundred gold gulden for the benefice of St Victor's in Mainz, although he had no idea where the money was to come from. Once again, in 1535 the same curia left this financially exhausted man in the lurch; and even his fervent entreaties for specific measures against the new doctrines produced only a few promises, but no action.

THREE

Decision for the Reformation
(1521–1525)

I. THE POLITICAL AND ECCLESIO-POLITICAL SITUATION

During the last years of his reign the emperor Maximilian had once again set his mind on realising his concept of the empire and its unity. He wanted to ensure that the vast superiority of the house of Habsburg–Burgundy would endure. He worked for the election of his grandson Charles as king of the Romans. Having himself acquired this honour in his own father's lifetime, undoubtedly a repetition of this arrangement would have meant a significant strengthening of the idea of the monarchy and the development of the empire into an hereditary dynasty.

Once again the electoral princes rose in opposition. This was understandable. Less edifying, however, was the manner of opposition. With the exception of Frederick the Wise, elector of Saxony, who jealously guarded the completely independent right of election of the electoral princes, every vote could be bought. At the *Reichstag* in Augsburg in 1518 Maximilian made a deal with Brandenburg, Mainz, the Palatinate and Cologne; but as the Spanish gold did not turn up, the deal remained ineffective.

And then the emperor died in 1519. Everything had to start from the beginning again, and now within the larger framework of an imperial election. Now the great world powers entered the arena, bringing their incomparably greater weight to bear upon the deliberations. But the same deal went on with the electors, whose votes were bought by bribery, and diplomatic or military pressure.

The Habsburg candidate was not the Archduke Ferdinand, but Charles I of Castile, Aragon, Burgundy and Sicily. It was not the power of his thrones, but his right as first-born and something indefinable, his youth and the mysterious power of imperious command, that was the reason for the choice.

Inevitably there were two opponents to this candidate – the pope and France.

The pope had to object because he had to do all in his power to prevent the states of the Church being encircled by a single power. This would happen if the occupant of the throne of Naples and Sicily obtained the imperial feudal lands of Milan. And so the pope decided to support the king of France. He persuaded him with very powerful diplomatic means, and also with those methods of 'reward' which were so much taken for granted at the curia that, as we have seen, they were decisively used in the campaign against Luther. Cardinals' hats were dangled in front of the electors of Trier and Cologne, on condition that they voted for the French king. It is true that they also received from the curia instructions which contained a formal command to vote for the Frenchman. This was a blunder, for it aroused the opposition of the lords of the Rhineland and a measure of national awareness.

There was nothing too unusual about a French king seeking the 'German' imperial crown. For long enough Maximilian had worked to gain the crown of England. The manner in which the electors allowed themselves to be moved by the frivolous and pleasure-loving Francis I proves that they were very far from looking upon a French emperor as an offensive idea. Nor was the plan the outcome of a foolish lust for power. Obviously the ancient rivalry between Germany and France played its part; but the fate of France was also at stake, for France was already encircled by Habsburg–Burgundy–Spain. If the ruler of Spain became emperor, the circle would be complete, and the sole possibility of mobility outwards, the Milan possessions, would also be threatened. And it was precisely the acquisitions in northern Italy that could not be better protected for Francis I than by a French emperor. On the other hand, there was the fear that under a Habsburg emperor the Burgundian challenge instead of being directed at Germany, would turn against France.

Moreover, the French imperial plan was but the logical continuation or resumption of universal political designs of the French monarchy upon a united greater Europe in the style of Charlemagne.

At the end of the thirteenth century the Cologne canon, Alexander of Roes, had already seen the danger that Pope Martin IV might make a Frenchman emperor. And now in 1518 the ambassadors of Francis I did not forget, when approaching the German princes, to declare their king's legal right to the crown of the great Frankish emperor.

At first French money flowed more abundantly. But in Germany there were the Fuggers. This family, a mighty power in Europe, had been financing Habsburg policy since 1490, and continued to do so until the Schmalkald War. From the moment when the Spanish Habsburgs resolved to do business with this German firm, the best financial security in the world at that time was on their side, and their cause had won. The election cost the Spanish Habsburgs some 850,000 gold gulden. About half of this sum was spent on straightforward bribery. The Fuggers' detailed accounts of how the money was used are most instructive. It went to the electors (Mainz received 103,000 gulden), and to councillors and servants, who, in the case of Mainz, received 10,200 gulden. It was an undisguised piece of haggling, with frequent defections from one side to the other (cf. the Brandenburgers, for example).

There was only one elector who could not be bought: Luther's territorial ruler, who was determined to do nothing other than his duty, while at the same time yielding none of his independence. None the less, even he was not left empty-handed.

Later, Jacob Fugger had once boasted in front of Charles V, that without his co-operation he would never have become emperor. It was true. But it was not true to say that he had made the emperor. Other forces had been at work also. Rudimentary national consciousness was already a force, even with the mercenary electors: after all, Charles was Maximilian's grandson. Besides this, the servitude of French absolutism was hateful to the

German estates. The autonomy of their territories, which they had defended and developed so successfully under Maximilian, might be seriously threatened by the extremely energetic French senates. In 1515 the Swiss had been defeated by the French at Marignana; now Francis had taken Milan; they were determined not to be encircled. The imperial adviser Van Zevenberghe plied them with money and promises. As clear as daylight they let it be known that they would recognise no one as emperor unless he were of German stock.

Finally: this time the Habsburg diplomacy was the better. They understood that this trial of strength had to be backed up by powerful instruments. They took over the army of the Swabian League, which, led by a Habsburg, had chased Archduke Ulrich of Würtemberg out of his domains,[1] and won over Sickingen and his knights as allies. This provided a healthy pressure which the bribed electors, casting their votes in Frankfurt, did not resist.

Once Pope Leo X had seen how hopeless were the chances of his own French candidate, he tried to obstruct Charles' election by another method. He launched a new candidate: the imperial administrator, Elector Frederick of Saxony. Eight days before the election he informed him, through the Saxon chamberlain, von Miltiz, of papal support for his candidature.[2] The pope hoped thereby to prevent foreign political influence in Italy from falling into a single hand. In the end he would be able perhaps to divide and rule.

The plan was quite impossible. Neither the intellectual and moral power of the Saxon nor the political power of his dynasty would have been anything like sufficient to hold in check the 'brood of German princes'. In particular he would have had to reckon with the irreconcilable and much more powerful opposition of the Habsburg–Burgundian–Spanish dynasty. Nor could the possibility be excluded of France making common cause with the

---

[1] This Ulrich, violating the peace pact, attacked the imperial city of Reutlingen immediately after Maximilian's death. France was behind this act.

[2] The details of the announcement are somewhat vague on account of the high-handed additions made by Miltiz. It would appear, however, that it was declared to the elector that the pope was ready to make one of the elector's friends a cardinal. The elector took this to mean Luther.

Habsburg when she had properly assessed his chances. The empire would have been broken up. Over and above the imminent con-confessional division, Germany would have been doomed to see a national division also. Frederick was clear-headed enough to see that his sense of patriotic obligation to his own principality would not be capable of filling out the whole framework of the imperial power and function. And so he declined.

The pope realised that Charles' election was inevitable; and he was pliable enough to bow to the force of circumstances.

As the theologians were gathering in Leipzig for the disputation, the electors were assembling in Frankfurt to elect an emperor. This was in June. The six electors and the ambassador of the king of Bohemia all voted for Charles I of Spain and Burgundy as emperor of the holy Roman empire. The first to give his vote was Albert of Mainz, who had received – in addition to monetary bribes – the promise of complete control of the imperial chancellery, and that application would be made to the pope for him to receive a fourth bishopric in Germany, and that he would be made papal legate to the empire.

The elector of Brandenburg alone remained loyal to the French candidate, for it seemed that Francis I would provide unusual possibilities for the aggrandisement of his dynasty within the empire. Would not he become Francis' regent in the empire and his brother, the archbishop of Mainz, the papal legate? In one respect a French emperor would have placed the empire ecclesiastically and politically in the hands of Brandenburg. In the end he too voted with the rest for the nineteen-year-old heir of the world empire, for he thought it imprudent to oppose him all on his own. None the less, he thought it perfectly consonant with his honour to register a secret protest to the effect that he voted out of fear and not from sound judgment.

This important election was supplemented by an even more important enactment, proposed, not, as previously, by any particular elector, but by them all. It might reasonably be supposed that the new sovereign would have to spend much time outside the empire. Should he leave his representatives in the empire it might happen that Germany would fall into alien hands. And so they took precautions. The German character of the empire, as well as their electoral privileges, was assured. Only born Germans could be given imperial offices by the emperor. He was not permitted to hold a *Reichstag* outside the empire. Within the empire the only official languages were to be German and Latin. In addition, he had to form an imperial administration. Once again the old idea of the estates was put forward, this time reinforced by national interests.

Charles' plenipotentiaries subscribed to the enactment. When he himself arrived in Germany at Aachen, he added his oath. We must distinguish his view of the nature of a prince, especially of an emperor, from that held by the electors. On their view the emperor ought to rule the empire in conjunction with the estates; or, the estates formed the empire and the emperor was added to it. Charles, on the other hand, regarded the German emperor as lord of the empire. At the *Reichstag* in Worms in 1521 he had it announced plainly that 'it was his will that Germany should have not many but only one master'. In his system of thought, which was by no means confined to the realm of theory but released political power, there was to be found the lively notion of *one* Christendom, with the emperor as its real, secular head, very much co-ordinated with the spiritual head. If we would understand Charles' political and religious activity throughout the course of his life, we must be quite clear about the way he looked at things. This is important most of all when we are considering the forties of the century, when he intervened so autonomously in the dogmatic and ecclesiastical movement.

Charles V was Burgundian and Spanish with a very small dash of Habsburg blood. From 1507, Maximilian's daughter Margaret had been regent in the Netherlands where Charles was educated as a Burgundian, speaking French and acquiring French culture. It is true that his tutor, Adrian of Utrecht, was a Netherlander, that is of German culture; but strict limits were set to German influence upon Charles because the German language was excluded. Charles never mastered German. And again, Adrian himself, later to be grand inquisitor and then pope, was the representative of a universal, medieval, ecclesiastical culture. He stood on a completely different plane from Charles' first highly important political educators and advisers, who were representatives of a French-style Burgundian culture, and who, like all the many princely councils in France and Germany, exerted an ever-increasing influence upon nationally or territorially conducted state affairs.

Just as the kernel of Charles' political power lay in the Netherlands, so, in accordance with his education, he could best be described as a Burgundian Netherlander. The first term would signify cultural influences, the second the geographical scene.

Even so, we still have not come to the heart of the matter. True, Charles was no German by blood, and he was not purely German in mentality and attitude; but it is equally wrong to call him a Spaniard. In Spain he was looked upon as a foreigner. Charles' deepest characteristic was indicated by the very fact that he was a Burgundian. Burgundy had never been a nation, but was, rather, a modern variation on an old, departed, universalist theme. His basic characteristic was his lack of nationality; and this was demonstrated by his world policy. The ultimate reason for this was his utterly uncompromising conception of one faith and one Church as the sole possible form of existence for a single Christendom. In contrast to all the Machiavellis of Rome, France and Holland, and at his own court, he regarded the Catholic faith as something inviolable, even in the political sphere. He was, in fact, a true Christian.

Being, then, neither a German nor a Spaniard, was Charles antipathetic to things German? Was it so difficult to pay more heed to over-all German interests, to use them, that is, less to gain one's own ends than did Joachim I of Brandenburg, the elector who was bought by France? In this Charles was no German: he was not motivated by petty particularist viewpoints, as were most of the German princes, whose thoughts did not go out beyond the bounds of their own territories, and who were intent merely on filling their own pockets.

For Charles the dignity of the German emperor was always the ruling factor in his thought and action. Can we say that to exalt this idea, which had kept alive the world sovereignty of the German imperial crown throughout the Middle Ages, to seek conscientiously and laboriously to realise it, was something un-German?

If the emperor worked at the same time for the exaltation of his own dynasty, this did not contradict the universal imperial programme. There was a shift of emphasis, it is true; but this dynasty was and was to be the vehicle for fulfilling a vocation on the grand

scale. The more autonomous the imperial house, the more effectively could the universal programme be carried out for the good
of a unified Christendom. It was a very different story where the
papacy was concerned. The unity of Christendom was directly
threatened by Clement VII's thinking and acting first and foremost as a Medici, for this was a flagrant renunciation of his universal obligations.

Charles' universalist attitude was outwardly expressed by his
choice of supreme councillors, from whom he so speedily and surely
withdrew, to become the classic example of the unapproachable
world ruler. These councillors were drawn from a great variety of
nations. No consistent national line is discernible in the sequence
of Dutchmen, Frenchmen, Italians and Spaniards; and the absence of German influence is undoubtedly significant. We might
well say that any patriotism Charles may have known, inclined
more and more towards Spain. His love for his Portuguese wife
played no small part in this. In harmony with this inclination, too,
was his religion. His later confessors, were without exception,
Spanish, and he favoured an Erasmian style of piety. At all times,
however, Charles remained the ruler of nations, not one of their
number.

Only thus could he rule over his lands. What was his colossal
empire? Above all it lacked unity. The only semblance of unity
lay in the person of the ruler. In Spain, however, political division, in terms of tradition and contemporary alignments, had
already begun. Spain was still very far from unity such as France
had already attained. Burgundy comprised an autonomous dukedom in the south and the Netherlands in the north: the two were
greatly divergent in every way – in terms of geography, culture,
economic and political needs. But we must think of all these parts
as linked up together. Austria on the frontier of the infidel, and
northern Italy – constantly having to be consolidated – no longer
formed a solid bridge between the east and Spain in the west, even
if the safe territory of southern Italy were included. The ultimate
burden, however, was this: the German territories very largely
felt themselves at variance with the empire and the emperor, and
the emperor himself was a territorial prince. Unified action
was obstructed by a host of almost irresolvable tensions. The explosive potential in these tensions was further aggravated by

imminent schism in the Church, and the emergence of new sects.

To fulfil his function successfully, as far as Germany was concerned, there was only one means that would be adequate. He had to create an all-embracing sense of nationhood. This could not be the nationalism of the humanists or of Luther, with its anti-Rome slant. It would have to be a sense of common obligation towards the empire in the hearts of those who possessed power, that is the princes. Unfortunately they had no such feelings. The dynastic egoism which we saw so callously at work in the unsavoury bribery of 1518 and 1519 dogged the story of the Reformation through many a disgraceful episode in the *Reichstag*, until it reached its climax in the shameful betrayal of German territory to France by the double-dealing Maurice of Saxony.

In considering their guilt, however, we must bear in mind the very bad example set the princes by the renaissance popes in their deals with the Turks. And it had been the imperial policy that kept alive antipathy to the French through stressing the French danger. In face of this danger, Trier, for example, had been insufficiently protected, and so, thrown on its own resources, had made peace with France to a certain extent. On the opposite frontier stood the arch-enemy: the Turks. It was Ferdinand's territory – Austria and Hungary – that really felt this pressure. Were France to enter into alliance with the infidel, this pressure would increase and these lands would press for greater agreement between the empire and France. This in turn meant that the ideas of the Burgundian emperor – doubly antagonistic to France – were by no means simply in harmony with the needs of the separate parts of his empire.

Charles' person and task significantly represented the fatal cleavage emerging between the universal Church–empire concept and the relentlessly advancing concept of nationhood. It was precisely this nationalism that was stirring and seeking expression in the reform of the empire, despite all aberration and egoism, and that appeared quite unrestrained in the humanists, amongst Sickingen's and Hutten's knights, and in the mighty popular Reformation movement of Luther. From the purely political angle, Charles would have great difficulty coming to terms with this Germany. This cleavage between the universal and the national, between the German and the European, found its consummation in the antithesis between the Catholic and the new belief. From the very start, Charles V's rule in Germany was destined, by the objective alignment of forces, for a collision. The period up to the peace of Westphalia contained all the fateful answers to the problem. Even this peace in 1648 was nothing but the admission of exhaustion, the admission that there could be no solution. And so a compromise was made legal.

It has been asked why Charles did not select a few of the problems presented by his territories and solve them completely instead of tackling an impossibly large-scale task. This sounds reasonable, and yet all practical politics contradict the notion. The traditional concept of the universal demanded that the situation be tackled as a whole. As soon as we begin to examine the separate issues tackled one by one by the emperor, we see that he could have ignored none of them without jeopardising the whole of his power. It is quite easy to prove that this was so in respect of the interior order of Spain, of resistance to the Moslems in North Africa, who threatened the granary of Sicily, which at the same time represented a most important interior link in the Habsburg state, and in respect of resistance to the Turks in Hungary. Could Charles have left Spain to suffer chaos, himself remaining in Germany during the twenties? This was a utopian dream. Without the ever-ready financial and military strength of a well-ordered and firmly occupied Spain the emperor's power would soon have collapsed in Italy and in Burgundy, despite the support of Flanders. The emperor would have become a shadow.

The necessity was already being discussed of a dispute with France over northern Italy. There were those who wanted to dismiss a battle against the religious innovators as suicidal. But that was a mere mirage. The emperor would have had to deny his deepest convictions and fail in his duty. It was impossible for him to acquiesce in what he saw would cause a split in the empire. He could not introduce a foreign body into his Catholic lands. And so fate left the emperor with an insoluble problem. None the less, as we shall see, he rose nobly to the challenge.

All of this enables us to see to some extent why all the German affairs and plans of Charles V went so unevenly, remained uncompleted, and, indeed, were doomed to end in disaster. The reason was that the empire formed but a part of his interests. It could never be more because he was never able to devote all of his time and attention and energies to the empire. In 1530 he made this entry in his memoirs: 'At this time there was much disagreement with the princes. Because the emperor realised that by reason of the vast kingdom and territories entrusted to him by God it was impossible for him to reside so much in the empire as he would have liked, and as he ought, he resolved to have his brother elected as king of the Romans.' The splitting up of functions and powers, the interior fate of Germany in general, became the fate of the German emperor as well. This had, in fact, been the fate of them all, throughout the entire Middle Ages. This, too, was the fate of the Church in Germany.

Charles was in Spain when he learned of his election. He was, indeed, no more than a claimant to Spain, to the inheritance of Ferdinand of Aragon in particular; but not until February of the next year, 1520, did the full uncertainty of his position become apparent. It seemed to contain within itself every possibility of highest glory, but to begin with it was full of danger. Aggressively, Francis I announced his claims upon Milan. Charles, he demanded, was to give him the fief on behalf of the empire, and in addition was to promise not to lead any armies into Italy. This was the first proclamation of that mighty dispute with France, that was to run all through Charles' reign, profoundly influencing development within Germany and upon her eastern frontier (in the war with the Turks). The acquisition of Würtemberg, annexed by the Habsburgs in 1520 in return for the refund of the war debt from the Swabian League certainly represented a considerable increase in strength; but at the same time it encumbered Charles with fresh dangers, which Philip of Hesse was later to exploit.

Charles' councillors countered France's move by turning sharply towards England, now celebrating the triumph of her middle course European policy under her chancellor, Cardinal Wolsey. While Charles, avoiding France, was sailing to the Netherlands, and engaging in his double meeting with Henry VIII, there broke out in Spain the uprising of the estates – the *comunidades* – against the monarchy.

This then was the very dubious situation in which Charles found himself when, on 21 October 1520, he set foot for the first time on German soil, and was greeted in the ancient ceremonial way by the electors. He was twenty years of age, pale and a bit puny. People had a poor opinion of his intellectual ability. He received the greeting in complete silence – a symbolic circumstance. Whenever he could, if the occasion was propitious, and even in violation of etiquette, which demanded that before princes, or the pope and cardinals, one should state one's case as eloquently as possible, Charles was from first to last a man of silence. In 1520 he may have been assailed with indecision or embarrassment; but already he was practising the silence of the unapproachable ruler, who knew himself to be the chosen one. He had a sense of consecration – strongly objective and having nothing whatever to do with personal arrogance. Between him and the geniality of his grandfather there was an immense gulf.

We have Charles V's memoirs – written in French – which clearly reveal his spiritual and intellectual image, mediated by the early scenes in Germany. He was unusually reserved, committed himself to few judgments, was remarkably level-headed and just in assessing the politico-military situation, even when it was unfavourable to himself, or in assessing the assistance given him by others (e.g. Admiral Doria in 1528). With the almost puritanical austerity of Spanish ceremonial, the figures of the queen mother and his brother Ferdinand appear and disappear, as do the various countries, without ever betraying any intimate contact with the lord and master of the world.

II. THE REICHSTAG AT WORMS

Charles was crowned king in Aachen on 23 October 1520. The solemn coronation vows assuring the basic rights of Church and state were made in the form of answers to six salient questions, which included: 'Will you keep and advance our traditional, holy, Catholic faith; will you be a faithful protector of the Church and her ministers; will you govern the empire with justice; will you give due submission to the holy father, the pope of Rome, and to his Church?'

By 26 October the cardinal archbishop of Mainz, Albert of Brandenburg, was able to announce that the pope had agreed to confer upon the new king the title of 'elected Roman emperor'. German princes crowded the court, and the young ruler behaved graciously to all, even to Brandenburg. It looked as if the great wave of trust and enthusiasm, which surged from the whole people, and which caused even Luther to place his hope in 'the noble young blood', was the beginning of true inner unity.

But the tough reality remained; the coronation itself reiterated the fateful question: 'Will you keep and advance our traditional holy, Catholic faith?'

On 28 September Charles had ordered the burning of Luther's writings in the Netherlands. Meanwhile the elector of Saxony had arrived at the court, and was being favoured before all the rest. Moreover, this elector was now in the act of receiving the bull of excommunication against Luther. The game of hide-and-seek over its authenticity was finished. Through the nuncios, Aleander and Caraccioli, Rome demanded the immediate declaration of Luther as a notorious heretic, and his excommunication with all attendant penalties.

Now a tussle ensued between the elector of Saxony and the papal nuncios concerning Charles' decision. The persistence of Frederick the Wise added to the difficulties arising from the power-political situation within Germany resulted in the demands of territorial churchmanship prevailing over the wishes of emperor and pope. The elector insisted that Luther, not having been tried in Germany could not be condemned on behalf of the empire. The battle moved to and fro. Aleander reported to Rome: 'Our business follows a fluctuating and hourly changing course . . . on every side are obstacles and personal passions, so that without the emperor we would be lost.' On 28 November the emperor agreed with Saxony that Luther should be examined again. He ordered Saxony to attend the coming *Reichstag* and bring his Wittenberg professor with him. At the end of December, however, the elector of Saxony himself began to be undecided. He entreated the emperor to spare him the embarrassment of a hearing before the *Reichstag*.

Meanwhile the act of burning had taken place in front of the Else gate in Wittenberg, and Luther had renewed his appeal to a general council. The period of grace granted him in the bull had run out, and he was now excommunicate. This provided the imperial chancellery with opportunity to proceed with greater energy. On 29 December a severe imperial mandate was issued against Luther; but it was not put into effect.

The mind behind this mandate was the papal nuncio, Aleander, and he was much more clear-sighted than the imperial council. He knew, or guessed, with instinctive certainty, what it might mean if German anti-Roman feeling was able to stage a final, symbolic demonstration by means of a dogmatic clash in the solemn assembly of the *Reichstag*. Day in, day out, he observed how things had changed since the days of Huss at Constance. It was his influence, too, that made the emperor qualify his acquiescence in Frederick's demands. Luther was to appear merely in order to recant. On 5 January 1521, in Worms, once again Frederick made the emperor change his mind. The mandate was forgotten. At the beginning of February Aleander again had the upper hand. But now the problems of power politics began to be more obvious in the *Reichstag*. The imperial council incorporated the Luther affair in their political calculations, in order to use him against the curia. From the Church's point of view, this was dangerous; for at the imperial court, as at the courts of many of the prince bishops, there were Lutheranising, if not blatantly Lutheran, councillors, who were secretly drawing pensions from the Saxon court. The danger was all the greater because the director of imperial policy, Chièvres, had so thoroughly learned to regard and to treat the pope as a political power. 'Take heed,' he said to Aleander, 'that your pope does not thwart our plans, then his holiness will gain everything; but if he does, he will bring upon himself such confusion. . . .' Aleander complained that the emperor paid heed to the German 'preference for Luther' in order to gain approval for the Roman campaign. When the plan became known that Brandenburg was going to marry his eldest son to the sister of the queen of France, the emperor's solicitude for the elector of Saxony increased even more.

In view of his own double-minded attitude. Aleander's voluble complaints cut little ice. He was convinced that without the emperor's intervention the whole of Germany was in danger of apostasy. He knew that the emperor's loyalty to the Church (he used the term 'conscience') was stronger than in any other man he had ever known. It is all the more astonishing, therefore, that he advised an external and calculating method of dealing with the emperor. For example, the curia were to treat the matter of Luther before the emperor as something not terribly serious, so that 'the emperor would not demand too much in return for his assistance'.

The elector of Saxony set the pace. On 6 March 1521 the estates having given their approval, the famous imperial writ was issued on behalf of the heretic, formally condemned by the pope, who had still failed to recant long after the sixty days' grace had expired, and who in addition had publicly declared himself as a defiant revolutionary by burning the papal legal code. Luther, moreover, had now been explicitly excommunicated in a bull dated 3 January, and an interdict had been laid upon any place where he resided. The emperor had been urged in a papal brief to 'publish an order throughout Germany. . . . The burgomasters of the towns, the regents of the states along with their officials and servants must publicly announce to all that they are going to take action against this Martin, according to the terms of our bull.' The writ was something quite unheard of; and this of itself shows how the mighty interior disposition of forces was bringing about a transformation even of the outward structure of life. The writ was subscribed by Charles and by the arch-chancellor, Cardinal Albert of Mainz. They addressed the heretic thus: 'Honourable, dear and devout brother, we and the estates here assembled, having resolved to receive information from you concerning the doctrines and books recently produced by you, do hereby send you our own and the empires' safe conduct here and back, with the desire that you would come to us within twenty-one days, fearing no violence or injustice . . . .'

A detailed guarantee of safe conduct was enclosed. Luther could travel in peace. It is beside the point that in 1524 Luther asserted that he stood before the emperor and the estates, knowing in advance that his safe conduct would be violated. This is but a further proof of how faulty his imagination was as a source of objective recollection of his own so passionate experience.

The *Reichstag* at Worms in 1521 was a parallel to that of 1495. Once again the centre of interest was the construction of a constitutional balance between the empire, that is the emperor, and the estates, by the formation of an imperial government. But there was a difference: in 1495 a promising beginning led to a positive result; now the result was a compromise, doomed to disaster. It was a compromise because the monarchically minded Charles would not agree to any real limitation of his powers by the estates. And so all that was created was an administration to act during his absence from the empire. The president was to be, not the estates, but a regent of the emperor – 'The emperor's government within the realm' (seat at Nuremberg as for the privy council). Nothing came of this because the princes would not agree to such servitude. They would not surrender to the empire or the emperor, the absolute juridical power that was rooted solely in their own territories. The struggle to resolve this tension, often dependent upon the world political situation – principally pressure from France or the Turks – lasted throughout the entire Reformation period. Indeed, it acquired its full meaning and importance precisely from the religious strife. No matter how much and how ruthlessly the political interests of the princes bedevilled the purely religious issue, there can be no doubt that in the end it was the impetus provided by the religious issue which enabled the princes to resist Charles' attempt to destroy their autonomy.

Once again the religious question was taken up in the *Reichstag* principally in the matter of the *Gravamina*. It was highly significant that the issue was clearly formulated by that specially loyal churchman, Duke George of Saxony.

And now the expression of hatred of Rome in Germany rose to a hurricane. On 2 April Luther set out from Wittenberg on the little cart put at his disposal by the town council of Wittenberg. He was accompanied by a few acquaintances, headed by Herold Sturm, known as *Deutschland*, one of the emperor's men, whose face is known to us from Dürer's portrait.

Aleander's observation that his journey was like a triumphal procession has often been repeated. This comment has tended, however, to obscure the true import of the facts. Throughout the entire empire the old religion was still taken for granted, and enjoyed every right to mould public life and enjoy the benefits of its institutions, for these institutions served none but those who professed the old faith. In every place the ancient liturgy was fully observed, and, in particular, holy mass was celebrated. Scarcely anyone thought of a real breakaway from the Church. And now one of those countless and much hated mendicant monks – for Luther was still a monk in dress, habits and life – was marching

L

through Germany, having already been solemnly declared a heretic by the supreme spiritual head of Christendom. This was a triumphal procession – and no mistake! In many cities he was solemnly acclaimed by the learned. Town councils, too, and much of the populace, applauded him as a liberator, with an enthusiasm that went far beyond mere curiosity. Aleander blamed the whole thing upon the anti-Roman Herold. There is no need to deny this, for Sturm was obviously in a position to make articulate the enthusiasm that already existed.

The journey was watched in Worms with rising tension. Would the great heretic really come? The atmosphere was full of foreboding, as before a mighty crisis. In Worms from the start of the *Reichstag*, under the very eyes of the emperor, the princes and the papal ambassadors, anti-Roman feeling was being expressed in ways that seemed to open the doors to a tumult of unrest. In Cologne Aleander had been given a hot reception. In Worms he was nearly stoned, and had difficulty in finding somewhere to stay. His name was erased from doors, and many other pranks were played upon him – the papal ambassador. He received nasty threats. In general there were signs of serious agitation. An unusually high number of murders occurred. Hutten incited the people to violence: 'Get out! (the nuncios) Do you not see that the wind of freedom blows, and people are sick of the *status quo*? They want something new.'

The papal party tried to avert the imminent episode at the *Reichstag*. The emperor's confessor risked a journey to the Ebernburg, which already harboured a nest of Lutherans, and was known as a 'haven of righteousness'. There he disputed with Hutten and Sickingen, who showed himself well versed in Luther's German writings, and also with Butzer the ex-Dominican. They agreed that instead of going to Worms Luther should come to the Ebernburg, where the affair would be settled through friendly discussion. Butzer took the proposal to Luther, who declined. In December, when asked by Spalatin, he had declared himself most ready to come: 'For there can be no doubt that if the emperor summons me it is the Lord that is calling me. He who preserved the three youths in the fiery furnace of the king of Babylon still lives. In this case we must think neither of danger nor of deliverance. We have only to take heed that the gospel upon which we have embarked is not mocked by the godless.' His idea now was that the emperor's confessor, if he liked, might interview him at Worms. He wanted to attend the *Reichstag*. He was full of the courage of his convictions, and also of a spirit of defiance born of a proud self-confidence, that we never see in the saints. 'Even if they kindle a fire that stretches from Worms to Wittenberg, I will still appear in the name of my Lord, and walk right into the very teeth of the monster' . . . 'defying the powers of hell'. 'I will go to Worms supposing there are as many devils there as tiles on the roofs.' He was undisturbed even by the elector's declaration that he ought not to come because he could not protect him. He trod his path with a complete assurance to the very end.

At ten o'clock on the morning of 16 April 1521 Luther entered Worms. Excitement grew in the city. Luther's followers were suspicious. Was the fate of Christ himself to be re-enacted in Luther? Luther was to appear in the *Reichstag* the next afternoon. The crowds were so great that he had to be brought there by a detour.

Luther was given a hearing before the emperor and the empire. The most significant thing about the proceedings at Worms was the mere fact that it happened at all, that the empire did not simply take action against the solemnly condemned heretic, but ventilated the question whether action should be taken against him or not, and then gave him a hearing. That the emperor and the imperial state formally considered this, and then acted accordingly, was the real threat to, if not the denial of, the foundations upon which Europe rested. This vacillation announced that the structure of Europe was on the point of disintegration. In comparison, the fact that imperial law had been insufficiently considered and that the consequences thereof had to be faced in the years that followed, is a mere bagatelle.

The full significance is seen in the fact that the people helped to bring about the structural change, and in some measure were aware of what was happening. In 1521 Worms was in the grip of a genuine, widespread, popular, public opinion. Aleander's reports are there for us to read. From him we learn what public opinion was and meant for a small well-defined area at the centre of a world event. We learn further to what extent the Lutheran cause had become a popular movement – under the very eyes of the imperial majesty and all the estates of the realm. 'The world has got into such a state that a mischievous villain and murderer, a criminal drunkard like Hutten can dress himself up as an improver of the state, and has the effrontery to say and do such things in the emperor's very face. If he were to be punished there would be a mighty outcry' (Aleander). The whole city was pervaded by anti-clericalism of the worst sort. Aleander affirmed that this had been the normal attitude of the Germans from time immemorial. While this mood was at its height the bishops were imprudent enough to aggravate this feeling towards the entire clergy by their arrogant way of life. 'A national uprising is threatened – the whole of Germany is in an uproar. Nine-tenths are for Luther, and the remainder, even, are shouting: "down with the Roman court!" They venerate Luther with religious fervour, hail him as sinless, buy and kiss his picture. This is not the Catholic Germany we once knew.' Aleander had found the perfect formulation of the whole problem; and then he exaggerated everything speaking as though conditions had reached a final and settled stage: 'The Germans have become convinced that they can remain good Christians, can even hold on to the Catholic faith, and yet rebel against the pope.'

The picture was, in fact, so grotesque that those in Rome, to whom Aleander addressed this report, took it for one of the rhetorical exaggerations of Aleander the humanist and diplomat. But the picture was perfectly accurate. The fact that those who were pro-Lutheran and antipapal for the most part had no idea of the far-reaching import of Luther's views or of their own sympathy for him did leave the way open for a future reaction; but to begin with it only heightened the danger.

The elector of Saxony summed up the feelings of all of Luther's sympathisers: 'It is only just that Luther should have an opportunity of defending himself. The condemnation of a German without any previous hearing is bound to rouse justifiable annoyance.' This demand was too weighty to be ignored. It expressed the longing for freedom that had long since been alive in every quarter. It had emerged in intellectual and humanist circles, in the realm of home and foreign politics, and now, augmented by rage and hatred, it appeared with great power in the sphere of Church politics.

The details of Luther's hearing at Worms are well known. His affair was overshadowed by the interests of high politics – the emperor's need of soldiers and of money, the necessities of imperial reform, and the *gravamina* against Rome. In spite of this the hearing followed its course according to its own rhythm.

On 17 April, the day after his arrival in Worms, Luther admitted authorship of the books laid before him, but asked for time to consider recanting. In this we may perhaps detect an element of anxiety in Luther's attitude. In reality, however, it betrayed a premeditated plan. Aleander may have enjoyed triumph, but it was short-lived. Granting the respite, the emperor asked Luther to consider 'the great danger, discord, unrest, insurrection and bloodshed that your doctrine has let loose upon the world, but which could be stopped by the suppression of your books'. The emperor was looking to the future, and expressing a thought that was constantly to recur in Counter-Reformation polemics.

On the next day, 18 April, the scene was acted, which made world history. Luther refused to recant. He did so first in German, then in Latin, in a well-phrased and neatly composed speech, which none the less clearly manifested the Reformer's style and attitude. Advisedly (probably at the instigation of Saxon councillors) he had included in the introduction to his address an anticipatory apology for the too great impulsiveness which he might possibly display in word or gesture.

In making his reply he divided his books into three groups. The real point at issue was contained in the second group – the books which attacked the power and the doctrine of the papacy. And here, for all his carefully weighed thought, Luther became abusive. No other process, no other declaration of the period shows so impressively how far hatred of Rome had gone in Germany, and how much it had become almost officially taken for granted, as does this section of Luther's address, in which a condemned heretic could dare to speak with such lack of restraint in front of representatives of the whole empire, the secular counterpart of the Church – the emperor and all of the princes, spiritual and temporal. He said: 'The pope is that power which by its abominable doctrines and bad example has ravaged, laid waste and destroyed the Christian world in spirit and in body. None can deny or disguise this fact, because all have experienced how the laws of the pope and his human doctrines have unmercifully enslaved, burdened and tortured the consciences of those who believe in Christ; and every tongue complains loudly of these things.'

At last the chancellor of Trier, John Eck, demanded a clear answer to the question: did Luther recant or not? This was the signal for a declaration of rebellion against the old Church. 'Unless I can be convinced by the testimony of scripture and of plain reason, I shall remain firmly convinced by the scriptural texts I have cited; and my conscience is a prisoner of the word of God. I neither can nor wish to recant, for to act contrary to conscience is inconvenient, unwholesome and dangerous. God help me. Amen!' He spoke the last words both times in German.

The whole episode was charged with colossal tension. As we follow the exposition of the texts we can sense how world history was being made. A new world was staring the old world in the face.

At a sign from the emperor, Luther was sent out. An uproar followed. Would they let Luther live? Curses were called down upon the heretic. It is reported that Luther waved his arms in the air and shouted: 'I'm through!' During the following night a bill was stuck upon public buildings. It ran thus: '400 noblemen have sworn to protect Luther. They declare war on the Romanisers and the princes. I tell you bluntly I mean to hit hard. I have 8,000 fighting men behind me. *Bundschuh, Bundschuh, Bundschuh.*'

What was the response of the old world? Only one of the princes present, the emperor himself, a representative of this world, fully realised the threatening tension, and reacted, in accordance with his rank, in an uncompromising fashion. He declared war. His eyes had been opened by the heretic's stubborn defiance of the empire. During the time that Chièvres had been ill, the emperor had greatly developed – as Aleander noticed. On the very next day in a document written in French in his own hand, he declared his opinion to the irresolute estates: 'My predecessors, the most Christian emperors of the German stock, the Austrian archdukes and dukes of Burgundy have all been loyal to the Catholic Church to their death, defending and propagating its faith, to the glory of God, and for the salvation of their souls. They have handed down the holy Catholic religion for me to live and die in. Until this day by the grace of God I have been brought up in this religion, as befits an emperor. That, which my predecessors accomplished at Constance, is my privilege to uphold. A simple monk, supported by his own private judgment, has risen up against the faith held by all Christians for more than a thousand years, and he has the audacity to affirm that until this day all Christians have erred. I have resolved, therefore, to enlist all my states, all my friends, and to put forth the strength of my whole body and soul, in this cause. And I declare to you that I am sorry to have delayed so long before taking action against Luther and his false doctrine. I will listen to him no longer, I have resolved to treat him and to take proceedings against him as a notorious heretic, and I require of you that in this affair you all behave as true Christians.'

But the theological situation was so lamentably confused, the Church so powerless, and Luther's cause already so closely linked with the country's destiny – peace or war – that the princes who were loyal to the Church did not like to think of Luther breaking with the Church, and so tried again to find a way out by having another hearing. Although he did not agree, the emperor consented; and a series of transactions followed. The participants varied, under the leaderships of the elector of Trier and the chancellor of Baden, Jerome Vehus. They tried to get Luther to admit the infallibility of councils, at least of the Council of Constance. Considering all that had happened this was a naïve attempt. The elector of Trier made four utterly fantastic proposals to Luther. Luther immediately withdrew within his ultimate citadel, from which he had declaimed his 'No' to the emperor. This was his conscience – the product of all his secret conflicts in the monastery, and wherein lay all of his stored up, now indestructible energies.

At last the whole perplexity of the old party became evident. 'How are we to deal with the whole business?' Luther pointed to the Acts of the Apostles: 'If this undertaking is of men, it will fail; but if it is of God, you will not be able to overthrow them.'

At this time an episode occurred, more far-reaching in importance than the official sequel. Cochlaeus was consumed with the ambition to beat Luther in a public disputation. He went quite over the score, urged Luther to decline his safe-conduct and dispute with him for his life. This suggestion so enraged Luther's companions that it nearly cost Cochlaeus his life. Ultimately the two faced each other in Luther's bedroom. Here, deeply moved,

Luther showed himself to be aware not only of the irrevocability of the cleavage but also of the tragedy of the situation.

Luther departed on 26 April. At the gate of the city he was met by a convoy of twenty knights. Four days later he sent Herold back. He wrote to the emperor, the electors, the princes and the estates of the realm. With exceptional skill he again affirmed that he was ready, as he always had been, to submit to any examination and trial and even to recant, provided that he could be refuted from the plain word of God. Equally skilful was his insistent, emphatic presupposition and demand, that the sole Christian norm had to be the free and unrestricted superiority of the word of God over all things, for 'the dignity and power of holy and divine scripture is greater than the capacity of the sum of all human intelligences'. Finally he worked round to the point that the issue was not a personal one, concerning him alone. He was concerned for the good of the whole of Christendom, of the emperor, of the empire and of the German nation.

At Eisenach, where he preached despite the interdict, he sent back the professors who were with him. Beyond Möhra he was apprehended and taken to the Wartburg, where he remained from the evening of 4 May until 1 March 1522, except for the period 2–12 December, which he spent secretly in Wittenberg.

A mere fourteen days after Luther's departure, the proceedings at Worms were published. Luther was the hero of the day.

What was the legal sequel? It took from 29 April until 8 May to work out and modify an edict against Luther. Political considerations constantly prejudiced the issue. At last Charles was able to put his signature to the document. Aleander at once revealed his total failure to grasp the situation. He imagined that the Church had been saved. He spoke of the complete stamping out of the Lutheran doctrine, which had already been largely disposed of and was diminishing day by day. He became almost jocular about this 'blessed mandate', this 'final instrument which human skill has devised and which the Blessed Trinity has poured out upon us from his strength.'

The Edict of Worms against Luther was an enormously detailed and ponderous document. Dogmatically it was based chiefly upon the *Babylonian Captivity*, and it enumerates Luther's errors for the most part as in the bull threatening excommunication[3] and in Aleander's Ash Wednesday address. In two different places the complaint is made that Luther had singled out the Council of Constance for special attack, and had insulted the German nation by calling this council a synagogue of Satan. Those who took part in it, 'our predecessor Sigismund and the holy empire of princes he called Antichrist and the apostles of the devil. Luther is no human being, but the evil one in human form, disguised under a monk's cowl. Because Luther has now become obdurate, we, the emperor, in everlasting memorial of this affair, have declared Martin Luther to be a member severed from the Church of God, and have unmasked him as an obstinate subverter and public heretic.' Then followed the prohibition to give him lodging, the outlawing of his followers and the prohibition to buy, sell or possess his books. All books that dealt even slightly with the Christian faith were to have the imprimatur of the local ordinary.

The edict was issued 'in virtue of the power of our imperial dignity, sovereignty and authority, and with the clear advice and consent of our and the empire's electors, princes and estates now here assembled'. The estates, however, had long since disbanded. In fact, only the elector Joachim had agreed to the edict in the name of the rest. In spite of this the edict was not only valid in imperial law, the emperor being obliged to take action against heretics, but valid also as an imperial law of the estates; for at Luther's hearing the estates had explicitly declared that the emperor might take action against Luther, should he refuse to recant. On the other hand, the edict was not included in the resolutions of the *Reichstag*, and this damaged its authority – even in the eyes of the loyal churchman, Duke George of Saxony.

From this moment on, Luther was under sentence from the pope, the emperor, and in terms of imperial law.

Bezold has described the Edict of Worms as Charles V's farewell to the German nation. How true is this statement?

Enthusiasm for Luther corresponded to the hatred Germans felt for Rome; and we know how enormous this hatred was. We have

---

[3] Considering that Dr Eck helped to frame the bull, and made it his business to publish it as widely as possible, it is interesting to note that he sharply criticised the way in which Luther's errors were set out in the edict.

also sufficiently explained how this enthusiasm for Luther embraced the widest variety of confused and conflicting tendencies. The Edict of Worms expressed loyalty to the ancestral Church and to the fundamental laws of the empire. Automatically a widespread defection from Luther resulted from the recognition of his apostasy from the traditional faith. Those who continued to support him could not claim to be the sole representatives of the nation. Furthermore, it is impossible simply to discount the overwhelming Catholic majority in the estates at the *Reichstag* of Worms in 1521.

On the other hand, we may not exclude the plainly attested fact of threatening political and social insurrection. In view of such a threat, was it not the duty of those who saw it coming to remove one of its chief causes?

Luther was a revolutionary. In the extraordinary inflammation of these months and years his moving utterances against a corrupt clergy, and against good works, and his views concerning the summary expiation of sin – which he had preached in a sermon at Erfurt as he travelled to Worms – might well precipitate revolution. A small illustration of this was provided by the events in Erfurt immediately after Luther's departure. We are too much inclined to underestimate the social and political power of Luther's speech. This power was its very essence. Throughout his whole life Luther never felt that he had raged enough against every grade of cleric. Those holding secular authority, too (1523), were a target for his revolutionary diatribes. It is hard to understand how Luther was able to let loose such undisciplined and wild statements as he did on this subject. It is even harder to understand how people think they must disguise the revolutionary element in these writings by appealing to passages which speak of obedience to our secular rulers. The flood of inflammatory material, indeed, sweeps away the other passages. He castigated the perverted minds of the princes who withstood his gospel, he heaped strange sins upon these 'murderers of Christ, these great fools, not one of whom shows the least signs of wit or piety'. Luther publicly threatened an imminent revolution: 'Be lost then! We will not, we cannot endure your tyranny and malice any longer. Dear princes and lords, who still know how to save yourselves, God will not suffer it any longer. The world is no longer what it was yesterday, when you hunted the people like wild animals.'

This does not alter the fact that, in spite of the edict, the Church was bound to lose the day at Worms. The immediate cause lay in the fact that the council of princes, the most capable of whom, John of Schwarzenburg, was a thorough Lutheran sympathiser, directed and carried out the real work. They did this in matters of improving the imperial administration and creating new sources of income, and so they took the initiative likewise in dealing with Luther. It is worth noting on this point that there were several of Erasmus' disciples close to the emperor. But a deeper cause lay in the fact that with the party upon whom the interests of Christianity depended, comprising the emperor, the estates, the curia, practical and external instruments of political and diplomatic calculation played far too great a part. We know what Aleander's views were about this, and, in particular, his lack of deep religious concern. In his despatches he does indeed ask for a few fervent *Paters* to implore God's direction of the whole affair, but the sentiment is such an afterthought that it sounds a bit insincere. Shortly before Luther's arrival in Worms he saw clearly that 'on account of the Lutheran question the salvation of Christendom was at stake', and he feared that 'a universal dissolution was setting in'; but even this does not seem to have heightened his religious earnestness; instead, against the whole background of events, the discrepancy between the task to be done and the means for doing it becomes more and more apparent. It is painful, considering Luther's conscientious attitude, to find so much diplomatic calculation in the representative of the curia. These things were, indeed, part of his task, and, placed in an atmosphere of animosity and lies, he had to try to fulfil his task as best he could. 'And so he made unscrupulous use of the emperor's secretary, Spiegel, without actually relying upon him.' He accepted without a word much that Butzer proposed; he presented a completely trusting front, and quietly went his busy and crafty way.

Unfortunately this was no accoutrement for an urgent religious mood. Aleander reports, for example, the following wicked proposal. 'Luther made certain statements to the archbishop of Trier under the seal of confession; the archbishop therefore refused to confide these things to the emperor. None the less, relying upon my intimate relationship with the archbishop, I will try to persuade him that he should secretly pass on the information to the pope for the glory of God and to advance the peace of the Church, as he is not bound to uphold the sacrament of penance for the benefit of one who destroys confession, a notorious heretic who has been expelled from the Church.' In one of his despatches (26 May) one is pained to discover a flippant mood, the intermingling of pious verses with others from the *Ars amatoria* of Ovid, reminiscent of the unseemly letter which Eck sent from the Leipzig disputation to Hauer and Burchard. In both cases there is a depressing absence of any sense of the seriousness of the situation.

On the one side, Aleander, on the other, Luther; the humanist over against the revolutionary *homo religiosus*. This contrast expresses the whole tragedy of the Catholic situation. We must bear in mind the religious, ecclesiastical, sacramental impotence of humanism in the style of Erasmus, if we are to assess the mortally dangerous weakness of the old Church as she went forward officially to face her challenger. The papacy, which had made no move against Erasmian relativism, against the spirit of non-dogmatism, now sent out as field marshal, a representative of that very spirit.

It would have been in harmony with the emperor's declaration of war after Luther's trial, and with the importance of the affair, had the execution of the edict been regarded by the emperor as a matter of urgency. Did he so regard it? At all events he turned his attention to Spain and France. Political circumstances forced him to do so. He left Ferdinand to represent him in Germany and travelled to Spain via the Netherlands. He was away for nine years. Bereft of their most powerful and most active representative the Catholic powers in Germany had no real leader.

III. IN THE WARTBURG

It was the elector Frederick of Saxony who had to have Luther taken for safe custody to the Wartburg. For the sake of his professor he defied the imperial decree. Why was he attached to Luther? He had hardly ever seen Luther face to face. Even later on he never fell under the spell of the superman.

Whatever considerations moved Frederick to act thus, the fact remains: he was the saviour of the Reformation. Without him Luther would have been lost in 1518, and again in 1521, and with him, the Reformation. From 1518 onwards the elector constantly and unfailingly protected Luther. This faithfulness is scarcely conceivable apart from some positive relationship to Luther's views on the Church and on religion.

The university of Wittenberg was this elector's darling creation, and Luther an important professor at that university, gradually winning European renown by his universal appeal to the studious youth of every land. It cannot seriously be affirmed, however, that this dutiful territorial prince and elector, Frederick the Wise, would have defied an imperial decree merely to keep a celebrity at his own university. Stronger motives must surely have been there in things that served the ends of this rising and struggling principality. When, a day after receiving the summons to Rome, Luther appealed to his territorial overlord, this provided an excellent opportunity of increasing his own ecclesiastical power.

In view of the election of the king and the emperor, Luther had become a decisive figure upon the political chessboard: his elector's support of him becomes more understandable. Again, after the election of the emperor, Luther's own public influence had become so great, as a result of the far-reaching effect of his views on religion and the Church, that the elector was able to appeal to the threatening popular mood.

The most important thing of all, however, was this: independent as the elector was, he was not the sole author of his decisions. His relationship with Luther provides a direct disclosure of the significance for the progress of world history of the creation of an intelligent and legally informed class of officials. We have only to think of the precisely regulated behaviour of Luther at Worms, where he was constantly supported by Frederick's advisers, to see this force at work, which then continued to play such a prominent part in carrying out the Reformation, including the secularisation, which did such harm to the old Church. In the case we are now considering this class of officials were particularly influential. Frederick's right-hand man was his secretary, Spalatin – George Burchard of Spalt. Luther had made his acquaintance as early as 1514. Spiritually he was completely sympathetic to Luther. We cannot exaggerate Spalatin's importance for the spread of the Reformation. He was one of its true fathers.

Luther did not exactly make it easy for the elector to protect him. Take the question of indulgences for example. At that time the elector might have regarded Luther as a troublesome adversary, for he was destroying the value of his whole collection of relics, and accusing him, indirectly at least, of having a totally unchristian outlook. In addition, in his letters to the elector Luther often vehemently expressed a self-willed defiance that could easily have strained their good relations. Soon Luther was to leave the Wartburg and visit Wittenberg, contrary to the elector's wishes. Consider, too, the tone in which he announced his decision. In truth, Luther here shows himself to be anything but a flatterer of princes.

It is the period at the Wartburg that probably best portrays Luther's psychological make-up: a singularly unstable and shaky conscience, the dangerous unbalance of which was held in check by an immense creative power. Sudden solitude following the excitement of so much recent turmoil, the natural reaction after fearful tension and physical excitement, the wine he drank so copiously, the constipation from which he suffered so badly, all of these things would have been sufficient to endanger a much more balanced and less eccentric mind than his. It is not astonishing that he faced fierce temptations. We can understand how his strained nerves would fire him to speak in superlatives. We must try to imagine the contrast between Worms with its world-shaking events, where the nation buzzed around Luther as their leader, and the anonymous sylvan solitude of the Wartburg. It was as though he awoke on a different planet; and he was an outlaw in the empire – no small consideration. His depression is understandable, as is the fresh sense of sin over trivialities, anguish over the fire he had kindled, and about which the devil was now worrying him. Conversely, he was harrassed by the thought that perhaps he had displayed weakness before his judges in Worms, that he might have attacked them much more vehemently. Undoubtedly, for him belief in the devil was central. Within the plan of redemption, by God's decree, the devil possessed enormous significance. This, too, was an idea that Luther had freshly formulated from his own experience and from the teaching of the Bible. The world was, indeed, full of devils, and in the Wartburg they now set about a concerted attack upon Luther.

We cannot overlook the unbalance of such a badly controlled

excitement. In addition there was, as in all of Luther's trials, that overpowering sense of the wrath of God which pressed upon him in temptation. Above all, however, temptations were, so to speak, his affair alone. In face of all of the factors making up public life, within a short time, from his Patmos he became more or less master of the situation, in spite of his enforced anonymity. In 1520 he had presented the nation with a comprehensive programme, and in defiance of pope, emperor and empire had staked his life for the cause. Having survived the first shattering convulsions he appeared once again in his old mood. And now the last restraints of the supposed humility, to which he had so often appealed, were cast off. So little did he feel himself the underdog, that he exploded in rage when, during his secret stay at Wittenberg, he discovered that Spalatin had not delivered letters or sent his manuscripts to the press: 'What I have written will be published!' He also attacked the elector who saved his life, denouncing his favourite endowment, the church of All Saints in Wittenberg, as he denounced that of the cardinal of Mainz, calling it the 'idol in Halle'.

That is but one, perhaps the least important, expression of his inner power. His literary works are a more essential expression of this power. They constitute primarily a continuation of his oral and literary pastoral work of 1518. They are, moreover, of the highest importance, revealing as they do a quality that is seldom found in tempestuous revolutionaries, for most of them, although able to argue, are unable to consolidate, having no understanding of how to let things grow; but Luther the revolutionary, who had no sense of history, possessed in pre-eminent measure the gift of consolidating and building up. Without pausing in his effervescent and violent attacks (against Latomus, Ambrosius Catharinus, the Parisians) he was able to build positively and progressively in a significant fashion. The new collection of his sermons and the translation of the New Testament form the core of this work, the aim and achievement of which are obvious: the permanent influencing of his followers by the regular reiteration of those thoughts and that awareness of salvation which had accomplished his own conversion.

The peak of Luther's religious activity was his German translation of the Bible. On 12 December he returned from his secret trip to Wittenberg to the Wartburg where, in the space of a mere ten weeks, he finished translating the New Testament.

Today we are well informed about the vast amount of work that had been done on translations of the Bible before Luther's day. We know how foolish it is to speak of a creation *ex nihilo* by Luther. Moreover, we possess, too, the equipment to assess the objective influence of the very early translations. It is false, in respect of the religious as of the linguistic development of Germany, to assert that Luther was the first to give Germany its Bible and its language. We ought to speak more precisely; and the sooner we do so, the easier it will be to preserve Luther's true renown. With a diligence that we might envy, Luther read deeply in holy scripture. He lived and moved in it. The rule of St Augustine held him to this, and he fulfilled the rule's requirements far more faithfully than by the mere study of the *Sentences* of Peter Lombard.

For Luther the Bible thus became the real power centre of Christianity. It was not simply an account of that power but the power itself – the sacrament that transforms. It transformed and yet did not transform; for this thoroughly real transformation was ultimately a transformation of mentality, not of being. Luther did, it is true, understand this mentality as supernatural faith bestowed by God – as something objective. This faith is at the same time the most personal surrender to the Father; but it is not created by the infusion of a transforming elevation of human substance. It is brought about by the word, but man's substance is and remains corrupt. The fulness of the word may well be intensified in the powerful manner in which Luther did intensify it; ultimately, however, the distinction between mentality and being remains, a distinction that was to prove the seed of schism for centuries.

Luther had grown up on the Bible. Reproducing this, his deepest treasure, in the German tongue, he created a living thing. None before him had been able to do this with such tempestuous life.

The result cannot be disputed. It followed both from the religious turmoil that Luther had unleashed and based upon the word, and from his mastery of language, which placed his translation far ahead of that of any of his precursors. Luther had evolved an inimitable cadence which blended the strange words in the most beautiful marriage with the German idiom, striking both mind and ear with amazing power. Even Cochlaeus forcibly admitted that

Luther's German translation of the New Testament had stirred up the religous sentiment of the people, and created a true hunger for the word of God in the ordinary man. Here was the religious centre which Luther produced to go along with his movement, that was so largely geared towards secession.

With regard to the dogmatic assessment of Luther's translation the important thing is not isolated alterations in the text (Rm 3 : 28, 4 : 15, 8 : 24). To enumerate these was the method of the fussy defensive polemics of the sixteenth century. What they overlooked was that St Thomas himself had translated Rm 3 : 28 by 'faith alone'. What is much more important was that this marriage of specifically Lutheran language and outlook with the word of God had been accomplished. It is true that in this Germanising, which is much more than a philologically exact translation, Luther saw the objective word as the chief thing. He had no intention of propounding his own doctrine, but that of Christ. In spite of that, in the inner rhythm and outward cadence the German, as it lived subjectively and uniquely in Luther, asserts itself subjectively and individualistically in the translation. The relationship between the Latin of the Vulgate and the Greek is quite different. In this sense we may say that Luther tied the timeless and suprarational truth of divine revelation too closely to nature as expressed in one particular language. Luther's subjectivism, dangerous as it was rich, had penetrated the translation. Here, too, the great man's plan of unlimited service had not succeeded.

This was all perfectly logical. The preface to the translation opened up the most radical approach to a destruction of the canon of scripture. Luther himself had already launched a radical attack; but the fatally decisive thing was this: he did not accept the whole of revelation equally, but looked for what was *essential* in the doctrine. This procedure is a faithful reflection of Luther's dogmatic outlook and of his theological method in general. This concept, however, necessarily produced its opposite: the *non-essential*. Thus from the whole corpus a core was chosen: St John's Gospel (understood in a one-sided manner as a parallel to the Epistle to Romans) the First Epistle of John, St Paul's Epistle to Romans, Galatians and Ephesians, and the First Epistle of Peter. The value of the rest shades off until we come to those that Luther wanted to reject or of which he could make nothing, because they said nothing to him: the Epistle of James, and the Apocalypse of St John.

We feel some amazement. Is this the same Luther who constantly reproached the pope for inept human adaptation of the divine word, who, for his part, wished to rely solely upon the immovable word? Here is a colossal contradiction, made no less by the fact that Protestant scholarship, largely accepting the foundation of this whole system, and enjoying the quite inexhaustible treasure of the German Bible, has scarcely paid any attention to this aspect of the question.

We reach the same result from examination of details. According to Luther there is an absolute, sublimely free predestination of man for hell. But in 1 Tm 2 : 4 we read that God desires all men to be saved. Luther quite simply applied this to the elect; and that is no less than to turn the text into its opposite. He justified this by his general viewpoint. He felt the irresistible need to relate everything to a few fixed points – to a single point indeed. By following this method, however, he contradicted the foundation of all his ideas: that the words of the Bible were to be taken baldly and naïvely at their face value.

We need not be surprised to discover further that this eminently religious and pastoral work bears traces also of polemical controversy with various opponents of the Reformation. But it is the style of the music that interests us now. In the apocalypse (1522) the 'great whore' already wears the triple papal crown, and papal Rome goes up in flames and collapses. Even so this is but a mild foretaste of the colossal grossness of later polemical imagery used in attacking the papacy.

The vast labour of translating the whole of the Bible into German went on until 1534; and the complete edition was not published until 1541, after a revision of the previous work and the enlistment of help from collaborators.

It was at the Wartburg that Luther made his most characteristic utterance – an utterance that was to be much misunderstood, and unjustly or one-sidedly turned against him. Melanchthon, unsupported by his strong master, was stricken with fear, and unable to cope with the turmoil within and beyond the university. Assailed by temptations on every side, he complained of his sufferings to Luther, who wrote: 'Sin bravely, but believe even more bravely.'

Its paradoxical audacity made this a truly Lutheran saying. On the one hand it expressed his conviction of the invincibility of concupiscence, on the other the all-conquering power of faith. There is the conviction that the tree is good – the tree of faith, that is – and can bring forth only good fruit, but it is burdened with the unresolvable inner contradiction of persistent sin. At an early stage Luther had already preached: 'We need not fear that Christ will be idle: no, there is none more active and busy than he.' And then in 1523 he said: 'It is impossible that there be not true Christians wherever the gospel is preached, no matter how few they are or how frail and sinful.'

In the exaggerated moralism of the preachers, who spoke of nothing but morality, and good works, Luther saw a distortion of the faith. Correctly, he objected to the order of precedence: morality – faith; but he himself falsified the picture by his radicalism. He allowed faith to triumph in isolation, even over sin which persisted.

Amongst the extreme fanatics, in particular, we see most plainly how inadequately morality was safeguarded in such a system. Ludwig Haetzer, leader of the iconoclasts against Zwingle in 1523, expressed this conviction in a single stanza, which sums up the nominalistic externalisation of the process of justification.

> True, says the world, there is no need
> for me to suffer with Christ; for he
> himself has suffered death for me, and I
> now draw on his account.
> Dear brother, all that is a fable
> devised by the devil.

We do Luther a grave injustice if we interpret his remark to Melanchthon as being deliberately antinomian in intention, as advocating moral laxity. It would be extremely difficult to prove that Luther had indulged in laxity during his heroic period. When an old man, he wrote to the aged Spalatin: 'Until now you have been far too refined a sinner, having had a conscience only over common, petty sins. I entreat you, therefore, be one of us, who are great sinners, well and truly damned, and do not think so little of

Christ as though he could help us only with petty, childish, artificial sins.' That is to say, he is concerned with the recognition of the real sinfulness in man, which consists in man's separation from God by original sin, and so goes infinitely deeper than the lapses of any individual man.

Luther's view is fundamentally somewhat similar to that of Augustine when he said: 'Love God, and do what you like.'

It resembles Augustine's view, but the difference between Luther and Augustine is particularly instructive, and brings out the essence of Luther's thought: his fatal, unrestrained readiness to accept responsibility. Augustine is positive: if we possess love we will not sin. In contrast, Luther said: even if we sin mightily, faith will save us. This betrays the same spirit of rash daring, as we find in the same letter to Melanchthon in the statements which precede the words quoted: 'Nothing will separate us from the forgiving mercy of the Lamb of God, even if we fornicate and murder a thousand times a day.' And there is another unhappy sentence which stands in cross contradication of Luther's customary concept of the burden of sin: 'What does it matter, then, if we commit a sin?' Or further on: 'On occasion a man has to drink deep, gamble, jest, must indeed commit sin to defy the devil, so as to leave him no scope to let us become conscience-struck over petty affairs' (1530, to Jerome Weller who was stricken by depression).

Faith, powerfully exaggerated to the point of contradiction, threatened the factor of morality with extinction. There is no denying that Luther had a real sense of the enormity of sin; and yet, by these statements he removed the horror from sin, making sin itself appear not so terrible after all. Such an attitude led logically to an underrating of morality by the masses. Later on, in plain words, Luther was to lament the declining morality of his congregations. Indeed, he used the same sort of superlatives as he used against the papacy. A fairly even distribution of this lamentable development can be verified for every region in Germany. It is true that Luther's complaints are full of his characteristic exaggeration; but Protestant theology itself recognises that Luther could not possibly have had a genuine moral doctrine; and it does so with greater certainty the more it goes back to Luther himself, seeing the pastoral ethics, that began with the end of the twenties of the sixteenth century and developed throughout later generations, as a watering down of Reformed theology.

In Luther himself, moreover, we can detect a lessening of fervour in his later years. The older he grew, the more he entered into the spirit of his own doctrine. Although he never allowed the certainty of salvation logically to exclude the uncertainty of salvation, he relied more and more upon his conviction as upon an assured possession, he was less fearful of the world to come, less anxious about his eternal bliss, less scrupulous and much less anxiously engaged in doing all he possibly could to turn away God's wrath. In this we see plainly the danger inherent in the overstress of his point of departure.

IV. THE EFFECT UPON HUMANISM

The Reform writings of 1520, with their radical attacks upon the substance of the Church's teaching; the papal bull threatening excommunication; Luther's burning of the papal legal code; his refusal to recant at Worms; his being outlawed: all of these things made quite plain his radical break with the Church and the old faith, and compelled his former adherents and fellow-travellers to make up their minds. Day by day the theological question presented itself more and more unavoidably. And it produced its greatest effect in that place where, on the one hand, Luther was acclaimed most loudly as collaborator and leader, and, on the other, the theological foundation had been most obscure – within humanism. Luther's effect upon humanism was, as might be expected, diverse, not to say contradictory.

What was Luther's own relationship with humanism?

Luther owed a great deal to humanist scholarship. His progressive criticism of the Church was in part tied up with it, and the effect of his writings were dependent, quite basically even, upon the preliminary labours of humanists.

On the other hand, it is false to affirm that Luther's personal revolution was essentially determined by humanism. It is important to be clear on this point. The freer Luther's interior revolution is kept from accidental ingredients, and the more purely it is allowed to appear as a personal act of the struggling and perceptive conscience, the more clearly are his inexhaustible reserves of power revealed. To explain his own revolution it is enough to see that he read holy scripture in his own unique way. This was an activity arising from the depths of his being, and was quite independent of humanist influence. The Latin text, which the justified man read in faith, was sufficient. There was no need at all for the new interpretation of penance as *metanoia* (change of heart), based upon knowledge of Greek.

Luther could not have had any deep relationship with humanism, for it was precisely the human element, the power of man's free will, that Luther denied. Grace alone remained. For him the affairs of the soul – that is faith – were much more serious than humanists allowed. For Luther polemics was no merry game of ridicule as it was for the authors of the *Letters of Obscure Men*.

Luther did not immediately recognise this contrast to humanism. It was only natural for him at first to feel himself to some extent a member of this broad movement, which took its stand against abuses in the Church and in scholasticism. After November 1517 he often adopted the humanist form of signature 'Eleutherius' and his commentary upon the indulgence articles brought him very close in spirit to humanist theologians like Pico della Mirandola and Reuchlin.

This alone does not signify much more than that in the Heidelberg disputation he preferred Plato and Pythagoras to Aristotle. It is all of a piece with his preference for the *Theologia deutsch* before scholasticism – the antithesis to the attempt, even the claim, to master Christianity intellectually and so destroy all mystery. Again it was quite simply the preference for a more full-blooded, more emotional and less rational treatment of Christian problems. At that point, however, where this more full-blooded approach began to show itself as humanistic, as founded upon human capacities, there came a disavowal. Luther was never a humanist except in a few marginal remarks.

The relation of the humanists to Luther was quite another matter. Their enthusiasm for him did not mean that they had understood his thought. In 1521 when Luther stopped at Erfurt on his way to Worms, Eobanus Hessus appealed thus to the city: 'Rejoice O sublime Erfurt, adorn yourself with garlands, he is coming, who will deliver you from dishonour.' And yet it was not until 1524 that Hessus threw in his lot with Luther. He returned to the Church, then ended up as an Evangelical professor at Marburg. On entering the city of Erfurt. Luther was received by a deputation of forty members of the university, headed by Crotus Rubeanus, the rector at that time. In this man's eyes Luther was 'the avenger of evil; and to be allowed to look upon his face was like a divine revelation'. The same Crotus Rubeanus, however, in true optimistic humanist style described Luther's work of faith as the purification of 'true piety'. When the heresy of Luther's doctrine became apparent to him and he had to decide for or against the Church, 'with the help of God' he decided in favour of 'the communion of the holy, Christian Church'. Eck, a man in whom the humanist mark is so easily overlooked, was the first to make a definite stand against Luther. We know about Cochlaeus' challenge, and Cochlaeus was a universally recognised humanist. In addition, there was that notable representative of the new spirit, Jerome Emser, court chaplain to Duke George of Saxony. He became one of Luther's first polemical opponents. Later he was followed by the leader of the Nuremberg humanists, Willibald Pirkheimer, who, shocked at the violent statements and intolerance of the new faith, found his way back to the old Church. Soon after Worms, the Augsburg Dominican, John Faber, realised that in his report of 1520 he had judged Luther far too favourably, and so he opposed him and parted company with the humanist party. Many others retreated along the same path: Zasius, the very man whom Luther had most acclaimed, Billick, Haner, Egranus, Glareanus, Jodokus Clichtoveus. 'Every country is full of such men, learned and unlearned, who having gone into things more deeply, discover that they have been building upon sand.' Witzel, too, was one of these – their most important representative. As long as the destructive consequences of Luther's doctrine for the Church remained hidden, the Erasmian patricians went along with Luther, as they had done in Augsburg in 1518. As the issue became clear, in all of the towns it was the aristocracy who provided a retarding and antagonistic element in face of the guilds, who were on the side of innovation.

The real problem of 'humanism and Reformation' arose only at points where humanist interests had become the determining factor; but it did not arise amongst those scholars for whom it was merely a useful stimulus or even just an insignificant embellishment of their intellectual life. As little did it arise amongst those who possessed real interior freedom and balance – Thomas More, John Fisher, or even Contarini and his humanist associates in the work of Catholic reform, for these men set humanism, from the very start, in complete subordination to the Church, which had left man free to fulfil his proper place in the scale of creation.

The first of these groups was doubly split by the advance of the Reformation. First, there were the section who removed humanism from the centre of interest, moved by the Christian appeal of the redemptive religion of the cross. The representatives of this section became Evangelical theologians like Melanchthon, Zwingli, Butzer, Oecolampadius and Capito. A second section at first remained loyal to the humanist view of life, and some maintained that loyalty for good. These were rebuffed by Luther and his turbulent revolution, because their primary goal was not religion but education and peaceful evolution. Amongst this section was to be found that representative humanist mind – Erasmus. This cannot be counted much of a success on the part of the Church, and we have already seen why. But even this type of humanism was conquered by the Reformation: it turned the interests of life imperiously back to religion, so that no niche remained within the new Church for non-dogmatic humanism.

On both sides there resulted a common and highly distressing state of affairs: the rapid decline of humanistic studies at the universities, and a decline of the universities themselves. The numbers of students fell with astonishing rapidity; many universities saw their numbers drop between 1520 and 1525 to a twentieth or twenty-fifth of their former total. Those affected in this degree were Erfurt, Leipzig, Frankfurt, Rostock and Greifswald. In 1515 Vienna had 600 matriculated students, in the twenties it had twenty to thirty.

Winning Melanchthon's support was probably Luther's greatest single success. Throughout his whole life. Luther never found anyone better able to spread his doctrine. Melanchthon's value was twofold. First, he brought with him the intellectual and systematising powers of the classical scholar turned theologian; and then, as a recognised light of the humanist world, he brought a significant section of that world with him, canalising their hatred of Rome into fruitful support of Luther's doctrine of *sola fides*.

At the age of twenty-one Melanchthon took up a professorship in Wittenberg, where he immediately fell completely under the influence of Luther's personality. Very soon he was to see his life's work as the service of Luther's cause. He no longer wished to return to the south of Germany, as his uncle, Reuchlin, desired, in order to wean him from heresy. 'I must turn my eyes where Christ is calling me, not where my desire leads.' In the charming phrase of Spahn, he became 'Luther's quiet craftsman'. He harnessed the unrestrained effervescence and contradictory paradox of Luther's profession within the comprehensible framework of a doctrinal and catechetical form. Luther combined a power of direct and immediate appeal with the danger of chaotic, revolutionary confusion. Here Melanchthon became the explicit mediator and compromiser – a man of inestimable value to Luther's cause. It is true that he deprived Luther's grandiose one-sidedness of much of its original power, and so contributed to the obscuring of the most fruitful products of Luther's theology – his Christology; but very few, apart from Luther himself, were aware of this, and then not until some time later. To begin with, Melanchthon was the one who persistently made the breach with the Church appear as something not so terribly radical after all.

On the Catholic side it was the humanist, Cochlaeus, who sensed the full import of the Lutheran ascendancy. 'Although my rage against Luther, the destroyer of our fatherland, has countless just and deep reasons, nothing rouses my ire more than that he has ensnared Philip in his Hussite barbarism and Godlessness.' This feeling became so intense that later on the controversialist, Cochlaeus, lost sight of Luther to some extent, and saw Melanchthon as the more dangerous. 'The more adroitly Melanchthon, by his pleasant manner, ousts Luther in the eyes of scholars, and the more moderate he is in his doctrine, the more dangerously does he threaten the Church's cause.' For, 'Melanchthon is more gifted, more moral, than Luther, is no renegade, no married monk.'

In reality there was a vast difference between these two men. Their natures were quite opposite. From the core, Luther was irrational, but Melanchthon could harmonise antitheses – so much so, that it could be a bit awkward. Fundamentally Luther was concerned with faith, so much so, that moral concerns were unduly suppressed. Melanchthon, however, represented Lutheranism in a more ethical, humanist form. He could say that his only purpose in practising theology was to make men moral. In many ways the Evangelical theologian Melanchthon was an Erasmian. This is true obviously of his philological activities. He was, that is to say, accommodating; and this characteristic marked the tone of his polemics also. If Luther set to work 'with an axe', Master Philip followed 'with a plane'. In his inaugural speech at Wittenberg, he had called Dr Eck a typical sophist. But there was no hatred in Melanchthon's make-up. As late as 1535 he had renewed his friendship with Cochlaeus, although Cochlaeus did not keep it up for more than a year. He had sympathy too, for Charitas Pirkheimer and her nuns. When he had ascertained that she was not a slave of work-righteousness, but relied wholly upon grace, he said: 'She might as well find happiness in the cloister as in the world.' The only strange thing was the impatience he showed over quite small differences of doctrine in the Strasburg – Zürich school, and that at a time when he was ready to compromise with Catholics.

It was in keeping with this vacillating intermediate position that a rumour should have been spread in 1527–28, that Melanchthon was parting company with the Lutheran movement. In 1530 representatives of the curia tried to win him over. It was only logical that later on he became representative of the *adiaphoria*, and fell foul of the radical Lutherans, Flaccius, Amsdorf, Wigand and Gallus.

This style of humanistic Protestantism achieved world historical importance through the confession of Augsburg, the first official Lutheran code of belief – to which we shall return later – and through Zwingli.

Huldreich Zwingli (1484–1531) was a humanistic Protestant, for whom faith was cast in a rational or rationalist mould, and the Reformation of the Church was closely linked with political endeavour for the common good of his native land. He has been well characterised in his portrait by Hans Asper (central library, Zürich): 'Supporting the good of my country by doctrine, I fall by the sword of an ungrateful fatherland.'

Like Luther he was a religious reformer, but in his own characteristic way. For Luther, religion was a primary and all-embracing preoccupation. That is to say, even if through education it was closely bound up with a particular theology, this theology none the less flowed directly from an absolute relationship to God and revelation. He was constantly setting up religious subjectivism. Zwingli on the other hand, was influenced by a much stronger critical and humanist cast of mind. The difference between the two is seen at its clearest in their interpretation of the Lord's Supper. Luther accepted the words 'this is'; Zwingli took them to mean, 'this signifies'. Luther made no attempt to explain away the irrational elements in Christianity (the devil, hell, original sin), but placed them at the very centre of things. Zwingli was infinitely more rational than Luther. He fell completely into the Erasmian trap. Luther's paradox, and his eternal warfare between God and the devil, fade away in favour of an orderly system, which, once established, leaves no room for vacillation about personal election. He denied the guilt of original sin. Luther's politics were never autonomous. He never wished them to be. The real propaganda in which he indulged remained tied to the preaching of the word. Despite the colossal excesses of his coarse fulmination and dangerous agitation against Rome and the fanatics, his preaching was left essentially to the interior power of the Spirit, and supported by a magnanimous trust in the immanent power of the truth, which was able to stand up for itself. Beyond this he was content to attend to his own personal administration and domestic economy, and then to act as counsellor of the Saxon electoral government and other magisterial powers. In his eyes politics was a worldly affair. Unlike Melanchthon he did not see its importance, but remained shut up within provincial patriarchism. The greatness of his approach lay in its containing a secret power which possessed a totally unsought world application.

Zwingli, on the other hand, was an independent and autocratic, leading politician – a foreign politician, what is more. He represented a very active city, one of the many south German cities in which a similar process was going on. They were all engaged in a civic reformation in the sense of the unification of the new form of civic life in all of its departments, including religion and Church affairs. Zwingli, therefore, was more a man of action, intent on external freedom, pressing on for the expansion of his cause. We cannot measure his religious power by the standards of Luther. He was too much of a rationalist. But it is only the absolute that has power to conquer; and today, from the religious point of view, only a very small section of Protestantism lives by that which was specially attributed to Zwingli.

None the less he was an important personality. He found the way to 'the gospel' on his own. On the other hand, there can be no doubt that he learned much from Luther, and that his work made very fundamental use of Luther's.

In some degree Melanchthon forged an alliance between Protestantism and humanism in the work of Luther. Would this alliance become universal, or would humanism attain an independent position within Lutheranism? These were life and death questions for the further development of Lutheranism; and this was the very issue that Zwingli and his denomination – pressing energetically from Switzerland into Germany – were posing. As the controversy over the Lord's Supper demonstrated, this issue concerned the very core of religion.

Zwingli recognised the necessity of a political unification of north and south if the Reformation was to succeed. In this politico-religious negotiation, Strasburg became an important link. It was there that Martin Butzer (1491–1551) was working. He was a humanist. His accommodating tendencies in politics were in harmony with his mediatorial ideas in the sphere of Church and theology. This theological humanist sought to achieve utter simplification – beginning with himself. He was completely relativistic, and with him theological distinctions lost all weight. He was a disaster for Protestantism, for he was unable to avoid this relativism – as Trent had been able to do for the Catholic Church. And so the notion that dogmatic distinctions were irrelevant gained more and more ground. From the fruitlessness of confessional and intra-Protestant heresy-hunting emerged an atmosphere suffused with the humanist concepts of Zwingli, Butzer and Jakob Acontius, so that the notion of revelation was directly and basically damaged.

We already know what Luther's relationship was to Erasmus, the chief representative of German humanism. Now we must follow this relationship up to the stage of enmity.

In spite of the essential contradiction between their temperaments and ideas, Erasmus had become of prime importance for Luther and the Reformation. Even if we say that the Reformation was the most characteristic thing of the century, the figure of the great humanist retains his deep symbolism and power as a precursor of this whole epoch; for it is not the separate items desired, which alone determine the interior aspirations of an age, but intellectual and spiritual formal attitudes. Amongst these are some which made both Erasmus and Luther exponents of the sixteenth century. We think of the revolutionary and effective awareness that thoroughgoing renewal was overdue in Church and theology, a renewal, moreover, that was bound to bring about greater freedom and also greater simplicity, and hence a more essential purity of life and doctrine. We have sufficiently explained the great measure in which Erasmus prepared the way in this respect for the Saxon Reformer, by his anti-Church polemics, and his individualistic and subjectivistic mentality.

Conversely, precisely because he was a humanist, i.e. one who stressed human capabilities, he was bound to be the opponent of Luther. In 1517 Luther had already succinctly expressed this fact: 'Human things means more to him than divine.' However, Erasmus wanted to be neither friend nor enemy. His public reaction to Luther and the Reformation is a classic proof of his characteristic noncommitment. He did not want to throw in his lot with any side. He preferred, he said, the role of onlooker at the tragedy, enjoying the dispute between the two camps. In the end his decision was empty, for he was almost forced to take sides.

On the one hand: 'If, as we deduce from the mighty advance of Luther's cause, God desires all of this, and perhaps requires just such a rough physician as Luther to cure the decay of these times, then it is not for me to resist him.' He requested the elector of Saxony, however, to desist from supporting Luther (1519). In Cologne, in the following year, after the coronation, he expressed support for Luther's doctrine in twenty-two axioms, and summed up his judgment of Luther's attitude to the Church in a light-hearted but clever saying: 'Luther has sinned on two scores. He has struck the pope on the crown, and the monks in their bellies. Luther's cause is that of the sciences.'

On the other hand, Erasmus reiterated that he had never read

Luther's writings. In May 1519 he explicitly declared to the Reformer that he neither approved nor rejected any of his doctrines. 'I seek power to remain able to be of use in the new blossoming of study. It seems to me that more is to be accomplished by attractive moderation than by turmoil. Thus did Christ conquer the world.' Erasmus was described as a Lutheran by Catholics, especially by Aleander. He was quick to be seen in the company of Catholics, so as to clear himself of suspicion. He tried to consolidate his position in Rome. At Worms he denied being the author of certain Lutheran books, but this only strengthened the rumour.

Aleander treated him kindly, but had sized him up and reported his real views to Rome: Erasmus was the chief corner-stone of this heresy, and had written more damaging things against the Church than Luther had. His misleading people concerning the authenticity of the bull of excommunication was in harmony with this view.

As the strife increased, Erasmus' affirmations that he did not support the Reformation became more insistent. He asked Luther himself not to make use of his name, and Luther agreed. Meanwhile the demands of Catholics that he declare himself against Luther were pressed with greater urgency. Those who adopted this attitude included Henry VIII, Duke George of Saxony and Adrian VI. For a long time Erasmus himself had been sickened by the turmoil. Characteristically, what he most found lacking in the movement was moral improvement. 'At times I saw the audience come away from the sermon as though possessed – raging in anger, ready to stir up strife.' In contrast he was moved to sympathy by the renunciation of force and the blameless lives of the peaceful Anabaptists.

In April 1524 there was a strong rumour that the great scholar was about to write an attack upon Luther. At this point Luther addressed him: 'If it suits you, just remain what you have always said that you wanted to be: a mere onlooker at our tragedy.' Luther well knew the blow it would be to his movement should the prince of humanists finally turn his back upon him. In the end Erasmus made up his mind, and acted. He wrote against Luther. The outstanding merit of his theme was the way that it went right to the mark and uncovered the most profound conflict between Luther and humanism in the problem of free will. At the same time he laid bare the crucial antithesis between Catholicism and

Lutheranism: the incorporation of nature as the point of contact for grace in contrast to the utter destruction of nature in the process of redemption. Erasmus certainly did not, however, present a completely adequate Catholic view of man's struggle for salvation, as rooted in the religion of revelation and redemption.

Luther accepted the challenge. He composed the most systematic of all his works, which he dedicated to his father. It was entitled *The Enslaved Will.* He wrote this in 1525, shortly after marrying the ex-nun, Catherine von Bora.

V. WITTENBERG, TROUBLES AND ANABAPTISTS

Luther had sowed the storm. Now he was to reap the whirlwind. To comprehend the radical Evangelical movement, which failed to consolidate the Church, we must look at it in much greater detail than is commonly done. These things were more than just interesting episodes. They belong to the explosive forces which gave birth to modern times.

First let us consider the movement at that most significant seat and origin of Luther's work – Wittenberg. Here the movement did not proceed at all in the direction or at the tempo he would have liked. Luther was far more attached to the past than his heretical tone often suggested. He was a highly conservative revolutionary. His colossal contempt for papal and ecclesiastical tradition found its most significant counterbalance in an acute hatred of external, turbulent revolution. Without realising the fact, he remained a Catholic at heart.

This was, indeed, an expression of Luther's highly personal, unique double attitude. His hatred had a much more powerful effect upon his followers than he himself desired. The word once uttered, was no longer under his control. Quite serious-minded men could very easily become fired with the notion that there was only one right course of action: the speedy destruction of all that was Catholic.

Luther's absence from Wittenberg provided proof of this. At once the fundamental danger in Protestantism appeared, a danger rooted in Luther's doctrine: schism. Schism appeared in two forms: (1) in tumult; (2) in mystical fanaticism.

The first development of the religious innovation at Wittenberg followed Luther's conception entirely, although he might not have approved of everything that happened. Initiated partly by the town council, partly by the university and partly by the religious houses, a process of practical decatholicisation was begun. Clergy in Wittenberg began to marry, to neglect the divine office and the saying of low mass. The elector, some of the professors, and even Karlstadt himself, energetically opposed the dissolution of order that was setting in. It is true that Luther was enraged when jurists of his own party at Wittenberg declared the marriages of priests to be null and void, and their children illegitimate. Then came a most significant swing of the pendulum: the social and economic possibilities which the Reformation and the eventual secularisation of monasteries opened up for the civil authorities, now for the first time really struck the German mind, and were affirmed by the town council of Wittenberg. Monastic property became a welcome assistance in organising a system of poor relief under the direction of the authorities (24 January 1522, *Decree of the City of Wittenberg*; prime mover – Karlstadt). A new Christian community life, directed by the civil authorities, began to be formed, and included in its aims the suppression of begging and of public immorality.

And now a serious problem, hitherto insufficiently considered as a result of the dominant mood of criticism, demanded a solution. Most of Luther's followers still felt that there was a tremendous difference between the marriage of a secular priest and that of a religious. But the inner logic of the principle, once established, made it impossible in practice for disintegration to stop short at that institution which critics, even before the Reformation, had most ruthlessly attacked. In the fifteenth century it had become quite common for people to forsake their monasteries. After the publication of Luther's revolutionary treatises this practice was bound to become exceedingly widespread; and, according to Luther's teaching, marriage was permitted – was inevitable – as a further and justified consequence. Very soon, indeed, in Wittenberg the religious, too, were casting off the habit and marrying. In January 1522 the momentous general chapter of the German Augustinians took place in Wittenberg. This granted monks the right to leave. They were to work as preachers or teachers, but were to earn their living by manual work. At all events, begging was done away with. Even this was an inept attempt to arrest the development and save monasticism in some form or other.[4] Luther had destroyed the foundations of monasticism too thoroughly. The spirit of rebellion could no longer be directed along regulated lines. Moreover, in connection with this denunciation of the strongest and deepest ties, a violent reforming spirit began to take a hand in the process of laicisation. The abandonment of the cloister by monks became a turbulent affair, in which Luther took no real delight. Likewise, the attack which Luther had so vigorously led against the 'idolatry' of the mass, now began to assume a violent expression. The electors took action against those who violated the mass, but with no permanent success, for the psychological causes went too deep. Criticism, desire for reform and material destruction did not abate, but became more intense. Luther's criticism, prepared for and exceeded by that of many humanists had turned radically against the 'Judaism' of works, which included ceremonial and most of the sacraments. The logical conclusions to all this were now being drawn in Wittenberg: the oil for extreme unction was being burned, and the side altars in the Augustinian monastery were removed. With the removal of pious pictures and statues the excitement of innovation turned into an ideological battle, in which Karlstadt was one of the moving spirits.

It was no longer astonishing to find on all sides an acute resurgence of the old temptation to violent anticlericalism. Many succumbed to this temptation. The extraordinary agitation of the years from 1517 to 1525 was no episodic, accidental, isolated phenomenon, but nothing less than the climax of a process of rising aggravation, which had been going on for decades, and which was founded upon a broad intellectual, social and religious basis. In Luther, this process had found the mightiest and most revolutionary expression possible. This revolutionary power was bound to explode in tumult. For long enough now the danger of revolution had been recognised at successive *Reichstags;* and always, if general taxes had to be voted, the danger had been exorcised. The endless complaints at the *Reichstag* in Worms in 1517 made it clear that

---

[4] Martin Butzer (a Dominican) and Ambrose Blaner (a Benedictine) had both received a dispensation before forsaking the religious life.

perhaps it might not be possible to correct the evils. In 1518 a young student rejected Luther's new theses with the observation: 'If the peasants hear this they will stone you.' In 1520 Latomus, like almost all of the Catholic controversialists about him, made this criticism: 'The new liberating preaching of faith alone will produce tumult, but no improvement.'

At the time, this had not disturbed Luther in the slightest: 'The Jews, too, spoke thus and failed to improve themselves. Ought Christ, therefore, to have kept silent?' But Luther was by no means for tumult. Just as in 1520, in contrast to the weak town council, he had taken a firm stand against the excesses of his students, so in the same year he had rejected Hutten's offer of armed support. The gospel was not to be spread through violence and bloodshed. The creative and purifying word of God alone would be his instrument. While Luther was secretly at Wittenberg in 1521 he wrote saying that what he saw and heard pleased him. None the less he gained a clearer impression of the uneasy mood of the town, and he heard of the fears for the future. He was forced to issue 'a faithful admonition to all Christians, to refrain from riot and insurrection'. He was disturbed by rumours of an imminent revolt by the common man, armed with flails and clubs, bent on the destruction of priests, monks, bishops and the whole clerical estate. Nor did he want the exercise of any power save that of the princes within their own territories. Power exercised by subjects was against God. 'Insurrection never brings the improvement aimed at, for insurrection has no intelligence and as a rule strikes the innocent . . . hence no insurrection is just, no matter how just the cause it stands for. I support, and will always support the party who suffer the insurrection, no matter how unjust their cause, and will always oppose the party who make insurrection, no matter how just their cause, for the reason that insurrection can never happen without the shedding of innocent blood. The revolutionaries have not learned their trade from me; they ought to read my doctrines correctly and understand them. The ordinary man ought to keep calm and refrain from passions and words that lead to rioting. We can do quite enough harm to the priests with words and writings, without resorting to cudgels and daggers.'

But there was another, strongly emphasised idea, alongside this, militating against it. The gospel is not peace but a sword. Even in his speech before the emperor at Worms, Luther had not softened this idea in the least, but had sharply accentuated it: 'I have fully considered the danger, the strife, the insurrection, which, as I was told yesterday, are latent in my doctrine. It is proper that God's word should stir up envy and strife, for Christ came not to bring peace, but a sword, to set son against father, daughter against mother. . . . ' As well as these cautious admonitions, taking precedence over them, indeed, was the penetrating expression, in his own words and in the words of scripture, of the inevitable and eternal wrath of God directed against the pope. Luther might try as he would to dissuade men from rioting, but his blazing picture of the wickedness of the papacy and of monks, and of the supernatural punishment they deserved, could all too easily inflame minds and hearts that were already agitated and outraged. This was notably the case when he began to say that such rioting was far too mild a punishment to mete out to the clergy, who could expect nothing less than the judgment of God. When, in addition, Luther demanded that the princes rise against the clergy, he was bound to fan the flame of insurrection even more vigorously. The threat contained in his words was for ever being enhanced by his tone, which was the result of violently blazing emotion. On Shrove Tuesday in 1522 the students let derision run riot over an effigy of the pope. Luther thoroughly approved. In June 1521 there had already been antipapal demonstrations in Erfurt, and in Wittenberg there had been unrest amongst the students on 3 December, the instigator being Luther's colleague, Karlstadt.

This man has been misjudged. The over-estimate of his character, which has long been current, thanks to Hermann Barge, belongs to the series of distinguished reactions, which have turned our attention to men of second and third rank, and to the stirrings of the uneducated masses.

At the Leipzig disputation Karlstadt affirmed as a basic principle that one must treat holy scripture *ex integro*, that is in the light of the essentials contained in it. This meant that one ought not to quote learned authorities on scripture, but seek and savour the Spirit contained within the letter of scripture itself. In this he himself had displayed an appealing religious zeal. He was a seeker; and his disparaging arrogance with regard to philosophy in theology only partially detracts from this quality.

In 1520 his seeking led to a far more revolutionary demand than any that Luther had made. The Bible must be the rule for every aspect of life.

In December of 1521 he married, being forty-one years of age. At Christmas in the collegiate church at Wittenberg, without preparatory confession, and dressed in secular clothing, he held his first public celebration of the Lord's Supper. In this celebration the canon of the mass was omitted, so that there was no consecration; and the sacrament was distributed under both species.

It was not surprising, therefore, that Luther's literary warnings were powerless to arrest developments in Wittenberg. They followed their own tumultuous and fanatical course.

Meanwhile, revolutionary forces bearing a strongly religious and social stamp were coming into Wittenberg from outside. With these, schism within the new religious outlook and structure began to be officially recognised. Prime agents of these new forces were the preachers who came from Zwickau at Christmas 1521: Nicholas Storch, Mark Thomae (Stübner) and Thomas Drechsel. These, much more than Karlstadt, who rejected the use of force, drew radical conclusions from Luther's theses. In particular, they carried Luther's subjectivism to its ultimate conclusion. They appealed to Luther, it is true, but wanted all of their action to be directly guided by freely illuminated resolve – by 'the Spirit'. In this city this was a dangerously explosive doctrine, for since Luther's departure the city had been in a state of feverish excitement. In the countryside all around, too, the agitation found expression under cover of the tradition-breaking Reformation doctrine. The new gospel did indeed claim these expressions for its own, but, as Luther said, they were mere profligacy, that could do religion no good. It would, however, have been astonishing if Luther's unique attitude, which so autocratically presupposed the separation of the religious and the non-religious, the spiritual and the secular, had not caused autonomous reforming concerns to spill over into other areas. It would have been equally astonishing if radicalism had not led to brutal consequences, inescapable as they were capricious, and far from anything that Luther had in mind.

Following the order of the Wittenberg town council in January 1521, the populace now roused by the preaching of those illumined by the Spirit, immediately flew into a ferment. In these, however, Luther recognised his great new enemy, whom he named indiscriminately and vaguely, 'the rabble' or 'the fanatics'. Gradually these seemed to become more of an enemy than the papacy itself.

Precisely in respect of these, we see how serious Luther still was, in his rejection of force. When the elector asked him what he ought to do to suppress this tumult, Luther answered that now no one knew who was master and who was servant, because far too much human scheming had got mixed up in the whole affair. This was not pleasing to God. Luther remained faithful to this viewpoint, event to the extent of adopting a tolerant attitude. In this first case he realised the demands which he had theoretically expounded in 1520 in the manifesto, *To The Christian Nobility:* 'One ought to overcome a heretic not with fire but with arguments, as was the method of the ancient fathers.' In controversy with Karlstadt, too, concerning the new form of the mass, he was, to begin with, for freedom of conscience, and opposed to compulsion.[5] Even in 1524 during the bitter struggle with Müntzer, he professed his belief in freedom of speech: 'Doctrine is defended by verbal battle. The elector, therefore, ought not to impede the ministry of the word. Let minds meet and clash. Some may be led astray, but that is the way of warfare.'

And now, emerging from the Wartburg he himself made determined and decisive use of this freedom of speech. Amid the rising flood Melanchthon had felt himself at a loss; but Luther came out to confront it. Against the elector's wishes, he appeared in Wittenberg, moved by enormous self-confidence and trust in God's guidance: 'I would like your electoral Grace to know that I come under much higher protection.' From 9 April until 10 April he thundered against the disturbers of the peace, calling them the 'prophets from Zwickau'. On 1 May he was in the market-place at Zwickau, preaching against 'the Spirit' and on the true way to God. It is highly significant, theologically and from the point of view of mass

---

[5] It is true that in 1525 he was to denounce the mass as blasphemy before the secular power, and demand that it be punished and suppressed like any other form of blasphemy, by the authorities.

psychology, that even in this situation he wanted the conviction of faith to be utterly free from all coercion.

This attitude had its dangers, it is true. His later phrase, just quoted: 'Let minds meet and clash', reveals that Lutheran defiance, which did not quite give way even before the workings of divine grace. Here was a frank departure from the spirit of the whole of ancient Christianity, which took the danger of contamination by sin so seriously, and never allowed the grace of faith to be carelessly jeopardised. This attitude corresponds in a deeper sense to Luther's defiant separatism vis-à-vis the old Church. The subjective element comes fully into its own, bringing with it the danger of further schisms.

Over and over again we find that the chief characteristic of German history is its complexity. Geographical and political diversity, and the resulting diversity of intellectual and cultural expressions and endowment, were bound to produce a wealth of idiosyncrasy in the sphere of religion, as a result of the colossal release occasioned by Luther's renunciation of the old Church. German particularism, aggravated by the subjectivism of Luther's basic principle found expression in a wealth of religious differentiation.

Following the pattern of the extraordinarily varied forms of late medieval, spiritualist, apocalyptic, socialist movements, and of Hussitism, with their forms that diverged towards opposite extremes, Luther's Reformation led to a rapid succession of important divisions. There was the Wittenberg of Karlstadt after 1522; then Karlstadt's unique and exaggerated laicism; Zwingli; the variety of autonomous forms of Church life which emerged in the cities; the influence, on the one hand, of the relativistic precursors of James Acontius (Strasburg: Butzer, Capito), which was doubly important for future development, and, on the other hand, the polished compromising dogma of Melanchthon; and finally, there were the radical fanatics (see below). Undoubtedly Luther had introduced simplification and centralisation of piety on a large scale. With tireless sarcasm he drew attention to the complexity of the outward forms of devotion in Catholic Christianity, which he found not only ridiculous but scandalous. In so doing he indulged in completely unrestrained exaggeration. Frequently we find ourselves perplexed at his impossible affirmations – as though this

heap of indulgences, processsions, fastings and payment for dispensations were the Church. In this we see how one-sided criticism
misses the mark. The complex, individual power of the Germans
threw itself upon the one central thing which Luther stressed.
With an inner necessity there emerged in Germany that multitude
of Protestant denominations, who in some measure mutually rejected one another, and yet for the most part lived by the sense of a
common allegiance to the pure word of the gospel. The exposition
of the content of this scriptural basis, however, led to violent and
essential dogmatic differences.

This schismatic tendency was taken to its most logical extreme
by the groups of fanatics – who in turn began to split up – and by
the Baptists and Anabaptists. We are badly informed about these
movements, for they affected the uneducated mostly, and their
teachings were handed on as a rule by word of mouth, from the
very start. All of this made for vagueness and contradiction. In
addition, when a sect disappeared, so did its literature.

All of the fanatics display a radicalisation of the new religious
spiritualism in terms of a communistic principle. As well as making
revolutionary demands, communism can signify complete, self-
sacrificing love. The later fanatics of Münster, for example, were
to display both.

We have always tended to dismiss these forms of fanaticism as
totally unhealthy symptoms, not worth consideration. Luther himself adopted this attitude; but the rage which this form of new
Christianity kindled in him clearly shows how he recognised his
real foe emerging from the heart of Protestantism itself. He thundered against the danger of uncompromising radicalism. In fact,
the fanatics had the strength of greater consistency on their side,
not merely in their exploitation of the subjectivism, which Luther
was now soft-pedalling, but also in their realisation of Lutheran
religious zeal in the formation of a stricter morality. It was not just
lack of insight into practical ecclesiastical life, which allowed
Melanchthon to be so deeply impressed by the Anabaptists of
Zwickau that he had to ask whether they possessed the Spirit of
God, or that of the devil. Very properly he was impressed by the
directness of their outbursts and their radicalism. In a quite naïve
fashion, these prophets were in deadly earnest with Luther's
demand that the whole of the Christian's life be placed under the

Word; that is, for them there was no longer any such thing as a secular life, but only a spiritual life. The gospel was directly binding upon the entire structure of life, even of economic and social life. Nothing can be considered Christian except what is explicitly recognised by scripture. The new life was to be realised in a 'little flock', in a holy congregation, as the new Zion, and utterly separated from the world. They desired to live a truly Christian life in all things. For this reason Hans Denk suffered such disillusionment when he was forced to admit that the fruits of a holy life were still lacking amongst the Anabaptists. This same religious and moral zeal together with the biblical principle, taken to its logical conclusion, led to the rejection of infant baptism also, and so to the introduction of rebaptism. Baptism, as the decisive act of incorporation in the supernatural kingdom, can be received only through a personal, responsible decision. Infant baptism was regarded as an inadmissible human contrivance.

The essence of any age can be discerned elsewhere than in its formalised energies. Part of the essence lies in the fructifying soil that lies beneath. In the sixteenth century it was precisely this formless Christianity of the fanatics that supplied an important component in the total economy of the Reformation. It provided one of those mysterious anonymities, without which great spiritual movements cannot thrive at all, least of all within Christianity. The Lutheran Church may have persecuted the Anabaptists harshly,[6] and for their part the Anabaptists may have made no mark upon the political, and historical ecclesiastical, structure of the time, but none the less they formed a most important part of the reserves of power of biblical and Reformed Christianity; and frequently they were granted far too few religious rights in the official Reformation of the states and cities. This power revealed itself most strongly at those points that will always be the most decisive in any movement: in the radical integrating points of doctrine and life, of ideal and reality, and hence also in martyrdom, a factor which Luther disregarded where the fanatics, and Zwingli, were concerned.

The fanatics were the sixteenth-century expression of the recurrent temptation in the history of the Church to present Christian law in separation from external forms – involving a settled

---

[6] The most striking example is the later attitude of Melanchthon – in spite of his many links with the fanatics.

authority and fixed particular doctrines – as the product of the
Spirit alone, working, not in the general mass of people but within
a small congregation. The central thing was opposition to the historical genesis of Christianity, and an insistence upon mystical and
charismatic experience. As so often has happened, even this kind
of spiritualism turned into a massive legalistic religion, or carried
the seeds of such a religion within it. The significance of the fanatics is made abundantly clear by two things. First, there was their
real religious power and the remote effects that resulted from it.
Second, they appealed vigorously, if often with inflammatory
venom, to the socially and spiritually deprived, who had not always been sufficiently considered by the other Christian denominations. The rich clergy, living in luxury and externalised religion,
provided a most significant legitimation of their fanatical, proletarian sallies. In both cases their effectiveness was derived in large
measure from what the Bible said about the poor.

What has been affirmed is not refuted by the fact that these elements had outwardly such a destructive effect. Frequently they
succumbed to unrestrained sensuality, but this only proves the
necessity of having fixed forms. In themselves the Anabaptists
would have been a destructive force – as they were in Münster –
only if they falsified their principle of having nothing fixed and
turned that principle into a fixed law, seeking to make palpable
history out of their spiritualism. In both Catholic and Reformed
Germany, however, this danger was adequately avoided; and for
this reason it was left to the mystical fanatics to exercise the important function of a fertile soil lying beneath the surface. The fanatics were indeed the silent ones in the land. Radicalism and fury
were aberrations, but it was on account of these things that even
the peace-loving amongst them were bloodily persecuted.

The fanatics did indeed follow out Luther's attack upon the
Church without any compromise. Within the Reformation it was
the fanatics who represented non-dogmatic Christianity. This non-
dogmatism did not by any means, however, exclude the fanatics
from the general fabric of Reformed Christianity. It is true that
Luther maintained that they did not know Christ – as he maintained of Zwingli, Oecolampadius and Butzer as well; but their
biblical Christianity and their strictly antipapal attitude remove
all doubt. In many respects their roots go back to Luther's human-

ist counterpart, Erasmus. Their strict moralism and hence their opposition to the notion of justification by faith alone, and to the denial of free will, because both of these view tended to discourage moral effort, their extreme love of peace, their non-dogmatic inclination towards toleration, and a certain mysticism, all point in this direction. There were, however, undoubted Reformation forces which certainly retained Erasmianism in a more marked degree. We think of Zwingli, Oecolampadius, of Zürich and Strasburg. 'These, my dear children and brothers, are the factious spirits and fanatics who, it seems to me, would have known nothing sound either about Christ or his gospel, had it not been for Luther's writings.'

On the other hand, it is a mark of the Anabaptist movement that it defies historical classification. Its boundaries are flexible, its characteristics appear in various combinations; and this is of its very nature. The Anabaptist movement was a release of the spiritualising elements of Reformed doctrine, and from time to time a reaction against the strict harnessing of Reformation energies, as these soon became expressed in the variously 'politicised' new Christianity of the states and cities.

We are reminded of the unusually widespread, excited apocalypsism, of spiritualism and of Christian socialism, with its demand for man's original, natural right to freedom and equality, and for poverty in the Church. These demands naturally came more clamantly from the socially depressed classes; and these were the very classes who, having become fired by Luther's preaching on the freedom of the spiritual man, and by the notion of the spiritual, invisible Church, were then described by Luther as fanatics.

Zwickau became a specially important centre of early Reformation fanaticism, which spread like an epidemic. Zwickau was near Bohemia, and this calls to mind one result of Hussite fanaticism which had allowed two extremes to develop simultaneously: the belligerent and violent Taborites, and the brethren who silently suffered all injustice. The cloth mills and the mines in Zwickau provided a specially favourable climate for apocalyptic and mystical ideas; and here, too, were to be found creative personalities, who alone could give a movement universality, unity, clarity and drive.

Outstanding above all of these was the local preacher, Thomas Müntzer (1489–1525). He was full of mistrust of the great Reformation slogan: 'faith'. 'The Lutherans never stop scribbling and chattering about faith, faith, faith.' On this point he, the mystic, spoke with great sobriety. The extreme spiritualist made the demands of a severe moralist. He enquired into the psychological process of the act of belief; he showed how in the supreme biblical example of our Lady, the believer completely preserved her justifiable autonomy by her questioning the revelation addressed to her, only reaching faith after first disposing of objections. This faith came through the direct testimony of the Spirit, through the 'interior word', which is the very antithesis of the dead word of scripture. 'They speak directly to God,' derided Luther. Müntzer's final rejection of Wittenberg – 'that dangerous corner' – was brought about by the fundamental antagonism between those justified by the Spirit and the professional theologians. Müntzer was the complete social revolutionary. All his efforts were made on behalf of the poor, common man, to whom he appealed over and over again. His words were addressed to 'poor Christendom' . . . 'The laity must become prelates and priests.' He had fled Wittenberg on account of its viperous race of scribes. Jesus gave St John no other justification for his doctrine except to 'point to the common people' 'But our scholars would like to send the testimony of the Spirit of Jesus to the university; they want to judge faith by their stolen scripture, having no faith at all, neither with God nor man. They are all seeking honours and riches. And this is the reason why you have to be taught, O common man.' The true gospel is only for the wretched and the oppressed and those who are denied education. The dispossessed are the elect; they must separate themselves from the world and from the Church, to become a little flock. None may be found amongst them who has not come to faith by his own, independent, earnest endeavour. The gospel has not annulled the law but thoroughly fulfilled it.

This non-professional theologian had gained a deep insight into basic requirements of scriptural exegesis which Luther had largely lost sight of. He took as his starting-point the elementary fact of the complexity of truth, and thus of the multiple connotation of the word. 'Each proposition contains its own exact opposite. When these opposites are not synthesised, neither can be completely understood, no matter how clear it is. This is the basic diet of all malicious separation.' Even if, for want of a living teaching authority, Müntzer, just as much as Luther, was bound to fall into one-sidedness – although from a different angle – that does not make the principle enunciated any less correct and important. It contains one of the strongest criticisms of the whole fundamental attitude of the Reformation.

Müntzer was an important manifestation of religious subjectivism. He resolved the synthesis between dogmatism and subjectivism, formulated by Luther, almost entirely in favour of the inner testimony of the individual. The realisation of faith in the depths of the soul is the only thing that is able to produce true faith. Admittedly, in contradiction of this fundamental view, it is still the Bible which provides outward confirmation of the inward Spirit. None the less faith does not really seem to be tied to the Christianity of the Crucified. More exactly: it is tied to it only in the fundamentally relativistic manner of Erasmus. 'The faith of Christ is identical with all the elect, whether they be Jews or Turks, and whatever their race or creed.' From this angle, the most obvious parallel to Müntzer is Erasmus – a spiritual father of fanaticism. Within this identity of relativism and moralism lie, indeed, the sharpest distinctions. Erasmus was primarily a philosophical humanist, an advocate of education, a champion of tranquility, and his morality was marked by a mild tendency towards a rarified spirituality. Müntzer was a religious and militant force through and through. He opposed education, conscious that he was its adversary, for it was to the uneducated, to the poor, suffering congregation that he spoke. His morality came from the Old Testament. The threat of the law, and fear, were given full weight within the life of faith and in external conduct. He seemed almost to delight in this severity. He did not disapprove but supported, riotous revolution. The principle of simplification that was one of the basic motive powers of the age, was expressed by Müntzer in the radical form of egalitarianism.

The simple consideration that there was much local diversity in the ceremonies of the mass within the Catholic Church, and that many nations or groups of nations celebrated mass in their own languages, moved Müntzer to be the first to celebrate public worship in German. This was in Allstedt. The servant of God has been given power 'to exercise a public ministry, not to hide beneath a furtive cover, nor conceal anything from the whole Church and the whole world.' 'Paul had his epistles read publicly before all, and Christ our Saviour commanded that his gospel be preached, uncomplicated and unspoiled, to every creature, neither in Latin nor with any additions, but in his own tongue as each can understand.' Considering the narrow clerical and ecclesiastical leadership, the exploitation of the people by the clergy, which had been customary until this time, and considering also the social discontent which had developed, what a powerful effect such a principle was bound to have! Let all be shared out amongst all.

There is very little variation in Müntzer's theses. They contain one or two ideas to which he repeatedly returns in his sermons and writings. His subjects are treated with tireless agitation, and his imagery is vivid and varied. He knew well how to make a powerful impression. The popular songs he composed carried his agitation right through the sixteenth century. A theme that constantly recurs is the strict obligation to fulfil the law of God, a law which he sought more in the Old than in the New Testament. From the first theses on indulgences Luther had attacked the false security and ease of the way of salvation as embodied in the papacy. Müntzer for his part now found Luther's Reformation lacking in zeal. Luther, he affirmed, was making it too easy for men, preaching of nothing but 'the honey-sweet, half Christ'. 'He who refused to accept the bitterness in Christ will die of eating the honey.' To him, Luther was 'Father Pussyfoot . . . the devil's high chancellor.' It is easily seen that Müntzer had failed to grasp Luther's *theologia crucis* as completely as he had failed to recognise Luther's zeal for a truly Christian life. Does it not say a very great deal for Luther that in his statement to the electors in 1524 he made no attempt to make any false apology in respect of morality? 'We admit that we do not do everything that we ought, because spirit and flesh war against each other in us.'

Müntzer was not merely the exponent of the fanatical splitting up of Bible religion. Equally, he was a perfecter of social revolution and of revolutionary self-betterment. He preached iconoclasm and did not stop even at the rights of the princes. 'The princes are not masters but servants of the sword. For this reason the people too must be present when anyone is truly judged according to the law of God.' 'Observe how our lords and princes are the root of all usury and thieving, for they take possession of every creature: fish, fowl, and the vegetation, and so oppress the husbandman and the tradesman.' With Jeremias he preached 'the rooting up and discomfiture of kings, princes, and priests. Marvellous will be the vanquishing and destruction of the mighty, godless tyrants.' The mood and aspiration are now clearly audible, which accompanied the rising of the peasants, whom Müntzer declared himself ready to help – only to go down with their cause. He was the demagogue who signed himself – somewhat ridiculously and yet so appropriately – Thomas Müntzer with the sword of Gideon' or '. . . with the hammer'.

Müntzer's demand for revolution and his encouragement of it were the signal for Luther to fall into line. He reacted by producing the *Epistle to The Prince at Saxony from the Spirit of Insurrection*. In this he now demanded that force be met with force. The authorities must intervene, 'for these are not Christians who want to go beyond words and use their fists rather than be ready to endure all things'.

The move of the Zwickau town council against the disorders that had begun turned Müntzer into a homeless itinerant preacher. In Allstedt he found a new sphere for more intensive work. The elector drove him out of this place too. He went to Mühlhausen where he thoroughly converted the town council to his view, and involved them in his own destruction in the Peasants' War.

Meanwhile Karlsadt in Wittenberg, deposed by Luther's return there, was developing views that were very close to those of the fanatics. He was specially impressed by the idea of the fervent Christian life, in which theory and practice must be one, and by the picture of the poor, uneducated man. Following out Luther's paradoxical criticism of the whore reason, to the point of logical self-destruction, he condemned all theology. For himself he renounced all the outward marks of the theologian: the title of doctor, and academic dress. He wanted to become one of the new laity. He recommended that his students give up their studies. Since the Fall, the only thing that God wants of man is to till the earth. He himself wanted to become a farmer. Because the Lord has revealed to the simple what is hidden to the wise, he let uneducated men teach him the meaning of scripture. And so, in the very first years of the Reformation, the biblical principle and faith-spiritualism, were already displaying the divisive power of their one-sidedness. Luther temporarily arrested the effect of this, but he was unable to overcome it.

Karlstadt, too, was exiled. A passionate enmity had developed between him and Luther, as between Luther and Müntzer. Karlstadt wrote secret attacks upon Luther. In 1522, a few days after his triumph on account of the rousing of the mob in Wittenberg, Luther replied: 'I fear not Satan, nor any angel from heaven, and certainly not Karlstadt.' But in 1525 he gave violent expression to his enmity with his one-time colleague and brother in arms, in his *Against the Heavenly Prophets*. Karlstadt had already become a man of no fixed abode. In 1541 he died of the plague.

VI. KNIGHTS AND PEASANTS

(a) The Reformation had now become the concern of every social class. At first it was entirely an open question, which class was going to come out on top. Even the declining knighthood were still in the running. Since 1520, and especially since 1521, Hutten by his indefatigable activity, his stirring literary polemics, and also his management of the knights, had acquired tremendous influence over emergent public opinion. The year 1521 saw the publication of his *Conversations* and also the German edition of his *Dialogues*. By 1522, before Sickingen's fortunes began to wane, he had become completely irreconcilable. He threw down a public challenge to the papists, especially to the Dominicans – for example, at the gate of the church of our Lady in Frankfurt, where his former student companion Cochlaeus had worked. Hutten was always primarily the literary champion. His influence upon the knights, urging them to take up arms in the cause, cannot be compared with the success of his propaganda in the world of ideas.

As well as Hutten there was Sickingen. In the art and practice of public declaration he was much the inferior of the vagabond poet-knight. In him there was scarcely a spark of the national idealism which inflamed Hutten. On the other hand, he was somewhat more strongly stirred in the religious sense by Luther, for Hutten saw Luther only as the enemy of Rome and the rouser of the nation. As we know, in 1521 Sickingen had been able to defend

Luther's ideas in his interview with the imperial confessor at the Ebernburg (see p. 314).

For him, too, however, religion was clearly not the ultimate thing. His characteristic, meticulous self-interest allowed him to follow no uniform line of development. He vacillated this way and that between the Habsburgs and the French; he fought for Duke Ulrich of Würtemberg, and he fought against him. He served the emperor in the first war against France; but in September he failed him at Mézières, and, falling into disfavour with the emperor, it was all the easier for him to return to a state of autocratic rebellion. When Cochlaeus said that Luther put more reliance in Sickingen than in any other prince, he probably exaggerated, just as Aleander did by his categorical affirmation that Sickingen was the scourge of Germany. All the same, Sickengen was a substantial military power, after the style of the other knights, but on a grand scale; and this power would gladly have claimed princely status. Proof of this is provided by his campaign against electoral Trier.

(b) In August 1522 the 'fraternal union' of imperial knights of the central and upper Rhine, led by Sickingen, threw down their challenge to the elector of Trier, Bishop Richard of Greiffenclau. By September they were encamped before the gates of Trier; but, under their militarily competent bishop, the city held out, to be relieved by Hesse and the Palatinate.

Sickingen's action constituted a serious violation of the territorial peace. If such behaviour could be condoned, all efforts to restore the Land Peace, especially to uphold the decrees of Worms, were in vain. On 1 October Sickingen was outlawed as a violater of the Land Peace, and his followers were overpowered by the princes, and their castles destroyed. In April 1523 Sickingen found himself confined in the castle of Landstuhl, west of Kaiserslautern. He was badly wounded, the castle was destroyed, and he died in the ruins, upon which the victorious princes had mounted in person.

This catastrophic episode possessed deep, symbolic significance. This challenge by the man elected leader by the council of knights at Landau was the very last attempt made by the knights to restore their power within the imperial union, vis-à-vis the princes. The collapse of the knighthood was confirmed by the campaign of the Swabian League against the French knights.

In the second place, this challenge is a significant illustration of how small a part religion often played in what went by the name of the Evangelical Reformation. It showed how Luther's religious movement could be used as cover for very many things. The chief motive of Sickingen's challenge had been to take up Hutten's earlier ideas thoroughly and make an opening for the gospel by force of arms. In the name of a crusade for Christ against the enemies of evangelical truth, they set forth on what was straightforward, colossal plunder.

In the third place, Sickingen's overthrow in 1523 showed the true alignment of forces even amongst the princes. During these years the religious and ecclesiastical situation might well serve their purposes, if it were able to bring them political or financial advantage. For the rest, the tone was set by the sheer egoism of the princes. On these terms in 1525 Philip of Hesse and Duke George of Saxony were to form forces against the peasants, and Catholics were to join forces with Protestants against sedition in Münster in 1535.

The old warning which had been sounded from the start by the curia, Aleander, and every German opponent of Luther, that religious anarchy was bound to destroy political and social order – as in Bohemia – was reinforced by the challenge of Sickingen. Large sectors of society began to pay heed, not least the princes. The long justified fear of an uprising of the common people increased.

There was good cause for this, for the powerful agitation, which we have recognised as a basic feature of the times, had not abated. Every day ominous discoveries were being made of deep-seated disorder in Church, state and society. These things were proclaimed in the *Reichstag*, in sermons and in literature. Fanaticism spread these ideas in an inflammatory way amongst the socially depressed classes. For years all this had been fermenting. By 1523 the fear of revolution in the empire had become general. Cochlaeus predicted a civil war of the very worst kind.

The beginning of the sixteenth century was not a particularly significant juncture in economic circumstances in Germany. The discovery of America and the influx of precious metals from that continent, as well as the outlet from the German silver mines, did not put any burden upon the German economy until the forties of the century. There were, however, other economic and social disturbances. These came from two totally different angles.

One cause lay in the early capitalism of wholesale and foreign trade. All of a sudden there grew up the vast and ever-increasing fortunes of half a dozen German firms. In the six years immediately preceding the Reformation (1511–17) it is calculated that the profits of the Fuggers were over fifty-four per cent, of Haug & Co., forty-seven per cent. After the death of Jacob Fugger, the Rich, their estate swelled to two million by 1527, and to its peak of four and three-quarter million gold gulden in 1546. That is the equivalent of about 300 million goldmarks – ten times as much as that owned by the great Medici bank in 1450.

Such concentration of capital was bound to lead to monopoly. No practically effective method was found of arresting this tendency. The agitation amongst the princes, the impoverished nobility and the poor scholars, was accompanied by many schemes to curb these vast fortunes, but none was ever realised. Examples like the transfer of the St Peter's indulgence to Albert of Mainz, or the election of Charles V as emperor, clearly display the reason for this failure; people required the capital provided by the banks. In addition, the number of well-off citizens was greatly increased as the cities rose to greater prominence.

Greater and deeper grew envious embitterment against those who had become too rich, as it did against the rich prelates, whose unspiritual lives of luxury provided special fuel for the fire of hatred.

The second threat to social equilibrium came from the attitude taken up by the lesser nobility to their peasant subjects.

About 1500 the peasants were quite well off. As we have remarked, the phrase 'poor peasant' was inappropriate at the beginning of the sixteenth century. Sebastian Brand informs us that in his day the peasants, who formerly drank water, now drank wine, had plenty of cash, ate meat, and shared in the general luxury in clothing. This may well be a bit of an exaggeration, but Dürer's etchings and those of his German contemporaries do portray peasants as very well dressed. Many of them must have been in comfortable circumstances. The outcome of the Peasants' War leads to the same conclusion, for many peasants were in a position to pay fines of several hundred gulden.

We must add to this the more developed self-confidence of the peasants. Not long before, the peasant-troopers had defeated the celebrated Swiss mercenaries. The requirements of natural law contained in medieval socialism, and the Bible's extolling of the virtue of poverty had been directly applied to the peasants. 'I praise you, O noble peasant, on behalf of all creatures and all the lords of the earth; the emperor must become your equal.' The pre-Reformation scholastic, Biel, had already recognised the divine right of the poor. The Thomist tradition of the Dominicans, too, displayed a dash of socialism. Cajetan and Conrad Köllin attributed to peasants the right to protect themselves against damage done by game. The princes were obliged to recompense them for such damage. Should they refuse to honour this obligation they could be refused absolution. One of Luther's friends, the Franciscan, Eberlin of Günzburg (1470–1533), wanted to set the peasants alongside the nobility as an estate of the realm, and to allow both to follow but one occupation: farming.[7]

On the other hand, the peasant class shared fully in the general discontent. There was still plenty of poverty to be found within their ranks. The lesser nobility had long been trying to curb the independence of the peasants, and even to turn them into real vassals. Social burdens had become more oppressive, the administration of superiors' rights too arbitrary. Proposals of the electors and of the imperial reform of 1502 speak of the great burdens suffered by the ordinary man through 'forced labour, deductions, and taxes'. Balthasar Hubmaier, who had once served the cult of our Lady in Regensburg, demanded, on the strength of our natural equality, that access to water, pasture, woods, game and wine, which had all become the property of the landlords, ought once again to be granted to the ordinary man. He wanted to reinstate the 'ancient law'; and the chief support of his claim lay in the divine law contained in natural law and in revelation.

[7] Very soon (1522) he realised the dangers of his views when he saw the unbridled release of popular passions in the Wittenburg iconoclasm; but this was too late to reverse the great stimulus he had given to radical socialism.

This discontent, allied to the self-confidence, from which it could not be clearly distinguished in the late medieval social and religious scene, found expression in a series of peasant risings, which shook the structure of German society, and played an important and unique part both in the eruption and the direction of the religious Reformation.

As well as those disturbances that are well known by the titles of '*Bundschuh*' and '*Armer Kunz*', the religious–peasant–proletarian operations of the fanatics (and to some extent the movement centred around Hans Böhm) heralded the coming convulsions. The first socialist-political reform programme was 'the fifteen confederates' of Eberlin of Günzburg. This dates from 1521. Karlstadt's agitations and eccentricities led on to the activities of Thomas Müntzer (see above, p. 355) in 1524, when he fought 'against the soft life of Wittenberg', which in turn ended in the more all-embracing social revolution which we know as the Peasants' War.

The writings which enjoyed the modest circulation in the twenties, and encouraged discontent and readiness to revolt, include the *Reformation of Emperor Sigismund*. This work foretold a liberator who was to come from the Black Forest. Swabia lay at the centre of this region; and it was there that divine law was inaugurated in December 1524. In the last half of that year peasant risings had been spreading in upper Swabia, Würtemberg, Alsace, Thuringia and in Franconia, until, early in 1525, they attained a climax of intensity and extension. The whole of upper Germany from Vogesen, the Harz and the Alps, to the far east of Austria, were in the grip of this movement. Its power was so great that not only lesser nobility but important abbots and bishops (Fulda, Hersfeld, Bamberg, Speyer) and mighty princes like the electors of Mainz and the Palatinate had to go along with it in some measure. Not that the power of the masses was all that great; it was rather that the widespread conviction that a revolutionery rising was imminent was having its effect. Prophecies had been repeated for decades. The spirit of the age was filled with apocalypsism. And now the time seemed to be ripe, the revolution inevitable.

In addition, there were sections of the nobility who made the peasants' cause their own, as had happened in the Hussite wars, when nobles and peasants had fought shoulder to shoulder. Florian Geger, Götz of Berlichingen and Archduke Ulrich of Würtemberg were of this group.

The parallel revolt of the *petit bourgeoisie* of the cities, however, seemed, in South Germany and along the Rhine, to have no direct connection with the revolt of the peasants – with a few exceptions such as Würzburg, Bamberg and Augsburg. In many respects it was simply an anticlerical revolt. Cochlaeus had to flee Frankfurt. In Augsburg John Fabri, the anti-Reformation preacher from Heilbronn, was deposed from the town council.

The actual bands of revolutionaries were not composed homogeneously of peasants. In their ranks were to be found men like Karlstadt, Eberlin of Günzburg, who preached a return to the land as the ideal of all life, and also ex-monks, fanatics and wandering folk. Amongst the peasants themselves, moreover, it was not the poor who were the real instigators of the movement but those who were a little better off.

From the geographical point of view, the peasant movements were exclusively a south German affair. It was only those more densely populated territories around the Roman *limes*, with their numerous smallholdings, and distinctive culture, that had bred the discontent required to produce an active, concerted attack by a sufficient number of peasants. On the sparsely populated expanses of the north and north-east, with its less ancient civilisation, the preconditions for a peasant rising were lacking.[8] Most of all, in the north there was an absence, for the most part, of that unscrupulous deprivation of legal rights which formed the chief cause of the discontent of the peasants; for in the north, a few great barons administered vast territories in which they kept the nobility and the clergy under control. Besides this, as Günther Franz has pointed out, the spread of the Peasants' Wars was more or less coextensive with the recruitment area of the mercenaries: 'The south was ripe for the Peasants' War, the north was not.'

The area we have mentioned was not uniformly affected by the rising. There were peasants who stood aloof. A huge tract of upper

---

[8] The disputes in Thuringia, which formed a climax in the drama, do not contradict this statement. The revolts there were a consequence of the northward spread of the infection, and of the effect of a single, independent personality – Thomas Müntzer.

Germany, the one really important self-contained state there, remained almost entirely unaffected. This was Bavaria, where the lot of the peasants was no less hard, but where their legal situation was more ordered and they were not exposed to the unbridled caprice of the petty nobility, for these were kept firmly in order by the dukes. Moreover, Bavaria had refused to become affected by the revolution within the Church.

What were the peasants demanding? The Peasants' War was a social and also an intellectual and religious dispute with the property owners. In this respect it was essentially a continuation and reforming revival of the late medieval movements, which had attempted to change forcibly the conditions of life of isolated strata in society, and which attacked all who tried to hold on to the 'old rights'. With resistance to real or imagined infringements of rights had become linked general views or theories about what constituted justice as applied to the living conditions of the peasants. These became crystallised into specific demands. That is to say, the movements we are discussing rested upon a conservative-historical, and a progressive-abstract, principle. Old rights were to be won back, new rights overthrown. The ideal of the equality of all men had become operative, although with many graduations. Appeal was made to natural law and also to revelation or 'divine right'. The vehicle of these aspirations was the 'ordinary man', as apostrophied in the popular apocalyptic writings of Hans Böhm and the corresponding literature of the fanatics. The form in which these aspirations was cast clearly manifested the unity of medieval life, as rooted in religion. The variety of socialistic views and aspirations were all completely intertwined with religion. The inscription upon the *Bundschuh* banner demanded: 'Nothing but the justice of God!' It bore an image of the Crucified, attended by John and our Lady, with a kneeling peasant looking up at the cross. Membership of the league brought with it the obligation to recite certain prayers (five Our Fathers, and Aves). The tone was set by the idea of the common Christian dignity of all the redeemed. Thus, the oppressors, the aristocracy, as true Christians ought to make the peasants free men. This interweaving of Christian and secular interests and ideas remained a feature of the peasant risings of the Reformation period.

In our understanding of the events of the twenties of the six-teenth century we must avoid the all too common notion that truly communistic economic demands took priority. The progressive peasant classes were not sufficiently interested in these things. The concept of a radical peasant must always to some extent be a contradiction. In the areas where they originated, the peasant risings were and remained tied to the soil and its needs. This made any sort of universal radicalism impossible.

On the other hand, we must not underestimate or ignore the emerging radicalisms, for economic amelioration was indeed a very real and by no means accidental issue. Certainly it is quite wrong to see the heart of the battle in a contention for the economic minimum. The issue concerned rather the basic rights of the social and political order of life. The battle was for law against tyranny and lawlessness. But when the liberty that was sought seemed to express itself in a denial of the decalogue – found, not in the New Testament but in the Jewish law – that obviously would have meant a most lucrative change from the economic point of view as well. Even with the rapidly accomplished wide dissemination of the most religious sounding *Twelve Articles* (see below) we can observe how, for many people, the ostensible religious-social aim was but a cover for a much more revolutionary aim. When the movement became co-ordinated in the Christian Union, radicalism manifested itself in the negotiations. Many wanted to demote the rulers to a position of complete powerlessness and turn the peasants into masters forthwith.

In the principal region, south Germany, it is true that to begin with the desire to succeed without the use of force had the upper hand. The Christian Union not only shared its constitution with the Swabian League but expressly renounced every use of force. Unfortunately the counter demands of the League were so uncompromisingly rigid that the radical elements amongst the peasants were able to carry away the disillusioned on the side of force. And then, with a suddenness that seems truly incomprehensible, there ensued those violent plunderings of everything of cultural value in castles and monasteries, which determined the picture that later generations would have of the peasant revolutionaries. A general process of interior Reformation history was repeating itself here within the social sphere: what had been holy yesterday – persons, institutions and ideals – suddenly became offensive and hateful, to be persecuted with all possible rage and fury, and, if possible, destroyed. We cannot honestly say that the unleashing of the lower propensities to unrelenting hatred and destruction amongst the peasants stopped short at sacred things or things of cultural value.

This radicalism did not prevail, however, in the places where the risings originated. It was in Thuringia that it manifested itself as a system, and there it derived primarily from a type of piety that was moulded by spiritualist and fanatical, and economically radicalised, influences. In short, it was the child of Thomas Müntzer, whose revolutionary reforms of 1523 had already announced the beginning of the convulsion to the people of Allstedt. None of the leading figures – Florian Geger, the half-honest, half-dishonest Götz of Berlichingen, Frederick Weigand, Wendel Hipler, Balthasar Hubmaier, or the anarchist, Jack Rohrbach – came anywhere near him in strength of mind or power to captivate the masses.

The name 'Peasants' War' denotes a host of individual actions, even including completely isolated and dimunitive risings, all different, according to region and idea. The peasant armies displayed a unity neither in mind nor in organisation. This fact symbolised their essence: the mass of peasants lacked a clearly conceived aim. Over and over again they rose on account of local grievances; nor had they a leader who could survey the whole scene and forge the diversity of aims into a unified project. Even Müntzer was unable to do this. And so the colossal, unwieldy power remained in pieces and easily fell a prey to the better organised and more skilfully operating aristocracy. The peasants were a real force, had compelled mighty lords and cities to compromise with them, they possessed weapons and fire-arms, could use these like experienced soldiers, had overpowered many castles and monasteries, and yet in the end they were easily vanquished. The Swabian League was able to annihilate the separate bands, one by one: the upper Swabians, the Würtembergers, the Franks (by George, the steward of Waldburg), the Thuringians and the Alsatians. By the end of June the resistance, even more, the will to resist, of the peasants had been broken. The actual Peasants' War 'scarcely lasted a

quarter of a year' (Franz). It is worth observing how the rising con-
vulsed spasmodically to its death. On 15 and 17 May there were
battles at Frankenhausen and Zaber; on 24 May Freiburg surrendered to the peasants; on 25 May Mühlhausen in Thuringia
was taken, and on 27 May Müntzer was executed; but throughout
the whole of June and July, and even in September and November
of 1525, there were bloody clashes, with a victory for the peasants
on 3 July at Schladming in Styria.[9]

The antagonists in this struggle were quite plainly the rulers and
the vassals. It is true that in the ranks of the discontented the only
active religious support came from adherents of the new religion.
Amongst the aristocracy, however, no division according to faith
was discernible. Just as the Swabian League were a confessional
mixture, so the critical battle against the Thuringians under
Müntzer at Frankenhausen was waged jointly by Elector John and
Duke George of Saxony and Landgrave Philip of Hesse.

It is credibly estimated that the dead on the peasants' side
numbered 100,000. The executions which ensued after the rising
had been quelled, those, for example, conducted by the bishop of
Würzburg, who travelled through his 'pacified' territory accompanied by his hangman, seem to us particularly harsh and unworthy.[10]

If history were determined only by those things that are consciously grasped or have visible results, the Peasants' War would
rank as relatively unimportant. Anonymous sacrifice, however, is
one of the most powerful driving forces in history, and the tragic
failure of great and just claims is a most worthy subject for consideration. For this reason the Peasants' War remains one of the
great themes of German history. Its importance reaches out far
beyond the brief outward events, which can so quickly be described.

Despite the lack of a greater unity, examination of the conflict
must search deeper than the episodic manifestations. We must try
to hear the complaining voice of the German peasant as an

[9] For Austria the crisis came a full year later at the battle of Gmunden/Pins-
dorf, 15 Nov. 1626.

[10] A specifically Jewish pogrom was associated with the peasant risings only
in Alsace where Jewish influence was particularly strong. It is probably true,
however, that individual Jews in all regions may have been robbed.

expression of the awakening nation demanding its rights, as the voice which, consciously or unconsciously, was protesting against a social class that was tending towards social injustice, against those who had legimated exploitation and the oppression of the common man by means of entrenched privileges.

There was a manifold and often complex interdependence between this ferment amongst the peasants, and the Reformation. On the more superficial, but most decisive level, the Christian Union was expressly appointed by the Reformers for the regulation of ecclesiastical and religious affairs (Luther, Melanchthon, Zwingli, Osiander); and the Thuringians were led by Müntzer, a product of the religious Reformation. At a deeper level, the Reformation as a whole was a revolutionary phenomenon, breaking through centuries-old institutions and laws, regarding its own conviction as sufficient legitimation. By this means and by preaching the liberty of the Christian man, and also through the spiritualist character of its concept of the Church, and its battle against good works and clerical privilege, Reformation doctrine supplied a welcome basis for every kind of revolutionary unrest. With an inner logic, Luther, whom men regarded as the champion of liberty, became the man one could trust, the man to whom the peasants at first looked with such naïve expectancy; and the revolutionary declaration of the coming of age of the laity, in opposition to a tyrannous hierarchy, became a stimulus to the attempt to achieve the social independence of the peasants from their feudal masters. Finally, the Reformation granted an equal share to all in the whole Christian and ecclesiastical life. There was a general striving for liberation from all form of tutelage, but no class was so oppressed and so much deprived of a fair share in common rights as were the peasants. The ideas that all were imbibing could be specially convincing in respect of the peasants.

The most significant single expression of the link between the peasants' risings and the Reformation was provided by the *Twelve Articles of the Peasantry of Swabia*, the 'basic and true principal articles of all peasantry and tenants of spiritual and secular superiors, by whom they consider themselves to be oppressed'. In these articles, setting aside all special local demands, the aspirations of the peasants found unified expression. They set out a programme that must be taken seriously: they completely rejected radicalism, fully recognised the peasants' obligation towards their superiors, and contained nothing in their demands, put forward as requests, which would have unduly prejudiced existing rights. 'It is not as if we wanted to be utterly free and acknowledge no superiors.' These various complaints, however, were deeply justified. They asked that arbitrary punishment cease, that the death tax of the best animal be discontinued, so that widow and orphan be no longer shamefully deprived of their own.

This programme might well have led to the reasonable satisfaction of peasant demands, and also to the integration of the power of the peasantry in the total energies of the nation. It was essentially a religious scheme, and based upon the Bible, although the relevance of the texts cited was not always very clear. For the sake both of outward propaganda and of spiritual effect it was enough that all demands appeared to be consecrated by Christian ideas. All their hope was placed 'in God the Lord, who alone can fulfil our hope'. Once again we hear the strong consonance of religious and social themes which had already produced such a strong effect in the fifteenth century.

Christianity as here represented was sheer religious renewal. Every parish was to choose its own pastor and have the right to depose him. 'This elected pastor is to preach the holy gospel to us clearly and plainly, so that we may come to God only through the true faith.' According to the twelfth article, should any of these articles be found not in conformity with the word of God, they would reject it, once the lack of conformity had been proved from scripture. All articles proposed for their acceptance must also be in conformity with scripture, otherwise they must be declared null and void at once. On the other hand, the right is reserved of making fresh proposals should such arise from scripture. It all displays a touchingly naïve and unworldly confidence.

Reaction came most powerfully as a result of the enormous disillusionment that Luther had in store for the peasants. And so the future ecclesiastical progress of the peasants ran either back into the old Church or into the non-Lutheran, non-ecclesiastical, fanatical sects. There can be no doubt that, as a result, Lutheranism lost much of the productive power it would have enjoyed from contact with the true native soil.

How did it come about that Luther failed the peasants? The answer is clearly provided by Luther's two treatises on the subject, written in 1525. In the preface to the first he formulates his theoretical view. This is faultless, from the Christian as from the theoretical point of view; and it is open-minded as well as cautiously critical. First of all, to Luther it seemed perfectly clear from the outset, that not all of the peasants took the biblical trimmings to the *Twelve Articles* seriously, 'for it is impossible that such a vast mob are all good Christians; many of them lack the right spirit to match their courage'. In the second place, he attached considerable importance to the situation because it might become critical for the existence of Church and state especially in Germany. In the third place, it was also a question of listening to the truth in view of the impending wrath of God who once again will soften our hard skulls.

The first part sets out his summary prophetic theology – full of zeal, but full also of self-will. He addresses 'the princes and lords'. It is they – especially those who do not follow the new faith – who are entirely to blame for this unrest; and 'it is not the peasants, dear lords, who set themselves against you, but God himself. If you have sense now, you will abate your anger for the love of God. A hay cart keeps out of the way of a drunk man. You ought, therefore, to desist from rage and foolish tyranny and treat the peasants wisely, as you would a drunk or erring man. Do not pick a fight with them, for you do not know where that will lead. Come to an amicable settlement.' All in all, he believed that the economic and social demands were reasonable.[11]

Part two, addressed *To The Peasantry*, once again concedes the grisly injustice of the superiors, but he is astonishingly reticent on the subject of any kind of self-betterment. This reticence arises from his *theologia crucis*, which for its part is but a concise form of trust in providence. This is his thesis: the Christian may have all the justification in the world for demanding justice, but it is his place only to suffer. M 5 : 39 ff., and Christ's example on the cross forbid him to procure justice for himself. What motivated Luther

---

[11] On this Luther remained true to his standpoint which excluded the civil power from the province of the preaching of the word. It was not the business of the secular authorities to decide whether preaching was true or false.

most of all was his concern for the gospel; and that might be supported only by the power of God, not by the solicitude or assistance of man. He himself had always relied upon God alone: 'and
now you are all about me wanting to assist the gospel, and do not
see that you are a prize hindrance to it'. The danger had emerged
of the peasants doing more damage to the gospel than pope or
emperor were able to do. If that were so, 'then you would be my
enemies'.

Luther attributed to the peasants the determination to better
themselves at all costs, a radicalism which did not by any means
inspire all of them, least of all those who upheld the *Twelve Articles*
sincerely. 'You say that you will leave them enough to live on. Let
him who will, believe it – I do not.' According to him the second
article is 'sheer thieving and open highway robbery', and the
leaders of the peasants are wily prophets of murder, and rabble
rousers.

'All of your articles can easily be answered thus: they might all
be right and reasonable according to nature, but you have forgotten the Christian law, and do not master it and carry it out
through patience and prayer, as befits Christian people, but
instead seek violently to destroy and coerce the authorities by your
impatience and crimes.' It is obvious that Luther's whole attitude
depended upon the strict separation of the secular and human
from the spiritual. The peasants, he affirmed in this first treatise,
were threatening 'to drive away Christian freedom'. Both sides
were in the wrong, both incurred the wrath of God. All who fell
in this unchristian battle would go to hell.

When at last the peasants were led on to use force, Luther wrote
his second pamphlet: *Against the Thieving and Murdering Peasant
Rabble*. 'Therefore smash, choke, stab secretly or publicly if you
can, remembering that there is nothing more poisonous or shameful or devilish than a revolutionary – it is just as if one were destroying a mad dog. If you do not strike, he will strike you and the
whole country with you. Stab, strike, strangle them wherever you
can. If you die while doing so, it is well with you. There is no more
blessed death than to die in obedience to the divine word.' Luther
did not think this an exaggeration. At various times he showed
himself of the same mind: 'The peasants, although numbered in
thousands, are utter rotters and murderers.' 'Whoever condemns

this treatise, betrays what he has been seeking all this time in the gospel.' Of the severe punishment of the insurrectionists he commented: 'It is sad, but necessary, that fear and awe must be spread amongst the people. . . . Do not be so worried about it, for many souls, who are now terrified, will benefit.' 'If there are innocent ones amongst the peasants. God will save them. If they do not pay heed, they will get scant mercy from me. Let the bullets whistle amongst them. . . . '

These are hard words, but no more than the logical consequence of the first thesis. However we judge Luther's views, we cannot say that he departed an inch from his severity for the sake of propagandist advantage. We have to recognise the absoluteness of the demand. In Luther's view, the authorities had been installed for the very purpose of punishing the wicked, protecting the virtuous and putting down disturbances. It was consonant with this view, therefore, that the obedience of subjects involved the renunciation of all attempts to better themselves. Even in mind, they ought to show submissiveness. Christian liberty was a spiritual, not a physical thing. Just as Luther would not revolt against, or even resist, the emperor as lawful ruler, so he could not allow others to do that sort of thing. This was particularly true of revolution accompanied, as this was, by bloodshed, destruction and also the abandonment of all spiritual discipline. Since 1522 his fury with all forms of fanaticism had been growing; and in 1525 he gave vent to it. And so his attack upon the peasants was filled with rage because he wanted to hit at the fanatics too. In 1524 he had reminded Frederick the Wise of his obligation as a ruler with regard to Müntzer, the disturber of the peace: 'Therefore, your Electoral Grace must not sleep or delay, for God will require an explanation for such lenient use of the sword entrusted to you.'

What was the response? Certainly the peasants made a mistake in appealing to Luther. The justification of their demands from Reformation doctrine were the first misinterpretation of Luther's views that was important for the course of world history. But this misinterpretation came about almost of necessity. Luther had fulminated in a revolutionary manner against the special privilege of the clergy. He had made most noise about the large-scale unjust use of oppressive laws. By so doing, was he not calling upon the laity to rise and improve their own lot? In preaching his doctrine and setting up his Church had he not frequently attacked the papacy, with quite undisciplined rage? Had he not filled the whole atmosphere with this ruthless tone? Those whom he now judged so harshly frequently thought – as in Zürich in the controversy with Zwingli – that the religious innovators twisted the scriptures more than the pope had done. In practice, it was quite impossible to separate the foundations of morality so utterly from faith, and to preach so vehemently the freedom of the Christian from outward restraints, or to tear the old Church apart with such reckless power, without the majority of the socially oppressed drawing conclusions as the peasants did. In an atmosphere of demagogic agitation, charged with hatred and unrestrained criticism, these doctrines were bound to provide a stimulus to insurrection. Iconoclasm was but a step away from the sacking of monasteries.

> Martin's advice is to
> Roast parish priests
> Above blazing monks,
> And pull the nuns into the street, Kyriolieson.

Added to this were the terrible attacks upon the princes, which Luther had presumed to make in writings of 1523 and 1524. The princes were portrayed as raving fools, upon whom God's wrath would be poured out; and the people would scarcely have been human beings had they not been prepared to take their just grievances to the point of riotous insurrection. Luther's outbursts of hatred – even in his sermons – against any, including secular rulers, who did not agree with him, were bound to lead to the weakening of authority in general. The new gospel had created a kind of common mind amongst all who were making demands. Without this common mind even the widespread general undermining of order, which did so much to make revolution easier, the peasants would hardly have achieved even the slight cohesion they did, which alone enabled them to abuse it. To indulge in unrestrained criticism and to stir up the masses against the existent order, in the name of eternal salvation, and at the same time to keep them within the confines of a settled, disciplined order, which in turn was recognised to be unjust, was an art never mastered by Luther, and one which, in his indifference, he never even tried to master. Indeed, things had gone so far that all of this might have been able to impose restraint upon him in his condemnation of the peasants.

The wave of rebellion itself was soon spent, but its effects ran deep. The outcome of the Peasants' War helped to prevent the Reformation becoming an affair of the entire empire.[12] The region actually affected by the Peasants' War, south Germany, remained predominantly Catholic, as did the unaffected region of Bavaria.

It is true that once again the curia deceived themselves, and along with them a great number of Catholics within and outside Germany, for they thought that Luther's heresy had been disposed of with the peasants. But here was the very point where the power of the Lutheran Reformation revealed itself once again. Its central religious basis was manifest, and declared itself to be tied neither to social nor political issues. The revolt of the peasants had arisen in the name of the gospel, and Frederick the Wise, the only ruler who showed any signs of meeting the peasants half-way, had died at the height of the storm, in May 1525. The reaction of the victorious rulers was unanimous and thorough. Erasmus and his followers and all Catholics were on their side. It seemed at this moment that on the side of the Reformation there was no power and little influence. Luther's prestige had suffered a severe blow. If the Reformation movement survived this catastrophe and even won back lost positions (imperial cities) it must at that time have had deep roots in the native soil and in the spiritual life of the people, and must have rested upon religious conviction that could not be destroyed by physical force. This fact remains, even if we take into account the reinforcement of Reformed forces in Germany by the foreign policy dictated by the war with Italy.

(h) The liberation of the peasants failed, as indeed ought the Reformation as a whole to have failed. In both cases an attempt at radical revolution produced a similar result: the old might, challenged by the new, curbed even more oppressively the freedom

---

[12] On the other hand, the Peasants' War prepared the way for the further development of the Reformation. Many monasteries had been plundered and were now left empty, so that they fell an easy prey to secularisation by the authorities.

formerly granted. In respect of the old Church this operation was taken much more seriously, and had very little to do with egoism. The Church's very existence was threatened, and she had to prune back private rights of persons as well as those of groups within the ecclesiastical organisation. This, however, was the highway of providence leading to unity. Trent led to Vatican I. Could it be otherwise in the social sphere? Their fall earned for the peasants a mighty economic loss. The dues demanded in money and kind were enormous. The danger was past and the victors learned nothing or very little from the shattering upheaval. They sought no really deep, plenary remedy for the illness. The important proposal at the protesting *Reichstag* at Speyer in 1526, which made an attempt to remove the cause of abuses, was never carried out. The princes and lords did not honour the assurances given during the disturbances – with the sole exception of Nuremberg. They did not, it is true, instigate a general worsening of the lot of the peasants – the most accommodating were the Swabian League in Allgau; but their only interest within and without the Reformation movement was to consolidate their own princely power. In the end it was the power of the princes alone which put down the rebellion. Neither the absentee emperor nor his important imperial government under Ferdinand had intervened. The princes had stood up for themselves. What a mighty stimulus for the future! Centralism, serfdom and absolutism, were on the way. The advancement of the peasants and of 'the people' had been set back centuries, to the detriment of the nation.

For the inner structure of the Reformation this meant the epoch-making diversion of the Lutheranism of independent congregations with free election of pastors into the Reformation of the princes. In the end of the day the secular overlord took the place of the bishop. The Church had been surrendered to the secular power, which meant the abandonment, in practice, of some of Luther's important basic ideas.

Chief amongst the enemies of public order was fear, which had greatly increased. The fanatics had to pay. They were persecuted still more severely, although often they kept rigorously free from any participation in disturbance – as in Zürich. Luther, for his part, was specially disquieted by the ghost of Müntzer. Five years after Müntzer's execution he still feared that 'another like Müntzer might sprout, for his spirit lives'.

VII. EXPANSION: FORCES AND RESULTS

The work of Luther and his colleagues was dangerously threatened several times even after 1525. In spite of that the years up to 1525 were the heroic years of the Reformation and those which, in a deeper sense, decided its power of survival. They demand, therefore, a specially thorough description, and so we must examine them in greater detail.

We have already seen how the new doctrine spread in specific centres and amongst certain classes – amongst the humanists and the peasants and in the form of fanaticism. These expressions of the new belief themselves presuppose some such spread of Evangelical ideas, so that we may no longer speak of isolated anti-ecclesiastical phenomena. In these the Reformation already appeared as a decisive characteristic of the times.

No single strata of society, however, may be described as the complete representative of Luther's world. The questions remain: which direction did the Reformation take in those persons, circles and classes, who set the pace for the life of the cities and the states? To what degree did it spread and take root in town and country, and which were its most successful methods?

We do not intend at the moment to give an exhaustive answer to these questions, for that would require too much detailed information. The state of affairs and the means by which it was realised must be described, however, so as to make visible the characteristic marks of the revolution. In doing this it seems advisable to look, if need arises, a little beyond the time limits we have stated, including in our survey the entire Reformation period, because certain methods affected the progress of the Reformation in exactly the same way as they had affected its early years. The vast sphere of politics, of the *Reichstags* and the confessional leagues will be mentioned only occasionally, for the most part being held over for examination in their particular contexts.

The fact of the spread of Lutheran ideas and their penetration through many channels into the structure of the common life is plain to our eyes. We are confronted with an astonishingly rapid, tempestuously advancing conquest. Incomprehensibly, quite suddenly in many cities, states and monasteries, amongst princes, lawyers and the secular clergy, the old faith and the life proceeding from it became questioned and collapsed.

We have already stressed explicitly that the approval which resounded about Luther in 1521 as he travelled to Worms did not by any means indicate a general agreement with his dogmatic views. But consider the picture painted of this side of the revolt by Aleander himself in his despatches. 'Countless numbers have ceased to go to confession. Students and even, women, openly defy the Church's teaching, and commit violence against Catholic preachers. A Franciscan in Ulm preaches strict orthodoxy: no audience. He takes up a Lutheran theme: the whole city runs after him.' The world seemed to have got out of joint, the whole of Germany had been incomprehensibly changed. 'There is no one, neither prelate nor prince, who is not completely against us, or if for us, dares to declare his support in public: everyone is in the grip of deadly fear. The whole world, boys and girls, old and young, run after Luther. The people are possessed by such a mad infatuation for this monk, that they would believe the devil himself – who drives them all, anyway – were he to speak in praise of Luther.' On entering Worms, Luther received true religions veneration. Hard as it was for him to do so, Aleander had to admit that 'many believed that Luther was full of the Holy Spirit'. Lutheran pamphlets were poured out daily. In Worms these were the only books that were sold and read. Even the imperial court provided no exception.

Aleander had an important explanation – one we are now to hear over and over again. The cause was the zeal of the Reformers and the fact that 'The people are amazingly united.' Is it not instructive that a non-political man like the devout Cochlaeus in Frankfurt-on-Main should suddenly cease to be greeted in the street when he returned from Worms where he had become known as Luther's adversary?

We may prune away some of Aleander's superlatives, but the essence of what he said is fully corroborated. It is true that in his negotiations with Aleander the elector, Frederick the Wise, fully played up the mood of the people, but he could not have done so had the agitation of the masses not been a reality. The threatening poster stuck up in Worms after Luther refused to recant is evidence of the alliance between the turbulent nobility and the people. From fear of riots amongst the people the Bavarian archdukes, like many bishops, refused to take the strict measures against Luther, which the bull of excommunication demanded. Such riots did indeed take place. The university of Vienna used the same argument when they refused to take proceedings against Luther.

The deluge of pamphlets in the following years reveals an overwhelmingly strong and independent adherence of members of every social class to Luther. It has been correctly pointed out that a great section of the nobility (Hartmut of Kronberg), of the burgesses (Lazarus Spengler), of former monks (Eberlin of Günzburg, Henry of Kettenbach), of the peasants ('Karsthaus', 1521) and of the students used this thoroughly effective instrument to prepare the way for the Reformation. The support of these like-minded people counted for more than their numbers merited, because there was no counter affirmation. The burgesses who were loyal to the Church, along with their episcopal masters, remained inactive. Duke George said that they were asleep.

The true sign of any revolution is that it bursts through the accepted framework of social stratification and the associated avocational differentiation. And so the Reformation aroused a host of men, filled with a new idea, who learned to see things afresh, and who, without any previous schooling, suddenly found themselves with the gift of oratory. Frequently they used this gift with horrifying one-sidedness; but they were inspired by a fanatical faith which endowed them with the art of persuasion. Without any effort the great drama of Luther found its reproduction in miniature in many towns. One or more gifted preaching agitators were able to cast the kindling spark into the masses, and so to enlist the immanent possibilities of explosion on the side of the Reformation. Men like Murner, who remained loyal to the Church, observed all this with indignation: 'The lowest are now all learned; those who could not read . . . now fight against the honour of Christendom.' These non-theologians, drawn from every manual trade, pioneers in every place of the religious change,[13] were of special importance.

---

[13] Elsewhere, too, those who spread the new doctrine were often artisans, as in Venice, where a joiner and a French shoemaker found powerful protection from the aristocracy who were enemies of the pope.

These show that every social class was in a religious and ecclesiastical ferment, and that the Reformation could list considerable successes in all of them.

At the beginning of 1523 Archduke Ferdinand informed the emperor: 'Luther's doctrine has so taken root in the whole empire, that today not one person in a thousand is unaffected; things could not be worse.' At the end of 1523 he wrote: 'The Lutheran sect rules the whole country, and good Christians are afraid to oppose it.'

This popular movement did not remain unorganised. Very quickly it was accepted, utilised and strengthened by the intellectually and politically determining forces. In many places it was, indeed, replaced by the autocratic activities of the princes or even of town councils. The biggest and earliest initiative was taken by the cities.

We can form a picture out of examples from all parts of the empire at different decades.

In 1521 the important city of Basel had freed itself from its bishop. This was the climax to a series of efforts which had begun with its joining the confederacy in 1501. From 1521 onwards the town council ceased to be solidly Catholic, and the city became a centre for the printing of Lutheran literature. By 1522 Oecolampadius was preaching as a Lutheran. The appeal of several of the clergy against reforms instigated by the bishop was used by the town council as an excuse to intervene. By 1525 there were open riots against adherents of the old faith. This caused the town council and Oecolampadius to proceed more cautiously, but the general development was undeflected from its course towards the new faith. In 1526 a new calendar was introduced, which weakened the Catholic imprint upon everyday life. At that time there were still about 200 priests in Basel. Civic taxes were now imposed upon them, and the economic activity of the monasteries was restricted. The clergy thus took their place on the common economic front, with one of their greatest privileges, that of immunity, removed. With the death of the bishop, Christopher of Uttenheim in 1527, the Reformation made more definite progress. In 1528–29 the Catholic members of the town council were chased out in the course of a popular riot. In February 1529 Catholic public worship was banned, the monasteries dissolved, pictures, statues, crucifixes and altars recklessly destroyed by the mob.

In Bern the course of events since 1523 had displayed a host of contradictions. In the end, however, the logic of radicalism was bound to prevail. The moderate town council could do nothing to stop the process. In 1523 it was already possible for people in Bern to dare to put on the carnival play *The Pope and His Gang of Priests*. Gradually Reformation doctrines permeated the community, and then won over the town council. Following on great religious discussion in 1528, the Reformation came out on top. In Graubünden the way had been prepared for the Reformation by an expressly anticlerical policy. The clergy had become regulated by the ordinary laws and subject to ordinary obligations. Congregations had the right to elect or depose their pastor. In Glarus there had been great confusion for years. Valentine Tschudi said mass and at the same time preached Lutheran doctrine. In St Gallen, where the humanist and Evangelical physician, Joachim Vadian had been mayor since 1526, preachers like the much-travelled theologian John Kessler were stirring the people up against Oswald Wendelin, Dominican preacher at the collegiate church, to such an extent that for years he did not dare show himself in the street.

We must return later – because of its political importance – to the development in Zürich, which had already become Reformed by 1523. Zürich provides a specially good presentation of a characteristic of the Swiss Reformation – its patriotic tone. It was fighting for freedom against foreign rule.

In Constance the cathedral preacher, John Wanner, was inclined to favour the Reformation. In addition to him there were another three Evangelical preachers in the city. The bishop put the capable Dominican, Anthony Pirata, in charge of the cathedral pulpit; but in 1524 the town council used this battle of preachers as a pretext for interfering. They ordered that nothing be preached 'except the holy gospel, plain and clear and according to true Christian reason, without the admixture of human accretion'. Because Pirata stubbornly refused to attend a disputation before the town council, he and his whole convent had to leave the city in 1526.

Strasburg had long been the home of severe anticlerical criticism. Sturm, later the Reformation leader of the city, admitted to being the person through whom Geiler, Brant and Wimpfeling had become estranged from the Church. In 1521 there were already adherents of the new doctrine in the town council, and by 1522 the first Evangelical preacher was at the cathedral. In 1523 Wolfgang Capito appeared, and shortly after, Martin Butzer, already married. In the same year the town council here began to take charge of religious life by a series of well-designed police regulations, and to mould it into the Reformed pattern. In 1524 a new regulation was issued concerning almsgiving, and also a decree against images and the mass.

It was Butzer who became the real creator of the new Church in Strasburg, and from the congregation which he built up there by force, Calvin took his model. This congregation became the stimulus for the successful structure developed in Geneva. By the forties of the century, however, it had lost so much of its power and support that a 'second Reformation' had to be attempted from 1546–50.

We have seen that since 1518 the climate in Augsburg had been particularly favourable for the Reformation, and that Lutheran preaching had been well received there in 1520 (see above, p. 269). In 1522 Augsburg had made similar attempts to pave the way for the Reformation by social legislation, for example the new regulation of mendicancy. In Memmingen, too, Zwingli's friend, Christopher Schappeler had been preaching since 1520, and in 1525 the city declared for the Reformation. In 1528 it was put in charge of Ambrosius Blaner (see below). In Esslingen in 1531 the town council claimed the right to examine all preachers. The officiating Dominican preacher, John Burchard, who did not bother much about his duties, was forbidden to preach and prevented from the saying of mass. He had to leave the city. In Ulm Henry of Kettenbach joined the Reformation. In 1530 the Cologne Dominican, Conrad Köllin, a native of Ulm, was travelling to Augsburg with Cardinal Erhard of the Marches, bishop of Lüttich. They stopped at Ulm, but the town council forbade the Dominicans there to give hospitality to their co-religious from Cologne.

In 1522 Albert of Prussia was travelling in Germany on the lookout for assistance against Poland. In Nuremberg he was won over to the Reformation by Osiander. In 1523 he was with Luther in Wittenberg, and in the same year, two years before the official break, he called John Briesmann to Königsberg as Evangelical preacher.

In 1522 Ambrosius Blarer (b. in Constance 1492) was converted by Melanchthon, and left his monastery. He became the Reformer of Constance, Lindau, Memmingen and Ulm. In the same year Brenz became a Reformer in Swabian Hall and produced the first Evangelical catechism.

In 1523 Hans Sachs produced his *Wittenberg Nightingale*. It bore a motto from Luke 19: 'I tell you, if these were silent, the stones would cry out.' This added tremendous impulse to the popularity of the Reformation movement. In the same year George Polenz, bishop of Samland, went over to the Reformation. At the same time the Reformation began in Sweden under Gustavus Wasa. The cities which protested to Charles V in Spain over the tax imposition decreed by the recent *Reichstag*, had to defend themselves against the accusation that Augsburg, Nuremberg and Strasburg, had become Lutheran. At the same time they also dared to appeal to the ordinary man, who was thirsting for the gospel.

This reproach was justified. About 1523–24, it was the cities that could be said, most emphatically, to be sympathetic towards the Evangelical Reformation. In July the assembly of imperial cities in Speyer was quite frankly Lutheran. The same was true of the assembly in Ulm in December, where mutual aid was pledged in defying the Edict of Worms. In 1521 in Ghent an Augustinian eremite was preaching Luther's doctrine in all the streets as the doctrine of St Paul and of Christ. The dioceses of Utrecht and Münster seemed to Aleander equally badly infected with the heretical disease, as were all of the lower German dioceses, not least, those in Holland – significantly the birthplace of Erasmus.

The new imperial government met in Nuremberg. To it fell the task of carrying out the Edict of Worms. We might have assumed that it could have obstructed the spread of the Reformation at least in the city which was the seat of government. The opposite proved to be the case. We can see in detail how in Nuremberg many forces had combined to produce a climate favourable to the Reformation, and how the town council (and the *Reichstags* of 1522–23 and 1524) had exploited it. In 1521 the humanist, Pirkheimer, made war on the emissary who brought the papal bull of excommunication. From 1522 onwards the humanist, Osiander, preached about the Roman Antichrist. The Augustinian monastery opened its doors to the Reformation. The town clerk, Spengler, a first-rate mind, wrote a defence of Luther in 1521, and moved the town council to share his views. In spite of the prohibition, Luther's books were being read – as they were everywhere. Dürer was awaiting the rebirth of Christianity, which Luther was supposed to inaugurate. And there was Hans Sachs, whom we have just mentioned. In 1524 the papal legate Campeggio, who had already visited the empire in Maximilian's time, found a different Germany. He, the papal legate, was ridiculed by the mob in Augsburg, where they displayed a cartoon of him. There was no longer any Church celebration to welcome him, and they even told him that he need not give his blessing, 'considering the way things now stand'. We have seen how the official conversion of the city, that is of the town council, to the Reformation, had been unusually well prepared. In this we see the fatal results of earlier defects. The council now extended its late medieval authority over the Church (gained partly through direct negotiation with Rome) so far, that after the religious discussions led by von Scheuerl in 1525, it was complete master of the situation. Then followed the surrender of most of the monasteries, and the forcible dissolution of those that would not comply (see below, p. 410).

In 1524 Magdeburg, Breslau, Memmingen, Nuremberg and Strasburg all officially banned the mass and had already set in motion the secularisation of Church property. Philip of Hesse had been converted by Melanchthon. The imperial report for this year declared that the estates would enforce the Edict of Worms 'in so far as they can'. The estates in lower Austria pledged their life and property to their overlord Ferdinand, but requested that he do not 'burden them with carrying out orders or prohibitions in matters touching their souls'. The most glaring illustration of all this is the fact that in the same year Luther, an outlaw and under excommunication, dared to resume teaching at the university of Wittenberg, with the consent of his feudal superior. In December he gave up wearing the religious habit.

In 1525 the Prussian religious province was turned into a secular dukedom by its general, Albert of Brandenburg, who thus broke his religious vows. The Catholic king of Poland stood godfather to this new creation, for the sake of political gain.

In this year a Reformed version of the New Testament appeared in English. As everywhere outside the empire, the Reformation showed signs of spreading. In 1521 Aleander reported the appearance in Antwerp of a Spanish translation of Luther's writings 'at the instigation of the Moorish merchants there'. In September of the same year Adrian of Utrecht, then regent and general inquisitor in Spain, had demanded that Charles and the Spanish estates suppress the Lutheran literature which was penetrating Spain in translations.

A unique state of affairs developed in Ratisbon. Almost everywhere cathedral immunities had proved an effective hindrance to the spread of the new beliefs. These privileges protected the canons and their houses and schools from the town council. For this reason, it always represented a most important step forward, if the council succeeded in banishing the prebendaries from the city. In Constance they were able so to restrict the living space around the cathedral that the canons were forced to take lodgings in the city; in Breslau they seem to have tried the same tactics. But in Regensburg there was not one but five, direct imperial immunities (bishop, cathedral chapter, duke, abbess of Obermünster, abbess of Niedermünster). And so it came about that great complexes within the city remained independent of the religious changes. At the same time, the Reformation made considerable progress, if only later, for the council in this city showed the same dangerous Lutheranising tendencies as elsewhere. Before the introduction of the Reformation many of the inhabitants had been going to hear the new sermons in neighbouring Beratzhausen. To begin with the council, under Bavarian pressure, had to expel a Protestant preacher; but this led to the presentation of a petition by many Ratisbon burgesses asking the council to call a preacher. Nobles had Evangelical worship conducted at their courts within the city. After the chalice had already been given to the laity for several years in two churches the practice was introduced in 1524 by a formal resolution of the town council. At that time the Jesuit Father Jajus was banished from the city, the people threatening to throw him into the Danube. (He replied that he hoped to get to heaven by way of water, too.) All the severe counter-measures applied by the Bavarian dukes were unsuccessful.

Conditions in Bavaria in general, followed a peculiar course of development. The territory as a whole, as we have said, remained unaffected by the change. A considerable section of the nobility, however, as in Austria, were for Luther. The bishops were inactive, almost to a man. The opposition provided by the dukes, that is by their chancellor, the eminent Leonard of Eck, was far too political in motivation. Of the burgesses, Hubmaier could assert in 1523 that 'amongst us in Bavaria there are many who preach the gospel with enthusiasm'. In Munich itself were a few individuals who dared go so far as to preach heretical views in public. Arsacius Seehofer of Munich, who supported the doctrine of justification by faith alone, and denied free will, was a master at the university of Ingolstadt and taught along with Melanchthon. In the same city were several of the clergy who found their way to Luther at an early date. In Straubing, too, the Reformation was busily at work. Stepehen Kastenpauer (Agricola) was converted to Lutheranism in 1520. In 1522 he was arrested and surrendered to Cardinal Lang. He worked and married in Augsburg. In many places there were reports of schoolmasters striking up Protestant hymns at public worship, and of the congregations joining in. We already know about the beginnings of the Reformation in Augsburg, where the Zwinglian, Dr Gereon Seiler, a diplomat in the employment of the Landgrave of Hesse, was city physician. We will hear more later of Käser from Raab, who was killed at Scharding/Inn. And then, in Bavaria there were to be found important centres of sedition in various small estates, directly subject to the empire: the dukedom of Ortenburg and Haag, and the lordship of Hohenwaldeck.

A more detailed example of the Reformation of an imperial city is provided by the case of Frankfurt/Main.

The youthful William Nesen, a pupil of Erasmus, became schoolmaster there in 1520. His interests were wider than the mere witty satire of the humanists. He longed for a rebirth of religion and morals, and his instruction of the children was in harmony with his outlook. On the way to Worms, Luther visited the school of his supporter. In the very same year the pastor of the cathedral, who had been a bitter opponent of the new belief, and the Dominican, Dietenberger, were driven out of the city. In their place, in 1522 a Lutheran preacher was installed in the church of the monastery of St Catherine by two of the city fathers, with the consent of the aldermen. This preacher then began to denounce the clergy of the old Church. Knights from the surrounding district demanded that the corporation protect the preachers. The defeat of Sickingen and Hutten brought about a reaction; but once again the pulpit at St Catherine's was opened to a preacher.

In 1524 there were street riots which, in 1525, assumed the proportions of a civic parallel to the peasants' risings. The guilds presented the town council with forty-six articles which, in their linking of religions with social demands, and their stressing the value of the word of God, show similarities with the *Twelve Articles* of the peasants. Then followed an attack upon the monasteries, where the cellars were looted. The town council were powerless, and had to approve the articles. It is true that when the Peasants' War came to an end, a reaction set in, but the movement in the direction of the Reformation went even further. Two Zwinglian preachers went on with their radical preaching, and one of the preachers married.

In 1527 in the church of the Barefoot Friars, where the guardian, Peter Comberger, had come over with members of the community, the Lord's Supper was dispensed under both kinds. The Corpus Christi procession of the Catholics was mocked, with the connivance of town councillors. Two years later the town council installed a fourth Evangelical preacher.

In 1530 the town council church was closed so that the sessions of the council were no longer preceded by the celebration of mass. They had not subscribed to the protest of 1529, nor to the Augsburg Confession of 1530. The Frankfurters also declined to join the Schmalkald League on the truly Lutheran grounds that, 'the Lord teaches in his holy word that we ought not to fight, but rather to suffer'.

In 1531 the cathedral was split between the two confessions; but the Evangelicals had a way of putting the Catholics at a disadvantage on occasion; at Christmas in 1531, for example, a lengthy Protestant sermon got in the way of the first mass.

The originator of this device, the preacher Melander, became more and more clamant in his demand for the removal of Catholic worship. His denunciations led to riots, breaking into churches, and the damaging of altars and relics. Luther wrote attacking these blind Zwinglian leaders, but Melander promulgated the excommunication of the pope and Catholics.

A vote of the guilds in 1533 for the abolition of the mass reveals both genuine conviction and sheer calculation. The furriers made the proviso that no action against the emperor be implied; apart from that they cast their vote the same way. The town council abolished the mass, the cathedral was closed, then reopened for the Protestants in the same year. In 1535, however, once again it was shared out between Catholics and Protestants. In 1549 during the interim it became Catholic and has remained so ever since.

In the few cities of the north the spread of the Reformation gathered momentum later, but once it started, it was worked out in the same way as in the south. In Rostock it was the town *syndicus*, a professor of law, who led the battle against the old Church. The Catholic duke wanted to overthrow him. The town council punished two friars who knew of his plans but failed to inform the council. The council forbade the friars to wear the habit outside their house (1531). It arrested the rector in order to force the surrender of all valuables. After the town council, step by step, had gained possession of the property and the rights of the friars, it still regarded its action as lenient, compared with that meted out in many other principalities.

In all cases, the victory or failure of the Reformation depended, in a critical degree, on the attitude of the territorial rulers. Most of them were slower than the cities to follow the innovation. The very thing which makes much of the political history of Luther's work so enigmatic, is that, despite a Catholic majority in the *Reichstag*, even there Luther's cause ultimately won the day. Take as example the *Reichstag* at Speyer in 1526. The resolution of the council of princes not to wait for a council to clear away abuses but to take the matter in hand themselves, shows a dangerous self-assurance in Church matters. The entire proposal of the secular clerical committee shows how receptive the mood was for the Reformation, even for its dogma, how strong was the feeling, that is, that the elementary Christian doctrines of the innovators were Catholic. The significant thing here was not that people wanted the chalice for the laity, the marriage of the clergy, and the use of the vernacular at baptism and communion. They also wanted private masses abolished, and to know that scripture was being interpreted exclusively by scripture. People were aware of the impotence of the emperor, who, on account of the pope's alliance with France, was unable to present the old doctrine in a good light before the estates. Everything conspired towards the estates' accepting the evasive formula, which in the end became the official basis of the Protestant territorial ecclesiastical system. But there was another force at work here: the counsellors, especially Hans von der Planitz from electoral Saxony. It was he who resisted the execution of the Edict of Worms, in defiance of the elector of Brandenburg. He was 'just like Luther', they said. All the same, he acted in conformity with his commission as an electoral adviser. Many of the counsellors of the prince bishops were much worse. Carlowitz, who betrayed the loyal duke George of Saxony in 1539, went so far as to say that he cared nothing for the Roman Church, which had indeed departed from the teaching of the apostles.

We already know the position taken up by Frederick the Wise. His successor, John, and John's successor, John Frederick, actively supported Luther without any signs of vacillation. They were the chief princely foundation of the German Reformation. By June 1526 the German mass had been uniformly introduced in electoral Saxony. In 1527 the territory received its first visitation, accompanied and followed by doctrinal direction given to the pastors. This pattern was then followed by many new forms of Church organisation.

Philip of Hesse joined up with Saxony. He had been the only prince who had dared to visit Luther personally in Worms in 1521. At that time Aleander had not regarded him as an adversary. In 1523 Eck still listed him in his survey for the curia as one of the unaffected German powers, although he did require a little warning. In the next year, however, Philip distinctly professed allegiance to the Reformation. Amongst the princes, he was the second great pillar of the Reformation, and undoubtedly he had the greater power of initiative.

Even in those princely circles that later turned their backs upon the Reformation, the Reformation made important conquests to begin with. At any rate it had enough time to take root; for consider how little real responsible Christian zeal lay behind the official, traditional profession of many Catholic princes.

The emperor's own sister, Maria, wife of the Bohemian king Ludwig who was killed at Mohacs, is an example. After her husband's death Luther wrote to her, for she read his books and had asked him for advice in matters of conscience. After 1530, when she travelled to Augsburg, she had a Lutheran preacher accompany her. From 1531 onwards, now regent of the Netherlands, she was once again a Catholic.

The emperor had another sister, wife of Christian II of Denmark, Norway and Sweden. She received the chalice of the laity, and her husband, whose opposition to the clergy until his deposition had been a sheer matter of power politics, became deeply influenced by Evangelical doctrine in Germany in 1523 through the agency of Melanchthon. For a time he had Karlstadt in Denmark as a Reformer. In 1530 he renounced the Reformation in order to win back his throne through the influence of his imperial brother-in-law. Meanwhile the new king of Denmark, Frederick I, duke of Holstein, and uncle of the deposed Christian II, had similarly been converted to the other side. He had, indeed, bound himself on his election to oppose the Lutheran Reformation, but allowed the Reformation to develop, and gave his daughter in marriage to the Lutheran duke Albert I of Prussia in 1526.

The further Reformation of the states, beginning with Würtemberg (1534), then the duchy of Saxony (1539), Naumburg-Zeitz, Hildesheim, the duchy of Braunschweig-Wolfenbüttel, Pfalz-Neuburg (1543), was very largely the work of a Protestantism that had already become politically organised. We will describe it, therefore, in that context. This development displays the prime importance of the princes in the spread of the Reformation.

There were two regions of more or less Reformed structure that had already evolved along these lines by 1525–27. These were the cities of the south, especially of the south-west, including Switzerland, and the states of Saxony and Hesse. The critical year for the spread of the Reformation in these regions was 1527. That year was the climax in a highly important period: 1524–29. The final resolutions of the *Reichstags* of 1524 and 1526, together with the general advance of the Reformation, were bound to bring about a mighty spread and quasi-legal consolidation of proselytising. In fact this period, taking us past the reaction to the Peasants' War, was the period of the great territorial expansion of the Reformation and this expansion was made possible by its political establishment through the confessional leagues, which soon took place. It was this development that finally made the lords spiritual aware of the real issue at stake, and brought about the overwhelming majority of those loyal to the Church in the council of princes and elector at the *Reichstag* of 1529.

It is out of the question that the Catholic powers had lost all initiative. We have already made some important discoveries on that subject, and later we shall return to examine it in detail.

However, cheering as it must be for all Catholics, and for all Christians indeed, to see modern scholarship proving that the Catholic life of that time was much greater and better than had formerly been supposed, the fact remains that victory went clearly to the Reformers.

The cause lay both in Catholic negligence and in the zealous initiative of the new Church, which in turn was greatly fortified by the sense of progressive victory.

First of all let us consider Catholic failure. The literary work of Cochlaeus is full of complaints of this sort, not least against the bishops. This theme had never been absent ever since John Eck raised it in Rome 1523 (especially against the bishops of Bavaria) at the orders of his dukes.

For the most part, as we have already explained, the bishops were ignorant and powerless leaders. Whether German or Scandinavian, the bishops in general felt themselves religiously and theologically powerless in face of the Reformation. They showed almost no interest in anything other than the retention of their worldly possessions, and none at all for the thousands of souls entrusted to their care. The sacrificial mood of the Reformers appeared in marked contrast. 'In two years the apostate archbishop of Cologne had staked more money and labour on the cause than all of the German bishops together in twenty-five years. Even so the bishops are going to lose their worldly possessions' (Cochlaeus).

The most important means of strengthening religious life were the schools, the press and preaching, and an increase in good priests. On all three scores the appointed shepherds – bishops and religious superiors – showed downright indifference. Cochlaeus' loudest entreaty met 'besotted shepherds' all along the line – a judgment which we encounter in Eck, Duke George, in Carafa and many others as well. Germany's first churchman, cardinal of Mainz, up till 1524 had taken no initiative to stop the coming conflagration. When, much later, the Reformation of electoral Brandenburg affected his own dioceses of Magdeburg and Halberstadt, he left them to the Reformation without giving it a thought.

Luther was delighted to see how many a bishop was at first pleased with his action against the power of the pope, and the privilege of monks. These bishops had not Eck's theological perspicacity and zeal, and had not learned the wisdom with which Cochlaeus ended his commentary on Luther: 'Catch the foxes while they are still young.'

The failure of the priests was a direct consequence of the clerical proletariat at the beginning of the sixteenth century. There could be no loyalty in clergy such as these, and they were carried away with the storm. It is true that apparently few of them were fired with religious zeal, but merely by the hope of a freer life. In addition, there was the decline of the Catholic cathedral schools and the Lutheranising of many parish schools. Catholics could no longer compete with the new schools, well endowed out of the proceeds of the secularisation of Church property. Thus, for example, the humanist cathedral school in Breslau lost capable teachers to the Protestant schools. Rapidly there developed such a scarcity of priests, that a few years later the cathedral had to admit that out of fifty parishes, scarcely one could any longer find a Catholic pastor. Monasteries and convents decayed through stoppage of income and lack of recruits. The shortage was so serious that even Cochlaeus – at the end of the thirties admittedly – suggested that the only remedy was to discontinue the celibacy of the clergy. Not until 1543 in Eichstätt did he discover just how weak the Church had become. In the preface to the *Schmalkald Articles* of 1538 Luther cleverly referred to this ever-worsening shortage of priests, about which 'neither bishops nor princes' bother.

The miserable activity of many bishops in face of the Reformation was encouraged by the Erasmian bent of their advisers. On the other hand, we know of Protestant-minded clergy who, until well on in the Reformation, had allies in the Roman curia itself, from whom they received many favours.

Whatever the various reasons for this failure of Catholicism, the same weakness appears over and over again: failure to make the proper decision at the right time. This happened in the vitally important period of the first growth of the Reformation, and bishops and curia were both to blame. After the bull of excommunication the emperor was out of the empire and as a result no real decision was arrived at by the *Reichstag;* then there were the final resolutions of the *Reichstags* of 1524 and 1526 in Speyer, with their 'as far as possible'; once again the same weakness was displayed by the repeated postponement of a general council, which ought to have met immediately after the *Reichstag* of Speyer. Events were pushed along the same course when Charles (1525–27 in Italy) and Ferdinand (1526–27 in Hungary) were almost forced by the pope, France and England to leave German affairs to themselves. In practice, the phrase 'as far as possible' is the slogan which explains the situation.

All of our statements about the growing Reformation movement, no matter how profoundly they characterise the struggles of that epoch, are as tame statistics when compared with the enormous sense of victory, which is expressed powerfully, inspiringly, and arrogantly in Luther's words and actions. For him this warfare had become his natural element. He threw himself straight upon his foes; and with menacing rapidity he became increasingly conscious of work performed and success achieved.

First of all, an incomparably important fact: Luther's writings, which possessed immense power to excite and inspire the nation, were distributed in almost two thousand editions in the years between 1517 and 1525. We must think what this colossal number of editions meant in those days, when the population was so small and printing was in its infancy. Any book was liable to produce a far greater impression than books do today. Moreover, these books of Luther's were not simply sold as commodities in a shop but displayed as a profession of faith. The travelling booksellers, who spread the new Reformation hymns, like the itinerant preachers, were in fact propagandists of Luther.

By 1522 Luther well knew that if the pope laid hands on all of his followers there would be an outcry in Germany. 'Look at what I am doing. Have I not broken the power of pope, bishops, priests and monks far more by my words, without ever drawing a sword, than have all the emperors and kings and princes of former days, with all their power?' With astonishing ease he finds himself saying that certain people will be too hasty to describe themselves as 'good Lutherans'. Along with this there is the other and more dominant thought that people ought not to choose his name as a badge, but to call themselves Christians. 'What is Luther? The doctrine is not mine. I wish to be no one's master. Christ alone is our master. It is not our work which is going on now in the world. It would be impossible for a man to undertake such a thing. Things have got so far without my planning and advice, they shall go on further also without my guidance, and the gates of hell will not stand in the way. It is another who drives the wheel; the papists fail to see this and put the blame on us.' 'The devil has been afraid of these doctrines for a long time, and has issued many prophecies against them, which some apply to me.'

In 1524 in the dispute with Müntzer he assessed what had been done, and seemed to speak as though, since Worms, there had been no religion except Lutheranism. 'Since being driven out, Satan has been running around these cities for a year or two . . . ' He felt deeply that God was making his army bigger and bigger, and that of his enemies smaller and smaller. Success carried him on. It is true, he reckoned on an even greater deceitful opposition to his doctrines by false brethren, after his death, but he did not worry too much about that. 'All these festering vermin are destined to destruction. How narrow and short now is the cover beneath which the papist can crawl!' Two years more, and 'Christ, through us, will have killed the papacy. We will write without more ado: *expiravit*' (1522).

Later on, too, in the *Table Talk* and other reminiscences, the consciousness of victory won, of a completely new era, of a Lutheran epoch, was loudly expressed. This consciousness was certainly not uniform, and was ever and again restrained by the necessity of defence; but the opposing forces in the end were reckoned by Luther to be of little importance. At all events it was astonishing how mean was the estimate of scholasticism, which supported his consciousness of triumph over the theologians, for that same scholasticism, incredible as it may seem, once ruled the day, when the 'cleverest men' gave voice to nonsense and sophistries, which now were said to have become unknown, barbarous and impossible. This was directed not against scholasticism alone, for

Luther goes on: 'Amongst these theologians we can include the greatest blether of them all – Thomas.' It is shattering, also, to observe how falsely he represented the plainest and most essential things in Catholic doctrine, thinking that he had destroyed this idolatry.

The spread of the Reformation over a vast area was rapid. Had it been a political affair, the chief question would have been answered: was it victorious or defeated, was it successful or not? But of the Reformation we have to ask the question; was the victory, when it occurred, the result of inner conscientious conviction? Was the change spiritually complete, or was it the result of outward compulsion? Were the motives entirely, or mostly, pure, based on knowledge, faith and zeal for the house of God, or were they adulterated with selfishness, violence and deceit? Is the case before us one of conversion, or of unscrupulous change of side?

This is not one but a whole series of questions of graded importance; and a satisfactory understanding demands that we answer them all.

In many individual cases the sudden breakaway from a Catholic piety, hitherto practised with deep loyalty, is utterly baffling. This happened in the case of the Ebners in Nuremberg or of the town councillors in Strasburg, to whom it quickly became clear that they had a say in matters of faith also. How quick they were to forget their so recently held contrary opinions. There is the amazing fact, that after duke George of Saxony died, his territory went speedily over to the Reformation. Is it sufficient explanation, that the new ruler commanded support for the Reformation, or was it that the 'crowds were easily inspired by the new doctrine'? It certainly is true that mistrust of all in authority was deeply rooted in the popular mind, and that its love could very easily turn to hate. This very illuminating suggestion is still not sufficient explanation. The subject, it seems, has to be examined again, more closely, and more distinctions will have to be made.

We know how much confessional polemics was at pains, from the very start, to call in question the sincerity of one's opponents' convictions. Catholics looked for Luther's and his followers' motives in the most personal areas of life; conversely, the Reformers were unscrupulous in casting suspicion upon the defenders of the old Church. It was insinuated that Cochlaeus, who had fought so hard and then paid dearly for his lifelong loyalty, had been bribed by the curia.

In great measure the questions asked are answered by Luther's earnest, spiritual evolution, by the fact that to begin with he stood alone, that he employed only the words of the gospel and his own words, that his preaching was carried along by a deep sincerity, and that he made heavy demands of faith.

In addition to these things we know what the intellectual and religious atmosphere was at the beginning of the Reformation. There was a spirit of destructive and flippant criticism, but also a great searching, much interior striving for the truth, and for a purified Church. We know how Luther's words spread over the country with astonishing speed, how people seized upon them as if this was just what they had been waiting for. We know to a certain extent, the effect of Luther's disputations, his correspondence, his lectures and sermons, and also how some of his disciples operated. We know the surprising way in which many lay people not only read the Bible more fervently but got to know it and spread its new interpretation. The pamphlets written by noblemen, and artisans who had no formal education, are full of unexpected surprises in this respect. *The House of the Wise and the Unwise* by Hans Sachs (1524) has eighty verses, and there are fifty-six scripture references in the margin. Letters of Argula of Grumbach display a quite unheard of wealth of Bible knowledge, which it handles with such ease, and from which it draws such a pointed interpretation of life.

A great danger lies in the historico-ideological, and particularly the theological, analysis of the Reformation; for the impression could be gained that we are dealing simply with a multiplicity of separate forces, which can be relatively neatly described. The mystery of that period, however, was that, in its decisive years it constituted a revolution. It was a revolution not merely in the sense that revolutionary ideas were thought up in one or several heads, and then spread abroad victoriously, but in the sense also that all of life fell under the spell of a revolutionary mood of the greatest intensity, that a longing for revolution was alive in all groups, that the existent social stratification of life spontaneously strove to find a new arrangement, and that any religious and revolutionary thought was bound to have transforming consequences in the social and political sphere. True revolution in its complexity is no mere accompanying phenomenon on the fringe of a great reforming event, but the living form in which the decisive reformation is expressed. The chaos, the intellectual infection, the mysterious subterranean quality of many impulses, which accompanied the period, the upheavals and the co-operation of the lower strata of society in the spread of the new attitudes, the general agitation of the years until 1525, were all part of the essence of the Reformation break-through. The same is true of the immediate seizure of other sections of the population by fears and indignation, by the open or secret oscillations of public opinion. This was seen in the fact that, quite naturally it seemed, the books of the new belief dominated the market, whereas Catholic books, if they appeared at all, were more or less assumed to be out of date and inferior. Enthusiasm for the new religion was expressed also in fervent missionary zeal. The word of the new gospel, with truly magical power, kindled a fire far into the ranks of the uneducated, and engendered an army of learned and unlearned who knew the text of holy scripture, and who were ready and willing at all times to work for the new interpretation. None of these things was subsidiary, but of the essence of the Reformation event. A simple method of bringing this complex process directly under our gaze, is to read long passages from Cochlaeus' *Commentary*. In recent times Herte has brought this work into fresh prominence.

The fact remained that the religious question summed up all the deepest cares and desires of the times. This question was not, however, a 'purely' religious question, but pre-eminently a question concerning the Church. The living manifestation of the question was the separation of the laity from the clergy, ending in unbridled hatred of the former for the latter. This meant that the dispute was not theological only, nor yet politico-diplomatic only – although these two aspects ultimately dictated the form of the thing – but was a popular dispute. This precipitated the theological Reformation into the liveliest and widest reality. In turn, hatred of the clergy exerted a lively influence upon the Reformation. From this angle for many people, profession of the but dimly comprehended new doctrine became quite simply an affair of the heart.

Schisms within the Protestant movement obviously constituted a severe obstacle to consolidation. We must not, however, allow diversity to blind us to the common element which ran very deep, nor to the fact that the wealth of variety which emerged within the framework of what was common, was of great assistance to the penetration of Reformation ideas into the most variously delimited areas of German life and the German landscape.

The conquest of Wittenberg by the fanatics was never more than an episode. Wittenberg was Luther's city, and we cannot over-estimate its importance as centre of the Reformation. While Luther was raging against the universities, the youth of Germany were streaming to him, to his young colleagues, and to his new traditionless university. The numbers swelled into the thousands, until Wittenberg looked like an appendage to the university. This was where Luther's 'system' was alive. From this place his audience returned to every part of the German-speaking world. There is no need to point out that, in spite of the mediocrities who soon began to hang around, this was a centre of intellectual creativity. Think of how Melanchthon had lured the youth to this place by his voice and his pen; and he had turned them into preachers and teachers of Lutheranism. There are many individual cases which prove that the first to bring the new doctrine to a district was a preacher, who was then joined by one or two more. These were pupils of Luther, who had either heard him lecture or read his books. In this way the new slogans spread to the people.

Cochlaeus was one of the first to recognise the importance of the Wittenberg seminary for national and international Protestant propaganda. Just as Cochlaeus' appeal for Catholic printing presses went unheeded, so was his demand for a thorough campaign against the university of Wittenberg ignored. He was able, through the agency of Polish bishops, to have attendance at the university prohibited by King Sigismund II; the Bavarian duchies and the duchy of Saxony issued a similar prohibition; but in the forties John Eck still thought that Rome had not made full use of the possibilities of taking action against this 'breeding ground' of the Reformation. Here again we see that Catholic apathy against which the Augustinian, Hoffmeier, inveighed so vehemently.

Catholics were the *beati possidentes* and slept. The Reformers had to win their inheritance and were at their posts. Thus they seized instinctively for the best weapons, or used old weapons in a more lively form: the word, the printing press, the school.

The general weariness on the Catholic side was expressed by the breaking up of the alliance between Christian faith and humanist, pedagogical vigour, which had set the tone at the end of the fifteenth century. The decline of Catholic schools as a result of the indolence of the bishops, the ignorance, neglect and immorality shown by the lower clergy, was an accomplished fact even before the Reformers increased the number of their schools and equipped them so well, so that the old schools could no longer compete in the race. In the time just before the Reformation a much freer, and ultimately anti-Christian, humanism had taken over the schools; then the Reformation itself succeeded in enlising in its own cause this humanist energy, in its most decisive form – the school. As a result of the keenness of the humanists who were well disposed towards Lutheranism, years before the dogmatic breach could be clearly recognised, precious territory was snatched from the Church and annexed by the Reformation. Thereafter the substance of the new belief was carried to the people by the schools with their religious instruction. Sturm's solitary effort in Strasburg, and Melanchthon's outstanding contribution, represent an incalculable gain for the Reformation. (Sturm was a product of the Brothers of the Common Life, and his work was based upon medieval humanism.) The old faith was left lagging behind. In any age it is a difficult art to combine conservatism with the spirit of renewal, to maintain close cohesion alongside the spiritual freedom of creative progress. Even that man who more than any other ought to have had an eye for this aspect of a Catholic defence programme, the schoolmaster, Cochlaeus, never mentioned the revival and exploitation of the educational system in the reform programme which he sent to the curia in 1523. In the territories of Duke George, where on occasion there was greater readiness to make sacrifices on the part of bishops and prelates, a more suitable Catholic plan was never carried out; for reliable teachers could not be found; and in the end of the day the indifference which characterised most of the bishops prevailed.

The result was a victory for the Reformers amongst the youth. 'Amongst our German Catholic youth, faith has become a rarity' (Cochlaeus).

The majority of those won over by the Reformation to be participants in the intellectual fight, were of assured subjective sincerity when they enlisted for the new beliefs. The very tone of their writings and sermons and of the disputations that were constantly being required of them, prove this fact. A considerable number of capable monks – most of them, it would appear, from non-observantine houses – went over to the Reformation from inner persuasion, and became the most valuable supports in polemics and in the consolidation of the movement. We have already got to know some of these. Whereas at the beginning of the twenties these ex-monks, like Butzer and Blarer, still tried to preserve a connection with the Church, revolutionary independence now began to grow with extraordinary rapidity.

Let us mention a few names by way of illustration. Augustinians: Casper Güttel at Eisleben, Wenzel Link – close friend of Staupitz and his successor as vicar general – at Altenburg and Nuremberg, John Lang at Erfurt. Franciscans: Frederick Myconius (Gotha), Stephen Kempen (Hamburg), Henry of Kettenbach (Ulm), Eberlin of Günzburg (Ulm), all of whom were a credit to the Observantine Franciscans; and there was Calixtus who preached in Styria (1525). Dominicans: the most important Martin Butzer and Osiander. Benedictines: Ambrose Blarer and the prior of the Nuremberg monastery. Cistercians: John Brenz, who had fallen under Luther's influence in Heidelberg. He went through a severe inner conflict while resisting Luther's doctrine, and then gave in after reading *The Babylonian Captivity* several times. 'The whole world has been blind.'

The same holds true of those who were martyred for the new faith, or bore witness to it by heavy sacrifice. There were the young Franciscans Henry Voes and John of Eschen, who in 1523 had already been executed in the Netherlands, and seemed to regard Luther as a hymn writer. ('We are taking up a new song.') Leonard Käser, hitherto a fickle character, was executed in 1527, showing resolute Christian courage in face of death by fire. On hearing his condemnation he said: 'I would rather have heard other news, but let God's will be done.' His testament was wholly concerned with an admonition to love, obedience, peace and solicitude for his mother and kindness to the poor. Luther wrote to console him: 'You must cry with confidence to God and support yourself with the psalms of consolation. Brother, be strong in the Lord and let his mighty power comfort you . . . , you will be set free, or you will not.' Käser followed this advice. As he went to his death he found comfort in the Latin psalms. Looking at the crowd who were waiting to see the execution he cried out: 'There is the harvest for which man should labour. Beseech the lord of the harvest to send reapers into his harvest.' He asked for forgiveness, and for prayers that he would die in the true faith, and said: 'Christ you must suffer with me, you must support me, otherwise all is in vain.'

A less edifying example was given by Adolf Clarenbach, executed in Cologne in September 1529. On the one hand he steadfastly refused to buy his life and freedom by taking an oath, on the other hand he took refuge in lies. But when the Dominican, Host, his opponent in the disputation was leaving, he said: 'Pray for me, and I will pray for you in heaven.' Then he bravely paid with his life.

All of these, no matter how many there were of them, belonged to the élite. The Reformation won its victory however, because it attracted the masses. What was the spiritual worth of this defection from the old Church?

Let us begin with what was positive. We have already discussed the spread of revolutionary infection (above, p. 398). Let us now find out quite clearly, what religious power was possessed by Luther's principal formulae, those which were the banner for his campaign, and which he addressed to all. For religious men, and for public opinion at the time as well, there could have been no more rousing or undisputed slogan than 'God's word alone!' 'God's word against the ordinances of men!' Considering the extraordinary, far advanced enlargement of the organism of the Church in life and in doctrine (and the many unjustified accretions therein), the battle for 'the word of God that endures for ever' against human ordinances had a never-failing power of attraction. In countless declarations, debates, confessions, precepts, hymns, proverbs and imagery, this demand was constantly sounded out with that air of perfect self-evidence which carries with it the sense of victory; and it was a demand which seemed so utterly Catholic. Eck once admitted in his reform proposals of 1523, that at first 'the brilliance of the Lutheran gospel and of the Pauline doctrine had captivated many'. It is certainly highly instructive that the slogan of 'the word' was a permanent feature on the Catholic side too. After thirty years of battle against the Reformation, King Ferdinand still did not like to speak of the 'true doctrine of the Church', which must be added in good time to an increase of clergy, if the Church is to be saved, but of 'the uncorrupted doctrine of holy scripture'; and scripture alone was proposed (to St Ignatius of Loyola, 1550) as a subject of instruction.

We must try to feel the anathematising energy with which the polemical literature of the Reformers made the most of the antithesis between the word of God and the ordinances of men. With the lack of restraint of those who believed themselves to have been deceived, as of those who were merely giving rein to their hatred of the pope and of monks, it was hammered into the readers that the pope had shamefully twisted the word of God – had 'crucified' it. More than this: the idea was urged upon the reader that it was a Catholic doctrine, that the pope was justified in altering the gospel. How victoriously then the pure work of God and his pure word could dissociate themselves from this work and word of man! Henry of Kettenbach can be allowed to speak for thousands – although it is painful to hear him give as basis for his assertion: 'as I am told has been preached here in public'. We can see how, independently of the honest conviction of the writer, the excited readers, too, fall into a misconception. To achieve reasonable completeness on this point, we would have to go right through Luther's whole presentation of Catholic doctrine, and that provided by contemporary Protestant theology. Over and over again we are disconcerted by so much misunderstanding, by such cross distortion of their own Catholic past. What a caricature of the doctrine of the sacrifice of the mass! How the graph of these misinterpretations rises as Luther grows older. This victorious distortion of Catholicism by Luther, out of zeal for a purified Christianity, is the foundation upon which the tragedy of the Reformation and of the Reformed epoch in Germany history is laid. For it was nothing other than the mighty words of Luther that mediated an image of Catholic doctrine to his own agitated age – an age that was in revolt against Rome. He imparted this image to souls who on the one hand were filled with justified indignation, and on the other with pure Christian trust in God.

The most varied means contributed to produce the result. To-day, we may see through the legends that were current in Erfurt concerning Luther's alleged miracles; but at the time they were extraordinarily effective in gaining for him the reputation of being a 'man of God', and in surrounding him with that mysterious, religious aura, which made it so much easier for the faithful to transfer their allegiance to him. This was all the more effective in the context of his powerful, fervent and popular preaching, as well as the context of so much laxity amongst the Catholic clergy.

In the course of history it has often turned out that apparently unimportant things have had undreamed of consequences. Details of personal politics became important long before anyone recognised their connection with the Reformation. How irrevocably, on occasion, the future destiny of a city and of the Church was sealed by the appointment of a certain individual to some position. In 1520 William Nesen, a pupil of Erasmus and Cochlaeus, then dean of the *Liebfrauenstift* in the city, applied for the important position of city schoolmaster in Frankfurt/Main. There was no question of the town council at that time being dogmatically behind Luther. But we may well ask, as Spahn did: 'What would the fate of the Reformation have been, had the mighty Frankfurt remained Catholic, as Cologne did.' Not least of the impulses towards the Reformation was provided by Nesen's influence over the youth and the town council of Frankfurt.

Ignoble motives and means now began to play a part in the victorious spread of the Reformation. How far would the masses have been led away from the Church without deception, and with-out the hushing up of changes, and without constraint from above?

There can be no doubt that the Reformation mass conversions brought in much that was external with them. It was almost the 'basic evil, that the new Church embraced so many who had become members by external reform and without real inner conversion' (Köstlin – Kawerau). The problem was first posed, and in an acute form, by the colossal apostasy of monks and chaplains. Luther stated crudely that 'he knew of few monks who remained in their monasteries; those who went in for the sake of their bellies want to come out now for the sake of the flesh'.

Nor can there be any doubt that in 1525 and even later there were crowds of people who bandied about slogans like 'gospel' and 'the plain word of God alone', but did not attach to them the doctrinal concepts which Luther did. They were neither dogmatically nor intellectually capable of doing so. In addition until the thirties and forties and even later they still kept many Catholic ceremonies. In particular the elevation at 'mass' was often retained, the old vestments were used wholly or partially (alb and stole), the old chants were sung, often in Latin, by Protestants in almost every province of Germany. In fact, they acted as though they were celebrating mass. By this means the people held on to the illusion that they still had their ancient Church liturgy. In such a milieu, the violent anti-Roman mood did not prevent many from regarding the Reformed sermon as good Catholic doctrine. Thus in a suspiciously large number of places people showed mighty little generosity towards the new religion. Luther himself compared the colossal open-handedness of earlier times towards monasteries, collegiate churches and the clergy, with present indifference: 'The great mass of people despise the gospel; the Lutherans themselves think only of how to fill their own pockets.' When Luther says that the gospel is despised by all, we must make allowances for his customary demagogic rhetoric and exaggeration. But it is to be noted also that he said this not just once or twice, but frequently in the years between 1525 and 1545. Moreover, Luther was well aware of the fickleness of the mob: 'The mob is easily persuaded, and ever eager to hear something new'; he knew that with a couple of sermons he could convert them all back to the pope, to mass, and to pilgrimages (1532). At the very beginning of his movement he said that in the surging battle between papists, the rabble and Lutherans, 'the poor silly people waver between heaven and earth, do not know what it is all about nor which party they ought to follow'. As well as this he knew all about the vacillating type who stuck to the view that the Church had not yet decided which of the two partners was in the right. This would be done by a council. The world is full of such people (1537). Nor did the Luther of later days remain for all men, the fixed and all-conquering centre of attraction. On the contrary: 'Amongst many who would like to follow our cause, my name stinks.'

As soon as a new conviction moves out of the relatively small circle of independent originators and becomes a mass movement, there appears beside the process of intellectual determination, one of infective public opinion, of resentment against the old. Ideas that were originally purely religious are carried over into peripheral areas. There comes about a confusion of religious and non-religious forces and interests, and hence that imponderable area wherein a mixture of conscious and unconscious, direct and indirect, pressure operates. In taking in this vast phase of Reformation development, so various in content, and marked by so many changes and reactions, lies the real, enormous difficulty of deciding conclusively about the moral and religious value of the conquest of the masses in those days. Was the attack upon the Christian and ecclesiastical substance sufficiently motivated by religion, zeal and conviction, or was it motivated rather by non-religious, material, economic, princely, self-interest? Did the structure of the Reformation revolt, directed decisively by the power of the princes and town councils, include an important or essential measure of coercion? Was the final result of the Reformation an adequate expression of the desires and convictions of the population who had been led to the new faith?

First of all, one or two warnings. Ever since Aleander and others around him asserted that the princes merely used Luther and his doctrine as a pretext for plundering the Church's property this colossal indictment has been all too frequently repeated without proper qualification, and so has lost its meaning. As a generalisation it is false

To arrive at a true understanding we must not define the term 'self-interest' too narrowly, especially when we come to assess the Reformation and secularisation in the cities. We must not suddenly forget the battle of the corporations for their freedom and their politico-economic independence from bishop and cathedral chapter. These battles had no need of a deeper justification. As there, so here there was more at work than sheer unbridled self-interest when an imperial city tried to make greater inroads upon Church endowments, for its access to these things was implied by the close medieval interweaving of Church and world. All sorts of civic and social moves towards liberation from clerical jurisdiction, from papal and episcopal taxation, and from clerical privileges, operated together. Admittedly everything depended upon the value people put upon religious matters. Melanchthon had, it is true, already asserted of the cities, what Luther had asserted of ex-monks: their chief interest was economic, and they enquired little about doctrine and religion. Then, admittedly, one reaches the conclusion that the least important factor in the motive force of the Reformation was religion. Very often religion was merely the signboard or outward jusification. How often was downright deception of the people practised under cover of the slogan: 'God's word and God's law alone', the fundamental breach with the old Church being disguised through the retention of outward liturgical forms!

In the end coercion had to come. Butzer and Capito, in Strasburg, at least, felt strongly the need to enforce attendance at sermon – 'in this state of dissolution in which we find ourselves'.

At this point, too, a distinction is required. The Reformation presented a different picture, and possessed different merit, in different cities. Just as the emperor surpassed the princes, and Philip of Hesse his colleagues, in power of political imagination, so there were cities and town councillors who assumed prominent parts in the German drama of these days, and who wrestled through the fundamental experience released by Luther, regarding it as a great matter of common concern. This does not mean that the religious issue was always sufficiently positively assessed; but it does signify a limitation or overcoming of petty egoism. The best minds amongst those town councillors took a lively share in the critical process of the growth of Germany, which had long since been adumbrated in the emergent self-consciousness of the community life of the cities and corporations. These men stood within the great tradition of independent, secular-clerical community life, as this had developed parallel to the autonomous concept of the state, as expression of the great secularising process of the late Middle Ages. But we must understand this concept neither as merely anticlerical, nor as the reverse, as though no room had been left for religious ideas. The central force was the consciousness of their own character and rights; and this force rose to special activity under the influence of the new, antipriest religion, that was being preached in German, and which so greatly enhanced the authority of the secular power.

Within this context the temptation to indulge in petty parochial politics was much reduced. It is true that such parochial Church politics were able all the more surely to take the steps necessary

to suppress Catholic Church life, long before the aim was consciously recognised. A classic example is provided by Basel in the
years 1525–27.

The spread of the Reformed doctrine was all too lightly dis-
missed by Catholics as a question of apostasy from the faith. This
way of approaching the question necessarily obstructed an understanding of the colourful variety of the concrete course of events.
The prime necessity is to see this real historical process of development; then one would scarcely subscribe to the view that Luther's
immediate environment, or a particular imperial city like Nuremberg, was full of specially sinful people who because of their sinfulness fell away from the Church; nor would one think that the
aged who remained loyal were more devout on average than the
impious youth who went over to the Reformation. In fact, this
remains one of the most distressing facts we learn from the history
of the Reformation in Germany: in this battle which, in virtue of
its magnanimous origin (in Luther's conscience), was supposed to
be a battle for the purity of Christianity, the decision whether a
whole region was for or against the old faith was governed in not
one single case by any essential difference in the personal moral
and religious condition. On a wide view the moral and religious
condition was the same everywhere. In the end of the day the
ecclesiastical and religious fate of a province was decided by the
ruler; and it would be hard to say of any particular ruler that his
decision arose from a strictly religious alignment. The purest intentions were those of the Saxon elector, Frederick the Wise, on
the one hand, and Duke George, on the other. And the emperor
surpassed them both. . . .

We must keep our observation of the natural process of the
growth of all convictions within the context of hard, visible and
tangible realities, and not flee off into the realms of the theological
virtues. Even the genesis of these free, grace-given theological
virtues is embedded in nature and to that extent bound to the
processes of life.

There were other developments in which blatant lack of commitment predominated. The Machiavellianism of the times which
had found universal expression in politics, and much in relativistic
humanism, too, had spread further as a result of the religious
and ecclesiastical dispute, with its attendant bickerings. Things

had gone so far that the question of true faith had become a matter of sheer calculation. The crudest example is that of Biberach at the *Reichstag* in Augsburg in 1530. The representative of this city had orders to declare whether his city was Lutheran, Catholic or Zwinglian, according to the decision made by the mayor of Ulm.

The progressive extinguishing of the life of the old Church is best seen, perhaps, as it went on in the well-defined limits of the monasteries. This process, too, displayed an extraordinary variety, far beyond what one would have expected, after the main issue had been settled. The variety was shown in respect of the point of time when Reformation or secularisation began; in respect of the speed with which it was carried out, or the reaction to it; in respect of the consistency, or the irresolution, of the means employed. We see a city falling to the Reformation, and close by a monastery holding out for decades. In completely Reformed cities, or regions, like Mecklenburg we see vestiges of Catholic life persisting in the most varied conditions of life until the seventies of the century.

As always, practice fell far short of the ideal it served. This was specially true because the process was one of revolutionary, ecclesiastical rearrangement. The practical spread of the new religion was anything but a straightforward victory for Christian idealism. It was very largely a chain of tragedy and harship. It was not as if the old religion still possessed life only where it was kept alive by the power of the territorial ruler. Just as in Catholic regions there were the beginnings of Reforming tendencies, which were suppressed, so in emergent Protestant regions the old Catholic faith was to be found. Whether one describes this persistence as loyalty or stubbornness depends on whether or not one has a real feeling for loyalty and freedom of conscience. We ought not to forget that Luther's mighty campaign was waged in the name of the inexorable demands of conscience; and we must take this imperative more, not less, into account, in the case of those intent upon upholding tradition.

There were little bands of brothers forcibly expelled from their monasteries wandering about the land, exposed to ridicule and a most uncertain life; there were priors who scoured the countryside trying to protect the rights of their monasteries in spite of everything, and to secure in some measure the existence of their

o

scattered brethren, and help orientate them in their new situation; there were small communities who made an attempt to return to their cloister in the midst of a Reformed region, because the attitude of the magistrates had become a little more sympathetic to them; there were nuns who, despite humiliating oppression by the magistrates, remained faithful to their vows, their observance of the choral office, and who doggedly defended themselves, even using force if such means was available; there were the last survivors of once flourishing convents who preserved the ties of that community life to which they had once vowed themselves, although now scattered far and wide over the countryside; there was the regular, slow closing down of many convents by simply cutting off all recruits who might have joined the elderly who stuck firmly to the old Church. All of these present a picture of real spiritual greatness and genuine loyalty. Qualitatively as well as quantitatively they form an important part of the events of the Reformation. It would be wrong to ignore this force, simply because in the end it was largely stifled and so could no longer contribute to the external picture.

The individual story of the closing down of such religious houses is often highly dramatic. There were the Cistercian nuns at Dobbertin whose suppression began in 1556 but which took twenty-two years to complete. Visitations were for ever being resumed; individual nuns were tried; the statues of saints were removed from the church; the sisters were allowed time to make up their minds to come over; they were threatened with forcible expulsion if they did not come to hear the word of God. The sisters maintained that they had been hearing this word all their lives – in company of Augustine, Ambrose, Jerome and Gregory, and that the new doctrine was 'mere vanity and invention of men'. In the end force was used. The nuns shut the door and blocked the entrance to the choir. Inflamed peasants were set to attack them, and the nuns defended themselves with stones and water. There were repetitions of this sort of thing, and to make divine office impossible, the sacristy door was blocked up. During a visitation in the presence of the dukes, the sisters were ordered to receive communion under both kinds. Whoever refused to comply was to be removed by brute force from the convent and sent to her relatives. The nuns pleaded on bended knee, saying that they could not in conscience obey the command, but to no purpose. As visitations continued the nuns were gradually worn down; some of the younger nuns gave in; one of them, we know, immediately became an enthusiastic advocate of the new ideas; but the older generation remained firm. In the same year (1562) the sisters who remained Catholic were finally removed from the monastery. Ten carts were provided, but the sisters preferred to walk. Three Catholic sisters stayed behind with the eleven who had become Lutheran. Even those who had become Lutheran were obviously anything but clear about their new faith. Not only did those who remained in the monastery deny the stereotyped charge that they had previously been living in unchastity and idolatry but they insisted in keeping up the seven hours in choir as before, and on having only a celibate preacher. It was quite in keeping with these Catholic tendencies within the monastery that the expelled Catholic nuns were brought back through the good office of the dukes' Catholic mother. There were even new entrants and the making of professions. In the end, when the nuns had been examined individually in Lutheran doctrine, a convenient solution was found: the old members were allowed to die out, and the young were indoctrinated. In 1578 the nuns finally capitulated, promising to give up wearing the habit.

Unfortunately, we have no record of the interior attitudes of these sisters during this whole process. We can only guess how much martyrdom had been produced by this encounter with the rising new religion.

This gap in our knowledge is filled by one celebrated case, set right at the heart of the great Reformation event. This is the sad story of the suppression of the convent of the Poor Clares in Nuremberg, the superior of which was Pirkheimer's heroic and intellectually great sister, Charitas. The Catholic piety of this convent was irreproachable, and, in the best sense, an expression of the gospel. Melanchthon appreciated this; but not so the city fathers. A letter from Charitas to Emser was falsified and maliciously glossed. Suspicion was coarsely cast upon the relationship of the nuns with the Franciscans, who were confessors to St Clare's, although there was no evidence to support such calumny. The battle of the town council against this convent became more and more of a disgusting brutalisation of conscience: 'Is it not a deplorable thing that they want to force us to accept a faith that is not in our hearts?' The request of the sisters for freedom of conscience was met by the town council with coercion. The mob were incited against the convent. In Nuremberg under Reformed rule many Catholics, including Willibald, who had returned to the Church, as well as his sister, Charitas, had to die without the sacraments. This was the very opposite of toleration.

One of the most important facts established by modern historical study of the religious orders, is that loyal monastics, like those we have mentioned, were not the exception. In every province, in very many cities there were monasteries, fully occupied, which observed their rule and remained loyal to the Church, and which had to be overcome by manifold and extreme physical pressure. The prior of the Carthusian monastery of Marienehe put up an heroic fight against the town council of Rostock and the duke of Mecklenburg from the beginning of the thirties until his death in 1576. The Dominicans who were driven out of Rostock in 1534 returned there with their prior and took in the surviving Carthusians who had been driven from Marienwerder. The Cistercian nuns of Holy Cross in Rostock drowned the sermons of their Lutheran preacher by their singing and bell-ringing, and even the oldest of them held her own in the disputation ordered by the council.

The Dominicans and the Franciscans of Nuremberg held their ground. The Augustinians, Benedictines and Carthusians gave up their monasteries to the city. Then the Carmelites capitulated after their prior had been expelled. He was Andreas Stoss, along with Charitas Pirkheimer, the life of Catholic resistance in the city.

In Starnberg the prior of the Augustinian monastery was first to go over, and continued to live in the monastery with his wife. This created a great scandal, however, and he was forced to move out.

In Mecklenberg several Franciscans, in contrast to the loyal Dominicans, declared for the Reformation. As early as 1520 Fr Stephen Kempe was preaching Lutheran doctrine in Rostock. He then travelled to Hamburg on business relating to his order and worked for the Reformation there. The council in Rostock, for its part, unlawfully deposed a guardian, made an inventory of the monastic property, and installed an apostate guardian in place of the one they had deposed.

In Basel, too, the town council hastened the disappearance of religious by means of frequent visitations of the monasteries. They asked if anyone wanted to leave. At least the people of Basel knew better how to keep up appearances. The town council did not close the monasteries, nor did they enrich themselves at the expense of the occupants of the monasteries. What they did was to offer economic security to those who did leave; their dowries were repaid; those who never had even that were given the necessary means of earning a living. There were parallels to this in the north as well. The last abbot of the Doberan Cistercians certified that he had given up the monastery freely and without compulsion. The monks were compensated, and the abbot got a pension of 1,000 gulden per annum; but he kept his old faith, unlike his colleague at Dargum, James Baumann, who became a pastor, married at the age of seventy-one, and was found to know absolutely nothing at the visitation examination in 1560.

Certain loyal women's convents were coerced by being deprived of the services of a confessor, or being forced to listen to a Reformed preacher.

Another method that was often used was the expulsion of monks who were particularly active in the Church's cause.

Ignoble self-interest was by no means the constant motive in the secularisation of the monasteries. It was present, however; and indeed, that egoistic, economic and political motives played a great and even normative part, is proved beyond any doubt. All too frequently secularisation was accomplished for the benefit of someone's own pocket. This happened, moreover, in careless opposition to the ecclesiastical institutions which had been gradually emerging since 1528.

Secularisation was an old idea. In some form or other it had been well known to princes all through the Middle Ages. In the rising crisis of the late Middle Ages it had often been demanded in quite a radical form – as, for example, by the 'Revolutionary of the upper Rhine'. This makes the harsh and often quite hateful happenings during the actual Reformation in the sixteenth century all the more comprehensible, although it does not excuse them.

The process of secularisation by the princes came about something like this. As soon as a territorial prince went over to the new religion the prelates ceased to be invited to join the cities and the knights in the territorial parliaments. A battle for the monasteries in the territory went on between the princes and the gentry, in the course of which the latter were not slow to accuse the princes of having made private gain out of the closed-down monasteries.

In these proceedings all of the partners adopted thoroughly pious language, speaking of religious motives, and high Christian and moral aims, that were to benefit the whole of society. We must not be too critical of this. The diplomatic tradition of the chancelleries at that time demanded the constant use of such jargon. From long years of practice, perfect facility had been achieved in its use. In any case, now more than ever the religious and theological reasons were the most relevant.

This, however, we may take as self-evident from the start: there was something very suspicious about this utterly unqualified appeal to religious reasons. To say that the protesting princes, and later, the Catholic princes, did not see how they stood to gain, in power at least, is to cast a grave slur on their political sagacity. The prospect of complete independence from the curia illuminated the extraordinary possibilities that were at hand; for in reality this independence signified control, in one or several forms, of the wealth and extensive rights of the Church.

In 1530 at Augsburg the emperor demanded restitution of secularised Church property. The princes refused, saying that they were under no obligation to do so because this was a case of conscience, in which the question of a property right of the one robbed did not arise. It was not difficult for the emperor to refute this argument: '... no one may take another man's property on the strength of the word of God, of the gospel, or of all papal and civil laws.'

Things were not always so blatant as in the case of the margrave Albert Alcibiades of Brandenburg, who regarded merchants, clergy, and the Church's property, all as fair game. All of his acts of secularisation were downright robbery. His appeal to the gospel was sheer cynical cant.

There were many grades of this sort of secularisation, none of which, however, could truly be made to harmonise with professed zeal for the pure word of God. A few months before the *Reichstag* at Augsburg, the margrave George of Brandenburg-Kulmbach had all of the golden and silver vessels, the monstrances, the pictures and statues, the vestments, the pearls and precious stones, removed from the churches and monasteries within his territory. The proceeds were used to pay off the gambling debts (50,000 gulden) and other liabilities of his deceased brother Casimir. George's son, Frederick, drew about 190,000 gulden from ecclesiastical endowments.

Following the closures of Doberan and Dargum in 1550, the duke of Mecklenburg wanted to Reform, that is to secularise, Marienehe also. With him, the need for money was just as powerful a motive as his Lutheranism. He allowed the infantry and knights to storm and plunder the wealthy Charterhouse, and drive the occupants out to suffer great hardship. Amongst these were many old men. The prior fought resolutely to keep his community together, and the duke ordered him to be imprisoned.

The story of self-interested secularisation includes also a load of indictment from the ranks of the Protestant preachers themselves, amongst whom we number Melanchthon – curiously double-tongued in this respect – Luther and many unknown names. We must not ignore Janssen's material simply on account of his one-sidedness. Again, while giving that its due place we must not ignore the material contained in the three volumes of Döllinger either. Certainly the contemporary Protestant indictments collected in these works are often exaggerated, just as pre-Reformation Catholic literature fell into exaggeration when describing the religious and moral abuses of their times. It must also be remembered that for the servants of the Church and the preachers, their livelihood was at stake too. In spite of this, after due criticism, the material remains serious enough. Many of the new rulers of the Church, who frequently gained possession of Church property without sufficient legality, grew fat on this property just as shamefully as the unworthy prelates had done at the end of the Middle Ages. A new simoniacal fiscalism had emerged which aimed at the retention and aggrandisement of personal power and property, to the detriment of schools and charitable institutions. Churches, built by their forefathers' money, magnificent furnishings and vestments, were allowed to fall into decay, or turned to the most profane uses. In stressing the violent religious assault of the first decades we must not overlook the striking decay of the succeeding period. How surprising and painful was the comparison of the end of the Reformation period with the preceding, much despised Catholics period; how distressing the emergence amongst Protestants of the question: 'What good has the gospel done us? It has kindled revolution and torn the images out of the churches.' The frequency of these complaints does not indicate a simple self-deception concerning the good old times. It expresses, rather, the bitter realisation, of how far the actualisation of the Reformation had lagged behind its ideals, of how little had been gained by much of its destruction. The statements of Luther and Melanchthon are guarantee of the accuracy of the facts stated.

In the Reformation period there had been riots, and there were even more acts of secularisation. Has mankind ever experienced riots in which the egoistic impulses did not obviously find satisfaction? Is it the rule or the exception that the integrity of a man's views is seriously prejudiced by the possibility of enhancing his own economic power and that of his office? If we deny the validity of this universal principle in the case of the spread of the Reformation, saying that naked egoism did not influence princes and town councils in the process of Reforming whole states and cities and the majority of monasteries, our thesis would be seriously undermined. No one, however, has succeeded in proving that the universal principle does not apply to this case.

Through the whole history of the German Reformation we can trace a long series of shameful examples of how Reformed town councils made common cause with the elements in the mob who were opposed to order, so as to make life intolerable for the monasteries. Sometimes it was the council who exploited the agitation which had arisen through various causes, sometimes it was the mob who urged on the council. The inflammatory attacks of the preachers stood somewhere in between. Revolutionary outbreaks were an almost inevitable consequence of the massive, vaguely defined calumnies contained in sermons, popular pamphlets, songs and woodcuts. In 1520 Luther had already taken up the theme when he called upon the emperor, kings and princes to take up arms against the old Church, in whose blood he and his followers desired to wash their hands. Those words and many others, although an echo of biblical ideas, were dangerous, spoken when the times were seething with revolution.

In Breslau the 'popular mood was at times so menacing that

Cochlaeus feared there would be plundering and destruction of the churches and dwellings in the cathedral precincts'. In Mecklenburg in 1525 one of the apostate Augustinians was dragged forcibly into the pulpit by the mob. In Rostock the menacing attitude of the mob forced the council to give free course to the Reformation. In Ribnitz the new doctrine was first preached in 1526 when an apprentice blacksmith demanded that tithes to the churches be withheld. The ducal abbess Dorothea was able, however, to have him expelled. In Lübeck the council were forced to accept the Reformation by the riotous mob, and in this place events followed a stormy course under the leadership of the radical elements.

The forcible Reform of the nuns at Biberach by means of discrimination and ultimate expulsion, the forced Reformation of the clergy at Esselingen in the twenties, the severe punishments meted out to Catholics, who heard mass, had their children baptised, or went to confession, outside the territories of their Protestant rulers, the ruthlessness with which the dying were refused confession and holy viaticum, the violence with which, on the other hand, clergy were compelled to administer holy communion to the excommunicate, all added up to much more than severity; and such things happened every day.

The final resolution of the *Reichstag* of 1530 officially required the re-erection of forcibly devastated bishoprics, monasteries and churches, and the reinstatement of forcibly expelled bishops, clergy, monks and nuns. In 1531 the town council of Rostock informed the clergy that they were no longer able to protect them from the rude violence of the mob. In 1534 after all monasteries in the town had been closed, the council forbade all inhabitants of Rostock to hear mass in Marienehe or other Catholic centres. The mob forced the council to deny the sacrament of penance to the Carthusians at Marienehe. In Wismar the mob caused violent disturbances at worship in order to force the council to alter the service. To 'prevent the use of violence' the council demanded the removal of 'certain ceremonies'. At first vespers at Christmas the mob made a riotous disturbance during the sermon. On the second day of the festival they sang profane songs in church, threw stones, snowballs and lumps of ice into the choir, chased the organist out of the organ loft, and tore off the altar covers. The council blamed the mass for the uproar, and demanded surrender of the key to the silver. They closed the monastic church until such time as the community decided to accept the Reformation. The monks appealed to their consciences and their duty to God and man. A brief respite came as a result of a warning by Duke Albert. In 1536 the storm broke afresh; a slow process of erosion went on until 1575 when the prior died, still a Catholic. In Stralsund, too, severe measures were taken against adherents of the old faith.

The expulsion of the Franciscans from Altenburg and Zwickau, where Luther personally directed the Reformation, was marred by intolerance and cruelty. 'Luther gave the orders, his disciples executed them without mercy.'

The successor of Duke George of Saxony reformed and secularised 'like a Turk or a Tartar'.

In Soest the mob got the upper hand more than once. In September 1531 even the Lutherans' lives were threatened. At the end of that year a renegade Minorite was able to stir up riots. Both burgomasters were taken prisoner, and the mob ruled the town.

The Reformation of the Cistercians of the Holy Sepulchre by the elector of Brandenburg was brought about by sheer violence.

The Reformers suceeded in preventing Catholic sermons being preached even in churches into which they could not penetrate. In St Gallen in 1524 they so stirred up the people against Wendelin Oswald, the preacher at the collegiate church, that he dared no longer appear in the streets.

Hildesheim was the last loyal Catholic centre in lower Saxony. Here, too, the issue was decided by the town council. In 1533 an advance by the new faith was repulsed; a Catholic mayor was elected. After his death, however, affiliation to the Schmalkald League was urged. A committee on 'religious affairs' took possession of valuables and documents in the monasteries. In consultation with the six peasant communes the town council arranged for a settlement of the religious question. The vote was in favour of the new religion. On the very same day the valuables were confiscated, and the following month the monasteries were closed. The people were forbidden to enter the cathedral during the time of public worship. There were frequent plunderings of the Charterhouse. The monks were imprisoned for five days, forced to put off the habit, and to listen to a Reformed preacher in their own church. Not one of them abandoned his faith, and so the prior (Loher) had to be removed. In 1545 he was banished from the town.

In the same manner the Carthusians of Maria Saal at Memmingen were plundered several times, and Loher and his procurator, who had moved there, were compelled to get out. The celebration of mass was stopped by armed force, and the wearing of the cowl forbidden. Thrice a week the brothers had to listen to Evangelical sermons. A Lutheran was installed as superior, and lived in the monastery with his wife and family for two months. The supplies were all used up, valuables stolen and turned into cash. The farms, and ultimately the monastic buildings, were mortgaged. Here, too, the monks remained steadfast.

It would be farcical to ask whether the Reformers possessed a legitimate title to properties acquired as a result of such proceedings as these. Indisputable legal rights had been violated, not in the name of a higher end but out of sheer self-interest. In these cases the Reformers used the new profession of faith as an excuse for robbery, physical and moral violence, and debauchery.

This sort of oppression carried out by the authorities or with their support was only possible because of an extensive hatred of Catholics which was there ready to be exploited. This alone can explain the extent of violent opposition to the old Church system. Many things were to blame for this mood. The whole agitation of the pre-Reformation and of the Reformation period played its part, as well as the rigid attitude concerning the treatment of heretics, which had far-reaching repercussions in the popular imagination.

Powerfully active in encouraging lawlessness and rioting were the evil habits of self-aggrandisement inaugurated by the robber knights. Utopian reform programmes, too, played their part: the broadsheets of the earlier Franciscan, Eberlin of Günzburg, with his radical demands for freedom and equality. There was a universal expectation that foes would be overthrown, and chief amongst these were the clergy. The coming emperor-saviour was to persecute the clergy in such a fashion that they would cover up their tonsures with dung. . . .

But the spark to kindle this great heap of hatred had not yet appeared. That spark was to be Luther. What we have said about his share of guilt for the outbreak of the peasants' revolts is even more applicable in respect of the direct assault upon the monasteries. His unrestrained tone undoubtedly threw open the gates, letting loose a flood of baser impulses, of hatred, intolerance and rioting amongst the citizens – as no other could have done. Luther knew that people were accusing him of being a Bohemian insurgent, or, as Murner said, a new Catilina. 'Yes, this is all your fault. You started it all, and there are the fruits of your doctrine.' He had to defend himself even more vigorously from this accusation when, in October 1530, the Catholic resolution of the *Reichstag* was published, and he could see that war and revolution were inevitable. None the less, he did not change his tone: 'They will not frighten me. I will frighten them. My life will be their master; my death their devil.'

In illustration we may cite Luther's fight with the Jews also. Because he regarded their interpretation of scripture as lies, and because they paid no heed to his more moderate demands, he commanded their synagogues and houses to be burned, their books to be confiscated, and their rabbis prevented from teaching. Their freedom of movement should be impeded; better still, they should be exiled. He had severe decrees passed against them in Saxony and Hesse.

Luthers' later warlike imagery is unspiritual, highly inflammatory and aggressive, the antithesis of the gentleness, which he said was to be his sole instrument with people.

Unfortunately, in the matter of the forcible expansion of his doctrine by the authorities, Luther did not remain true to his original ideal. In the controversy with Reuchlin he energetically espoused the cause of the freedom of scholarly opinion, for otherwise, 'these inquisitors will strain at gnats and swallow camels as they please, regarding the faithful as heretics, in spite of all their professions'. In May 1521 he wrote to Melanchthon saying, that although it might be a good thing to coerce the unteachable godless, yet to use force would bring infamy upon the gospel, and arouse just resistance. We know of his brave renunciation of sanctions imposed by the authorities in his battle with Müntzer, and of his championing of the freedom to teach at that time. Even when war threatened on account of the Packschen forgeries, Luther and Melanchthon again refused to use force, for that would dishonour the gospel. Luther adopted the same attitude on the question of an alliance with the Zwinglians: 'The emperor remains ruler, even if he persecutes.'

As early as 1521, however, the tide was beginning to turn. From the Wartburg Luther was inciting Sickingen to the bloodthirsty use of force. His attitude to the question of a religious war was clearly changing. The change came about quite slowly, but in the end Luther unconditionally demanded the use of force against the Anabaptists. 'The secular authorities are bound to mete out corporal punishment to the Anabaptists.'

To speak exclusively of the use of physical force betrays an inadequate grasp both of the alignment of forces and of the problems involved. The examples cited teach us that the oppression of Catholics in favour of the new religion in cities and states used every means, material and moral, of obstruction, including the most comprehensive and ruthless application of the *cuius regio* principle. This was in harmony with the widespread anti-Roman feeling and the universal revolutionary agitation of the times. We have already noted the severe distress caused by the denial of the sacraments, especially to the dying. In the intellectual sphere there was the suppression of Catholic printing presses. Duke Henry simply allowed the Catholic printer, Wolrab, to be arrested. The poor man was compelled to put his press at the disposal of the Protestants.

Indeed, if we approach the question of Reformation and secularisation from the angle of hard practice, we discover countless cases which cast a shadow upon the Evangelical cause. Appeal was constantly made to holy scriptures, when people were in reality using it as a cover for their own designs. This hypocritical practice did untold damage to the authority of sacred scripture itself. When in 1548 at Augsburg, the Frankfurt ambassador, Humbracht, appealed to conscience against the interim, in defence of his remaining true to the entire Protestant faith, he was answered in these significant words: 'You have consciences like the sleeves of the Barefoot Friars: they could swallow up whole monasteries.'

The question of Evangelical secularisation must be examined from the theological angle as well.

Was the transference of the property of the old Church to the Reformers justified? Politically, that is but a part of the all-embracing question concerning the rights of territorial princes over Church property. These rights had greatly increased, both with and without papal consent, especially since the schism and the concordat with the princes. The exemption of the orders and certain parishes from the jurisdiction of the local bishop had directly opened up a legitimate way of limiting episcopal power; and the cities confirmed this limitation. The right of patronage over a church could be bought or extended. Parishes could make themselves autonomous by becoming elevated into provostries. The principle of *cuius regio, eius religio* had already been well prepared. If this principle were accepted as valid, the right of those who followed the ruler into the new religion to take over possession of Church property, followed logically.

Canonically, the basis for transference was always found in the proposition that in fact the Church was the owner of all pious endowments. We know the grotesque ideas to which this intrinsically great conception gave rise in the course of the Franciscan dispute over poverty, as a result of the complicated circumstances of real life, and especially as a result of the spirit of secularisation which had invaded the curia. The concept had become mixed with untruth. The rule of thumb, the all too material notion of the benefice system, with its well-known fiscal abuses, was utterly opposed to the spirit of true poverty, and had nothing at all to do with the original conception.

None the less, the principle we have mentioned held the field. The parties had slowly been trying to exploit it, each in his own interest. In the *Gravamina* handed over to Campeggio by the estates at the Nuremburg *Reichstag* of 1524, they complained against the pope's permission to Ferdinand to apply one-third of the clerical income to the war against the Turks. This was unjust because the estates, bestowed upon the Church by emperors, kings, princes and other of the faithful, 'was dedicated to the honour of God, ought always to remain in the Church, and ought not to be alienated without the consent of those who had bestowed it upon the Church; in such impermissible things they owed no obedience to the pope'.

For a long time now the curia had been accustomed to control dying or refractory monasteries in their own interest. It was in line with this practice, therefore, when in 1523 Eck proposed to the pope that the Augustinian eremite monasteries, which followed Wenceslas Link, be turned by the civic authorities into hospitals, or used for some other worthy purpose.

The Reformers, in turn, drew the opposite conclusions from the same principles. Because Reformed doctrine, too, stated that there was but one Church, and because the Reformers were convinced that they had not started a new Church but were themselves the one, ancient, apostolic Church, from their point of view the demand, that Church property be transferred to them, was just. On this argument it was true that the transference of Church property from the community of old believers to that of the new left the relation of ownership fundamentally undisturbed.

The matter had, however, its civil side; and here the question became considerably more complex. The benefices of the Church and the endowments of the monasteries were in great part tied to specific obligations – the saying of mass, and that at a particular altar, divine office, burning the eternal light – or had been bestowed upon a particular monastic order (the Cistercians, for example), or linked in some way with a pastoral function in a particular place.

It could by no means be taken for granted that some sort of centralisation of these properties was justified, either in terms of the spirit or the letter of the endowment documents, or that the endowments might be diverted from sacramental, ecclesiastical institutions to purely educational or charitable purposes, such as schools, hospitals and charitable institutions for gentlewomen. This became even more problematic as the legal association of the schools, for example, with the Church, had universally become dissolved. Justification of the Reformed solution became really dubious, however, when the lawful owners of these endowments refused to accept the new faith. This held true even of individuals or minorities, who did not want to fall into line with the new fashion.

In any case, the Reformed concept of the Church, in so far as it bore a Lutheran stamp, was fundamentally opposed to any form of theological reason for the transfer of property; for a juridical constitution could never form part of the essence of the community of the redeemed.

The whole process of the transfer of Church property really did take on a completely new aspect when the rulers went on to effect actual secularisation. As has been demonstrated earlier, in this process we frequently find acts of sheer self-aggrandisement and robbery, such as have occurred in every age, casting their shadow over great conceptions.

Luther himself was not competent to judge strictly legal matters. As 'worldly things' they were too far removed from anything that the 'gospel preacher' thought important. His attitude was bound to display a certain vacillation on the question of the diversion of the ancient monasteries, collegiate churches and endowments to new purposes. Private as well as public and legal alignments, the needs of religion and those of secular and public society, were too diverse. The practical question arose, not so much theoretically, as from case to case.

With an almost childish unconcern Luther was for ever pressing on to one central point in the problem. His expositions cannot be set aside as mere phantasies, no matter how much his exaggerations lead to non-juristic views and untenable conclusions. He said: Church property has been endowed on strict presuppositions and with specific obligations. If the owners of the endowments behave in a manner which would have horrified the donors, their title expires. Luther considered that this had happened: the diversion of vast sums of money to Rome was a shameless plundering of endowments, contrary to the intention of the donor. He appealed insistently to current canon law. He knew that simony was punished by excommunication. If, then, the owners of the endowments were *irregulares*, they became the most vicious thieves of Church property – and amongst such culprits were to be numbered the pope, bishops and others; for 'they observe not at all, those things for which the endowments were made, but the exact opposite'. 'They do not perform their office, and so they have deposed themselves; you have lost your property in terms of your own law.' If the endowments have already been applied to an unchristian use, it would be better if they were held and administered by 'emperors, kings, princes or lords'. 'They cry out that the monasteries and collegiate churches are being robbed. . . . That is true, and I, too, am horrified at such pillage and destruction. . . . I am especially displeased to see vicious men at the game, who deserve nothing; but I will not make an issue of conscience concerning those who work and are true servants, and who may get something out of it. There are, however, quite clearly two sorts of endowment pilferers and monastery plunderers: the outward and the spiritual. The outward are the vicious and unworthy men; the spiritual are the bishops, canons, and monks, who misapply their endowments in all manner of vice and lewdness, who abandon the position consonant with their office, and and send vast sums to even greater louts than themselves in Rome, thus shamelessly plundering the endowments.' This is not what the donors had in mind. Their object was rather to produce devout, chaste clerics, who would study, teach and pray. 'The stipends ought to support the office, not abuses.' 'Your own law teaches you these things, punishing misdemeanour with excommunication, and labelling it simony.'

Is it worth while discussing these exaggerations and inexact statements from a juridical point of view? Had the endowments been made in respect of the circumstances obtaining within the Roman and papal Church and its authority, with the special sacramental priesthood in mind, or had they not?

Such fundamental presuppositions no longer had any weight with Luther. When in 1530 the emperor demanded that the Protestants restore everything as it had been before, Luther retreated quite non-juridically and hence dangerously to an explosive religious principle, which simply called in question the *spiritual* justification of former Catholic ownership: 'All right then, first let the pope and the papists give us back Leonard Kaiser and all the others whom they have innocently done to death, all the souls they have led astray with lies, all the money and lands they have swindled us of, all the honour they have stolen from God by their blasphemies; then we will be prepared to discuss restitution.' In 1537 the members of the Schmalkald League expressed this same idea in their reply to the imperial vice-chancellor, Held, in this form, 'They felt themselves compelled to deprive of their endowments, those who so stubbornly refused to allow the reform of the Church; they could not tolerate the presence amongst them of Catholic monks and clergy.' In the end there remained the unchallenged conviction that true revelation, the true Word, surpasses utterly all other norms and drives all other claims out of the field. Such a conviction, however, could not be supported by existent law.

Luther dared to go further. In 1524 he wrote to his own elector concerning Müntzer: 'When the heart has gone out, and churches and monasteries lie desolate, let the ruler of the territory do what he pleases with them.' That made sense; but the Peasants' War, the impression of the visitations and political developments, caused other notions to mature in his mind. In 1523 he had already advised that in judging the doctrine of a pastor, and when deciding about his induction or deposition, one ought not 'to take any account of men, law, rights, tradition, customs, or authority'. In 1530, without any appeal to legality, he reached the same revolutionary solution: 'On account of such abominations and the blasphemous abuse of the mass, one ought to deal with endowed institutions and monasteries as Josiah, king of Judah, did with the altars of Baal. Not a stone should be left upon another. It would be fitting and right to do this, if one cannot effect reformation.' What bonds were thus being severed! By this stroke the deep interconnections of the whole life of the times were being cut, and the result would go far beyond anything that had been desired. Many would listen only to the negative denial of tradition. The congregation of Leisnig made Luther himself aware of the constant danger that churches and monasteries, endowments and lands, would not become common property, but that 'each man would hold on to what he could grab'.

On the broad view, the following characteristic lines appear. In the process of consolidating the Reformation of states, of the people, and of life, purely religious motives came last in order of importance. The most powerful impulse came from antagonism to the old canon law, and to all the economic rights deriving from it (seen as impositions by the Reformers). Even the popular demand for the chalice for the laity, and for clerical marriage, came behind this. The readiness of magistrates and princes to support the Reformation was sparked off primarily by these economic privileges. Added to this, and equal in importance, was the political battle for the retention and increase of territorial autonomy vis-à-vis the Catholic emperor.

There is no need to stress again that accidental factors played a part in many individual cases, both in respect of successful expansions and in respect of reaction and obstruction by the old Church. The personal ties that a mayor might have with an abbot, the pledged word of a prince to a prior, the fact that an abbess was of princely blood, all of these things at times determined the fate of a monastery for a whole generation. Much more important, however, were the radicalising misunderstandings which accompanied and made possible the first rooting of this revolution and the extension of its power over wider sections of the people. This function was shared by uneducated preachers and their uneducated hearers. These people took hold, first and foremost, of the externals, which they and their impulses much preferred; and they did this in a radical fashion. They gave a new interpretation to the gospel message. 'Faith alone' became a very convenient maxim. Evangelical freedom would, in any case, put an end to the payment of tithes and other dues. The simplifying imagination of the masses greatly helped on the Reformation movement.

Those living on frontiers found themselves facing a unique problem. The frontier traffic from Wittenburg to Jüterburg, to hear the indulgence preachers, had at one time played a decisive part when Luther's doctrine was made public. Later, the subjects of the Saxon elector and those of the Saxon Duke George, lived in totally different religious and ecclesiastical atmospheres. Those living on the borders of Bavaria were in a similar situation. The accident of a border stream could decide which religion these people and their descendants would profess. There was also the frontier traffic which broke through the demands of the ecclesiastical system. As counsellor of Duke George, Julius Pflug took this very seriously. Villages within the duchy often held their Church festivities in the electorate, and vice versa; and on all sorts of occasions people went to and fro – for baptisms, village feasts and annual fairs. And so the Catholics of the duchy got to know about Protestant life and assimilated it to some extent. Thus the Reformation expanded, as did a general uncertainty about religious matters. Here, and in the cities the fatal question arose, which in practice prepared the way for modern relativism. Men are much the same everywhere, neither better nor worse. Where, then, is true Christianity? Conversely there were, indeed, cases of intolerant dogmatism, which turned to hatred of one's neighbours, and which persisted for centuries, strengthening Catholic or Evangelical Christianity, as the case might be.

Exceptions, however, were more common than the norm.

VIII. LUTHER

We return now to one of the points from which we started. Luther was the German Reformation; and the German Reformation was Luther. That is to say: from Luther it received critical and continuous nourishment. The most essential nourishment, however, he supplied in the earliest years. This does not mean that the Luther of the second half of the twenties, and of the thirties and forties, had nothing more of importance to say. Even when older, Luther still possessed the secret of mental growth: the ability to start afresh. 'I have now become a fresh scholar of the ten commandments,' he wrote in 1530 from the Coburg, 'I am learning them again word for word like a boy, and see that their wisdom is beyond measure.' His really creative period, however, was that before 1530. In that year Melanchthon did not exactly assume leadership, but the conciliatory Confession of Augsburg compelled the regulation of the Reformed masses along a more moderate course. Even earlier, in 1525, when Luther parted company with the peasants and wrote his book on the enslavement of the will – a kind of summary of his doctrine – one sees the end of the heroic Luther in sight. For Luther's work, the later years of the Reformation are essentially the completion, or simply the continuance, of something already begun rather than the creation of something new.

It is proper, therefore, at this point in our exposition, to sum up our view of Luther and his work. We shall include the picture of the older Luther. There are many things about the Luther of the critical years which cannot be correctly described unless we see the later forms which evolved from the earlier beginnings.

Obviously a book like this cannot pretend to supply an exhaustive exposition. Its purpose is merely to cast a few sidelights on what we might call Luther's basic attitudes, his type, and the inner tendency of his powers. We shall do this chiefly within that sphere which became directly active for the Reformation and its history. In the process we will ever and again encounter the same kind of factor, over an astonishingly wide range. The massive complexity of Luther's life's work rests upon a few fundamental conceptions. Our subject compels us to be for ever returning to the same ideas, and frequently to those we have already had to speak of in respect of the young Luther. He makes repetition unavoidable. In order to minimise this repetition we will proceed, not chronologically but systematically.

The first and last impression Luther leaves behind him is one of pulsating richness. He is a phenomenon of life and certainly no schoolmaster. But the fulness of life is always complex, and cannot be framed within a system of propositions.

We are forced also to encounter severe tensions; and even this formula is not sufficient to characterise the facts fully. In Luther, tensions become sheer contradictions; and these contradictions are far from being ultimately resolved, but reach down, rather, into a dangerous abyss, giving rise to exciting and overwhelming realities.

It is understandable that Evangelical Christians should feel great distress when faced with assertions about the serious inadequacies in Luther's image. Such assertions arouse distrust. We cannot hope to please those who venerate Luther and regard the faults of the genius as of no importance. To those we may perhaps be allowed to say this much: by their attitude, precisely as Christians, they make the shattering fate of Germany in and as a result of the Reformation, largely incomprehensible, for they exclude the mighty complex of Luther's character from the problem of how to assess the responsibility for the appalling misdirection of forces. We may approach Luther with reverence, but dare not shut our eyes to his defects. This must be so, for the sake of truth, for the sake of Christianity, for the sake of Luther himself.

To discover the true Luther we must be able to penetrate the full extent of his virtues, and also the full depth of the faults which overshadow these virtues. The spiritual conflict, the whole complex of forces in this man's life, can only be comprehended within a picture that is full of differentiations, full of 'Yes' and 'No', of 'But' and 'In spite of'.

All portrayals of Luther ought to agree on one fact. He was a man obsessed by religion.

It is extraordinarily difficult to interpret this concept so as to be satisfactory from every angle. We can approach it, however, by saying what Luther was not. He was no politician, no lawyer; nor was he a mystic; and he was not a theological systematiser. We are left with conscience, firmly in the grip of the absolutely binding norm of the 'Word'; and with the prophetic profession of faith – Luther, preacher and confessor of his gospel. This gospel, however, is Jesus Christ, the God-man, whom we behold upon the cross, the revelation of the Father.

First we have to enquire into the sincerity and the power of this Christian piety.

Luther strengthened the good impression made by his struggles in the monastery, by that which we have called his theology of the cross. Because Christianity and the Christian are to be measured by their conformity with Christ, it is of their essence to suffer severe temptation. Christianity is not proved by victory but by the threat to which it must be exposed. What is of God must be thoroughly tried (1523). 'If the Christian does not recognise his distress and temptation, let him know that he is in the worst possible state.' Just as the Godhead turned away from Jesus in his hour of need on the Mount of Olives and on the cross ('My God why hast thou forsaken me'), so, when temptation becomes acute, Christ is taken away from us. Uncertainty about our election terrifies us, as Luther knew in the Wartburg. So, too, the true Church must suffer for the sake of the word of God (1530). That they felt this suffering laid upon them was taken by the Reformers as the justification of their actions. Rome's burden, however, was that she made the way of salvation too easy. Luther did not oppose the cross but its alleviation. He made the condition of the Christian more acute (but cf. p. 477 f.).

This was undoubtedly an important power-centre in Reformed preaching. Not even the radical theory about sin, which fundamentally denied all value to nature, and thus strangled initiative, was strong enough to checkmate this power. We cannot overstress the seriousness of Luther's theology of the cross, his opposition to all forms of complacent self-assurance, or the merciless and rigid way in which he forced men to the point of decision.

Admittedly this was a theory, although filled with power. We wait to see whether the practical life of the Reformer was consonant with this ideal, and to what extent the theology of the cross was accepted by the Reformation as a whole. As Luther himself warned, self-love in its refined or coarse manifestations is hard to escape, and the ideal can be reached only by a small band of the elect.

At the core of Luther's religious experience we find God. Luther sensed the majesty of God deeply enough to know, that no man can comprehend him. At the same time there was in his mind no shadow of doubt about God's existence. From his youth, the existence of God had been a fact settled once and for all. As a result of his fundamental experience of anguish there ensued a despairing battle, which came near to blasphemy against the relentless demands of this God, who had called man into being, burdening him with commandments, and in addition, predestining many to eternal damnation. Notwithstanding all this, Luther never doubted the existence of this God. 'An unbelieving heart finds ever new stumbling blocks.' Such a saying certainly did not apply to Luther himself. For him, God was the mighty power, the only true source of action, from whom come all things, and in face of whom man's powers do not even exist, do not even count, least of all in the process of redemption, which depends utterly upon God's mightiest act of love: the sacrifice of his own Son upon the cross, for us. Man fulfils the purpose of his existence when he annihilates his own powers of cognition and volition, when he disregards what seems valuable, and instead, considers what seems despicable. For, in revelation through his Son, God is a hidden God, and his deeds are seen precisely in those things which manifest lowliness and provoke disdain. The inversion of appearances and a progress through contradictions (the *contraria species*) are the sign of the divine. Luther conceived man not simply as the non-divine but as truely *anti*-divine. God and man contradict one another. The tension between God and sins becomes a tension between God and man. God's judgment is plainly the most acute antithesis to man, and hence man is intrinsically the adversary of God. Luther thought that the distinction between the divine and the human cannot be seen until it is recognised as sheer contradiction. Luther had to go to the extremes of exaggeration, and stretch antithesis to the breaking point.

We know already how little the natural knowledge of God, which Luther found in Romans 1:19 and expounds in his treatise on Romans, meant to him. It is true that the heathen have a vague feeling that there is a God, but as soon as they make any definite statement about him, they go astray. Scripture alone tells us of the one thing that is important for us: the process of redemption, which is complete in the trusting surrender of mankind to the heavenly Father through the Crucified. The formal statement of this is 'by faith alone', the ultimate essence of which is once again trusting surrender to God. Luther's life was filled to the brim with this concept, often in a shattering fashion, humanly speaking, and yet at the same time with a cheering childlike peace and purity. If this surrender had not been so destructively marked by the unbridled emotions of the tempestuous man, Luther the monk might have risen by it to the heights of sanctity. What a fulness and power is in this resting in the Lord, in this speaking and praying out of that fulness! This is what gives the interior man, the spiritual man, perfect victory over all that is external and of this world. Neither adversity nor prosperity is able to harm, the true, the spiritual man. Luther expressed these things in *The Liberty of the Christian Man* and in may other places as well. The immediate effect of this is to produce a mighty disinterestedness in material possessions, and the striving to persuade one's colleagues to learn the same kind of everyday piety. Luther did this in a particularly delicate and unobtrusive way with his friend Eberhard Brisger, for example. Luther's sharp attacks upon the worldly princes of the Church cannot be turned back upon him.

Nor does the terrible boldness of Luther, which we will discuss later, change things in the least. His awareness of being an unprofitable servant of his master, who gives all, the beginning and the end, remains unshaken. Luther certainly took Christianity in deadly earnest; and so he was right in regarding the worries of cardinals and bishops over their worldly advantages, and their disputes at a coming council as pathetically insignificant. (Obviously this is not altered by the fact that Luther lamentably restricted the field of interest of a council, and wrote: 'If a council were to deal with the primary things relating to the spiritual and secular estates that are contrary to God – impurity, usury, avarice, unchastity, luxury, gambling, disobedience, insubordination – they would have their hands so full that meanwhile they would forget all the nonsense about long robes, tonsures, broad girdles, bishops' mitres, cardinals' hats and croziers.')

Luther had no true doctrine of providence. He was aware of a marvellous reality in virtue of which he feared neither death nor the devil. He possessed a glorious and blissful trust, an irresponsible freedom from care. He expressed this with the power of an imperious sense of prophecy in March 1522 when, an excommunicant, he rode into the seething town of Wittenberg, against the wishes of the elector. 'No sword shall or can help this cause. God alone can prosper us, without any human care and assistance.' We have to consider what these words meant in the circumstances, and how his coming immense preaching activity in Wittenberg also proceeded from trust in God. We shall see, too, in more detail, how much this prophetic consciousness, this conviction that he fought and spoke in the name of God, this equation of his own work with God's command, stamped his action until the end of his life. The essential gaps and the growing weaknesses will modify as they complete the picture, but will not destroy it.

Even in thoughts which occupied Luther right to the end, the idea keeps breaking through, that God's thoughts are high above our thoughts, and his hearing far exceeds our petitions or understanding, 'for we do not know how to pray as we ought' (Rm. 8 : 26). The assurance of divine help rests not upon our understanding, but is given to our incapacity to comprehend.

These things applied also to the spread of his gospel, which seemed miraculous to him. The one stable and reliable thing was always the power of God, and trust in him. In those highly charged and critical weeks of the *Reichstag* at Augsburg in 1530, when Luther waited in the Coburg, and Melanchthon in Augsburg was 'crucified' with agitation and fear for the progress of the cause, he strengthened the faint-hearted with these words: 'Were the cause of the gospel never so great, he is greater, who began it and leads it, for it is not our gospel. If it is wrong we will recant, if it is right will we call him who has promised a liar, who desires us to be faithful – like men who enjoy sleep? For he has said: cast thy burden on the Lord! Has he spoken to the wind or to beasts? Christ once died for our sins; he will never die to justice and truth, but lives and reigns for ever. If that is true, why do we fear for the truth? God is mighty to raise the dead, and also to defend his own cause when it is weakening, to raise it up when it has fallen, to advance it when it stands still. If we are not worthy instruments, then let others take our place.' 'The outcome terrifies you because you cannot comprehend it; but God has set this affair under a concept which you have never learned in philosophy or rhetoric: it is called faith. This contains everything which man does not see (Heb 11:1). The Lord has said that he wishes to dwell in darkness. The *I* is too small. It is written (Ex 3:14) "I will be what I will be." Man does not see who he is; but he will become it, and we shall see.' 'It must be, therefore, that we do not know the outs and ins.'

The renunciation of reason stands at the beginning and the end of Luther's work. He, who had thundered against reason and Aristotle and scholasticism, declared in his last Wittenberg sermon: 'The devil will light the lamp of reason and lead you from faith.' Scholasticism had asked too many questions, and sought far too many fancy answers to 'devised and highly artificial questions'. Theologians, he thought, show far too little awe before the divine majesty. He, on the other hand, preferred a non-academic, biblical and religious approach to that of intellectual theology. Characteristic of this is his dogmatic confession of Christ as God. There is absolutely no ratiocination about the why and wherefore, about the relationship of the two natures. For Luther, such things were no more than a pursuit of the sophists, who are no Christians.

This is not denied by the fact that Luther himself retained considerable competence in the method of formal, scholastic thinking and disputation, as a result of his intensive university studies. The first essays of the young *sententiarius* – expositions of Augustine, 1509 – display an unusual power of architectonic, integrative and conceptual thought. All his life he could quote the schoolmen by heart. Nor did he forget, on occasion, to challenge his opponents thus: 'Luther, too, knows your philosophy and theology, for he applied his mind to them creditably for over twelve years.'

Luther was no theologian, but a preacher of the gospel. By this statement we do not want to be identified with the most superficial verdict of Aleander, who thought that the outcome of the Lutheran movement would be a justification or abandonment of the old theological, i.e. scholastic, categories. But the question whether Luther was a theologian or not is far from being a purely academic question. It becomes the chief theme both in the assessment of Luther himself, and in any fruitful discussion of the confessions. If we deny that he was a theologian we arrive immediately at the source of Luther's words and imagery, and see these things in their authentic style, as a product of his spiritual-intellectual work. Because he was no theologian, Luther was capable of containing the most violent contradictions within his fundamental theories, without any dishonesty, and without his statements utterly cancelling one another out. Protestants scholarship has taken this non-theological quality sufficiently into account, with the result that they reject Catholic theological proofs of contradictions in Luther as mere 'formal constructions'.

Luther possessed a mighty power of prayer. He was rooted in God, he knew the thoughts which God has made accessible to us through revelation in such depth, bore them about with him as such living possessions, that he never had to jump over any ditch before beginning to speak with God or about God. Fulfilling one of his master's highest aims, his believing mind turned against one thing especially: mechanical religion. This he was determined to overthrow. But relying as he did upon himself alone, in this campaign he destroyed much, too, of the essential content of revelation. He damaged the inviolable objectivity of religion. What purification this man might have accomplished within the Church, what a new birth, had he been able to remain loyal to the *una sancta*!

With his treatise on Romans he had already taken up arms against externalism in prayer. From this basis he then developed sound principles in that little work of 1534, which was intended to teach his barber how to pray. The deeply religious approach of this work imparts instant life to the principles. How delicately he first warms the arid and indifferent soul to prayer, leads sinful man to God, and draws everything together in the 'great confession', the Our Father!

There was a robust solidarity about Luther's prayer. He knew that God is influenced by our penance. Nothing could be stranger to Luther than a relativistic and deistic attitude. He interpreted many things in the Bible in a quite inadmissibly private way; but he did not play at Christianity.

Christianity makes absolute demands; and for Luther there was nothing apart from Christianity that was of any value at all. He meant, of course, biblical Christianity, as it had come once and for all into this sinful world. All nations, the heathen, share radically in this sin. They are utterly separated from Christ, for they are completely in the grip of error. It is only a philosophical interpretation of revelation which has qualified this absoluteness of Christianity, in favour of the heathen, who are said to have evolved towards Christianity. The conscientious reporter must, however, frequently note irregularities and contradictions in Luther's thesis. This applies now: not only were there 'individuals within the people of God, whom God himself had taught and awakened, but amongst the Godless and the heathen, too, were to be found men directed by God'.

On the other hand, Luther's fundamental religious thought contained the idea that a perfect equality obtained amongst all of the redeemed and baptised. This permits the immediate application of all that St Paul, for example, says about himself, to every Christian, and provides at once the broad basis for the doctrine of the priesthood of all believers. Because Christ became like us in all things, except for sin, the Christian is *the same as* Christ. For this reason 'to this day Christ continues to be despised, killed, scourged, crucified in us'.

By many routes, Luther's piety penetrated the circles of his followers and there began to show its effects. Several of his books must be given special mention: *On Good Works; On the Liberty of the Christian Man*, for example, and his catechism performed a great work of direct education.

His extensive work of reforming the liturgy not only formed a society but was the sign of a society already in existence. Luther approached this vast work much more carefully than did many of the hotheads around him. When concerned with the ordinary people and their corporate prayer, he always lost in great measure his presumptuous, reckless iconoclasm. He took the heart out of the liturgy when he deleted the canon of the mass, including the consecration, and thus deprived so many millions of the eucharist in the course of time; but at the same time he was able to stay within the atmosphere of ancient Catholic prayer; and the objective root of this was the real presence of the Lord in the Lord's Supper.

Luther's common prayer found a prominent echo in the new hymnody. Luther was a musician. His love for, and competence in, music was one of the many charming natural gifts which enabled him so easily to perform tasks that lay on the fringe of his real work. In addition, music played an important part in Luther's battle against psychological and physical depression.

Luther's contribution to Protestant hymnody in the Reformation period was considerable, in respect both of words and of music. The hymns composed or commissioned by him (twenty-seven in all) fulfilled the function of a rousing battle-cry. Not only did the tunes make these, first and foremost, a social force, but their whole conception was one of corporate prayer; and from this source Luther's subjectivism itself experienced significant modification. In the practical expansion of his doctrine he proceeded outwards entirely from the natural unit of corporate life, from the congregation. For him this represented the Church. He, who knew personal struggle, made the congregation into a group who struggled in prayer – like Israel in the psalms. He scarcely could be said to have activated the mind of the organism of the Church; but in public worship he still lived by the objectivity of the liturgical chants of Catholic times. In this way, the congregation sang the psalms and hymns in German, as chorales. Luther's hymns are worlds removed from the egotistic hymns of pietism. Like Luther's own faith they lived on the fulness of the facts of redemption, as these were formulated in the unaltered ancient creeds. It is certainly significant that the spiritual songs contained in the very first hymn-book of 1524 were aimed at an explicitly moralistic goal.[14]

Luther had a very poor opinion of human capabilities:

[14] The tunes are set for four voices because I want the youth to have something that will wean them from lewd songs and teach them something wholesome instead' (from a lecture).

'Everything in nature proceeds from weak beginnings to a mighty conclusion; but men go from mighty beginnings to weak endings.' Man takes this impotence with him into faith. So his own experience and his pastoral work taught him. To unbounded joy in believing, and certainty of salvation he added anxiety (Ps 127). This is an expression of that uncertainty of election which is a lifelong essential component of belief in election.

Man's impotence in the moral sphere is expressed by, and has its roots in, invincible concupiscence. We know that this statement must not be interpreted in an antinomian sense. Luther deliberately tried to preserve religious and moral endeavour, even within the context of a defective morality. His stress upon the primacy of faith over the moralism of the fanatical sects was so great, that he even warned against the notion 'that one may impugn a person's doctrine on account of the frailty of his life. This is not what the Spirit teaches. The Holy Spirit reproves false doctrine but tolerates weakness in faith and life, as St Paul teaches everywhere (Rm 14, 15; 1 Co 9:22; Ga 6:1). I would not bother about the papists if they would only teach the truth. Their wicked lives would not do so much harm. Because this spirit (of the fanatics) takes such offence at our frail life, and judges our doctrine so impudently on that account, it has sufficiently proved who it is.' No one who knows Luther will dispute that he himself carried on his battle with the papists in a totally different way. The theoretical foundation remains in spite of all, and it has definite value.

On the other hand, we know also that the formula of invincible concupiscence, taken literally, and in contrast to the former practice of good works, allowed many to slacken their efforts, that is to yield more easily to their impulses. This laid the foundation for moral decline. Luther's complaint[15] and that of other leaders concerning the 'carnal lives' of the Reformed, described fully by Döllinger, indicate the way things actually worked out. Melanchthon recognised a chief cause, which he noted in the Saxon visitation order of 1528: 'Nearly everybody misses out one piece of Christian doctrine: penance. In this way the people be-

---

[15] Also his 'heaviness of heart' at the 'terrible signs and wonders, which these times have produced', his small output or desire to work in 1534, and his pessimism.

come self-assured and fearless. This is a worse error and sin than any of previous times.' Luther expressed the matter thus: 'Most people understand doctrine and faith carnally.'

Luther had already tried to put a stop to this misinterpretation in a well-known passage in *The Liberty of the Christian Man*. 'If faith is all, and quite sufficient to create all piety, why are good works commanded? Shall we be good and yet do nothing? Not at all. A man must control his own body, and live amongst men: this is where work begins. He must direct and exercise his body by fastings, vigils, work and all discipline, so that he becomes conformed and obedient to the spiritual man, not opposed to it.' 'We must live as we teach.'

Unfortunately 'there are many amongst us who say: Lord, Lord!' After 1527 this recognition led to a greater stress being laid upon *works* and *mortification;* but there never was any place in Luther's system for a genuine moral doctrine.

Important for the fundamental direction of his thought was the battle against *work-righteousness, satisfaction, merit*; and this battle rested upon misunderstanding. Luther and the succeeding generations of Protestants were the first to impregnate these terms with a nuance of odious utilitarianism, which became a permanent feature in their use as ammunition against the old religion. In themselves, that is in the Catholic view, according to which they were conceived, they possess no trace of self-righteousness. Proof of this from the history of dogma extends with overwhelming cogency even into the realms of nominalism, although there an unchristian overemphasis on the part played by the human will in the redemptive process is undoubtedly at work. An even more impressive proof comes from our experience of present-day popular Catholic piety – taken almost at random. When a mother urges her children diligently to win 'merits for heaven' she does not in the least lessen their unconditional committal to the hands of God, whose mercy and grace alone can save us. Such exhortation merely spurs us on to cultivate the spirit of the good and faithful servant who, having done all, still knows that he is an unprofitable servant.

In 1530 Viet Dietrich wrote to Melanchthon from the Coburg to say that Luther spent a good three hours each day in prayer, full of reverence and profound trust. If we bear in mind his

constant study of holy scripture, we realise how this period must
have been steeped in prayer. It was a very special period. Luther
reacted to outward pressure by a more intensive formation of his
spiritual life. His many sermons, his devotion to the mother of
God, his numerous edifying discourses, all prove that the life
of prayer endured throughout his entire life. He was aware, too, of
a progressive sanctification of life – of 'elevation and growth'.
It is difficult, however, to tell from his examples and precepts,
how such progress is supposed to be realised in detail. He compressed the mind of Christianity into a few broad lines. These
were indeed capable of producing great fruit, but he did not
provide us with a technique of their application, so as to ensure
progress. In this, Luther felt himself uniquely removed from his
Catholic past: 'But I feel equally that now I do not pray to God
with the same diligence as I used to pray to the saints' (1537).
He had minimised also the little things of daily practice. It was
for succeeding generations, who so thoroughly renounced Luther's
Catholic vestiges (confession,[16] veneration of our Lady and the
saints), to carry this process to its sad ending.

Luther had split the Church by his doctrine. He did this
in spite of explicit statements that he was committed to the unity
of the Roman Church, and that its division could in no way be
justified. In the controversies about observance he had already
laid down the principle: 'Give way to wrath and let the weeds
grow up amongst the wheat! It is better to lead a few to salvation
in peace, than to precipitate everyone into turmoil for the sake
of the majority, and thus destroy the few. . .' In the *Instruction
in Some Articles* (1519), he again explicitly conceded that neither
the Roman abuses nor any other reason, 'no matter how great',
can justify the breaking up of unity. 'The worse things become,
the more one ought to exert oneself and hold firm; for breaking
away and contempt will improve nothing. No kind of sin or evil
we can name or think of, is sufficient reason to divide the body
and split our spiritual unity, for love can accomplish all things.'
It is true that these statements are followed by others which

---

[16] Cf. 1522: 'I would long since have been choked to death by the devil,
had I not kept up private confession.' Luther's lifelong confessor was Bugenhagen.

to some extent spiritualise the concept of the Church, thus minimising the importance of the visible Church, and of the *potestas
clavium*. But he retained his basic concept, that it would be a
sheer impossibility to separate oneself from the Roman Church,
which God has clearly blessed before all others. 'I have never had
any thought of a schism in the Church, and I never will. The
Bohemians are doing an evil thing, uprooting themselves from
the Church, as though divine law were on their side' (1519).

In the same year Luther was launching his sharpest attacks
against Rome. In spite of this, frequently and solemnly he protested that he wanted to say or affirm nothing except what could
be found in holy scriptures, in the fathers approved by the
Roman Church, and in the decrees and canons of the popes.
'I may err, but I will not become an heretic.'

In Augsburg in 1518, before his meeting with Cajetan he had
said to Cajetan's emissary: 'If I am shown that I have been saying
things that are contrary to the mind of the holy Roman Church, I
will be my own judge, and recant.'

Luther fulfilled his intentions badly. His own interior development and external forces led him away from it and beyond it.
He clung rather to views which in this problem, as in others,
reveal his theological vacillation. At the same time as he was
protesting his firm adherence to the Roman Church, he was
aware of the revolutionary qualities of his views. On 1 September
1518 he wrote to Staupitz: 'As with Rebekah; the children must
struggle in the womb, even if the mother's life is at stake.' In
January 1519 in a letter to the electors he roundly refused to
recant. This merely corresponded to the way things had gone in
his interview with Cajetan, and to the new definition he had given,
after the end of 1518, of the pope and the papal Church: the pope
was Antichrist and the Church his kingdom. However, the concept
of the one true Church was never abandoned. 'I thank the good
Lord that I have not invented any new doctrine, but have maintained the old, true doctrines.'

How real, we must ask, was this concept of the Church? At
all events the concept of the Church, as a unique entity, as an
organism prior to, and superordinate to, the individual, and
within which the individual Christian believes and prays, was a

P

concept that played little part in Luther's thought. As we have said, in the years 1517–19 he often declared that he had no desire to teach anything that the Church did not teach; but this was meant in a strictly apologetic sense. The reality which the word 'Church' denotes, eluded him. The part which Luther had discovered and declared was everything in his own eyes – all that ever could be. Precisely this defect in his approach is the foundation, as it is the most impressive expression, of his subjectivist conscience.

Luther's contemporary opponents were fully aware of this fact. Witzel, moved no doubt by resentment and other defective motives, declared, however, that he had parted company with Luther because 'I have seen how this monk has made the issue himself, pushes everything along according to this own notions, makes and mars, turns and turns again, affirms and denies, . . . all by himself, according to his own pleasure and inclination.' Luther understood this reproach. He replied with a general definition of the true Church, which Catholics could accept without hesitation: 'The true Church must be that one which holds fast to the word of God, and is prepared to suffer for it, as we do. Thus you ought not always to be shouting – "Church! Church! Church!" but ought to show that you are the Church.' Unfortunately it became impossible for Luther to give this proof himself after he had dethroned the living teaching authority of the Church and her tradition, and recognised only his own interpretation of scripture. This alone was enough to destroy the ancient concept of the Church, and establish its invisibility in the Lutheran sense.

The Church's means of dispensing salvation, too, so directly dependent upon the visibility of the Church, receded in a frightening way. If the Church is the mystical body of Christ, she possesses and dispenses divine life. In 1519 Luther had already arrived at the principle: 'God's law and Church are as gold and precious stones compared with wood and straw.' This was not meant simply to be a rejection of what was human, of the exaggerated curialism which was pressing into the sanctuary; it was not merely an example of Luther's common confusion of extreme casuistry or abuse with the Church itself; it amounted to an essential emptying of the very concept of the Church.

All we need do to gain a first-hand impression of how the

genuine concept of the Church had vanished from Luther's theology, is to read the great writings of 1520. There we see how autocratically Luther set himself above the Church by his own knowledge and interpretation of the Bible. We see how emphatically he made a measuring rod of his own highly personal searching, knowing and vacillating. For example, he lists amongst impediments to marriage which are of divine law, the vow of chastity; but he naïvely adds that he does not see perfectly clearly on this matter. What can this mean if not that the doctrine of the Church depends upon the greater or lesser insight of theologians? This question about impediments to marriage was in fact dealt with as part of the campaign to unmask the Roman Antichrist.[17]

We have now uncovered a position that is theologically untenable. Luther said: 'In questions not yet definitively settled I would not look for a definition by the authority of the pope or the bishops; but if two learned and worthy men agree in Christ's name on a doctrine and declare it in the Spirit of Christ, I would prefer their judgment to that of a council.' What are we to make of such ambiguity and vagueness?

We have already stated that the role which Luther assigned to the Christian congregation, invests subjectivism with a measure of objectivity. 'The word of the gospel has been entrusted to the congregation by the Lord. Through the Church, i.e. through the ministry of the brethren, the faithful hear the word of the forgiveness of sins. The congregation must be the co-judge, but . . .', and this 'but' has to be underlined . . . 'it confirms the gospel and the holy scriptures as a subject, not as their master and judge' (1530).

The same year, 1530, produced another definition of the Church, the first part of which clearly goes back to the ideas current amongst the supporters of the conciliar theory, and which utterly obscures the objectivity of the Church. 'Have we no faith, why do we not want to put up with the faith of others? There are bound to be others who believe if we do not believe, for otherwise the Church would have come to an end and Christ would have ceased to be with us upon earth, before the world came to an end.

[17] When Luther occasionally concedes that he, as an individual, cannot affirm his own views against all other, he means this to apply only to certain very secondary matters.

If he is not with us, where else is he in all the world? If we are not the Church or part of the Church, then where is the Church? If we have not the word of God, who has?'

Luther does not bear the entire blame for this theological defectiveness. In all of the material available for his theological education in the monastery and at the university there was no tractate specifically on the Church. The basic Catholic idea, that all private theologising was merely a presentation of the thought and prayer of the Church, and could emerge from this thought and prayer, had been displaced by a chattering debate amongst a thousand private opinions. At an early date Luther exaggerated this view to the point where he considered all the doctrines of St Thomas – as he knew them – as mere opinions, assuming the right of rejecting them as he would other opinions.

Only once in Luther's early development do we come upon essays which might have filled, in some degree, the gap left by the missing tractate on the Church. This was the quite rich, completely non-Occamist and fully papal material, contained in Biel's commentary on the canon of the mass. Unfortunately this work did not have a very profound effect upon Luther, nor could it have had. He studied it for only a few months: the period between his profession and his ordination to the priesthood. Whatever effect it did have was then obscured by his subsequent theological studies in the school of Occam. Above all, it changed nothing in his subjectivist, experiential approach to things; and this was the real cause of Luther's inability to understand the Church. Luther epitomised the individual person, the individual conscience, against the Church; and that was the kernel of his programme.

All mass movements need inspiring watchwords. For the Reformation to sweep away large sections of society it was imperative that Luther find a slogan that would reduce to a simple formula all the vast and variously caused discontent with Rome. The formula would also have to direct and consolidate these feelings, while providing it with the highest possible justification. It would have to be a slogan, unsullied by artificial propaganda, an adequate expression of the earnest endeavour to attain ultimate, world-shaping values.

Such a slogan was found in the endlessly repeated reproach about Roman ordinances of men. These were stubbornly and confidently condemned with the positive demand for God's word alone. 'Leave the Word alone!'

This motto had tremendous power. Its effect was all the greater because a great many of those who remained loyal to the Church had to admit it applied to so many of the practices and precepts of the curia, and to theological and liturgical accretions. In addition it possessed that world-historical, fatal ambiguity, for the emergence of which late medieval curialism had to share the blame, and which now made it so easy for criticism of peripheral things to overflow into the realm of dogma.

This motto began to echo from all the groups of followers who were now gathering around Luther. Theological tractates, like the pamphlets and woodcuts, were full of it, and the retinue of the Saxon elector and of the landgrave of Hesse wore it on their sleeves. We have only to read Dürer's effusions in the diary of his journey to the Netherlands to experience the power with which these words of Luther struck and stirred up his contemporaries. We see, too, with what incredible facility, frivolity even, and with what obvious vagueness (cf. pp. 156 and 233 f.) the papal régime and the Church as it had been known were equated with worldliness. Perhaps it is at this point that we experience most strikingly the fearful collapse of those things which yesterday had been regarded as sacred: ' . . . your false, blind doctrines, invented by men, whom they call the fathers.' 'God will have nothing added to, or taken away from, his word.'

On whatever front he declared it, the formula was the interpreter of all of Luther's attacks. Luther maintained that in scholasticism he had not learned the merest elements of Christianity. On the contrary, he had learned only what was false and contrary to the divine word. Indeed he had almost lost Christ as a result of this study (1519). It is the mortal sin, the anti-Christianity of scholasticism, that it distorts the divine word by means of human philosophy, out of a single biblical saying carving dozens of meanings. Revelation plainly demands that we leave Christ's words just as they are, just as he spoke them.

Only against this as background can we make sense of Luther's hate-filled and tragic battle against the mass. The relevant passage in *The Babylonian Captivity* clearly expresses this. In the mass Luther sees a 'good work', a work done by man, a sacrifice made by man: 'When we ought to be thankful for the promises we have received, we come boastfully to God with our good works, giving what we ought to be taking.'

It remains a mystery, however, how Luther was able to draw such false conclusions. Mark well the exact point in question. We ought fully to admit Luther's real solicitude about the perfect, exclusive uniqueness of the sacrifice on the cross. We should do this all the more gladly, as we learn how to appreciate the objectivity of his view of the eucharist, in contrast to psychological theories. All of this is deeply Catholic. Again, we must concede that the theory of sacrifice current in his time was defective. Many of its vague details not only sounded anthropocentric and moralistic but were so (cf. Part Three in Vol. II). None the less we can say: neither the Church nor any individual Catholic theologian had ever asserted that the centre of the mass was a sacrifice made by man. Nicholas of Lyra and Faber Stapulensis, whom Luther knew and used, and even more clearly, his teacher, Gabriel Biel, clearly stressed both the uniqueness of the New Testament sacrifice, and the identity of the sacrifice on the cross with the mass. They teach that when *we* offer the sacrifice of the mass to God, it is Christ who really makes the sacrifice. Luther boldly affirmed the opposite. Man's work has replaced God's work – 'it is the work which is effective'. He shows no understanding at all for the true and venerable tradition expressed in the canon: 'any old ignorant monk might have composed it'.

Thus he was left with not the least understanding of the 'papists' in general. Not only did they teach the rankest idolatry but Luther was in no doubt at all that they rejected his plain reasons and doctrine out of sheer stubbornness, and 'maliciously persevere in their abominations'. In 1530 under pressure of circumstances the most they would do was to weaken the sacrifice of the mass to become a 'symbol of sacrifice'. 'Who could tell anyway whether or not the priests really said the words of institution at all? It would be better for them to wash their anointed fingers with soap and soda and remove the mark of Antichrist.'

It was foolish of Luther to ask for a vote of confidence. We recall what he said about the holy mass in *The Babylonian Captivity*. It is true that this much is made clear, that Luther was attacking something central, something that was connected solely with his central proposition about faith. There he divested the mass of its special character and equated it with the simple communion of the priest. But he did this without in the least altering what men were everywhere accustomed to call 'the mass' – at least not in externals. The priest who is asked to say a mass ought to pay heed only to the spiritual intention of the sacrifice. This amounted to nothing less than advice to practise clerical deception. The priest is instructed to agree to say mass in a totally different sense from that which the faithful intend. He simply prays for this or that at communion; and we may call this prayer, praise and offering a sacrifice if we like. It may 'incite Christ to sacrifice for us in heaven'. Sacrifice in the objective sense has been eradicated.

Luther believed that in the mass of his time the most important thing, the memorial of the Lord's death, had become utterly submerged beneath human additions; and he argued: the mass is full of externalism – the whole of Catholic teaching is the same. He identified Catholicism with the widespread vulgarised Catholic practices of the time. He acted very properly when he inveighed against the greed which had got mixed up with the celebration of the holy sacrifice. By their multiplication of undevout hastily said masses, many priests had 'turned the altars of the Most High into an altar of Baal'. In practice, the faithful all too often regard the mass as magic. 'Some have mass said in order that they may become rich . . ., others because they think that if they hear mass in the morning they will be safe from all distress and danger all day long.' It is certain, too, that many priests out of avarice pressed for stipends when the money was badly needed by a widow or family. But when Luther affirmed that the ceremonies were introduced merely for the profit of the clergy, he was right off the mark. Above all we must note that the subjective worth or carelessness or guilt of the dispenser or of the recipient do not determine the objective validity of the sacrament. On this very point we can refer Luther to his own words in *The Babylonian Captivity*, and even more appositely to the relevent writings of the years 1527–29, which teach the objectivity and the objective efficacy of the eucharist in a fully Catholic way.

In 1519 Luther had already pressed his exaltation of holy scripture to the point where scripture alone possessed any validity. This was his biblical principle: we are forbidden to believe anything except holy scripture; 'what is not in the holy scriptures is an addition of the devil'.

This biblical principle underlay Luther's battle with the Church and the empire. No real refutation was possible on these terms; for all depended upon the interpretation of the texts, upon disputation. No one seemed to see then, that the biblical principle was the really revolutionary formula; for this principle denied and destroyed at one stroke the substance of the whole Church–state structure, before a word had been said on the subject. In fact, Luther's attitude and that of the Saxon elector and of the public opinion that was behind him rested almost wholly upon the much repeated assurance, that no word of Luther would stand, no proposal be carried out, if he were refuted from scripture – a proviso which Luther gladly accepted. Luther had never tired of stressing this, ever since he began to write, and he did so all the more vigorously after his clash with the historic power of Church and state. By this method he urged the world to face the question of the value of what had become historic, of the human element in the Church. The posing of the question carried far more weight than any negative answer. God's word versus human development; could there be any doubt over the answer? There were few who saw that this was a false question. For example, Duke George of Saxony did not see it in the critical moment of the Leipzig disputation, when the divine right of the primacy was being disputed (above, p. 236). Luther saw much more clearly on that occasion, and was able to make capital in his duel with Antichrist. As we have said, it was enormously clever and impressive, the way he once more drove home this point in writing, after departing from Worms, and then stressed, proved and demanded, that the one 'Christian norm' must be 'that God's word be free and unhindered above all things', for 'the dignity and power of holy scripture is greater than the powers of the whole of human reason'.

For Luther 'the word' embraced the sacraments also. He stated conclusively that 'our Church has been equipped by God's grace with the pure word and the right use of the sacraments'. We know how Catholics regarded this particular use as a fearful amputation. 'To me there is nothing in Lutheranism so distasteful as their painful destruction of the holy sacraments' (Charitas Pirkheimer). 'Five, they have completely done away, the others they keep, but so mutilated that they, too, will soon be gone' (Murner).

None the less, not only was infant baptism retained – an unmistakable recognition of the *opus operatum* – but so was the real presence of Jesus Christ in the Blessed Sacrament.

Once again we have to defend Luther's belief and preaching against much misunderstanding. Luther's doctrine of the Lord's Supper contains a departure from his subjectivism, that is specially important today. The words 'This is my body' had, for him, a truly objective power; for, according to Luther, this real presence of the Lord in the sacrament does not depend upon the faith of the individual but on the celebration of the Lord's Supper by the congregation assembled in the Lord, to whom his promises apply. Christ, then, is truly present in the bread even without the faith of the individual, so that unworthy reception of the true body and blood of Christ can take place. The faith of the individual is a precondition only of a sanctifying reception.

The conceptions of the word, too, and of a religion of conscience, in Luther's spirit and words, were not what his imitators or the Enlightenment and modern liberal Protestant theology have made of them: subjectivist picking and choosing. The word of God as it is imperiously presented to men, was for Luther, a powerful divine authority, the norm of all norms. There is no doubt whatever, that Luther felt himself utterly bound to the unchangeable, divine word, despite all its harsh demands, despite all intellectual difficulties, despite any personal wishes and desires. We might say that there was a powerful dogmatism in his subjectivism, or that his was a subjectivist dogmatism. He would gladly have given all his commentaries and those of every teacher, to ensure that every Christian accepted the scriptures, the pure word of God. 'Go in, then, dear Christian folk, for God dwells only in Zion. Amen!'

There are countless passages which express this idea. In *The Liberty of the Christian Man* there is a highly spiritualised description of the independence of piety from all that is external – rather, of its sole dependence upon what is spiritual and inward; and this has a highly subjectivist slant. An objective aspect breaks through in the fifth point, which announces the fixed norm: 'The soul possesses nothing in heaven or earth by which it may live devoutly and freely, and be a Christian, except the holy gospel, the word of God preached by Christ.'

For Luther and for his doctrine, the deepest and ultimate source of power was not his own personal faith but the mighty, objective reality in which he believed and out of which he believed. And this was – far beyond any theoretical definition – Jesus Christ, the Son of God, the Crucified, the redeemer of the world. Luther took hold of this person and preached *him* far more powerfully than he preached any doctrine; and that is Luther's power to this day. This, too, is the only thing which can explain Protestantism's grandiose contradiction of its own fundamental latent spirit of disintegration. In his Christology Luther provided this objectivism with a fruitful foundation by thinking of Christ as our example in the sense of a 'sacrament'. At this point Luther was profoundly affected by the spirit of the saying: 'I am the way.' This was what enabled him to overcome the dangers of a merely psychological piety, for in this form the saying contains far deeper realities than if it had run: 'I will show you the way.'

The strongest proof of Luther's objectivism and dogmatism is provided by his incredibly severe attack upon the fanatics, provided that we stress this more than is usually done. His declarations on this topic were so full of hatred, that he must have regarded the fanatics as professors of an essentially different belief. The fanatical subjectivism he so detested, made itself master over the Word. Luther wanted to be its servant.

There are deep causes for the neglect of these elements by the critics. Luther's objectivism was self-deception, a piece of illogicality. It was a deception because no religious objectivity is possible unless accompanied step by step by a living interpreter, an infallible, living, teaching authority. No objective norm can be built upon personal insight, even less when this insight is so uniquely personal and subjective and vacillating as it was in

Luther's case – as we can prove with certainty. Herein is the illogicality of Luther. He was the servant of the Word, but according to his own highly personal understanding. By setting up the Word in sublime isolation, he contradicted the pure concept of the servant of the Word, and he ceased to be merely its hearer. One of the commonest weaknesses of almost every Protestant picture is that, in spite of the contradictory variations in Luther's exegesis, they present his interpretations simply as the pure Word.

Very properly a great many Protestant theologians today oppose the view that Luther regarded the Word as a purely spiritual entity. They fasten on Luther's violent antagonism to the spiritualism of the fanatics, who believed that they possessed the Spirit of God without the meditation of the Word, and prior to it. Historically, however, this is not completely decisive. Much more significant is the question: how far was the spiritualistic interpretation put upon Luther's words justified? Luther's greatest conceptions did in fact contain the most stubborn interior paradoxes; the essence of his Christian preaching was paradox – as we have seen. The decisive thing immediately fastened upon in any statement, was anything that appeared new within the polemical situation. This, however, was always something that led men away from what was visible, from the institution, from the living, sacerdotal, teaching authority. All that was left was the Word and man's spirit. If there is no living teaching office, but simply the priesthood of all believers, then I can interpret the Word for myself; I must do so; or it may be that this or that congregation must do the interpreting. The basic problem of all interpretation of Luther is how to view together and hold together subjectivism and objectivism. On this point the critics part company. Luther himself was still medieval in his concept of the Church, or rather in his view of the authoritative objectivity of the Church (within the scope indicated). For him, neither the invisibility of the Church became absolute, nor was the Church's authority over souls completely denied. But his personal metamorphosis into the Reformer, by a process of scrupulosity which was highly subjective in its crediting only private insight, and his doctrine, were primarily subjective and recognised that objectivity only within specified limits. The whole was quite correctly understood and developed in subjectivist terms. With perfect logic, therefore, the sharpest differences of opinion emerged, and became expressed in a splintering of the Church.

Protestant variations began with Luther himself. The changes and contradictions in the 'many-headed' Luther, were from the start a fundamental theme in the Catholic counter-attack.

Aleander did not make much of this point. The imperial confessor made use of Luther's contradictions when he was working on Sickingen. In 1523 Faber wrote on Luther's contradictions. In 1525 Dungersheim in Leipzig expatiated on the same theme. Eck and Hoffmeister and Ambrose Catharinus, and the Franciscan John Findling, and all of Luther's opponents developed the theme further.

Cochlaeus in particular, with the most pedantic thoroughness, followed up and carefully noted all of Luther's variations. He wrote on this subject in 1521, 1522 and 1528. In 1528 the instruction to visitators was published, carrying an introduction by Luther. Cochlaeus thought that he saw here a return to a dogmatically fixed, orderly ecclesiastical system, which seemed to be *the* contradiction of Luther's doctrine and of his break with the old Church. No longer must we turn away from the Church; we must return to it. Thus in the *Seven-headed Luther*, Cochlaeus portrayed the Reformer's development in seven sharply defined steps. The self-contradictory statements of Luther on individual doctrines of the Church were quoted verbatim.

From what has been said so far in this book it must be obvious that I find no pleasure whatever in perpetuating the distorted Catholic picture of Luther which we owe to Cochlaeus. His collection of 91, then 132, then 500 changes in Luther's views contain many quibbles and even misinterpretations. This does not, however, destroy his basic thesis about Luther's considerable theological vacillation, of which Cardinal Stanislaus Hosius was later to provide abundant proof from Protestant sources.

In view of this vacillation, which was audacious enough to propose to replace the secular system of the Church, Cochlaeus forecast 'that we Germans will become much more confused in faith through Luther, than the Bohemians have become in over a hundred years'.

In contrast to the finality, so dear to Luther, the many deviations of the formative years 1518–20 and then 1530, which might however be explained as tactical accommodations, had a painful effect. (For example: Luther's *Instruction on Certain Articles* after his interview with Miltiz.) Obviously these sedulously avoid facing the real issues.

At the height of the stormy offensive of 1518, when Luther had already begun to draw the antithesis between the pure word of God and the pope as Antichrist, his position was so ill-defined that he admitted the inconstancy of his theological opinions: 'I see a few things, which Augustine saw, and yet I know that others who are to follow me will know more than I.' Unfortunately, in enunciating his new revolutionary theses he did not sufficiently accept the wholesome restrictions this thought might have provided.

We have seen how emphatically Luther rejected all suggestions of a split with the Roman Church, how he vacillated on this fundamental point, and quickly adopted a radically different opinion.

In discovering what the binding word of God is, the concept of inspiration is the deciding factor. On the one hand, Luther refused to allow full canonical status to the Epistle of James, on the other hand, he left others free to make up their own minds about it.

We have tried to define Luther's doctrine of predestination. No one would want to assert that all of Luther's statements on this topic are unanimous. Here we find undoubted inconsistencies that merge into contradictions.

How difficult it has always been to determine exactly and uniformly the details of Luther's views on the Lord's Supper. Very properly attention has been drawn to the many emendations Luther made to his manuscript of 'that these words . . . remain firm'. The Schwabacher Articles which claimed to be a binding confession, were the product of the opportunist machinations of the secular and ecclesiastical Saxon counsellors. In Marburg a much stronger stress was laid upon what was common to Luther and Zwingli. This was clearly a result of the political purposes served by the conversations which took place there. Even more suspicious is the fact that at the beginning of the forties Luther seemed to be prepared to come to terms with the ecclesiastical system adopted by electoral Brandenburg. The compromising spirit of this (in harmony with the truly non-religious character of the pliant Joachim II) was far removed from the demands he had been making.

Amongst these things, which could be endlessly enumerated, are many that may appear quite obvious to a modern historian of theology. Luther, however, did not emerge as a theologian disputing over theses. He accused the 1500-year-old Church, foundation of the structure of the known world, of radical and essential error in the most sacred things, and of blatant deceit. He appeared, claiming to bring at last the true light of the gospel, true Christianity, through grace alone, claiming at last to have unmasked Antichrist. He did this by a colossal exaggeration of this antithesis: the pure Word against the deceit of the devil. He identified his doctrine with the one narrow way of truth into heaven; any deviation led straight to hell.

In such an atmosphere even less important variations cease to be harmless. The founder of a religion in which the absolutes of the Christian demand appear so imperious and rigid and uncompromising, dare not have any variations, least of all such great variations, in his doctrine. They would destroy his claims.

Finally, this variation was a necessary consequence of Luther's basic views. If scripture is the sole norm, who, then, can understand it aright? In his commentary on Psalm 1, Luther declared unequivocally: 'If the doctrine is not preached authoritatively by the teaching office through living men, there would be as many doctrines as people.' On the other hand, he said: '. . . it is declared only to the humble and meek' – a character that can be variously interpreted. We shall soon see how strongly criticism can be made of Luther's own exposition, beginning with this very point.

Luther said: 'No one understands scripture, it must be experienced.' He added: 'We must listen to the words as though they had been written yesterday.' For whom had they been written? 'I must know and pay heed to the person for whom God's word was written.' 'One must indeed distinguish whether the Word applies to one or to all at once.' Who in the end is to make this distinction? The scholar of scripture who 'by reading, examining, and meditating (upon the Bible) becomes practised in knowing the truth, and powerful in expounding the holy scripture and instructing others'. Luther was such a lover of the Bible; so were Zwingli, Calvin, Osiander and Butzer. Whose judgment was the true one? Thomas Aquinas and Ekkehard, too, were scripture scholars, so was Cajetan. Where, then, is the right interpretation, if it is amongst scripture scholars that we have to look for it?

If Luther was the prophet of God, how could he get out of making the decision? As we have seen, however, he did avoid this decision. With reference to the book of Revelation (1522) he solved the problem in much the same way as with the Epistle of St James – the 'epistle of straw': 'I say what I feel. I feel a lack . . . . I cannot sense that the book has been composed by the Holy Spirit. . . . My own spirit finds no resonance in the book.'

Consider the immense field of allegorical exegesis. It is true that Luther rejected this on principle; but he was equally opposed to literal exegesis. Thus, all his life long, he was never able to refrain from allegorising. In this sphere who is to judge where the line must be drawn? It can hardly be denied that all of his statements leave plenty of scope for subjective and vacillating exposition, or even display this already in operation. It was impossible for Luther to escape the consequences of his subjectivism, which penetrated the very substance of the gospel.

His translating of the Bible into German was a most powerful and large-scale demonstration of this sort of thing. As Hirsch so well expressed it, Luther really did give birth anew in German to the Word that had lost its power for us. This was a noble act, and none has put the Word into a new language with such power as Luther did. But at the same time this creation was marked by what we have recognised as his chief characteristic: with the unrestraint of genius he poured forth his own emotion, captivating all; and his emotion so penetrated the German, that the result often was no synthesis of revelation and material speech but a victory for what was of nature, for the German language, which completely enmeshed the substance of revelation. It was not his majestic rebirth of the Word that was the fault of the work but his lack of restraint.

To gain any notion of the extent to which Luther's most unique genius made itself autonomous judge of a completely objective value, we would have to examine the whole of his vast work from this angle. To take but one example, for him, the validity of the proof of the existence of God seemed to be completely caught up in a subjective principle. It depended utterly upon the human disposition. 'If man is just, God is (i.e. seems) just. . . . Therefore, to the damned, he will appear unjust for all eternity.'

Let us once more recall that one of the marks of Lutheran theology is its tendency to reduce Christianity from a multiplicity of precepts[18] to a few essential points. In this Luther was continuing the process that appeared with the Platonic humanists of Florence: he did not listen to everything but chose what he wanted.

The non-radical streams within Protestantism (the ecclesial denominations) often object vigorously to the characterisation of Luther and his work as fundamentally subjectivistic. Is that not a contradiction of the proud affirmation that Protestantism is wholly a religion of conscience, which throws man utterly upon the decisions of his own conscience? Appeal to one's own conscience in the scrupulous style of his monastic years, was the source of Luther's strength, and the same appeal at the time of Worms became the hallmark of the Lutheran attitude. It is impossible to make this proud claim, and then reject its consequence – subjectivism with all its dangers and burdens – as soon as the one possible objective corrective is found wanting: an infallible teaching authority. Protestants may, however, with justice object at least to Luther's subjectivism being represented as sheer caprice, as modern liberal theology and Catholic studies of Luther, since the Enlightenment, have done. In the last analysis, for Luther, it was a case of 'If you believe, you have; if you do not believe, you have nothing.' But this faith is not free, but inexorably demanded. Luther was utterly convinced that these demands were objectively ascertainable in the Word.

The dissolution within Protestantism, that began with Luther,

[18] In the Schmalkald Articles: 'Therefore I have set down few articles, for over and above what God has commanded, we are obliged to do so many things in the Church, in the state, and at home, that we could never fulfil them all.'

Karlstadt and Melanchthon, that spread rapidly and produced permanent subdivisions, that ridiculed all religious conversations and concordat formulae, was no accident. It was the logical expression of the divisive principle latent in Luther's words and deeds, and above all in his fundamental attitude. In his own lifetime Luther saw this development coming: 'I am still alive and already false brethren are here turning my doctrine violently against me. What will it be like when I am gone?'

We cannot ignore Melanchthon's deviations as expressed in the various editions of his *Loci communes*. For example, in 1534 he stressed man's natural powers and his capacity for education. Less still may we overlook Butzer's relativism and how it was hushed up in view of the Wittenburg concordat. Nor can the fanatics be denied all right to existence, from purely Protestant principles. At the time Luther saw the issue more clearly, for he could not sanction state action against them. Even if we rule out their interpretation of Christianity as an arbitrary abuse of the scripture principle and of the religion of conscience, there still remains lamentable confusion even amongst the supporters of the Augsburg Confession.

It is true that Luther denied responsibility for this development. Quite simply he labelled the divergent theses 'lies contrary to his clear doctrine, spread by false brethren instigated by the devil'. This argument can scarcely be taken as refutation of the objections adduced; all the less so when we consider that Luther's whole intellectual and psychological make-up, his experimental approach, his lack of clear systematic power, was the perfect soil to nourish spasmodic growth, with its reverses after colossal advances, and that this make-up also seemed to demand deviations in his formulae. Luther's use of superlatives, too, leads further along the same line.

In propounding his doctrine, Luther's great mistake was to make a universally binding precept out of a highly personal conviction, itself the outcome of a unique process going on within the most singular personal psychological constitution imaginable.

Many details of this somewhat highlighted world of Luther's theological concepts may seem unimportant for German Reformainto history. We do not deny this.

Q

And yet – even these unimportant details, as all that we know about Luther, reveal that mental attitude which determined nothing less than the destiny of the modern world. It was not Luther who had introduced subjectivism as a universally operative power into Europe. What he did more than any other man, and in spite of his dogmatic ties, was to ensure the triumph of this power.

Subjectivism is the destruction of unity – the unity of the Church, of Christianity, of the world, and has led to the chaos of unfettered, modern life; and subjectivism split up Germany.

When we have recognised Luther's share of the blame for the fatal domination of subjectivism in modern history, we have completed half of our appraisal of his significance.

Subjectivism was no accessory to Luther's make-up but a basic element. A consequence of this, and a proof of it as well, is the fact that Luther's disposition and his work show a great number of characteristic peculiarities that are related to what is singular and personal, and alien to what is objective and universal. Together and separately they are all part of that peculiarity which we constantly encounter: Luther was no thinker but rather a man of temperament who felt things, and who was able by his words to set others on fire with his own concentrated experiences of the hour.

At the head of any exposition of these things would stand a study of Luther's power of empathy in general. It will suffice if we refer to what has been said. The striking way in which this gift, so precious to a professor and pastor, is already revealed in his inaugural lecture[19] remained unchanged in all the changing situations of the years that followed. Frequently this quality displayed a quite extraordinary capacity to hit the mark. Indeed, almost all that we still have to discuss will turn out to be an illustration of this power of empathy.

I shall begin with his polemics, which hitherto have always been taken to be the most characteristic thing in the external image of Luther.

---

[19] Preface to the lectures on the Psalms of 1513: on the way in which David, in contrast to the other prophets, described his inspiration.

When examining Luther's toleration and his opinion about the use of force in the spread of the gospel, we mentioned this vehemence. Even on this point, however, a true understanding of the confusingly rich, lively and irrational figure of Luther is attained only if we see him close up and in all his quite contradictory differentiation. In doing this it is absolutely essential to distinguish Luther's purely theoretical attitude to what he called 'antichristianity' from the sheer instinctive impulse which drove him on out of hatred and without Christian discipline, and which at least moulded his speech.

In order to exclude every possible source of error we shall first take note of whatever qualities of moderation, gentleness and humility there are to be found in Luther.

Luther made humility one of the foundations of his doctrine, to the extent that he completely annihilated man's own powers. Everything on the road to salvation, without any exception, happens by God's action alone. More than this: man remains an active sinner, even when justified. There is no room at all for any kind of reliance upon his own power. The confession of the unprofitable servant was pushed to the limit – and beyond. Selfishness in all its forms, especially in its more refined and dangerous forms, was more of less established as the essence of sin, and a renunciation of the *sensus proprius* demanded – to the point of contradictory quietism.

Luther put this into practice personally, as is proved beyond all doubt by the manner in which he wrote about this, and also by his frequently repeated profession that all glory is due to God, that all his own thinking and searching in the monastery had counted for nothing, and that God alone, through his grace, had given him enlightenment. The proof is further backed up by countless similar fervent utterances, which attribute his struggle and victory and difficulties to God alone. His admission, too, that the realisation of Reformed doctrine in life, that the striving of his followers for purity, lagged far behind the ideal, and his acceptance of a share in the blame for this discrepancy, is part of this story, for Luther expressly included himself as 'the least, and most sinful of all'.

As we have seen, the battle with Müntzer was to be carried on within the bounds set by the spirit Luther preached – the spirit of love, joy, peace, patience, kindness, goodness, faithfulness, gentleness, self-control (Ga 5:21). Even in face of rebellion the gospel is still gentle and spiritual, and must simply be preached. Luther expressly declined to have his name used to designate his followers: they were to be called Christians. 'What is Luther anyway? The doctrine is not mine. I was not crucified for anybody.' He wished also that consideration be given to the attitude and mental capacities of those to whom one preached. The gospel must not be pressed violently upon them, nor should the adherents of the old religion be rebuked in arrogance.

Until the end of his life, Luther was to be found expressing this attitude of humility, of Christian abandonment to the will of the Father. Even in one of the books that is an acute embarrassment on this score (*Against Hans Worst*) there occur such statements as these: '. . . because we truly believe that God's word is such a glorious and majestic thing, of which we are all unworthy – to think that such a mighty thing should be spoken and done by us who are mere flesh and blood!' In the same book he castigates the coarseness of Henry of Braunschweig-Wolfenbüttel, as the utterance of one possessed.

This is the true and authentic Luther. Catholics ought to know these things of which they have been so ignorant in the past. At the same time there was another equally real, perhaps more obvious, Luther. All humility has to be tested decisively by the practical expression of a man's self-assurance. How did Luther show up at this test?

If we are to avoid being unjust to Luther we must bear in mind the coarseness to which this age had become accustomed. The basic note of polemics in the sixteenth century was ridicule and destruction of one's opponent at all costs and by all available means (Eder). A dispute about ultimate problems, initiated so radically by Luther, could very easily, almost inevitably, provoke an excess of violence and acrimony.

We know Aleander's colossal reproaches against Luther: 'Arius, blackguard, basilisk, dog, Mahomet, Satan, villain, murderer, beast.' Cochlaeus, Eck, Augustine Marius and others, and not least, ecclesiastical decrees, had often used the same sort of language; and from the opposite side, too, people like Müntzer had loaded Luther with insults: 'mindless lump of flesh, raving envy, flattering scoundrel, *doctor ludibrii*, godless flesh, malicious raven, godless rogue, doctor liar, Father Pussyfoot, devil's high chancellor, sly fox'. Further splitting up within the new doctrine let loose intra-Protestant polemic of the most hateful tone. With apparent relish, each side anathematised the others as children of the devil and worthy of hell. Renewed bitterness was poured by both sides into the antinomion controversy, when it flared up afresh in 1536 (Agriocla *versus* Melanchthon–Luther).

The age was incapable of expressing itself except in vehement gestures; and it is not true that the geniuses of the day sublimated this vehemence by their greatness. With them, too, the tone often became cantankerous, petty and unbelievably coarse. Even amongst humanists of an Erasmian type the beauty of a mighty peace was known, as a rule, only in theory. When attacked they replied with great outbursts, defaming their opponents, the monks, with the most abominable, ruthless and damaging coarseness. Pirkheimer himself had composed verses in which he called for the hanging or drowning of his opponents. He did not live up to his own commendation of moderation in polemic if the least blow fell upon himself. Nor was this coarseness excused by the Catholic declaration that they ought to repay Luther in his own coin – as did Cochlaeus, Dietenberger, Paul, Bachmann and others.

Grobianus might well be taken as the patron of this age. A truly repulsive illustration of this is provided by the coarse, undignified, obscene and uncontrolled behaviour of many lords and princes, even at the height of Christianity's and the nation's battle for life at the *Reichstags*.

Luther was no exception to the general picture. For a long time he proclaimed allegiance to the principle of patient suffering under legitimate authority; and he was much displeased with Zwingli, 'the wild Swiss', for 'trying to advance the cause of Christ with Swiss crudeness'. But he himself became a master of this same crudeness. None surpassed him; indeed he surpassed the rest, and the fault was worse in him.

We have already seen enough of Luther's unbounded joy in criticism, and his arrogant assessment of his own talents in questions about eternal salvation; and we know how he would stand up and attack all the more vehemently if his adversary was a whole epoch or the whole world. In 1520 he told the pope that he hated bickering; a little later, after the bull of excommunication had been issued he wrote to Spalatin: 'My long maintained meekness is going to give out.' If we collect the mass of bold invective which Luther had hurled at Rome very shortly before the issuing of the bull of excommunication, these words do not ring true; but Luther himself did not see the contradiction; he was not lying. Once again we establish the fact that Luther was quite incapable of freeing himself from this own private images. In 1530 he was still able to represent things as though he had spread the mantle of love over the transgression of the opposing side, and to foretell that others would come, who would treat of the misdemeanours of the bishops in an unsavoury fashion. And yet in 1520 he had admitted that he 'had never sought to be considered modest or holy'. Certainly this was confirmed by his speech.

The chapter of abuses we have merely touched on reminds us first of all how justified violent indignation and ruthless attack might well be, and how such a response was almost inevitable in the case of a radical mind with deeply Christian principles. If we want to be fair to Luther we must keep this clearly and constantly in mind. Many of his destructive judgments were objectively justified. With Luther we have what might be called an objective crudeness.

This applies first to the battle against the real abuses in the Church, against those things, that is, which holy Church herself disapproves. The occasional, but not fundamental, criticisms found in the lectures on the psalms (1513–15), and especially the violent outbursts against the decadent curia in the treatise on Romans, show that Luther was in dead earnest; 'You may commit every sin, but you are still a good Christian if you uphold the rights of the Church (especially those over temporal goods). Money and power are the chief things. The leaders of the Church condemn it, but make no attempt to live Christian lives themselves. Ironically he mocks them: 'But, of course, depraved infamy, the monstrous accumulation of all manner of immorality, outward show, avarice, ambition, and sacrilege, are no sins to this whole curia.' He was deeply aware of the contrast between the present and apostolic times: 'If the prelates were worthy of all gifts, and were the worthiest of priests, they themselves would pay taxes and be subject to the authorities.' Here his criticism is all the more telling because he is able to avoid undue exaggeration: 'Not as though these rights were evil in themselves . . . , but because today they have been bestowed upon evil and godless men, who were only appointed for the sake of endowment.' Even at a time when he had long since rejected the papacy, he was able on occasion to give this same depth to his criticism: 'You must recognise your sins, which God in his strict justice has punished in these last days by those who rule you – as St Paul proclaims in 2 Th 2: God will send you teachers. . . . It is nothing but our own fault – all these things we suffer, at the hands of the pope and his crew, in our property, our body, and our soul.'

Luther was driven on from an early date by the Church's real need of reform. Gradually he came to the opinion that no individual – the pope – no group – the cardinals – but only the whole world, or rather, God himself was able to satisfy the universal need of reform. Even good shepherds could not effect improvement. The blazing wrath of God must appear; and Luther felt that he was the instrument of this avenging wrath. It was right, therefore, for him to hit hard; and he had to do so.[20]

At a very early date, in another way, Luther tried to achieve detachment in his struggle: 'I know that it is not the men who appear to oppose me who are the real originators of the shameful deeds; it is not them that I hate, but that *Behemoth*, the prince of evil who wants to use my downfall as a means of driving the truth out of his kingdom.'

That is true and important. Unfortunately it often remained pure theory, and human resentment was the thing that really counted; for Luther did not just stand looking on at the abuses, nor was he content to fight these with detachment. He attacked the system, and fulminated against people; and this he did with fierce passion. Was he right? Before we conclude that this was

[20] We must not conclude from this exposition that the abuses in the Church played a normative part in the foundation of the Reformation revolution. They may well have been normative, however, in the elaboration of Reformed doctrine, not just as a stimulus, heightening anticurial feeling, but, unfortunately, in that in important cases Luther mistook external things for the essence of the Church.

impulsive hatred and culpable distortion, let us first ask what was his basic conviction. We must keep the way open to distinguish between objective error and the hatred based upon it, and lies and mean spitefulness.

Now, initially Luther was able subjectively to provide a general justification of the acerbity of his attacks by the sheer sincerity of his Reformation revolution. This revolution was the basis of his future development, which followed logically from it. This whole development, therefore, shared proportionately in upholding that sincerity. There can be no doubt that Luther's bitter fight against all that was Catholic and Roman had its origin deep in conscientious conviction. In a very early sermon he declared: 'The heathen are those who do not want to offend anyone, but deceive people with soft words.' Taking his stand upon this conviction, he opposed all who cried out 'Peace, peace!' when he knew that their mood was nothing but careless indifference. As he preached the cross as the centre of faith, so he always had it on his conscience that one 'cannot be too hard on the wolves'.

At this point it is specially important clearly to separate subjective fancy from objective being and intention. A representative of the Counter Reformation, like Hosius, for example, provides proof of the excesses of condemnation to which purely objective and unimpassioned polemics can be driven (cf. vol. 2, p. 218). The more definitive the distinction in question, the more keenly must attention be turned to it. What is right for Hosius must be accepted in Luther also. He is constantly describing the pope and papists as Antichrist, the devil, and idolaters, but we must not fail to see that subjectively he might be in as good faith as Cardinal Hosius was, when he inflexibly denounced the Evangelicals in Christ's name, calling them children of the devil. If we take as our starting-point, that Luther was subjectively convinced in conscience, that he saw the papacy as a perversion of Christianity, then it is easier to understand why he was repeatedly carried away by such exaggerated statements. That which may be called Luther's coarseness, in the broadest sense, his revolutionary assault upon venerable traditions, carried out in a crude and contemptuous tone, was thus the product of the sincere awareness of his duty, upon the fulfilment of which depended

eternal salvation. Holy scripture asserts: 'The word of God is a
sword, is warfare, is destruction, is a stumbling block, is poison,
and like a bear in our path or a lion in the forest, it confronts the
sons of Ephraim.'

Admittedly, all we heard about Luther loudly proclaims
that he was not going to remain upon the even path of objectivity.
He was simply incapable of such behaviour. His temperament
forced him down to deeper levels.

In the early period, before his zeal had been poisoned by
public controversy, he reproached the Bohemian Picards that
they rejoiced like hypocrites over a public sinner, instead of
suffering with him. Unfortunately this type of sympathy was soon
to vanish from Luther himself, and with it, the corresponding
pastoral treatment of adversaries, whom now he castigated as
spoilers of Christianity.

Lest Evangelical readers too hastily meet the following arguments with unjustified strictures, let us recall that Catholic
short-sightedness and sensitivity was neither the first nor the
only angle from which the charge of downright crudity, of
vehement, impassioned agitation, was laid against Luther.

Melanchthon, indeed, who was saddened by the lack of restraint shown by his man of God, had sought, in his funeral oration,
to excuse it in terms of Luther's practical radicalism. This, he
said, explained the violent outbursts of the otherwise so gentle
Luther. In 1520 Peter Mosellanus saw things more clearly. He
concluded an extraordinarily favourable description of Luther
thus: 'All accuse him of the one failing: his scolding is too vehement and too biting for one who is trying to open up new paths in
theology, and it is unbecoming in one learned in divinity.' Chancellor Bruch described it in plainer terms as 'the blustering spirit of
Doctor Martin', or as his 'twelve pound axe manner', and he said
that 'in addition, by God's grace, he possessed a greater spirit
than other men'. Capito attributed a great part of the terrible
decadence of Christianity in the Reformation to Luther's hasty
impulse and ill-considered vehemence.

None of this will surprise him who knows to what depths of
unrestrained hatred the various trends within Protestantism
went in mutual denunciation, in Luther's own lifetime, and even

more after his death. Outbursts of this sort could fill a whole litany of desperate abuse, the quintessential refrain of which is the phrase 'children of the devil'. This started off with Luther's hatred, not only of the fanatics but of Zwingli, who was to be avoided like a plague of Satan's own invention, and whose writings were more poisonous than a viper, and whose book had been fathered by the devil himself, who was raging against Luther.

This was the tone of the dispute between rivals, and later between their imitators of the next generation. Osiander made a straightforward comparison between the pliable Melanchthon and Judas Iscariot. For his part, Osiander was laden with a flood of abuse: heretics, Antichrist, Jew, black devil, dragon, base fellow, criminal, enemy of Christ. In the guise of two dogs, two devils followed his every step. Those who as much as listened to him ought to be excommunicated and refused Christian burial.

As Luther attacked those who disagreed with him, so his opponents, Butzer, Oecolampadius and the Zürich men, for example, revolted against Luther's unbearable arrogance. Protestants as much as Catholics were up in arms against the *detractationes* in Luther's translation of the Bible.

This provided a foil for Luther's fulminations against the pope's Church. We have remarked that with him, exaggerated criticism was the expression of a universal characteristic. As a young *sententiarius*, how he had swooped down upon Wimpfeling. When still a young man he had written Aristotle off completely. Later he turned him into the *archistultilis* and the *archstultus*. In 1515 in his opening sermon at the general assembly of Augustinians at Gotha under the presidency of Staupitz, he let loose without restraint against the gossip of the 'little saints', in the course of which he resorted to the crudest comparisons.

In 1520 he directed a violent and bold diatribe against Prierias, master of the papal palace. 'The best medicine to stop your raving madness, would be for emperor, kings and princes to arm and make an end of the game, using weapons, not words . . ., and to wash our hands in your blood, so as to save ourselves and our posterity from eternal fire.'

Here are severe prophetic words from a passage written in

1521, but without base emotion: 'Listen to this O your unholiness the pope! God will destroy your chair directly from heaven and fling it down to the depth of hell. Who gave you the power to exalt yourself above God, to break and loose what he has commanded (dispensation from vows and oaths), and to teach Christians to be inconstant, perjurers, betrayers, villains and faithless, especially the German nation, who have been extolled throughout their whole history for their constancy and loyalty, for the nobility of their nature?'

All of this is highly significant in respect of Luther's self-assumed defiance, that ran so dangerously close to presumption; but a much greater weakness was his indelicate, rough and hate-filled tone, his passion, which destroyed respect and love, bred personal hatred, and damaged all that was pure and fine in religion. The essence of his fault was the unrestraint which turned his criticism into an emotional explosion, born of hatred. The end of it all was an avid self-indulgence in insults and even in coarse and obscene imagery – made much worse by the sacredness of the immediate context.

Detailed proof of this damaging emotional quality is abundantly provided by Luther's own works. After the Leipzig disputation he lost his temper with a poor Franciscan, and gave vent to common rudeness, saying that his doctrine was now 'being tried in the fires of their miserable little order, and damned as heretical by a couple of snoring brothers who probably had never seen a doctor of theology more than once in their lives'. In 1520 he wrote vehemently to Spalatin saying: 'I tell you again that I have never feared anyone, and have never tried to write what would please people.' At the recording of the admonition to the clergy at the *Reichstag* in Augsburg in 1530 he himself testified how his gorge rose and he had great difficulty in suppressing the ruffian in him. His unimaginably arrogant affirmations to Melanchthon, from the Coburg, accompanied as they were by protestations of sheer devotion to the cause, and his repeated rejection – in the filthiest language – of curial attempts at reconciliation, all make painful reading. It was as though he were violently unburdening himself of some terrible inner torment.

In 1532 he wrote a pamphlet against Duke George of Saxony, giving it the title *Against the Traitor of Dresden*. In 1522 he had already written defiantly against this Catholic prince (in his letter to the electors before leaving the Wartburg). In 1531 he stuck to his attitude of cursing and vituperation, in spite of the conciliatory deliberations at Grimma. 'We'll see, then, if I won't fight for it with my neck: let them come!'

Over and over again his love of superlatives ran away with him. In the crudest possible manner, every shred of goodness was torn from the pope's Church. Imperiously and in rage he threw himself into a frenzy of assault and rabble rousing.

Step by step he inveighed against monks and his own monastic past, until he reached a veritable climax of fury. In harmony with this mood, he affirmed that he himself had changed so much since the days of his monastic captivity, that when he now beheld a monk he saw a monstrosity. This avowal betrays the unreliability of the retrospective reports of his monastic period.

Luther's hatred was nowhere so great as in his denunciation of the papacy and its bulwark, the mass. His theoretical condemnation is not what is most significant but the way he heaps insult upon insult, multiplies crude images, and indulges in quite unrestrained presumption, mixing up the most sacred things with utter profanity. Along with *Wider Hans Worst*, the well-known slanderous images of the papacy form the high point in this vehemence. And Luther expressly claimed all this as his very own: this deluge of vulgarity he regarded as his testament. Nothing is gained by labelling these absurdities as 'the fitting expression of the agitated popular mood' or by excusing these 'obscene pictures' as 'the malicious fantasies of an old fool'. These images were indeed a scandal in the history of Protestantism, as the adulteries of Alexander VI were a scandal of Catholic history. There is only one possible course open to us: to turn our backs for ever upon such scandals.

Before investigating the inner motive power of this coarseness, we ought to recall one important thing: in his severe indictments of the Church Luther had produced a hopelessly inadequate description of Catholicism. It is quite shattering to see how blind he had become to all that was Catholic, and how he had pushed to absurdity his concept of the Church as the idolatry of Antichrist. Without a qualm he was able to identify the sum total of outrageous corruptions with the reality of the Church. In a purely theoretical disputation by letter with Melanchthon, when he had no personal adversary, and with no papist in sight, he described the substance of Catholic vows thus: 'Behold, O God, I vow to be unfaithful to you and to commit idolatry all my life long. . . . Such people clearly make vows not to the living God, but to their own lies and to the idols in their hearts.' The portrayal in *Wider Hans Worst* of the Catholic veneration of saints is the work of a sheer amateur.

In the past insufficient attention has been paid to the fact that concerning confession and penance, Luther concentrated entirely upon those aberrations which made them appear as 'human works'. On confession: 'You have told us nothing of the consolation of absolution . . . which strengthens faith and trust in Christ.' On penance: 'You have never paid so much heed to contrition and confession' (as to satisfaction through your own works). 'You must make satisfaction for your sins, that is, you must deny Christ, revoke your baptism, blaspheme the gospel, give the lie to God, cease believing in the forgiveness of sins, trample Christ's blood under foot, dishonour the Holy Spirit, in order to gain heaven by such virtues of your own. How can a soul do anything other than despair, when it learns that all its consolation in face of sin lies in its own works? How utterly nonsensical these words must appear even to the most merit-conscious Catholic.

'The man who can tell Christ that he is an heretic, and that his doctrine is of the devil, not knowing that Christ whom he blasphemes is Lord and God, is possessed not by seven but by seventy-seven, devils. This is precisely what the pope's Church does – deliberately and maliciously.'

Such blindness to the true nature of Catholicism was responsible also for failure to recognise the honest efforts at reform which were being made by their opponents within the old Church. His comments upon the famous 1538 reform bill of the cardinals, to whom he immediately denied any serious intention of reform, were sheer distortion. Destructive criticism had already become second nature of Luther. Were that not so he could never have recorded so casually the colossal misrepresentation, that the papal supporters themselves noted with chagrin how 'the pope would rather see all of Christendom lost and all souls damned, than reform himself or his cronies in the least degree'.

To a public, who in fact knew better, Luther asserted flatly that the ultimate *raison d'être* of monasticism was hatred of liberal science and scholarship. His criticisms of Catholic piety in *To the Christian Nobility*, are completely taken up with externals. His descriptions of Catholic pilgrimages in the admonition of 1530 depended essentially upon exaggeration. This admonition in general supplies a whole series of illustrations of our thesis. The basic falsity of the description of his own monastic life and of the official direction on prayer, fasting and humility, given him in his convent, is as well known as it is disconcerting in its radical contradiction of demonstrable reality.

For very good reasons we do not follow Denifle and say that all of this was lies. None the less it is shattering to see how most of the world at that time, including educated people, fell under the spell of the eloquence of this mighty wizard. They had such a poor grip of their Catholicism, were so confused and uncertain, that they seemed to forget one day what they had practised and revered as sacred the day before. In other words, the victory of the Luther legend was uncanny in its completeness. Ever and again Luther's voice was raised to guarantee the truth of his assertions that Catholicism was an infamous humanisation of the pure Word: 'I went to school with them myself; I learned these things; I was brought up in that way.' There was no end to this sort of tirade, and to the most nonsensical generalisations.

Murner felt the injustice of Luther's victory, won in this manner. According to the Reformers, Catholic teachers have 'spun a web of fables; all they have ever said was sheer invention; they have led Christendom astray . . .'. The fact that Murner fell into the same error ('anyone who can tell lies is sure to attract an applauding audience', 1522) only proves how decayed public utterance had become, but does not contradict Murner's original assertion.

This fact compels Reformation study, compels Protestantism, indeed, to make a serious decision. There can be no doubt that Luther's victory depended in great measure, upon his successful portrayal of the papacy as the counterpart of the pure Word. Even such deep and positive religious powers as Luther's can change great masses of people in such a short time only when assisted by emotion and hatred. This emotion was not released by theoretical criticism but by the exaggeration of abuses to the point of distortion of reality, a distortion which represented the whole state of affairs in the Church as one great affront to the people who blindly followed their self-seeking, mendacious leaders, the priests.

In fact, this fundamentally distorting Luther legend has dominated almost the whole Protestant mind down to Otto Scheel in our own century. Nor is it true, unfortunately, that the abandonment of Scheel's ideas has exercised a purifying influence upon the general Protestant mind to any great extent. On the other hand, it is certainly not true that the Luther legend was first created by Melanchthon. It originated with Luther himself – not just in the *Table Talk* but in his authentic, deliberate, printed works. Thus, if Luther's own progress, and the conversion to him of large sections of the people, rest upon essentially false presuppositions, then this error must be made good. That means at least that false portrayals of Luther must cease to appear in literature; and it also means that that which Luther and his followers attacked or rejected as Catholicism, in many ways was not the Catholic faith at all. And so the highest ideals of the two confessions in many points do not possess that exclusive antagonism to each other, with which Luther's faulty representation endowed them.

The deepest impulse which urged Luther on to exaggeration was pride in various forms, beginning with the early self-assurance, which we have already noted, and developing into a mystical sense of mission, both attributes lacking indispensable Christian safeguards.

Inward freedom preceded pride. It was not as a freedom-hungry revolutionary that Luther had learned and taught the great and fundamental concept of Christian freedom. He came to it, rather, from being a slave of duty and obedience. Unfortunately, therefore, his discovery was one-sided. In this, however, he satisfied his own deep need for utter independence, for the freedom of his own judgment. This deep need had been ever present, since his first ruthless and self-assured critique of Aristotle and the scholastics – a consequence of his own scrupulous nature, which allowed him to accept none but his own judgment.

In this the revolutionary is not far to seek: 'For my part they may have been holy and full of pious zeal (those who created the impediments to marriage), but why should the sanctity of others curb my freedom? Let who will be a holy fanatic, but he is not going to lay a finger on my freedom.'

This need for spiritual freedom was the basic feature of Luther's nature. It manifested itself throughout his whole life, often in a most uncomfortable fashion, in his utter independence of those who were his closest collaborators: Melanchthon, Bugenhagen, Jonas, Spalatin, Kate, the electors. How many close ties were there, and yet there is no evidence that he ever became trammelled by any of them. Above all, in large issues and battles, he preserved an almost absolute independence. The classic example is probably Augsburg–Coburg in 1530, when he was so truculent with his friends in Augsburg, leaving them in no doubt that if occasion demanded, he would go his own way entirely.

He maintained the same attitude towards the rulers. He had no time for their all too zealous interference. Multiplication of laws must cease; divine law plus natural prudence on the part of the rulers was enough to direct the people.

Luther was never at peace. It may have annoyed him a bit, when people said that he 'was only writing part songs and German sermons for the uneducated laity', but he knew how to reply: 'If I thought that I would accomplish more by it, I would gladly write weighty volumes, instead of popular sermons.' He was roused by other things entirely.

First of all there was that most important spiritual independence, absolutely necessary for the enlivenment of religious life, and which sought to read texts and see things in a completely fresh light; but in addition he was soon suffering also from insolent pride. In 1517 he had already stated explicitly: 'Who knows, perhaps nothing new has ever been produced without the aid of pride or at least the appearance of pride. They will not find that sort of humility in me (hypocrisy) which expects me to ask their advice and opinion before I publish anything.' Apparently at this time he had only the scholastics in mind; but a significant development followed, which betrayed his secret tendency: 'My work is the product not of human judgment and cleverness but of God's wisdom. If the work is of God, who can obstruct it?'

For the first time he signed himself 'Martin Eleutherius' – 'Martin the Free'.

This goes far beyond his mighty rejection of the 'generation of vipers', of the 'masked faces', and the 'theologians',[21] or, as he was to express it in 1522, of the 'lying tongues, corrupters, poisoners, the pope, Eck, Emser, various bishops, priests and monks. . . . Leave the dogs and swine alone (Mt 7 : 6).'

Luther's self-assurance became so imperious and impatient, that it pressed far too much into the foreground, and became utterly revolutionary. It is something to be able, in one breath, to affirm, that one is certain, by God's grace, that the scriptures surpass all the learning of sophists, and papists, and that: 'Hitherto God has graciously preserved me from pride and will continue to do so' (1524). Just before this at Worms he had seen his courage in a true light: 'How weak and poor I was then; had I known that as many devils had their eyes on me as there are slates on the roofs of Worms, still I would have gone there.'

When Butzer visited Luther at the Coburg in 1530, he was specially struck by Luther's stubbornness. He sought the glory of God with all his heart, but he refused to budge from his preconceived path. The more people warned and reproached him, the more petulant he became. 'This is the way the Lord has sent him to us: we must accept him as he is.'

When the discussions in Augsburg were in progress, Luther himself was convinced that not only had he supported the cause of God but had guided it so neatly that no one would have to forgive him for anything – 'as long as Christ and I remain one.'

From 1517 onwards (even from the sermon at Gotha in 1515) we find this identification of his own concerns with the cause of God. The letters, written in the critical years of 1518, 1519, 1520 and 1521, are full of this identification. With an astonishing self-evidence, in the most complicated and confused situations, he saw that his plans came straight from God, that it was Christ who directed his cause, which otherwise had long since collapsed at every step since the indulgence theses. He believed implicitly that God was drawing on him, was, indeed, driving him on, that he could do nothing better under God, than make issue with the Roman sophists and flatterers; and if the Wittenberg students

[21] Inaugural sermon at Gotha 1515.

revolted, that was an intervention of the devil, who threatened his work and was breaking into the midst of the children of God in Wittenberg. After receiving the bull of excommunication in 1520, he announced: 'God's cause is hidden, it lies within the spirit. In its own time it will recognise who has rejected and perse-cuted it.' In the same year he wrote to Staupitz: 'This is not the time to quake, because men are blaspheming our Lord Jesus Christ. You are too humble, and I am too proud. If until now it has been fitting to keep quiet and be humble . . .'

Luther's claim to be the first to rediscover true Christianity, must be seen as absolutely serious. He was not being rhetorical, but literal, when he told his father that hitherto no one had known that we are bound by nothing except the law of God. In 1535 in Wittenberg, at a common table with Bugenhagen and the invited papal legate Vergerio, who was seeking a council, he made the astonishing remark: 'By the Holy Spirit we are certain about the whole affair, and need no council; but Christendom needs to know the errors in which it has wallowed for so long.' 'I will come to the council all the same, and I will lose my head there if I defend my propositions against the whole world. That which pro-ceeds from my mouth is not my own anger, but the wrath of God.'

Throughout all the ups and downs of his restless life, he main-tained this sense of 'his gospel' in such strength that in 1542 he was able to assert that he needed no notary to make his last will and testament, for he was 'Doctor Martin Luther, God's notary and witness in his gospel, known in heaven, on earth, and in hell'. God had entrusted the gospel of his blessed Son to him, and made him faithful and true in the discharge of his commission, so that many 'in the world regarded him as a teacher of the truth . . . despite the rage of all the devils'.

Amidst all the seething rage of 1518–19, with all his nervous agitation, at times Luther reached a positively repulsive pitch of arrogance (e.g. his threatening letter to the poor Franciscans of Jüterborg). In the less acid outbursts of later years, too, there was a presumption that was most unwholesome.

In saying this we do not deny that the Luther who spoke with such arrogance and put himself so much in the foreground lived deeply in the reality of God, and worked and strove for him. It is something that he should have thought that perhaps the recognition of his work through a legacy of 150 gulden indicated that God meant to requite him for his labours in this life rather than in the next.

It is quite inadequate, as well as unjust, simply to write off all of Luther's exaggerations and outbursts of fury as religious and moral blemishes. Some, in spite of their agitated and immoderate style, are a moving expression of prophetic indignation. At the beginning of the process, that is when the incomprehensible fact that the Church, in practice and in theory had no place in his ideas, was slowly disclosing itself to Luther, these were frequent. We must not lose sight of the positive elements in Luther's trust in God. In another context, we have sufficiently expounded this. Nor may we forget his ruthless and severe attachment to his own conscience, nor his frankness. He often stated that he had conquered only by the power of God. 'How mightily the gospel advances, despite the raging of pope and emperor: I have taken up no sword, and exacted no revenge; but have taken God completely to my heart.'

A highly developed self-assurance is required to preserve unharmed the attitude of humility. The sense of mission is, for the one called, first of all both power and obligation. A daring trust in the immanent power of truth has always been one of the great energies of history, even of Christianity. The powerful and moving synthesis of humility and enormous self-confidence, with its attendant burden of responsibility, in St Paul, as in Gregory VII, demonstrates this in a most instructive way.

In Luther's case, we are repeatedly struck by the self-assurance which his words express. It is the self-assurance of greatness. We think of the way he equated his own cause unhesitatingly with God's cause, regarding himself, like Jeremiah (Chaps. 7 and 15) as under God's orders, no longer to pray for these papists; of the unconcern with which ever and again he disregarded the threat of riots and death: 'No one can harm me'; of the noisy, violence with which he announced his defiance: 'The worse they make things, the worse I will become . . ., the harder-headed they are, the harder will I be. They will not terrify me or make me weaken; I will terrify them. I will remain; they will collapse. My life will be their hangman; my death their devil. That is the way it will be; and they will know it. They may well laugh!' At the end of his life, when Luther surveyed the course of the Reformation, once again he believed that he saw the mystery of iniquity at work in world history. He saw all of the mighty opponents of his doctrine as fresh and powerful threats of the devil. On the other hand, in face of all doubts about his cause, coming from without or, even more, from within, he preserved his ready and never failing certainty. All of his adversaries – pope, bishops, *Reichstag*, a concourse of Catholic champions, his own physical weariness, his depression, inability to read, write or pray, his anxieties in the morning or in the evening, the battle for the confession at Augsburg, the unchristian dispute of the dukes of Mansfeld, Zwingli's opposition and programme – were simply instruments of Satan. And he was equally sure that all of these burdens were a heap of lies and injustice. Thus, belief in his cause remained serene, his confidence always unshaken, in contrast to the more conscientious uncertainty of many of his collaborators.

Luther was aware of the resistance he put up to all this 'gang', whom he defeated. He knew his power; but it was God's power: 'It was God, who constantly protected his flickering lantern and prevented it from going out.' 'It is not we, who are able to preserve the Church, nor was it our forefathers, nor will it be our posterity. It is he, who was and is and shall be, who said: I am with you until the end of the world.' The final word he wrote – in true Lutheran style – is a moving formulation of humility as the essence of being a Christian: 'The truth is, we are beggars.'

With the passage of time, Luther's years of utter despair in the monastery began to assume a more theoretical form, and became united with a strongly bourgeois concept of life, the foundation of which is found in Luther's theology of consolation. But the despair did not disappear. In the form of the theology of the cross, of faith's uncertainty of salvation, it remained with him all his life, in closest companionship with his immovable self-assurance. The man must have possessed enormous vitality, to be able to bear this antithesis .'Bear' is the right word, for he did not synthesise the two things.

Herein, however, would be found the whole answer, for such a synthesis is always the most difficult thing of all to accomplish. It becomes the test of ultimate genius, that is of sanctity, when gigantic powers of mind and soul become active in the process of redemption – in proclaiming redemption. Luther's work was the product of immense forces. Since 1521 he had known (in the aftermath of Worms) the dangerous formula: 'it has been revealed to me'. Nothing less than heroic humility could have guaranteed the required synthesis.

Unfortunately Luther did not even succeed to a sufficient degree in applying the theoretical humility of his system so as to ensure the attitude of basic humility in his own personality. In him, heroic, that is saintly, constant humility was lacking – as was sanctity in general. What there was of humility in Luther, did not permeate his whole life. Most of all, it failed to remove from his self-assurance that element which would have to go, before the required synthesis could be reached: the element of self-centred imperiousness. His trust in the immanent power of truth was so unbounded, his 'radiant certainty of salvation turned him into such a presumptuous hero', his 'effervescent zest at being a warrior of God', were so strong, his spiritual independence of tradition and of any court of appeal outside of himself, was so extreme, that he reached a dangerous abandon in destroying, a foolhardy boldness, presumption and audacity. This general attitude reached the height of arrogance in *Wider Hans Worst*.

This was no battle over human things, but over immutable revelation. Luther himself stressed this over and over again. This proved Luther's earnestness and commitment, but it also was to prove a mighty burden as a result of that colossal pugnacity, which made him seek to annihilate the 1,400-year-old tradition of the universal Church.

Our concluding verdict on the juxtaposition in Luther of humility and self-assurance can only be, that the fine line of demarcation separating mighty zeal for the house of God from belligerent contention for the rightness of one's own viewpoint, and separating trust in the heavenly Father from presumption, was absent in Luther from an early stage in his development, and that the two attitudes often clashed in inflammatory contradiction. Even utterances of profoundly religious humility, such as Luther often voiced, were not enough to close these gaps.

Luther bore a final and very special burden: his brash readiness to accept responsibility, which verged on irresponsibility, on account of its latent boundlessness. This expressed itself in the most sacred areas of life, and gave rise to the reaction into naturalism and secularisation, which we have already mentioned.

On this topic, the first thing to be mentioned would be the foolhardy boldness of the too negatively understood *pecca fortiter*.

This spirit, by its unbridled impulse all unintentionally removes the horror from sin, and, working directly counter to its own conviction, represents it as not so evil after all: 'Often Luther speaks as though abstinence from the works of the flesh were not a good thing, but rather rebellion against God's will and law' (Paulsen).

For Christianity, trust is as indispensable as holy fear. None demanded this more strongly than Luther; but whenever one element is overstressed, the other is endangered. According to the situation, Luther stressed now one, now the other, and often tore them asunder. Now an overstress on reasoned trust damaged fear. Certainty of salvation destroyed uncertainty. Luther was not logical in the development of his theory of the uncertainty of salvation. In practice, his behaviour often displayed such impudent presumption that it threatened to obscure the *tremendum* before the deity, rejected all uncertainty as the devil's work, and represented man as a jolly, defiant hero in the face of God. 'What of it then, if we commit fresh sin!'

Luther was not always happy, by any means, in striking the enormously difficult balance between frankness and delicacy. In the later Luther we do, indeed, find a wealth of humility of faith in the sole sovereignty of redemptive grace amidst the impotence of the sinful will. This humility is fundamental. To fulfil its function perfectly, however, it has to be embodied in a lively sentiment and practically portrayed, as it was in the young and struggling Luther. Of the older Luther we often gain the impression that he had settled down in complacency. He seemed to have become much more strongly ruled by the certainty of having once and for all won the victory, of having gained a position centred upon the certainty of salvation. The 'cheerful defiance of the hero' has its attractions. It is not the same sort of thing as the relaxed joy of a St Francis or a Philip Neri. The certainty of the older Luther was too often stripped of the ever-renewed striving to grow more deeply into God.

At the heart of piety is the sense of standing before God, the practical recognition of the absolutely superior, of the wholly other. In devout people this gives rise to the virtue of humility, which is by no means the same thing as impotence. It is essentially characterised, however, by a certain awe before the holy. Piety must be a reflection of the objectively holy, of the unapproachable. It is not permitted to lay profane hands on the holy. At this point description and evaluation of Luther becomes most difficult, for Luther mixes the sacred with the profane, not so as to sanctify every-day things, but rather so as to tarnish the brightness of religion. In a sense the devout man will always stand before the holy with eyes downcast. If he does raise his eyes, his strength and boldness must be the strength of God, and must be utterly joined with radical humility.

We have already cited *Wider Hans Worst* as the supreme example of crudeness. His revelling in abuse and in subumbilical imagery reaches an absurdity of immoderation. Luther's craze for exaggeration, his frequent lack of sober judgment and of balance are particularly crudely exemplified in this work. He was the slave of spiritual agitation and emotion. As an exponent of coarseness Luther was not master of his own moods. In fact, he was ruled by his emotions.

Not only did Luther pour out a stream of coarseness; he did so quite unconcerned and in the context of the most sacred discussions. He speaks in the one breath of our Lord's Redemption, of whores, liars, fools, drunkards and all manner of low life. The whole thing is an enigma. He displays a stupendous vitality, which each may assess according to his taste. Certainly he possessed an unusual, if coarse, forthrightness. This, however, did not increase but lessened the element of religious refinement.

This impression is heightened if we place Luther in company with the great saints. None of these exhibits this intolerable juxtaposition or intermingling of the sacred and the base.

In exoneration of Luther, people have pointed to certain crudities in the story of revelation, and its development in the Old Testament. The prophets (to whom Luther appeals) use coarse imagery, it is true, but on what a different plane! The image of the harlotries of the chosen people may be blunt, but the religious environment turns it into an effective warning example. If we read the prophet Hosea along with *Wider Hans Worst* we can seek in vain in the prophetic text for the unrestrained cursing, railing and lewdness, to which Luther has accustomed us.

Letting one's life be directed by passion, however, is the really sinful thing, is the antithesis to sonship of God through the Spirit in the kingdom of the Logos.

There are things which may properly be thought in private, but which ought not to be publicly declared, because of the danger of giving scandal. Luther was unable to maintain this distinction, but went far beyond the bounds set by prudence. It is true that this revealed a notable frankness, but such frankness is a virtue only when concerned with private opinions that are kept in their proper place.

Once again we encounter a deep contradiction in Luther. His theory of the lie of expediency, that is so often pointed out, depends upon the distinction between what does and what does not harm our neighbour. We may well ask: where is this caution to be found applied in the many examples of Luther's unbridled naturalistic utterances?

As the restorer of the true gospel, which he claimed to be, Luther ought to have been so bound by the spirit of this religion, that he never once damaged it. The colossal zeal of St Paul should have been his model. The word of God is a sword, and in that sense is not peace; and yet it does bring peace. Luther brought no peace. He smashed up unity. He harboured and spread passionate hatred. Many writers have stressed this fact, and pointed out the revolutionary disturbance arising from it. There are few, however, who have felt, as Murner did, the deep contradiction there was to the essence of the gospel, and under-lined, as he did, Luther's faulty picture of the Catholic view of the gospel. Murner spoke of 'the word of eternal life that Christ has given us out of love,' and he complained:

The holy gospel – what a happy story,
Wonderfully revealed by God – peace come down from heaven;
Now they have poisoned it – murder and bitterness in their hearts.
What was ordained for joy – now brings sorrow of heart.

Even the Turks could not have 'destroyed our sanctity as it has now been wasted away for us within Christendom'.

Obviously it is possible to become so enthusiastic over Luther's destructive power that we fail to see his enormous hatred and violent pride.

Luther himself went so far as to assert that in the midst of bitter and acrimonious polemics he had taken himself in hand and restrained his emotions. This is blindness. Nothing is a greater hindrance today to profitable appreciation of Luther's actions and aspirations, than this blindness. To fail to see the destructiveness of Luther we must first of all shut our ears to the Sermon on the Mount, which extols that meekness, which Luther praised so often, but failed to practice. 'Blessed are the meek.'

The character of any force is determined, not only by what it is but by the direction in which it is moving. The epoch of the young Luther was great – even setting aside the dogmatic issues – because it proved itself through adversities and won for itself a new level of existence by the daring of a revolution.

Luther, however, was unable to maintain this high level of subjective endeavour. This is shown by a certain resting at ease in the once achieved certainty of salvation. As Luther grew older, religious restlessness in God's sight became less and less. The change over from the Christianity of the little band of faithful, of the true Christian congregation, to the territorial Church of the princes' Reformation, cannot be described as an advance. This change was accompanied by a hardening, expressed in growing intolerance. In contrast to Karlstadt, Luther, in 1520 did not want to abolish the mass by force (cf. above, p. 349); in 1525 he denounced the mass to the rulers, as punishable idolatry. The important communications to the Augsburg *Reichstag* of 1530 and the Schmalkald Articles are very poor stuff, theologically; and his refutation of the doctrine of the Church is also extraordinarily weak. The pointed and genuine aphorisms of the one-time vigorous man of God became fewer and fewer.

As we have said, the youthful, heroic storm, turned more and more into sated and habitual self-assurance, to hardened hatred against the Church, and blindness to his own past. There is no evidence of a compensating increase in striving for a life of prayer or for moral perfection.

And it is the coarseness of which we have just spoken, that shows this downward trend most clearly. *Wider Hans Worst* and the lampoons of the papacy were produced towards the end of his life.

Reading Luther's lectures, we are repeatedly moved by the hidden power of his words. Wherein lay the mystery of their effectiveness?

The primary power of any movement lies in the self-confidence it has shown in its own purpose and in its capacity to accomplish that purpose. For Luther, the purpose was the most sublime purpose possible: to restore the allegedly corrupted pure word of revelation. His sense of power grew, through his own particular endowments, and also through the flood of his creativeness, and the visible results of his activity. There emerged also a curious sense of community between himself and the nation, all those, at least in Germany, who felt themselves oppressed in body and soul by the pope.

In one sense this grasping and activating of the historical moment might be said to indicate a kind of sense of history in Luther; in another sense, however, this sense was lacking. For him, Christianity was a fixed entity, given once and for all in its entirety, incapable of any kind of development in the course of the centuries. According to Luther, any other view implied a diminution of the sole majesty of God, and a falsification of human existence. The whole foundation of the history of salvation, in fact, is that human existence since our first parents has been annihilated at its roots by ever-present sin. This is what gives the thing we call Christianity its robustness and inviolability, so powerfully expressed by Luther; at the same time, however, it damages the most basic laws of life – the potential for organic development – so seriously, that the very inviolability is in danger from an inevitable reaction. Luther would exclude the richest energies inherent in the people, energies which could incarnate the Word naturally in a temporal organic process of growth. What was left was a one-sided process, which was bound to take revenge upon itself through atrophy and violent recoil into its opposite, and which found expression in the loss of popular religious practice, even the loss of a more active sort of religious life in broad sections of Protestantism itself.

The ultimate mystery of Luther's effectiveness was his own vitality.

His work was devoid of any trace of dullness. This liveliness was displayed in the most unexpected ancillary activities. We are astonished to discover Luther, the theologian and monk, a man apparently preoccupied with spiritual and theological issues, giving the most pertinent instructions on economic and administrative affairs in 1516, when he was given the job of district monastic administrator. How perceptive was his judgment of the prior of Neustadt whom he deposed; how solicitously he brought back a brother who had gone astray in Mainz; how remarkably he harmonised objective penal power and its exercise with his own sinfulness: 'On earth we are always having to punish sinners who are better than ourselves. . . . Therefore, in our hearts, we must preserve humility and kindness towards them, although officially our hands treat them with severity, because the office is not ours, but God's.'

We know what Luther's accent was in his own special sphere of theology and pastoral work. His polemic was brisk and versatile, never very solid, but impudent to the point of arrogance. With unerring instinct for what would produce the desired effect he even published Catholic attacks upon himself, providing them with comments, prefaces and epilogues. He made fun of his opponents, and outwitted them by his retorts before ever they could speak a word. He was fearless and loved to utter self-assured threats. He replied to Alfeld, saying that his words should be taken to heart even by the mighty standard bearers who were afraid to declare themselves. The climax of this sort of thing was his literary output of 1520, animated by colossal aggression, and best expressed, perhaps, in the defiant ending to *The Babylonian Captivity*: 'Let this attack, then, form part of my recantation.'

In order to understand the enormous success of Luther's polemic we do not have to extract the theoretical essence of his ideas. We must, rather, see his polemic as a living whole – its form, its accent and its consummate mastery of particular situations. At times Luther's irony became cumbersome, but the speaker was always in command of the situation. His refutations of important topics often depended upon arbitrary interpretations of what his opponent was saying, or upon the isolation of parts of what his opponent expounded. All this, however, produced an effect. He faced up to his adversary; with wit and cunning he won the laughter over to his own side; and those whom he made laugh were embittered in any case, quite apart from any stimulus provided by Luther. These, then, were all ready for a victorious attack upon Rome.

The most important thing of all is this: Luther seldom appeared on the defensive; he always called the tune, even when he did have to defend himself. He never went so far after his adversary that he had to step on to his ground. His sheer individualism helped him to stay on his own ground, so that all of his replies were vehicles for his own ideas. The ultimate explanation of this lies in the new construction with which he was necessarily preoccupied after his radical rejection of the authority of the old Church. This constantly prevented him resting in mere refutation. It is true, he ridiculed: 'I am being taught every day, for many distinguished masters heap their attention upon me. . . . I can see that they have plenty of time and paper, and so I will see to it that they find plenty to write about . . .' Then follows a declaration that is a most significant indication of the way things were going: 'But I will forge ahead, so that while these renowned champions are rejoicing over the destruction of one of my heresies, I will produce a new one.'

Luther produced an effect, too, by the speed of his production. His incredible, effortless capacity for work, and the creative tension of mind, which never left him in his great years, annihilated the slowness and dullness of his adversaries, of Prierias, for example, who spoke of writing a mighty treatise against Luther, but who never got it finished. In March 1520 he printed his reply to the condemnations of his theses by the universities of Cologne and Louvain, when these had only just appeared.

Cochlaeus complained that the Reformers wrote with so little attention to any system, that they poured out their statements in an uncontrolled stream, without paragraphs or order. He would have preferred to read treatises, to discuss with theologians of a

different stamp from Luther. But even such contempt turned to
the advantage of the Reformers. Luther had an argument with
Emser on this point; and he knew to whom he could turn for
support – to the common people. He poured scorn on his literary
opponents and all the while exploited them fully.

Luther was essentially an attacker. Even the attacks he suffered
from his opponents helped to drive him forwards. We have
already seen how Eck's assaults in Leipzig gave him a real push
forwards. It has been very properly observed that 'in Luther's
incontrovertible living certainty, ecclesiastical authoritarian
opposition was the most significant factor of all'. We may well
ask whether Luther would have ever become the founder of a
Church without his opponents. For his own part Luther was
talkative enough, but not fitted for purely scientific writing.
Important parts of his doctrine were hammered out only as a
result of conflict with others. On this question, the expediency or
otherwise of the manner of the Roman process, and of the style
of his literary opponents, is of the highest importance.

Life is found only where there is something fresh and new.
All created things, however, must wilt. This is true even of the
forms in which the word of God makes known to us God's never-
changing revelation. In response to this revelation the Church
must constantly realise the saying: 'Behold, I make all things new.'

No wonder, then, that the Christianity of the late Middle
Ages had become worn out, in the sense indicated. The formulae
had been used over and over again and become worn out; or
new ones had been invented, based not upon the word of God
itself but derived from formulae already at one remove from scripture. These sounded alien to the heart of the word of the Bible and
of the liturgy – curious, complicated, sterile.

As no other had done, Luther sensed this deeply. He felt
it with rising anger, all the more so because in great part these
were the formulae that had led him on into that painful process of
attrition, in which a solution was always denied him. The secret
of his success lay in his being able to break through this sterile,
outmoded, broken up conceptual language, and strike down
afresh to the roots of the gospel. He made things new; he spoke
a new language.

It was not just the external, formal aspect of his language

that was new; he rediscovered the life behind concepts – the reality of the Father and of the Crucified. In a significant, intimate and direct fashion, without the aid of philosophical restriction, he discovered Christ as the meaning and end of the whole of scripture. The complete reversal in the contents of Luther's mind was this: formerly he had been seeking the God of grace by various detours, through general experiences and theoretical reflections, through, for example, the concept of 'God', the notion of 'becoming sinless', the idea of 'God as judge' or at least of 'Christ the judge'; now – since the Reformation resolution – the historical event of the crucified God-man stood at the centre of his life, and this he preached and lived. In an heretical way he had discovered the central treasure of Catholicism.

Luther's excitability and scrupulosity betrayed a most unstable conscience. It is a fact also, however, that he was able to accomplish great things in the scientific and pastoral spheres. By this he gave ample proof of his mental health. That is to say: Luther was psychologically robust enough to endure years of assault by dark and dangerous forces, and to come out on top. He gave evidence of genius. Therein lay another important power of his words: his words were the expression of a gigantic recoil and eruption. By his struggles Luther's mind and soul had suffered years of compression. Even allowing for exaggeration – taken over perhaps from Tauler – we may well believe him when he says that often he felt near to destruction. The fact that he weathered the storm, that he was stronger than the destruction that threatened him, caused his strength to grow correspondingly. And so the years of struggle, ending in 1516, became the well-spring of his later power. The crisis in Reformation history was initiated by Luther in those years when the public at large knew nothing at all about him. His conscience was the focal point of the forces at work. The substance comprised Christ crucified, the revelation of the word of God upon the sinner, and of his redemption.

But a sound thesis is foolishly spoiled if we compare earlier scriptural exegetes with the painfully wrestling Luther, and declare them to be 'self-satisfied, assured and self-righteous . . . lazy-minded speculators'. We ought to maintain a more balanced judgment of St Bernard, St Francis, St Bonaventure and St Thomas.

In the last analysis the mystery of Luther's natural powers lay in the fact that he had fought for his knowledge, his profession of faith, his manner of life, in face of the threat of annihilation. His struggles in the monastery led him on through the dangers of spiritual collapse. In this he had overcome the danger of death, and his words became alive with this the strongest of all his powers.

This interior excitability, this innate endowment, was consolidated by exposure to the danger of being burnt at the stake. We have become so accustomed to hearing these facts stated, that we consider their meaning far too little. It is, however, an accomplishment of the most unusual human power, to persist in a defiance that could lead directly to the stake. In 1518 and in 1521 Luther was in this situation in varying degrees. At that time such steadfastness signified something other than it does in the twentieth century. Moreover, Luther provoked the personal hatred of his adversaries in a different way from Huss.

Luther's words bear the unction and power of bravery in face of death. He trod this path through the danger of death, not yet aware of the fact that he was outside the Church, in the good faith that he was serving the gospel. Unfortunately, in the battle which emerged, Luther's arrogant, revolutionary defiance was not consumed by the pure fire of service. His one-sided interpretation of the gospel was incapable of preserving the whole substance of revelation. The schism in Christendom was not counterbalanced and healed by personal zeal. His hatred and defiance made serious inroads upon the humility he himself demanded. These things are definitive in reaching a dogmatic appraisal; they justify the condemnation of Luther as an heretic; but no Catholic should allow this to blind him to the other fact, that Luther's words carry great weight, or to prevent him learning from the secret of their power. The word which the ministers of the Church preach must become their own deepest possession, if revelation is to be effective. The truth operates through itself; but, in the natural course of things, not through itself alone. It requires a living instrument.

In the end Luther's work will always have to be measured by the justice or injustice of his revolt against the Church. It is necessary when doing this, however, to see Luther as a whole, that is with his Catholic inheritance.

As we have observed, in his definitive development, Luther did not attack the Catholic faith (the same is true of his later years) but an allegedly Catholic thesis. On the basis of this false presupposition he was led to reject the Church and to propound heretical doctrines. In 1535 he admitted, for example: 'If the pope would concede that God justifies the sinner through Christ by grace alone, then we would not only applaud him but kiss his feet.' How close to Catholicism Luther seemed to be at this point. One-sidedness was his undoing, or, conversely, he foundered on the Catholic synthesis. This was because he took one side of the synthesis too seriously (the thesis that nothing can exist independently of God, that nothing is that does not come from him). Luther propounded one side of Catholic doctrine, taught it thoroughly with great depth, embracing a significant wealth of mystery, of imagery and of the power of the word of God. By declaring that this one side was the whole truth, Luther falsified his Catholic thesis and deleted the complement supplied by nature: the will, the priesthood and the papacy.

We said earlier that Luther was the German Reformation. In making this statement we must by no means forget the reservation that was stated in the same place: Luther became the Reformer because the nation responded to him (cf. p. 164). On the other hand, the response was not in the remotest degree simply the free assent of faith. The territorial Church system, which we have already seen as providing the fundamental possibility of the Reformation, will reveal itself, in our future study, as the very power which ensured victory for the emergent or already accomplished Reformation, and often by means that were not religious, but egoistic, coercive and violently revolutionary (see pp. 397 and 419). The propaganda methods and the allied calculated mobilisation of the mighty new potential of printing were often very far removed from the healthy growth of genuine religious conviction. Luther and Melanchthon themselves are evidence of this.

Many of these reservations apply to the early days of the Reformation. They apply with even greater force to the period to which we now turn our attention.

DATE DUE

OCT 84 77			
JAN 2 1984			
MAR 1 4 1991			
GAYLORD			PRINTED IN U.S.A.